CONCURRENT PROGRAM STRUCTURES

CONCURRENT PROGRAM STRUCTURES

David Bustard
John Elder
Queen's University of Belfast,
Northern Ireland

Jim Welsh
University of Queensland,
Australia

PRENTICE HALL

NEW YORK   LONDON   TORONTO   SYDNEY   TOKYO

First published 1988 by
Prentice Hall International (UK) Ltd,
66 Wood Lane End, Hemel Hempstead,
Hertfordshire, HP2 4RG
A division of
Simon & Schuster International Group

© 1988 Prentice Hall International (UK) Ltd

Printed and bound in Great Britain by
A. Wheaton & Co. Ltd, Exeter.

Library of Congress Cataloging-in-Publication Data

Data available upon application

British Library Cataloguing in Publication Data

Bustard, David
   Concurrent program structures – (Prentice
   Hall international series in computer science).
   1.   Parallel programming (Computer science)
   I. Title II. Elder, John, *1949–*
   III. Welsh, Jim
   005.1'2   QA76.6

   ISBN 0-13-167289-4
   ISBN 0-13-167080-8 Pbk

---

2 3 4 5   92 91 90 89 88

ISBN 0-13-167289-4
ISBN 0-13-167080-8 PBK

Contents

Preface   ix

1 AN INTRODUCTION TO CONCURRENCY   1

Concurrency – what it means   1
Examples of inherently concurrent applications   5
    Operating systems   5
    Real-time/embedded systems   6
    Simulation systems   6
Examples of machine-oriented concurrent programs   7
    Large-scale concurrent behavior   8
    Small-scale concurrent behavior   9
Summary   10
Further reading   11
Exercises   11

2 THE EXECUTION OF CONCURRENT PROGRAMS   13

The general problem   13
Executing concurrent programs in a sequential environment   15
Executing concurrent programs in an environment with asynchronous i/o   16
Executing concurrent programs on a multiprocessor   18
Summary   22
Further reading   22
Exercises   23

3 THE DESIGN OF CONCURRENT PROGRAMS   24

Requirements analysis and specification   24
Approaches to program design   25

What is a module?   26
   Module type (a): those responsible for physical objects   27
   Module type (b): those responsible for data structures   33
   Module type (c): those responsible for related program components   34
   Module type (d): those responsible for program actions   36
   A state module   37
Case study: a filling station control system   38
Summary   42
Further reading   42
Exercises   43

4   THE REPRESENTATION OF CONCURRENT PROGRAMS   44

Module representation: basic requirements   45
Dominant and subordinate modules   47
   Unshared subordinate modules: the envelope concept   48
   Dominant modules: the process concept   50
   Shared subordinate modules: the monitor concept   53
   'Look before you leap': a synchronization problem   56
   Explicit process synchronization: the condition concept   62
   Monitor exclusion: further details   64
Program termination   69
Specifying modules   69
Summary   71
Further reading   72
Exercises   72

5   THE TESTING OF CONCURRENT PROGRAMS   74

A concurrent sorting program   74
Modular testing   82
   Isolated module testing: sequential case   83
   Isolated module testing: concurrent case   84
Presenting program behavior   89
Summary   93
Further reading   93
Exercises   93

6   RESOURCE MANAGEMENT   95

Resource management concepts   95
Resource management modules: basic requirements   97
Allocating resources individually   99
   One resource defined   100
   One resource from N identical resources   101
   One resource from a subset of N similar resources   104

Allocating resources in multiple units 112
   M resources from *N* identical resources 114
   M resources from a subset of *N* similar resources 117
   M resources from sets of different resources 118
Dynamically defined resources 125
Sharable resources 126
Virtual resources 133
Case study: the dining philosophers 134
Summary 136
Further reading 137
Exercises 137

7 COMMUNICATION MANAGEMENT 139

Communications modules: basic requirements 139
Synchronized communication 141
   An example: pass-the-parcel simulation 142
Buffered communication 144
   Single item buffer 145
   Multiple item buffer 146
   An example: pass-the-parcel with two parcels 150
   The sort program revisited 152
Summary 152
Exercises 153

8 DISCRETE EVENT SIMULATION 154

Simulation models: basic concepts 154
Simulation models: some definitions 156
Simulated time 157
An implementation of the clock monitor 161
Presenting model behavior 163
Stochastic models 171
Random number generators 179
The dining philosophers: a simulation model 181
Summary 182
Further reading 183
Exercises 183

9 REAL-TIME SYSTEMS 186

Environment interaction 187
   User level interaction 188
   Environment level interaction 189
Time constraints on the response to external events 194
Case study: management of interaction with a VDU 195

Basic VDU handler　195
A higher level terminal handler　199
Real-time program simulation　202
Summary　207
Further reading　208
Exercises　208

10　GENERAL-PURPOSE OPERATING SYSTEMS　209

Operating systems for traditional computing facilities　210
The user accounts module　212
The interactive interface module　213
The filing system module　215
The command processor module　225
Distributed operating systems　229
Summary　231
Further reading　231
Exercises　232

11　THE REPRESENTATION OF PROCESS INTERACTION
Other approaches　233

Boolean variables, semaphores and conditional critical regions　234
Monitor-based programming languages　243
Modula-2　246
Directly communicating processes　249
Basic process communication　250
Accepting interaction　250
Selecting one from a set of possible interactions　251
Guarded selection　252
Directly communicating processes versus monitor-based
communication　253
Summary　256
Further reading　256
Exercises　257

Appendix 1　Pascal Plus definition　258
Appendix 2　Solutions to exercises　270
Index　319

Preface

A concurrent program contains components which may be executed simultaneously. This book is concerned with the construction of such programs. In particular, it deals with programs in which the concurrent components, or *processes*, have a relatively long lifetime. The most common application areas in which this type of concurrency occurs include:

- real-time (or embedded) systems
- operating systems
- simulation modeling.

The material presented here is suitable for a second or third year undergraduate course on concurrent systems or in any course on systems programming. The book can also be used as an introductory text in courses on operating systems and real-time systems. Its use in simulation courses is largely restricted to those in which a *process-oriented* view of modeling is taken.

It is assumed that the reader is familiar with the concept of a sequential program and has some experience of expressing sequential programs in Pascal. Most of the programming examples that are given are expressed in Pascal Plus – a language which extends Pascal with facilities for modular multiprogramming, based on proposals made by C.A.R. Hoare. Other languages with similar constructs include Modula, Mesa, Concurrent Euclid and Concurrent Pascal. The purpose of the book is not to teach a particular programming language. Rather, it is to consider how concurrent programs, in general, can be designed and represented.

Structure

The book has eleven chapters. Each chapter is concluded with a summary of its main points. Most chapters contain exercises which are intended to reinforce and, in some cases, extend the reader's understanding of the material covered in each chapter. Solutions to the exercises are given in Appendix 2.

The book may be read or presented in chapter order. Indeed, a course with this structure has been given several times. However, some variations are possible:

- Chapter 2, which deals with the execution of concurrent programs, may be covered anywhere between Chapters 1 and 8.
- The first part of Chapter 11, which gives an historical review of the early attempts to represent the interaction of processes in concurrent programs, can be presented before Chapter 4, which gives a *monitor-based* introduction to the representation of concurrent behavior.
- The remainder of Chapter 11, which deals with other representations for concurrent programs, can be considered immediately after Chapter 4.

The order in which the chapters appear in the book is an order which in our experience students seem to find most 'comfortable'. In particular, many are unhappy with an abstract discussion of concurrent activity and prefer to know at an early stage how concurrent programs might execute. Also, while a presentation of a range of programming notations is a more objective way of considering program representation, students seem best equipped to make comparisons after they have become familiar with one particular notation.

Chapter 1 introduces the concept of a concurrent program through a series of analogies and examples. A distinction is drawn between *small scale* and *large scale* concurrent behavior, as it is only this latter type of concurrency that is treated in the remainder of the book.

Chapter 2 provides a brief review of the way in which programs involving large scale concurrent behavior can be executed in a number of different environments.

Chapter 3 considers a design technique for concurrent programs based on the modular approach to program decomposition advocated by Parnas. Programs are designed as hierarchical groups of modules that may execute sequentially or concurrently.

Chapter 4 discusses how a modular design, as described in Chapter 3, may be translated into a monitor-based programming language notation. Some of the problems and pitfalls encountered when representing the interaction of concurrent processes are also discussed.

Chapter 5 describes how a concurrent program can be tested. The main objective here is to show how the behavior of a concurrent program can be constrained to follow an arranged test path. Also, a general technique for presenting concurrent program behavior is discussed.

Chapters 6 and 7 present a collection of techniques for handling process interaction. Interaction occurs when processes compete for shared resources or when they wish to communicate. Chapter 6 deals with resource management while Chapter 7 covers interprocess communication.

Chapters 8, 9 and 10 consider the use of concurrency in three application areas: discrete event simulation, real-time systems and operating systems, in that order. In each case the relevance of the material presented in earlier chapters is demonstrated and some additional technical problems posed by each area are discussed.

Chapter 11 provides a brief review of the ways in which concurrency control is represented in programming language notations. The review covers the early techniques involving the use of *Boolean variables*, *semaphores* and *conditional critical regions*, through to *monitors* and *conditions* and, finally the concept of *communicating sequential processes* is considered. In particular, the way in which this concept has been realized in the programming language Ada[†] is analyzed briefly.

Acknowledgements

Many people have influenced the content and structure of this book. The authors are particularly grateful to Howard Johnston who made many useful suggestions for improvement to a succession of earlier drafts. A recent draft was reviewed by Jane Hughes. Her comments prompted several changes which have undoubtedly improved the overall quality of the book. Most recently, Maurice Clint worked through the 'almost' final draft adding a polish to some of the chapters.

We are also grateful to Roy Calvert and Alan Stewart for commenting specifically on Chapter 8 and Appendix 1, respectively. Comments have also been received from students and, in particular, Daphne Campbell, Fergus Fitzpatrick, Paul O'Neill and Martin Patterson reported faults which would have gone unnoticed into the final text.

Thanks are also extended to Margaret Bustard who commented on an early draft and helped throughout with planning. Also, we are grateful to the staff of Prentice Hall for their patient support over a long gestation period and to Helen Martin, in particular, for her help in the crucial final stages.

Finally, and most important of all, we are deeply indebted to Tony Hoare whose ideas are an integral part of the material presented here.

[†] Ada is a trademark of the United States Department of Defense.

One

AN INTRODUCTION TO CONCURRENCY

Concurrent behavior is present in every human activity. Those who read this book, for example, will assess the information that it contains as they move their eyes over the text, turn each page, breathe air in and out of their lungs, and so on. Because concurrent activity is so much part of our lives it is not difficult for anyone with even a scant knowledge of computer programming to appreciate the concept of a 'concurrent' program – namely a program in which there are several activities in progress at the same time. The purpose of this chapter is to clarify this intuitive understanding through the use of a series of analogies and examples. The discussion covers the distinguishing characteristics of concurrent programs and considers, in general terms, what their execution involves.

Concurrency – what it means

The principles of computer programming are often introduced to complete novices by drawing an analogy between a program and the directions that are followed by someone carrying out an everyday activity, such as preparing a meal, changing a wheel on a car or knitting a sweater. The directions for one person trying to obtain a meal, for example, might be presented as in Figure 1.1.

The person, a man (say), first opens the refrigerator. If no food is available he goes out to a restaurant; otherwise he prepares an hors-d'oeuvre, entrée and dessert in that order.

This analogy introduces the concept of a *sequential* program as a col-

1

```
open refrigerator
if refrigerator is empty
then eat at restaurant
else
    begin
        prepare hors-d'oeuvre
        prepare entrée
        prepare dessert
        eat at home
    end
```

Figure 1.1 Obtaining a meal: a sequential algorithm

lection of instructions that are intended to be followed in sequence. The execution of such a program is performed by a *processor* and the pattern of behavior that results is known as a *sequential process*, or simply a *process*.

A large number of programs can be expressed acceptably in a sequential form. However, there are some classes of problem where it is essential, or simply more appropriate, to develop a program as a set of *cooperating* processes that have the potential to execute in *parallel*, or *concurrently*, to achieve the program's purpose. This is particularly true when developing a program for any problem in which concurrent activity is an aspect of the problem. Consider, for example, how we might describe the behavior of two people obtaining a meal. If the couple, John and Catherine (say), share the preparation of the meal by taking responsibility for different courses then their activity might be described by a concurrent algorithm of the form shown in Figure 1.2.

John opens the refrigerator and the couple decide whether they should eat at a restaurant or prepare a meal to eat at home. If they agree to make a meal Catherine prepares the entreé while John works on the hors-d'oeuvre and dessert. Then, when all three courses have been prepared, they sit down to eat.

```
John:                                    Catherine:
    open refrigerator
    if refrigerator is empty                 if refrigerator is empty
    then eat at restaurant                   then eat at restaurant
    else                                     else
        begin                                    begin
            prepare hors-d'oeuvre                    prepare entrée
            prepare dessert
            eat at home                              eat at home
        end                                      end
```

Figure 1.2 Obtaining a meal: a concurrent algorithm

One of the main distinctions between a sequential and a concurrent algorithm is that a sequential algorithm imposes a *total ordering* on the activities involved whereas a concurrent algorithm specifies only a *partial ordering*. In preparing the meal, for example, there are constraints that the person opening the refrigerator must do so before the couple can decide where to eat, and that the courses must all be prepared before eating commences. However, within these constraints the entrée might be completed before or after either or both the hors-d'oeuvre or dessert.

As a concurrent algorithm specifies only a partial order of activity it allows for the possibility that the timing of individual operations is not fixed. Thus, if a meal is prepared several times, following the algorithm given in Figure 1.2, the courses may be completed in a different order without violating the requirements of the task in hand. In concurrent programs we need the same flexibility because the timing of some operations is not known. This is obviously the case when user-initiated input is expected. It is also true of peripheral operations in general and there are even small variations in the time taken to execute individual machine instructions.

The uncertainly over the precise order of some events in a concurrent system is a property that is referred to as *nondeterminism*. The presence of nondeterminism in a program can create problems for its developer in that program faults may emerge as *transient errors*. A transient error is one that may or may not occur depending on the execution path taken in a particular activation of the program. The cause of a transient error tends to be difficult to identify because the events leading up to the error are often not known precisely and the source of an error cannot, in general, be found by experimentation. Thus, one of the skills in designing any concurrent program is to express it in a form that guarantees its correct behavior despite any uncertainty over the order in which some individual operations are performed. That is, there should be no part of a concurrent program whose correct behavior is *time-dependent*.

The algorithm in Figure 1.2 is incomplete in one important respect: it does not identify (clearly) the *interaction* that occurs between the two processes involved. It is this interaction which, in effect, makes the algorithm concurrent because otherwise we would simply have a set of sequential algorithms.

In general, process interaction occurs in three different circumstances:

(a) when processes compete for access to shared resources – just as the couple might compete for the use of knives and other shared utensils during the preparation of the meal;

(b) when processes need to align their execution – just as the couple delayed starting the meal until all the courses had been prepared;

(c) when processes exchange data – just as the couple might exchange ideas and pleasantries during their meal.

In all three cases it is necessary for the processes involved to *synchronize* their activity, either to avoid conflict, as in (a), or to make contact as in (b) and (c). In the case of resource management it is often essential to have restrictions on the way in which the resources are administered to ensure *fairness* and to avoid or recover from *deadlock*. Deadlock is a situation in which one process, having resources required by another, refuses or neglects to release them, thereby causing the other process to wait indefinitely. Fairness is achieved by allocating resources to processes of equal status in the order in which resource requests are made. If resources are allocated in any other order care must be taken to avoid *starvation*. This is a situation where a process is repeatedly overtaken in its attempt to obtain resources such that there is no guarantee that an allocation will be made in finite time. Deadlock and starvation are major concerns in the design of most concurrent programs.

In operational terms a concurrent program may be defined as 'a program that contains parts that are *designed* to be executed in parallel'. The key word in this definition is 'designed' because all programs exhibit concurrent behavior at some level of their execution. For the traditional sequential program, concurrency is often present in the operating system when it performs operations on behalf of the sequential program, and below the operating system there is concurrency in the hardware implementing individual machine instructions. Even a simple assignment statement of the form

```
I := 0
```

may be considered concurrent in that the bits in the memory location for the variable are cleared in parallel.

In general, there are two reasons why a designer might use concurrency in developing a program for a given problem:

(a) the problem may naturally suggest that a concurrent program is desirable, in that the program is required to perform operations that proceed in parallel, or handle events that occur unpredictably;
(b) the hardware of the computer on which the program will run supports parallel execution of operations, thereby enabling the execution time of the program to be reduced if it is expressed in a form that permits concurrent execution.

By analogy, case (a) in everyday life is the situation where several people are needed if a job is to be completed in a satisfactory way. For example, back in the kitchen, if one person is preparing a particularly volatile sauce which requires his or her full attention, then the other person might be responsible for making sure that nothing else suffers in the meantime. A second, less obvious, example of case (a) occurs when a meal is being eaten; having prepared the meal the couple eat together simply because they are both hungry, rather than fulfilling a need to dispose of the food in minimum time! Case (b) is the situation where several people are available to tackle a particular job, and where the work is shared out among them to minimize the time taken to complete the job, as in the overall preparation of the meal.

In the sections that follow examples of both classes of concurrent program are considered.

Examples of inherently concurrent applications

This section deals with applications in which concurrent behavior is a fundamental aspect of the problem area. The areas covered are operating systems, real-time systems and simulation systems, each of which is discussed in turn.

Operating systems

Anyone who has used a computer will have accessed its facilities through an *operating system*, which is the most commonly occurring type of concurrent program. A computer system consists of many pieces of hardware (processors, memory units, disks, terminals, etc.), all of which operate in parallel, and hence it is natural to write the operating system in a way which reflects that concurrency. The concurrent nature of an operating system is obvious in cases where it is required to support several interactive users simultaneously. However, even on single-user systems concurrent behavior is usually evident in facilities such as type-ahead on keyboard input (where the operating system accepts each character typed on a user's terminal while carrying out the user's preceding request) or in the ability to print text files in parallel with other forms of processing.

In some operating systems users are provided with facilities at the command level to enable several interacting programs to run in parallel. In the UNIX[†] operating system, for example, a command of the form:

    A | B

starts the concurrent execution of the programs A and B, using the data output by A as input to B. The data is transferred through a one-way communications channel, known as a *pipe*, which is represented by the bar '|' in the command. Likewise the command:

    A &

causes the program A to be run as a 'background' process concurrently with further commands input by the user.

Each individual sequential program may also trigger concurrent behavior within an operating system as a result of input/output data transfer requests. For example, a program statement of the form:

    Write ('Here is a message')

[†] UNIX is a trademark of AT&T Bell Laboratories.

may result in the text string being transferred to the output file by the operating system in parallel with the continued execution of the program statements following the write statement. Similarly, if a program opens a sequential file for input the operating system may read the data items into main memory in advance of any input requests by the program.

Operating systems have the typical profile of a concurrent program. That is:

(a) they have parts that operate in parallel – to provide a service to one or more users concurrently;
(b) the parts interact – reflecting the fact that, for instance, users interact, either when competing for shared resources (e.g. files), or when they pass information to each other (e.g. mail messages);
(c) the sequence in which the overall set of events occurs is nondeterministic.

Historically, the need to program operating systems in a systematic and reliable manner provided the impetus for the development of concurrent programming techniques and languages. As a result many language features provided for concurrency have their roots in operating-system technology. However, because the characteristics listed above are typical of concurrent programming problems in general, such features have proved to have more general application.

Real-time/embedded systems

Concurrent programs are also run on computers used to control equipment of various types, where the computers are possibly embedded in that equipment. It has now become standard practice, for example, to use microprocessors in the internal control of all forms of computer peripheral down to the simplest visual display unit. Outside the computing world similar control systems are being installed in cars, washing machines, video recorders and many other pieces of everyday equipment. On a larger scale computerized control systems are used in telephone exchanges, the automation of factory processes, in the guidance systems for air- and space-craft, and so on. Such systems are known as *real-time systems* since they receive inputs directly from their environment and must respond quickly enough to influence and, possibly, control that environment. In all cases concurrent programs of varying degrees of complexity are at the heart of these systems. They are concurrent because they need to be able to respond to events that may occur at unpredictable times.

Simulation systems

Another form of concurrent program is one constructed to model, or *simulate*, a complex system of interacting activities in order to gain a thorough understanding of that system, and experiment with variations of it. All of the examples given so far might first be developed as simulation models in order to check their logic and assess their performance under different test conditions. Simulation models may also be constructed to gain an understanding of complex management problems such as running the economy for a country, controlling passenger flow in an airport terminal, or perhaps simply deciding how best to prepare a quiche if two equally competent people are available to tackle the work. In all such applications concurrency is again the key to modeling the possible sequences of events in the real-world situation under investigation.

Examples of machine-oriented concurrent programs

Simulation, real-time and operating systems are classes of program that are inherently concurrent because the physical systems that they control, or reflect, are themselves concurrent. Concurrency can also be used in a program as a means of improving its performance. This approach is only worthwhile, however, if the machine on which the program is to run has suitable facilities for the parallel execution of program components. As a general guideline, the greater the amount of computational activity associated with the concurrent components of the program the more likely it is that modern general-purpose computers will be able to execute them in a way that gives an improved performance over an equivalent sequential program. As the active life of the components (or *grain of concurrency*) becomes shorter only special-purpose computers will yield any improvement in performance. For example, in the expression:

```
a*b — c/d
```

the calculation of a*b and c/d can, in principle, be carried out in parallel. However, it can be achieved only if the computer supports parallel arithmetic operations and has a synchronization mechanism to prevent the subtraction operation being attempted before the multiplication and division are complete. Computers with this type of facility have existed for some time (e.g. the CDC 6000 series machines), although they are not commonplace.

The remainder of this section gives examples of programs that have been constructed to take advantage of concurrent hardware. The examples fall into two groups:

(a) those involving *large-scale* concurrency, where the components that are executed concurrently are relatively long-lived;
(b) those involving *small-scale* concurrency, where the parallelism is at statement and expression level.

Large-scale concurrent behavior

As an example of a program involving large-scale behavior consider the problem of sorting a single list of data items. One straightforward way of introducing concurrency is to split the list into a number of sublists, sort these in parallel (using a suitable sequential technique) and then merge the resulting sorted lists. More specifically, if we divide the initial list into four parts the sorting program might operate as shown in the data flow diagram in Figure 1.3. The program operates in two phases as follows:

(a) the four sublists are sorted in parallel;
(b) the resulting four lists are merged into one sorted list.

Since a list of length N can be sorted in $0(N \log N)$ time, while the time to merge a number of sorted lists into one of length N is $0(N)$, the concurrent algorithm described should be faster for sufficiently large N than any traditional sequential algorithm.

Similarly, if we wish to locate a data item in an unsorted list, the list can be split into sections and the sections searched in parallel. The overall result

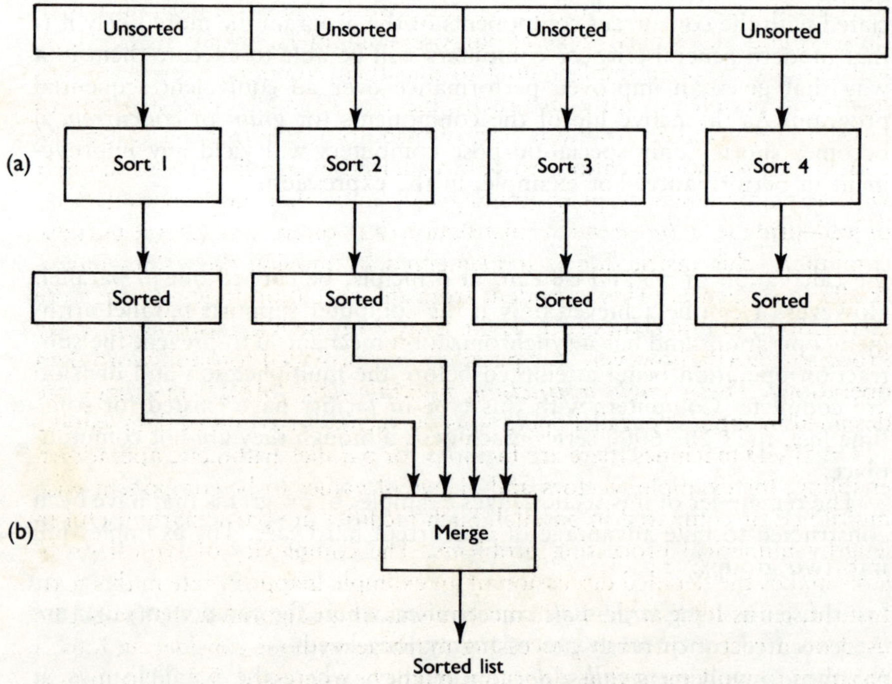

Figure 1.3 A concurrent sorting strategy

of the search is then determined by either:

(a) any one of the concurrent searches finding the item; or
(b) all of the concurrent searches failing to find the item.

On average, this strategy should be faster for lists of any length.

In both the sorting and the searching examples discussed above any assumptions about the improved performance of the programs concerned relies on suitable hardware being available to implement the concurrency specified. Without such hardware concurrent programs are likely to perform less efficiently than their traditional sequential counterparts. The next chapter gives a brief review of the types of machine architecture that support large-scale concurrent activity since it is, in the main, this type of concurrency that is treated throughout this book. Before that, however, let us take a brief look at small-scale concurrency in order to identify its characteristics before setting aside any further consideration of it.

Small-scale concurrent behavior

The instruction set provided by a computer reflects the general programming requirements of its users. If a particular class of program has to be executed quickly then the instruction set can be devised to suit that class. This is achieved by providing appropriate instructions of a higher level than those found on typical general-purpose computers. These higher level instructions are often implemented so that their component steps are performed in parallel, as far as is practicable. For example, an instruction to move a block of data from one part of memory to another may cause the contents of memory locations to be transferred in parallel. Those familiar with assembly language programming will know that most computers do indeed provide a *block move* instruction but often, on general-purpose computers, this instruction is implemented by moving the values individually in sequence. (This is evident from the execution time given for the instruction.) On machines such as the Cray-1 or the ICL Distributed Array Processor (DAP), however, true parallelism is provided for multiword data operations. These *single instruction, multiple data* (SIMD) machines are designed to support parallel operations on vectors or arrays of data values.

On SIMD machines there are facilities for parallel arithmetic operations, enabling, for example, vectors and arrays of values to be component-wise multiplied or compared in parallel. Such facilities are particularly useful in lengthy numerical processing problems. The complexity of typical problems makes the detailed discussion of an example inappropriate in this text. Instead, let us look at the basic mechanisms of an algorithm that might be used on a vector or array processing machine without considering how a program to implement that algorithm might be expressed. The algorithm is known as *Habermann's neighbor sort* (a parallel bubble sort) and is illustrated in Figure 1.4.

Pass	Phase	List							
		1	2	3	4	5	6	7	8
1	Odds	82 ⟷ 48	14	15	84 ⟷ 25		77 ⟷ 13		
	Evens	48	82 ⟷ 14	15	25	84 ⟷ 13		77	
2	Odds	48 ⟷ 14	82 ⟷ 15		25 ⟷ 13		84 ⟷ 77		
	Evens	14	48 ⟷ 15	82 ⟷ 13		25	77	84	
3	Odds	14	15	48 ⟷ 13	82 ⟷ 25		77	84	
	Evens	14	15 ⟷ 13	48 ⟷ 25	82 ⟷ 77		84		
4	Odds	14 ⟷ 13	15	25	48	77	82	84	
	Evens	13	14	15	25	48	77	82	84

Figure 1.4 Habermann's neighbor sort

Sorting a list of N numbers requires N *div 2 passes*, where each pass has two *phases* identified as *odd* and *even*. In the example there are eight numbers to be sorted so four passes are required to perform the sort. During the odd phase the odd-numbered elements of the list are compared in parallel with their right-hand neighbors, and exchanged if necessary. In the example, in pass 1, the pairs $1-2$, $5-6$ and $7-8$ are exchanged in the odd phase. Similarly, during the even phase, even-numbered elements are compared and swapped with their right-hand neighbors, if appropriate. In the even phase of pass 1 the pairs $2-3$ and $6-7$ are exchanged. After a further three passes the sort is complete.

In practice this program needs to be revised to take account of a limitation on current SIMD machines that parallel operations may only be performed in one instruction over a small sequence of data elements. On the Cray-1, for example, 64 numbers may be handled simultaneously, so a suitable sorting algorithm will sort a list in 64 number units and then merge the resulting sublists.

Summary

A concurrent program is defined here as one which contains parts that are capable of being executed in parallel *and* have been identified as such by a program designer. Programs of this type are either constructed to take advantage of hardware that supports concurrent execution or to implement classes of program that are naturally concurrent because the physical systems that they control, or reflect, are themselves concurrent. Programs of the latter type are quite commonplace, with the most obvious examples including operating systems, real-time systems and simulation systems.

The main concern in designing a concurrent program is the organization of the interactions among its concurrent parts. The sequence of events associated with most interactions is nondeterministic but a concurrent program must be constructed so that it operates correctly for all possible interleavings of events.

The actual run-time behavior of a concurrent program will depend on the nature of the underlying hardware support for the concurrent execution of program components. Small-scale concurrency, at program statement and expression level, is usually supported only on array and vector processors, and programs that are designed to run on such machines usually need to use special-purpose algorithms to take advantage of particular machine characteristics. Large-scale concurrency, as exhibited by programs containing a number of relatively long-lived processes, can be supported on most general-purpose computers and it is this form of concurrency that is primarily addressed in this book.

Further reading

Examples of inherently concurrent programs are discussed in detail throughout this book. The three specific application areas, real-time, simulation and operating systems, are covered in Chapters 8 to 10.

The architecture and programming of a wide range of SIMD and other types of small-scale parallel processing machine are discussed in:
- Hwang, K. and Briggs, F.A., *Computer Architecture and Parallel Processing*, McGraw Hill, 1984.

This book also contains many references to other recent work in this area.

The Habermann algorithm and its representation in the high-level programming language Actus, based on Pascal, together with other examples of concurrent algorithms are discussed in:
- McKeag, R.M. and Macnaghten, A.M. (eds), *On The Construction of Programs*, Cambridge University Press, 1980.

Exercises

1.1 Discuss, in general terms, the operation of a program to implement a parallel search for a data item in an unsorted list of such items. Identify, in particular, how the program might display the results of the search and also how it might terminate.

   (*Hint*: When designing a concurrent program it sometimes helps to picture how a similar problem might be tackled by cooperating humans. In this case, imagine how a search might be handled by a number of people inspecting a set of cards with several items of information on each card.)

1.2   Describe, in general terms, a parallel algorithm for searching for the exit from a maze. Consider the two cases where there are:

(a) a small fixed number of *searchers*, that can operate in parallel;

(b) any number of parallel *searchers*.

Two

THE EXECUTION OF
CONCURRENT PROGRAMS

A concurrent program contains a set of processes that are *capable* of being executed in parallel. If there is a corresponding number of suitable physical processors on the computer executing the program then the potential for concurrent behavior can be fully realized. If not, then the program must be executed by *time-slicing* the available processor power – that is, by switching each processor from the execution of one process to another, regularly, so that they all make progress over some specified period of time. This chapter provides a brief review of the types of processing facility available on modern computers and discusses how the execution of concurrent programs can be supported in each case.

The general problem

Executing a concurrent program on any computer involves the assignment of the logical processes in the program to suitable physical processors for execution, as suggested by the diagram in Figure 2.1.

The number of processes and processors present may vary over the lifetime of a program.

In general a number of different types of processor are available in a system. The two main categories are *central processors* and *input/output processors*, usually referred to as i/o processors. A central processor executes machine instructions while an i/o processor performs input/output operations on a particular peripheral device. One way to view the relationship between the two classes of processor is to assume that any ex-

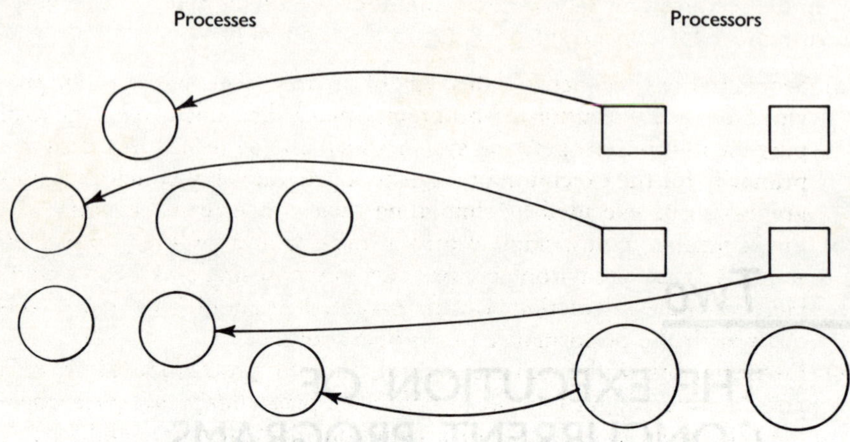

Figure 2.1 Assigning processes to processors

ecution of the machine instructions that initiate an i/o operation (by a central processor) causes the execution of the process involved to be transferred to the corresponding i/o processor for the duration of the i/o operation.

In practice, this means suspending the execution of any process initiating an i/o operation until the operation is complete.

The central processors are usually of the same type (*homogeneous*) but some may have particular attributes, such as high processing speed. These processors must be selected by the processes that need them and so they can be treated in much the same way as i/o processors.

The general strategy used for allocating processor power is as follows:

(a) Processes that engage regularly in i/o operations should be given ready access to a central processor to ensure that i/o processors are kept as busy as possible with the result that the concurrency in the system is maximized.

(b) Identical central processors should be shared *fairly*, so that processes with similar requirements progress at a similar rate.

(c) Identical central processors should be switched frequently from one process to another so that a reasonable illusion of concurrent behavior is presented. However, the processors should not be switched so frequently that the cost of switching becomes 'excessive' in relation to the time taken to execute the processes concerned. (Unfortunately, the definition of 'excessive' is largely subjective and will tend to vary from one application to another. In real-time applications any overhead whatsoever may be unacceptable whereas in simulation applications the overhead may be substantial and yet be considered acceptable if the required program behavior is achieved.)

In the sections that follow three commonly occurring types of execution environment for concurrent programs are considered:

(a) Sequential environments – the type of environment that is often provided for the execution of programs under the control of a general purpose multi-user operating system. Such an environment is designed primarily for the execution of sequential programs but concurrent programs can be executed by simulating their concurrent behavior.

(b) Environments with a single central processor and multiple i/o processors – the type of environment provided on most single-user computers. Here machine instructions can be executed in parallel, or *asynchronously* with the performance of i/o operations.

(c) Environments with multiple central and i/o processors. Here it is possible to distinguish between *tightly coupled multiprocessors*, where the processors have access to a common main memory, and *loosely coupled multiprocessors* where the central processors have only their own local memory. Computers with tightly coupled central processors have been available commercially for some time (e.g. Honeywell 60/66 and Univac 1100 series) while computers with loosely coupled central processors are becoming more commonplace. One particular development worth mentioning in this context is the Inmos *transputer* which has a central processor and main memory on one chip. A computer can be built from a single transputer or from several transputers connected together to form a loosely coupled multiprocessor.

Executing concurrent programs in a sequential environment

On modern computers, peripheral devices can operate in parallel with the processing of machine instructions and there may be several central processors available to execute sequences of such instructions in parallel. These facilities, however, are often either unavailable, or not easily accessible to programs executed on a multi-user computer with a general-purpose operating system. Instead, each program is normally presented with a *sequential environment* in which only one program activity can proceed at a time. That activity will involve either the sequential execution of machine instructions by one central processor or the execution of an i/o operation by one i/o processor; if a program initiates an i/o operation then its further execution is delayed until the i/o operation is complete.

In a sequential environment of this type concurrent program behavior is simulated by switching the processor regularly from one process to another. Often the switch will take place when the process that is executing is unable to make further progress. For example, if the running process requires data supplied by a second process, then the execution of the first can be suspended until the data is available, thereby releasing the processor for use elsewhere.

Sharing processor power in this way is relatively cheap but the resulting level of concurrent behavior may not be sufficiently close to the designer's view of how that program should behave. To achieve the desired effect it may be necessary to switch the processor from one process to another more regularly. In block-structured programming languages the processor switch might take place at procedure entry and/or exit. This method is simple to implement, and adequate for most programs.

One important side-effect of executing a concurrent program in a sequential environment is that its behavior is deterministic which makes debugging easier.

Executing concurrent programs in an environment with asynchronous i/o

On a computer with asynchronous i/o facilities i/o operations can take place in parallel with the execution of machine instructions. We can view an i/o operation as part of the execution of the process that initiates it and so suspend the process concerned for the duration of the operation. It should be noted, however, that there is no physical requirement to link a process with the i/o operation it initiates and instead we might consider the i/o operation as a separate process executed by the i/o processor concerned. That is, the process initiating the i/o operation would continue to run in parallel with the i/o operation. To see why this strategy is undesirable let us consider its consequences.

Figure 2.2 shows the interaction between a process A which initiates an i/o operation and the device concerned.

In this model the i/o operation is performed by the i/o processor in

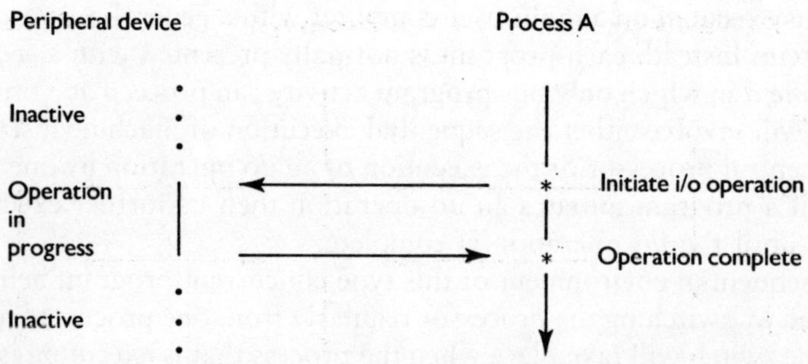

Figure 2.2 Making use of asynchronous device transfers: processing independent work

parallel with the continued execution of A by a central processor. The implication is that process A performs useful work throughout the i/o operation. However, in practice this is extremely difficult to arrange for the following reasons:

(a) the programmer may not know how much time is available during the i/o operation, especially if input is expected from a user through a terminal keyboard, or other input device;

(b) even if this time is known it is not easy to find work of similar duration to perform;

(c) even if work can be found, the resulting program is not portable since any change in the characteristics of the device involved, such as, for example, changing a printer to one with a faster baud rate, will require a corresponding change to the work performed during an operation on that device;

(d) the work performed by a process during an i/o operation must be independent of the data involved – if data is being copied into or out of main memory then no attempt should be made to use or modify that data until the transfer is complete.

Faced with these constraints most programmers will take the easy way out and either implement A to perform any convenient independent task (regardless of its duration) in parallel with the i/o operation or simply waste the time available in an idle loop that inspects the state of the device concerned until the completion of the operation has been detected.

In general, therefore, it is inappropriate to allow a process to continue executing after it has started an i/o operation. If the process is suspended then the central processor that was executing it can be used for the execution of one or more other processes until the i/o operation is complete. Figure 2.3 illustrates this strategy for two processes A and B.

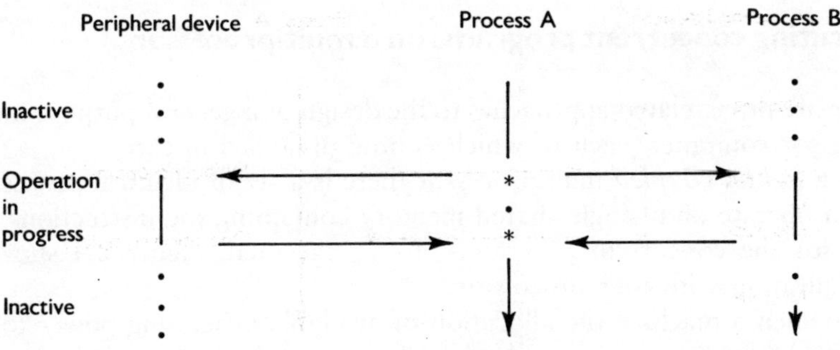

Figure 2.3 Making use of asynchronous device transfers: switching the processor elsewhere

A initiates an i/o operation which causes it to be suspended and the central processor that was executing it to be switched to the execution of B. B then runs throughout the i/o operation and in parallel with it. When the i/o operation is complete the central processor executing B is switched back to the execution of A, and B is suspended.

With this strategy the processor power available during an i/o operation can be fully utilized. At the same time, the programming of any process initiating an i/o operation is also made easier because, for the process, the i/o operation now appears to be immediate.

The end of an i/o operation is indicated by a change in the observable state of the device concerned and is also usually accompanied by a central processor *interrupt*. An interrupt causes a central processor to suspend its current activity and so allows it to continue the execution of the process that initiated the i/o operation concerned. This ensures that a process can respond rapidly to the end of an i/o operation without wasting time repeatedly inspecting the state of the peripheral device involved.

As in the sequential environment discussed in the previous section, it is again necessary to have a scheme for sharing processor power among the processes that are ready to run. For applications where the processor is rarely used to its full extent, as is the case in most real-time programs, it is often adequate to consider process switching only at the beginning or end of an i/o operation, or when a process can no longer proceed for some reason. In applications where there is more competition for the processor, more regular switching is required. One technique is to obtain additional switching points by using interrupts from a *real-time clock*. A clock generates central processor interrupts at regular intervals. When one occurs, the process that the interrupted processor is executing (if any) is suspended and another process selected. If the processes that are ready to execute are ordered according to the time that they have been waiting to run then the longest waiting process is always selected next when a processor becomes free. This technique is known as *round-robin scheduling*.

Executing concurrent programs on a multiprocessor

There are three related approaches to the design of a general-purpose multiprocessor computer, each of which is now discussed in turn.

In a *tightly coupled* multiprocessor there is a set of identical processors which operate on a single shared memory containing the instructions and data for the concurrent program(s) to be executed. Figure 2.4 shows a configuration with four processors.

On such a machine the allocation of available processing power to the processes of a program can be handled using the techniques suggested earlier, namely:

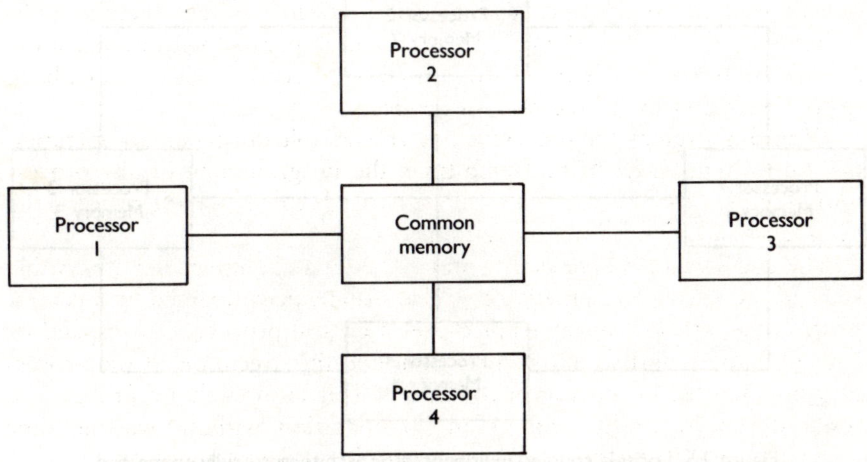

Figure 2.4 Tightly coupled multiprocessor architecture

(a) If processor power is plentiful then a processor need only be switched
     from one process to another if:
     • the process being executed initiates an i/o operation, or
     • the logic of the program is such that the process can only progress
       after some other process has changed the state of the program.
(b) If there is frequent competition for processing power then additional
     switching points must be found to give an adequate illusion of concur-
     rent behavior while keeping the switching costs involved to an accept-
     able level.

One limitation associated with a tightly coupled multiprocessor architecture is that the effective power of the machine is usually reduced through
memory contention. Only one processor at a time may have access to the
common memory and if two processors attempt to access it simultaneously
one will be made to wait momentarily. As the number of processors
increases the amount of contention increases and so more processor power
is lost in access delays.

The amount of contention can be reduced substantially by dividing the
memory into sections which have separate access control. Alternatively,
memory contention can be avoided completely by giving each processor its
own local memory. The resulting units may be connected in a *loosely
coupled* fashion, as suggested by the diagram in Figure 2.5.

A fully connected scheme is shown here, with each processor attached
directly to every other processor. This approach is satisfactory for a small
number of processors but, as more processors are introduced, the number

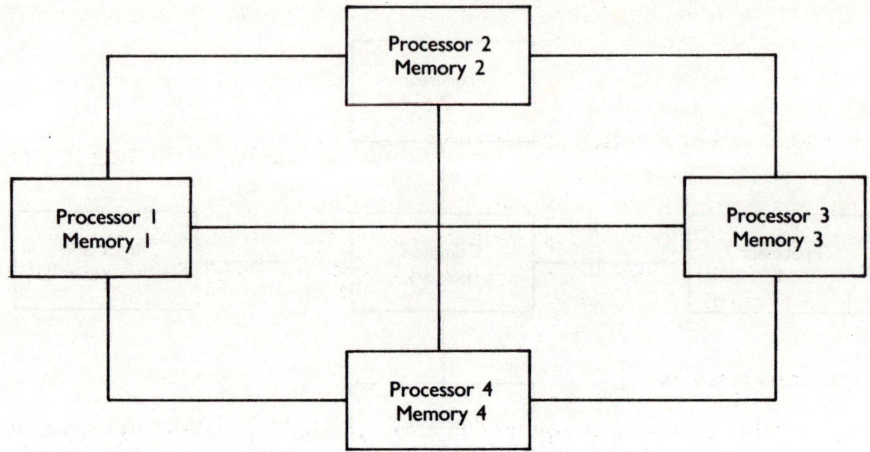

Figure 2.5 Loosely coupled multiprocessor architecture: fully connected
communication scheme

of connections becomes excessive, making it necessary to be satisfied with a
less dense connection scheme. One possibility is to connect the processors
through a central *switch*, rather like a telephone exchange, as illustrated in
Figure 2.6.

With any connection scheme the main administrative problem encountered on this type of multiprocessor is the efficient allocation of processes to
available processors. Unlike a shared memory multiprocessor, the assignment of a process to a processor now involves copying the instructions and
data of that process into the local memory of the designated processor. This
is a relatively slow operation so this type of multiprocessor is best suited to
systems where the allocation of concurrent program processes to processors
is relatively static and, ideally, arranged when the program is first loaded.

A second problem is that the exchange of information between program
processes running on a loosely coupled multiprocessor can involve more
data copying than in the tightly coupled case. Also, it is faster to pass
information in a shared memory and in some cases no copying may be
necessary if the data is left in an area to which the interacting processes have
access. Thus, a further constraint on any program that is to be run suc-
cessfully on a loosely coupled multiprocessor is that interaction among its
concurrent parts should be relatively infrequent.

A third type of multiprocessor is one that is simply a hybrid of the first
two, made up of a collection of processors each of which has its own local
memory and also has access to a common memory. This architecture is illustrated in Figure 2.7.

A hybrid multiprocessor can ease both the memory contention problem
associated with tightly coupled multiprocessors and the lack of communi-

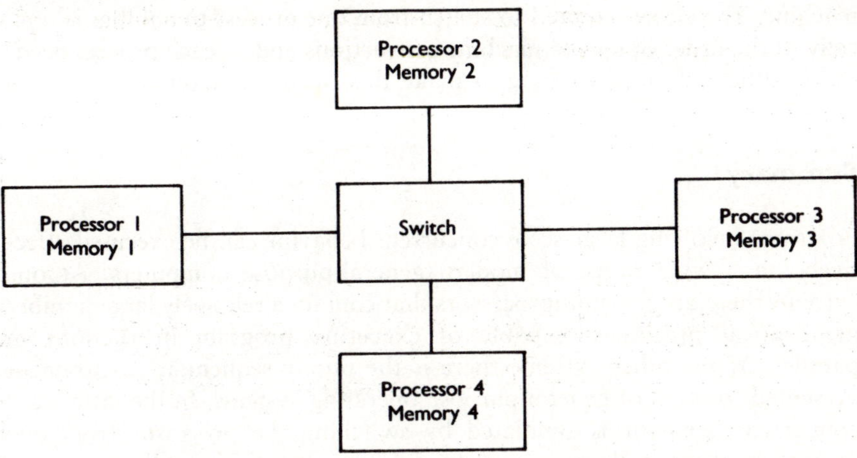

Figure 2.6 Loosely coupled multiprocessor architecture: switched communication lines

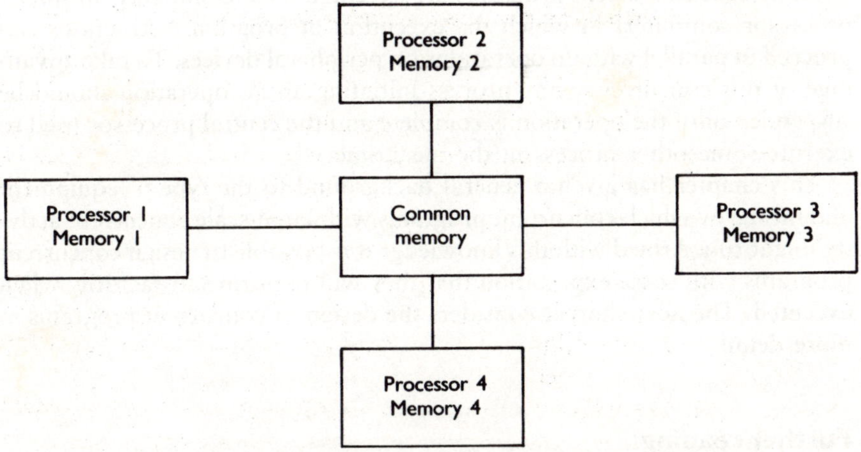

Figure 2.7 Hybrid multiprocessor architecture

cation speed inherent in the loosely coupled case. Memory contention is reduced by assigning the longer running processes to specific processors (by copying their instructions and data to the local memory of those processors) while communication speed can be kept high by exchanging information through the common memory.

Note that all of the machine environments discussed in this chapter are considered to be unsuitable for small-scale concurrent behavior because of the overhead involved in allocating processes to processors on these types of machine. The effort required to switch from one process to another is typically of the order of tens of machine instructions and so each process needs to be sufficiently long-running to make this overhead acceptable.

Summary

Programs involving large-scale concurrent behavior can be executed effectively on a wide range of modern general-purpose computers. At one extreme there are the multiprocessors that contain a relatively large number of identical processors capable of executing program instructions in parallel. At the other extreme there is the purely sequential environment presented to users of general-purpose operating systems. In the latter case concurrent behavior is simulated by switching the processor from one process to another. Even on a multiprocessor there are usually more processes than processors to execute them so it is necessary to share out the available power. In doing so the general objective is to achieve a reasonable appearance of concurrent behavior at an acceptable cost.

At present concurrent programs are executed most commonly on single-processor computers in which the execution of program instructions can proceed in parallel with i/o operations on peripheral devices. To take advantage of this concurrency any process initiating an i/o operation should be suspended until the operation is complete and the central processor used to execute some other process in the meantime.

This chapter has given a general background to the type of equipment and means by which concurrent programs with large-scale concurrent activity might run. Armed with this knowledge it is possible to design concurrent programs with some expectation that they will perform satisfactorily when executed. The next chapter considers the design of concurrent programs in more detail.

Further reading

The sharing of processor power among available processes is discussed in most books on operating systems. The part of an operating system with this responsibility is known as the *low-level scheduler* or *dispatcher*. For example, see:
- Lister, A.M., *Fundamentals of Operating Systems*, Macmillan, 1979.
- Deitel, M.D., *An Introduction to Operating Systems*, Addison Wesley, 1984.

For a detailed description of multiprocessor architectures see:
- Hwang, K. and Briggs, F.A., *Computer Architecture and Parallel Processing*, McGraw Hill, 1984.

This book also includes a section on *input–output subsystems* which describes various mechanisms for the low-level control of device transfers.

Exercises

2.1 How might a concurrent program be executed in a purely sequential environment but behave in a nondeterministic way?

2.2 Earlier in this chapter it was suggested that a switch from the execution of one program component to another in a program written in a block-structured programming language might be performed on entry to or exit from a procedure. Explain why this policy may not always be adequate and suggest a suitable method of switching that overcomes the problem.

2.3 Discuss, in general terms, a possible design for a concurrent program that is required to transfer the contents of a text file to a printer, assuming that the text file is held on disk and that the program will run in an environment providing asynchronous device transfers.

2.4 Not all peripheral devices generate an interrupt when a data transfer is complete. How might the end of such transfers be detected without the initiating program component being aware of this complexity if a real-time clock is available on the machine?

2.5 Suggest, in general terms, how the concurrent sorting program, discussed in Chapter 1, might be executed on both a tightly coupled and a loosely coupled multiprocessor. Identify the optimum number of processors required in each case.

Three

THE DESIGN OF CONCURRENT PROGRAMS

The task of developing a computer system for the solution of a given problem is rarely straightforward – even apparently simple problems will usually require a large amount of detail to be assimilated before a potential solution to that problem can be derived. The complexity resulting from this detail is generally kept under control by developing systems in an organized manner. Several development methods have been proposed for this purpose.

With regard to program design, most of the methods are based on the 'divide and conquer' principle of successively subdividing a program into smaller, less complex components, until each component can be coded directly. The main purpose of this chapter is to describe one such design method and to illustrate how it might be used in the development of concurrent programs. Before that, however, the next section gives some consideration to the *requirements analysis* and *specification* phases that must be completed before design commences.

Requirements analysis and specification

The starting point of all computer system development is an initial statement of the problem to be solved. In some cases this statement might provide nothing more than a general indication of what is required, while in other cases the problem statement may, in effect, define its solution.

The first phase of development, the *requirements analysis* phase, is concerned with identifying all of the requirements and constraints that must be incorporated in a solution to the problem being tackled. When this information is known one or more possible solutions may then be evident. For problems that are particularly complex, or novel, a *feasibility study* is generally performed to determine and examine potential solutions before selecting one, or deciding that no feasible solution can be found.

A 'solution' at this stage is largely in the mind of the person (or persons) analyzing the problem. The next step is to produce a precise *specification* of the requirements of that solution. For the software, a specification identifies the set of requirements that it must meet. These are made up of *functional* and *nonfunctional* requirements. Functional requirements identify functions, or operations that the software must implement while nonfunctional requirements identify other constraints such as, for example, stipulations of performance characteristics or an indication of the implementation language that is to be used. For example, a specification for a word-processing system might have the functional requirement that it should include a spelling checker and nonfunctional requirements that the spelling checker should be able to process ASCII text and operate at a rate of not less than one thousand words of text per second.

A specification should be unambiguous since it will often provide the basis of a legal contract for the development of the system concerned. This suggests that the requirements in the specification should be stated precisely and, where possible, be expressed *formally* in a mathematical notation. Ideally, the path from such a specification to a coded implementation of the software should also be pursued with mathematical rigor. In essence, this means that it should be possible to prove that the final implementation of the software (or any intermediate step in its development) satisfies the requirements stated in its specification.

Techniques for specifying software requirements formally do exist but these are, in the main, only suitable for defining *functional* requirements, while techniques for advancing formally from a software specification to an implementation are still the subject of research investigations.

Formal methods are not considered in this book; partly because of the space required to describe the various concepts, notations and basic mathematics involved and partly because the methodology is not sufficiently well developed to cope easily with the definition of the systems that are discussed here. Instead, specifications, where they are given, will be expressed in English and any arguments of correctness with respect to a specification will be presented informally.

Approaches to program design

A program design is developed by splitting the program into a set of smaller, more manageable parts. One approach is to divide the program into components that are intended to be executed in sequence. This is a general technique that can be used when subdividing most tasks, including those encountered in everyday life. For example, the task of completing a jigsaw puzzle might be divided into a sequence of three stages as follows:

(a) separate the pieces into two piles: those with outside edges and those without them;
(b) use the pile of pieces with outside edges to construct the jigsaw outline;
(c) complete the jigsaw with the remaining pile of pieces.

Similarly, program design by *functional decomposition* of the program involves subdividing the total task into a sequence of computational steps, or subfunctions which, when executed in order, implement the overall program function. For example, a program whose function is to sort a file of records might be subdivided initially into three subfunctions that read the records into main memory, sort the records and then write the sorted records to a file, respectively. These three subfunctions might then be subdivided into smaller subfunctions, in the same way, and the subdivision process repeated until each of the subfunctions can be implemented directly in the target language.

This technique is not adequate for concurrent programs, however, because their components have no defined order of execution. Instead we need a design method that allows program components to be defined without regard to their execution behavior. This chapter considers one such method – design by the *modular decomposition* of a program. This approach yields program designs in which the components, or *modules* may be implemented so that they can be executed either in parallel or in sequence. The remainder of this chapter attempts to explain what is meant by the term *module* with a view to giving some guidance on how modules can be identified.

What is a module?

A module may be defined in general terms as an *area of responsibility* within a program. As a step towards clarifying what this definition means in programming terms consider, by analogy, how we might describe the task of building a house. Taking a functional approach the description might outline the sequence of building phases involved, ranging from drawing up the plans and obtaining the required financing through to starting the foundations and finally putting on the roof and completing the interior. With a modular approach, the description would first identify those people involved in the construction, such as the client, the architect, the building contractor and the bank, and only then describe how the house can be built by their combined efforts. Put another way, we first identify the areas of responsibility required in a particular solution to the problem and then consider how these *modular components* can work together to implement this solution.

Most modules in a program fall into one of four general categories:

(a) modules responsible for physical objects (e.g. hardware devices);
(b) modules responsible for data structures;
(c) modules responsible for grouping related program components (e.g. related groups of type definitions or related groups of modules);
(d) modules responsible for program actions.

Modules in category (d) are similar in many respects to the type of component identified by the functional decomposition technique. The important difference is that components derived in the modular decomposition of a program are not constrained to have a defined order of execution at the design level and so may be implemented to execute concurrently.

Most concurrent programs have one particular type of module in common, a *state* module, whose responsibility is to record information about the current state of program execution. The *state* module is discussed towards the end of this chapter after four successive sections that deal with the four general categories of module identified above.

Module type (a): those responsible for physical objects

Often a module is made responsible for each physical device with which a program interacts. Such a module would handle, in particular, all of the low-level operations on the devices concerned. The amount of device handling in a program will vary from application to application but all programs have some form of external interaction, possibly requiring only the reading or writing streams of text. Some programs will have substantial amounts of code to handle devices. In particular, real-time programs are largely concerned with driving devices and responding to device input.

As a simple example of how a program can be developed in a modular fashion consider the following real-time problem:

A microprocessor-based alarm system is required to observe and display the temperature and humidity in a room and sound an alarm bell if either value exceeds some preset bounds. Temperature and humidity are shown on separate displays.

Additional points to note are:

(a) The alarm system operates for as long as power is supplied to it and so has no 'on/off' switch.
(b) The bell is a two-state device: for each signal it receives it switches alternately between the states 'ringing' and 'silent'.
(c) The temperature and humidity displays are updated as frequently as the hardware permits. In practice, the limiting factor is likely to be the speed of the sensor and display operations.

The alarm system involves five devices: a temperature sensor, a temperature display, a humidity sensor, a humidity display and a bell, as well as the microprocessor. These are shown in a *configuration diagram* for the system in Figure 3.1.

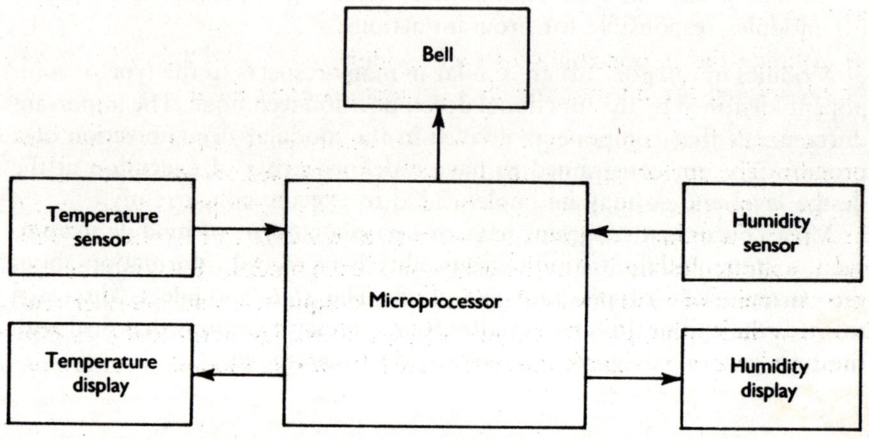

Figure 3.1 Temperature/humidity alarm system: configuration diagram

If a module is associated with each device the alarm system program, executed on the microprocessor, can be subdivided into five modules as shown in Figure 3.2.

This diagram is effectively an internal view of the microprocessor box in the configuration diagram. Connections are shown between each of the

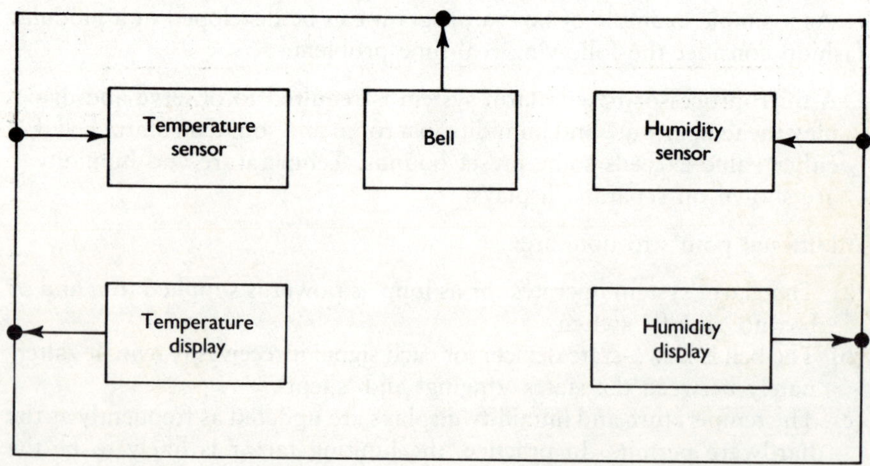

Figure 3.2 Temperature/humidity alarm system: device modules

device-handling modules and the edge of the box, denoting connections to the external physical devices concerned.

The next step in designing the program is to decide what other modules are needed, if any, and how the resulting set of modules can operate together to produce the desired program behavior. More specifically, this involves:

(a) defining the responsibility of each module;
(b) identifying the information that is passed among them.

The result is an *operational model* that describes the system design informally. The operational model that follows identifies one possible design for the temperature/humidity alarm system. The description is given in three parts: a module diagram, a summary of the behavior of the modules and a separate description of the behavior of each module. Each interaction between pairs of modules is identified by a unique reference number and an arrow indicating the direction(s) of data flow. The term 'data' in this context also covers signals that are passed from one module to another.

Temperature/humidity alarm system: operational model

Module diagram
See Figure 3.3.

Summary of module behavior
The *temperature sensor* module repeatedly takes temperature readings and reports each to the *temperature display* module (1) for output; if necessary,

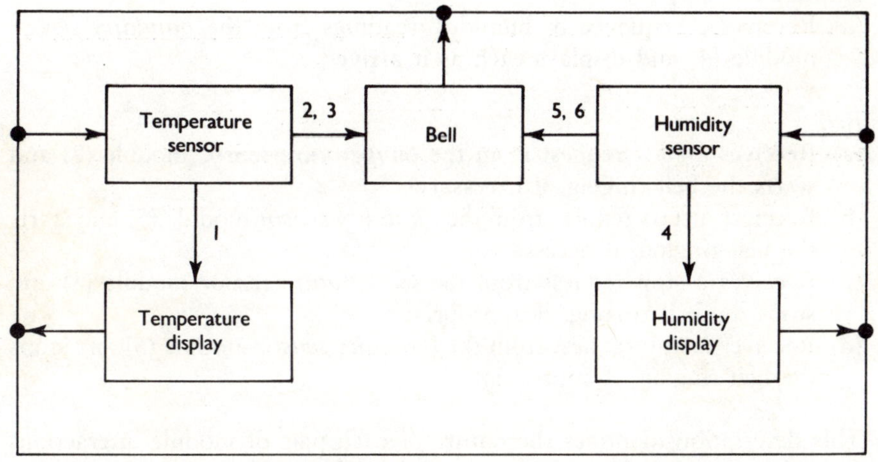

Figure 3.3 Temperature/humidity alarm system: module structure of concurrent solution

it interacts with the *bell* module to start (2) the bell, on detecting that the temperature is outside the defined acceptable range, and then to stop (3) the bell, when the temperature returns to normal. The *humidity sensor* module operates in a similar way.

Module descriptions

Temperature sensor
(a) Takes temperature readings repeatedly and sends each to the *temperature display* module (1).
(b) Sends a start request to the *bell* module if the temperature goes outside the acceptable range (2).
(c) Sends a stop request to the *bell* module if the temperature returns to the acceptable range (3).

Temperature display
(a) Receives a sequence of temperature readings from the *temperature sensor* module (1), and displays each as it arrives.

Humidity sensor
(a) Takes humidity readings repeatedly and sends each to the *humidity display* module (4).
(b) Sends a start request to the *bell* module if the humidity goes outside the acceptable range (5).
(c) Sends a stop request to the *bell* module if the humidity returns to the acceptable range (6).

Humidity display
(a) Receives a sequence of humidity readings from the *humidity sensor* module (4) and displays each as it arrives.

Bell
(a) Receives a start request from the *temperature sensor* module (2) and starts the bell ringing, if necessary.
(b) Receives a start request from the *humidity sensor* module (5) and starts the bell ringing, if necessary.
(c) Receives a stop request from the *temperature sensor* module (3) and stops the bell ringing, if appropriate.
(d) Receives a stop request from the *humidity sensor* module (6) and stops the bell ringing, if appropriate.

This description identifies the nature of each pair of module interactions from the viewpoint of each of the modules. This makes the text large but it has the advantage that the responsibilities and actions of each module can be understood in isolation.

A full design specification will include a precise definition of both the information passed among modules and the mechanism by which the information is transferred. Ideally such a definition should be given in a form that is independent of the intended implementation language. At present, however, there is no widely agreed notation for this purpose, so design decisions will be given here in the formal notation of the target programming language supplemented by suitable commentary, where necessary. A consideration of this aspect of design will be left until the next chapter which deals with a possible language representation for concurrent programs.

In the solution outlined for the temperature/humidity alarm system there is an assumption that the *temperature sensor* and *humidity sensor* modules execute in parallel to reflect the fact that such measurements can be taken simultaneously. Some or all of the remaining modules may also run in parallel, although the *bell* module does not have an obviously active role. In general, it is possible to divide the modules within a design into two types:

(a) those that are *dominant*, providing the motive force in a program;
(b) those that are *subordinate*, providing a service for the dominant components.

The decision as to which modules are dominant and which are subordinate in any solution tends to be influenced strongly by the implementation language used, so a further discussion of this point is delayed until the next chapter. For the moment it is sufficient to note that this possibility for distinguishing modules exists but assume that all modules run concurrently in a concurrent program.

In a sequential program there is only one dominant module. In some cases this module may be present in the design but in the temperature/humidity alarm system a sequential solution is best produced by introducing an explicit *driver module* (a module of type (d) according to the classification given earlier). All of the device modules are then subordinate, leading to the module diagram shown in Figure 3.4.

The driver module is connected to all of the device modules which are now independent of each other. The driver module will repeatedly sample the temperature and humidity in turn, display these values and switch the bell on and off, as necessary. All of these operations are performed through the appropriate device-handling modules. Notice that this sequential version of the alarm system may still appear concurrent to any observer of the system as the sampling rate is likely to be fast enough to make the temperature and humidity display changes seem simultaneous. Thus, in effect, the driver module is simulating concurrent behavior by switching regularly between temperature and humidity processing.

The sequential and concurrent designs for the alarm system have a similar modular structure but their respective modes of operation are quite different. In general, there is considerable choice as to how a design can

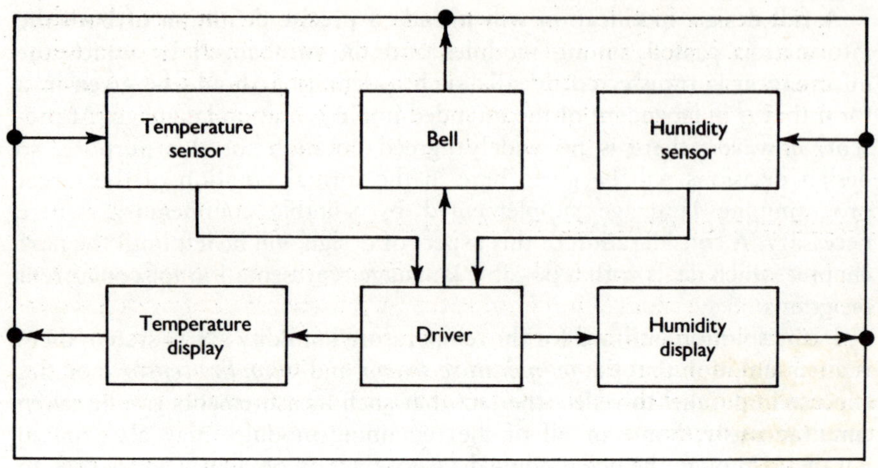

Figure 3.4 Temperature/humidity alarm system: module structure of sequential solution

be developed but, as yet, there are no guidelines to help steer a designer towards a recognizably best solution. Indeed, there are always vague conflicting requirements to be met in developing any program (e.g. small and powerful) so designers are really looking for one of many possible adequate solutions. The main role of a design technique is to provide a framework within which an acceptable program solution can be produced. Knowing that it is useful to associate modules with devices leads to an initial design diagram but it is then up to the designer to decide how the modules should operate together to produce the desired effect.

Finally, it should be noted that making modules responsible for physical objects such as devices yields a program structure which has several desirable attributes. In particular:

(a) It can help to make a design easier to understand because it establishes a direct link between the design structure and the physical structure of the system.

(b) It can make a program more portable and also easier to maintain, because the effect of replacing one device by another will tend to affect only one module in the system. The device module alone should be aware of how to drive the device. Any other module that requires operations on that device then goes though the device module. In this way device dependencies in a program are isolated. Such isolation of information is often known as *information hiding*. Program maintenance is also easier as a consequence of (a).

(c) Associating modules with devices can simplify the use of the device by the rest of the program. In general, a device module can serve as an *interface* to the facilities offered by a device, giving access to those facilities in a high-level abstract form. For example, in programs that use a graph plotter it is more convenient to operate on the plotter using operations that the plotter module provides, such as drawing a line or drawing a circle, rather than specifying the corresponding low-level operations actually needed to drive the device.

Module type (b): those responsible for data structures

A physical device is effectively a data structure in hardware. Just as it is useful to make a module responsible for each device used by a program so it is equally useful to have a module responsible for each data structure defined within the program. A data structure module isolates details of the implementation of the data structure and provides a suitable set of operations for its manipulation.

Consider, for example, a text analysis program that is required to identify and list all of the different words in a given text. Assuming that this program takes its input from a known disk file and directs its output to a file on the same disk then the program has only one device connection, namely, the link to the disk. The design will, therefore, include a disk interface module and may include, in addition, a module for each of the significant data structures present, viz. the input text, the set of words found and the output report. Assuming that these are the only modules needed part of the operational model of the system might be as shown in Figure 3.5.

Module summary
The *input text* module extracts a sequence of words from the text supplied by the *disk* module (1) and sends them to the *word set* module (2). The *word*

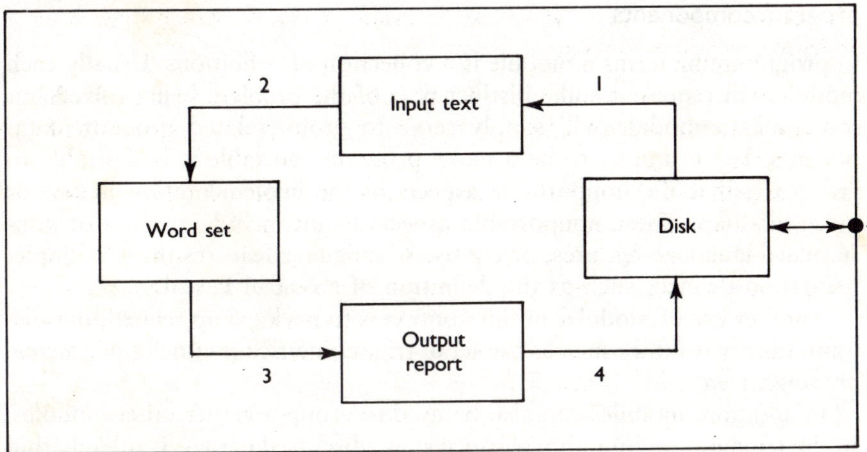

Figure 3.5 Text analysis module structure

set module analyzes the words it receives, builds the set of different words found and passes this set on to the *output report* module (3). The *output report* module produces a report from the set of words that it receives and sends the report to the *disk* module (4).

As mentioned already a design in this form is incomplete until a precise definition has been given both of the data involved and the method of its transfer between modules. This subject is discussed in the next chapter but two points are worth noting here:

(a) To maximize concurrent behavior it is desirable to pass on data from one module to another at the earliest opportunity. Thus, in the word analysis program the *input text* module should pass on words as it identifies them rather than waiting until the complete sequence has been found. The same argument also applies to the *word set* and *output report* modules, except that in the latter case it may be preferable to sort the words for presentation before producing the report.

(b) When a finite sequence of data values is passed between modules the end of the sequence must be identified in some way, e.g. an end-of-sequence data value.

The modular design that has been suggested for the text analysis program allows the modules concerned to execute in parallel. However, even if a sequential implementation is chosen the program structure is still in a desirable form in that each module hides some aspect of the representation of the data structures that it processes: the *input text* module isolates details of the representation of the text structure, the *output report* module isolates details of the report structure, and the *word set* module isolates details of how the set of words is maintained.

Module type (c): those responsible for related program components

In programming terms a module is a collection of definitions. Usually each module will represent some distinct part of the problem being solved but sometimes a module will simply serve to group related program components. For example, to help make programs portable it is desirable to group together the nonportable aspects of the implementation in one or more modules. These nonportable aspects might include any use of nonstandard language features, or the use of language features that are implementation defined, such as the definition of Maxint in Pascal.

Another use of modules in this context is to package up related, but disjoint, library routines such as the set of trigonometric functions *sine*, *cosine*, *arctangent* etc.

In addition, modules can also be used to group together other modules. In the temperature/humidity alarm system, discussed earlier, it is likely that the device modules will involve such a small amount of code that they can be implemented directly. In larger systems, however, the modules that emerge at the initial decomposition stage may be complex and so they too need to be subdivided in some way. Each module has the same structure as the program, in that it has a defined purpose and external connections, and so might be subdivided in the same way as the program. For example, consider a single-user interactive database system whose configuration diagram is shown in Figure 3.6. This system might be divided initially into two modules, as shown in Figure 3.7.

Both the *user interface* and *disk interface* modules are associated with devices, but as well as handling low-level data operations on those devices, they deal with the higher level interpretation of that data. The *user interface* module is responsible for handling all user interaction, and deals, in particular, with the input, analysis and response to any commands issued at the user terminal. The *disk interface* module is responsible for the representation, storage and retrieval of data held on disk. The connection between the two modules (1) denotes requests from the *user interface* module for database operations, such as the location or modification of a data item.

A suitable *user interface* module might be implemented by many thousands of lines of code, so it is desirable to perform some further breakdown

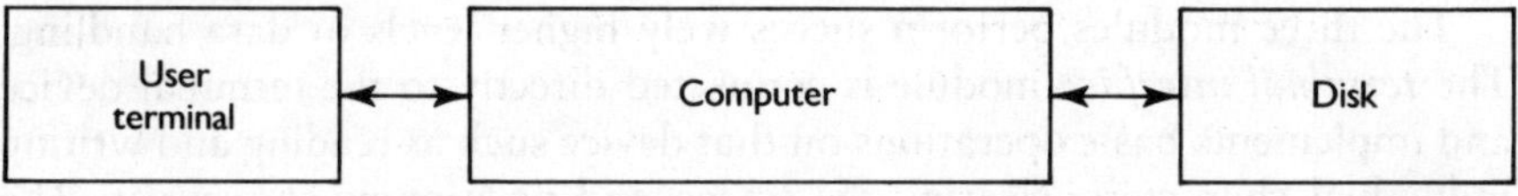

Figure 3.6 Database configuration diagram

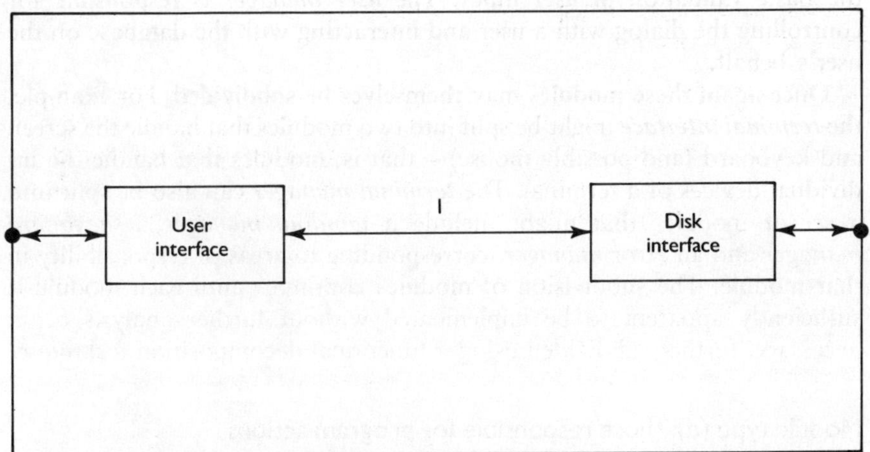

Figure 3.7 Database module structure

of its structure before coding it. One possibility is to subdivide the module into three parts as shown in Figure 3.8.

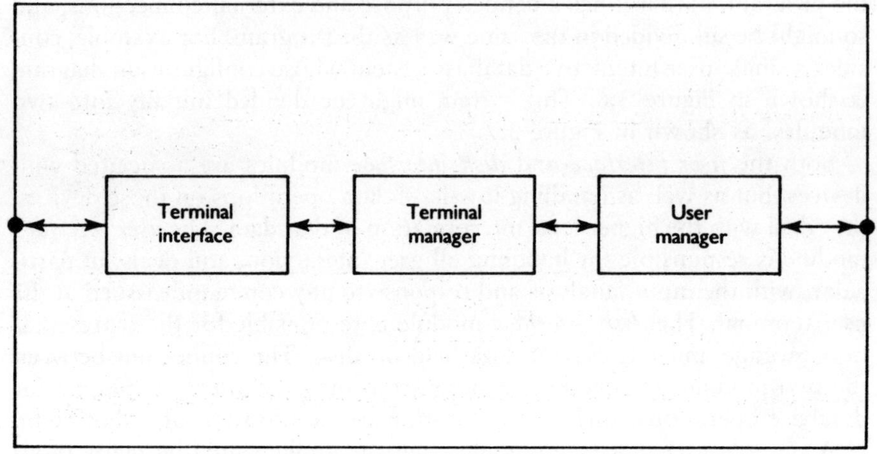

Figure 3.8 User interface submodule structure

The three modules perform successively higher levels of data handling. The *terminal interface* module is connected directly to the terminal device and implements basic operations on that device such as reading and writing individual characters, clearing the screen and positioning the cursor. The *terminal manager* module implements higher level terminal operations through the terminal interface module. These operations might include the control of text and graphic windows, the positioning of error messages and the basic validation of user input. The *user manager* is responsible for controlling the dialog with a user and interacting with the database on the user's behalf.

Once again these modules may themselves be subdivided. For example, the *terminal interface* might be split into two modules that handle the screen and keyboard (and possibly mouse) – that is, modules that handle the individual devices of a terminal. The *terminal manager* can also be split into a set of modules that might include a *window manager*, a *keyboard manager* and an *error manager*, corresponding to areas of responsibility in that module. The subdivision of modules continues until each module is sufficiently apparent to be implemented without further analysis or, if necessary, further subdivided using a functional decomposition technique.

Module type (d): those responsible for program actions

Modules of this type have already appeared in the examples used when discussing modules of types (a) and (c). The *driver* module in the sequential version of the temperature/humidity alarm system is a module of type (d), as is the *user manager* module in the database example. These are modules that provide a motive force in a program, whereas those belonging to types (a), (b) and (c) tend to have a subordinate role. It is difficult to give a more precise definition of this type of module except in the rather negative sense that if a module cannot be classified as belonging to (a), (b) or (c) then it must be in (d)! This 'definition' also mirrors the strategy followed when identifying modules in a program in that modules with types (a) to (c) are sought first with any remaining modules being classified as of type (d).

A state module

A *state* module is a repository for information about the current state of execution of a program. This information can be used to summarize the activity of the program and to detect when a terminating condition for program execution has occurred. A terminating condition might be reported directly by one module or deduced from information supplied by several of them. As an illustration of the latter case, consider the structure of a program simulating children playing the game of *hide-and-seek*.

One child is nominated as the *seeker*. The *seeker* allows the other children to find hiding places and then goes off in search of them. Each child who is discovered in turn becomes a *seeker* and the game ends when the last child hiding has been found.

A possible module diagram for the *hide-and-seek* simulation program is given in Figure 3.9.

The *child, seeker* and *hiding place* modules correspond to the entities

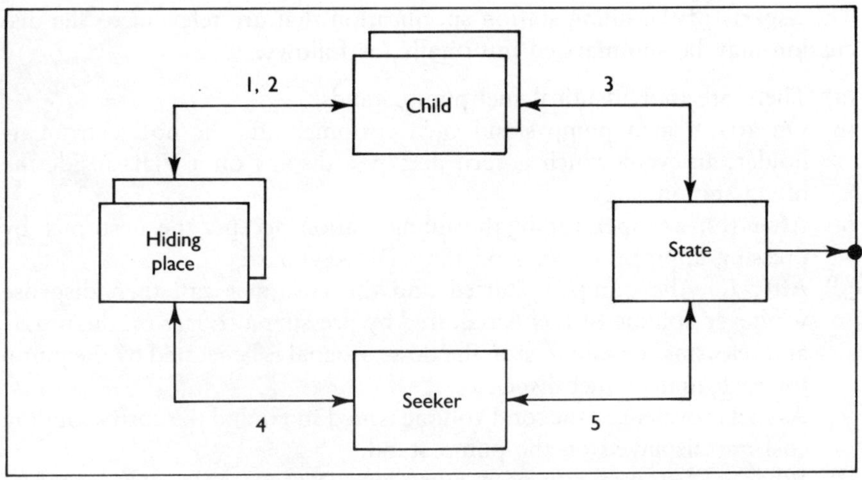

Figure 3.9 Hide-and-seek simulation program: module structure

in the simulation model. The *child* modules interact with *hiding place* modules to model the children both searching for hiding places (1) and, later, searching for other children (2). The *child* modules inform the *state* module each time a child is found (3). The *seeker* module also searches for children in the hiding places (4) and informs the *state* module of each discovery (5). In this way the *state* module keeps track of the number of children that have been located and so enables the terminating condition for the program to be detected and reported to the *child* and *seeker* modules.

The implementation of the *hide-and-seek* simulation program is set as an exercise at the end of Chapter 4 and a solution is given in Appendix 2.

Case study: a filling station control system

This section considers a larger example of the application of the modular design technique and provides further clarification of what is involved in developing and describing such a design. The filling station case study considered here and the other examples given later in this text do not address all aspects of an adequate solution for the problems being discussed. This is not altogether a result of laziness on the part of the authors. The purpose of most of the illustrations is to make specific points which would tend to be obscured by the amount of detail normally found in 'real' problems. This case study is best viewed as a treatment of some aspects of the operation of the filling station rather than constituting a close approximation to a complete solution.

Specification

The aspects of the filling station specification that are relevant to the discussion may be summarized informally, as follows:

(a) There are four identical fuel pump stands.
(b) On arrival at a pump stand each customer lifts the nozzle from its holder, an event which is recorded by a display on a VDU inside the filling station.
(c) After (b), an operator in the filling station accepts the customer by pressing appropriate keys on the VDU keyboard.
(d) After (c), the pump is started and the customer can then dispense whatever volume of fuel is required by pressing a trigger on the nozzle and releasing it again to stop the flow; a signal is generated by the pump for each unit of fuel dispensed.
(e) As fuel is dispensed the total volume issued so far and the corresponding cost are displayed on the pump stand.
(f) When a customer returns a pump nozzle to its holder the pump is switched off and the final charge details are displayed on the VDU in the filling station.

Operational model

Design: top level structure

Module diagram

There are two main areas of responsibility in this problem: the handling of pump operations and the handling of all communication with the operator in the station. There are two types of device involved: the operator's VDU and the pump stands, where each pump stand consists of a nozzle sensor, a pump and a display. As the four pump stands are identical it is appropriate to represent them as multiple copies of a single module, as shown in Figure 3.10.

The *pump stand* module has a 4 beside it in the diagram to indicate that four such modules are required. Each of the pump stand modules has three device connections: a nozzle sensor, a pump and a display. The *station operator* module has a single device connection to the VDU in the station. The responsibilities of each module are described below.

Module descriptions

Pump stand
(a) Detects the arrival of a customer when a pump nozzle is taken from its holder, and reports this event to the *station operator* module (1).
(b) Receives permission for a pump to be started from the *station operator* module (2).
(c) Starts the pump to allow a customer to obtain fuel and stops the pump when the operation is complete.
(d) Displays the amount of fuel dispensed and its cost as units of fuel are issued.
(e) Sends the total volume and cost of the fuel dispensed to the *station operator* module (3).

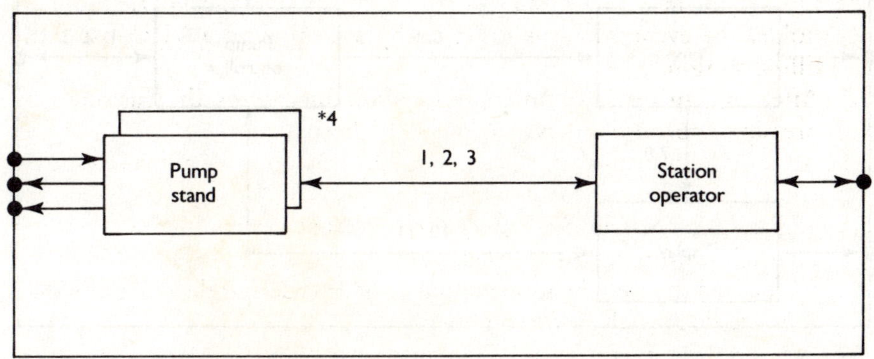

Figure 3.10 Filling station program: module structure

Station operator

(a) Receives notification of the arrival of a customer (1), informs the operator in the filling station, via the VDU screen, and awaits a reply via the VDU keyboard; on receiving a reply sends permission to start the appropriate pump to the *pump stand* module concerned (2).

(b) Receives details of a customer transaction from a *pump stand* module (3), and displays this information on the VDU.

Design: pump stand module structure

Module diagram
The *pump stand* module can be decomposed into four modules as shown in Figure 3.11.

Summary of module behavior
There are three modules handling the various device connections and a *pump controller* module handling communication between the devices and the *station operator* module.

The *nozzle* module sends a signal to the *pump controller* module if the nozzle is taken out or replaced in its holder. The *pump controller* module sends signals to the *pump* module to start and stop the pump. When a pump starts it informs the *display* module so that the display can be reset. Thereafter, the *display* module receives a signal from the *pump* module each time a unit of fuel is dispensed and the display is adjusted accordingly. The *nozzle*

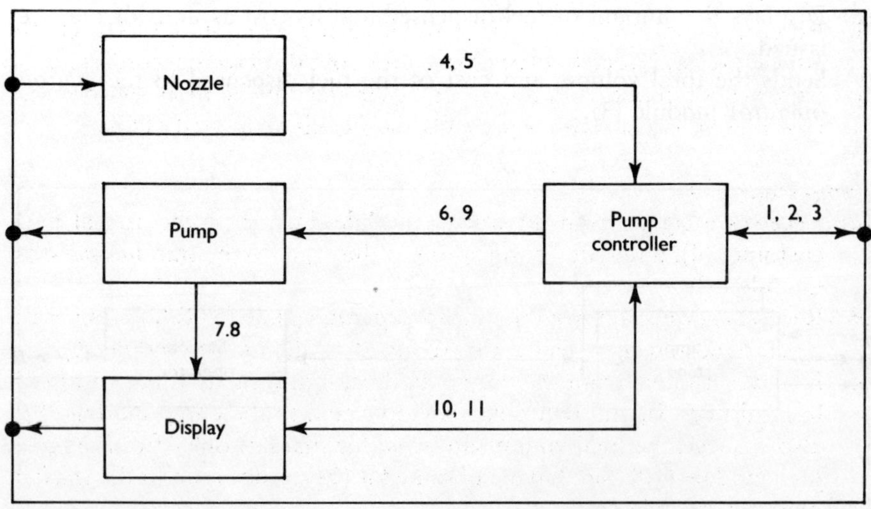

Figure 3.11 Pump stand module structure

module detects the end of the operation when the nozzle is returned to its holder. The *nozzle* module then reports this event to the *pump controller* module which sends a stop request to the *pump* module. The *pump controller* also obtains details of the volume and cost of the fuel dispensed from the *display* module and sends this information to the *station operator* module.

Module descriptions

Nozzle
(a) Detects removal of nozzle from holder, and reports this event to the *pump controller* module (4).
(b) Detects the return of the nozzle to the holder, and reports this event to the *pump controller* module (5).

Pump
(a) Receives a request to start the pump from the *pump controller* module (6), and then sends a reset signal to the *display* module (7) and starts the pump.
(b) After (a), detects each unit of fuel issued and informs the *display* module accordingly (8).
(c) Receives a request to stop the pump from the *pump controller* module (9), and then stops the pump.

Display
(a) Receives a reset signal from the *pump* module (7), and clears the display.
(b) Receives signals from the *pump* module each time a unit of fuel has been issued (8), and adjusts the volume and cost displayed accordingly.
(c) Receives a request from the *pump controller* for the total volume and cost of fuel issued (10), and sends the details requested (11).

Pump controller
(a) Receives a signal from the *nozzle* module, indicating the arrival of a customer (4), and sends notification of the event to the *station operator* module (1).
(b) Receives permission from the *station operator* module (2) for a pump to be started, and then sends a start signal to the *pump* module (6).
(c) Receives a signal from the *nozzle* module, indicating that the customer has finished (5), and then sends a stop signal to the *pump* module (9); also requests the final volume and cost for that customer from the *display* module (10) and, having obtained it (11), sends it on to the *station operator* module (3).

The *station operator* module in the top-level module diagram (Figure 3.10) can be subdivided into two connected parts: a *VDU* module, providing the usual device interface, and a *pump stands interface* module that is responsible for interacting with the *VDU* module by reporting the arrival of customers at the pump stands, sending permission for pumps to be started, and reporting pump transaction details. Once again a detailed description of the module responsibilities and interactions at this level can be produced, in the manner already illustrated for the other modules of the system.

No further modular decomposition is required and the design is ready to be completed by adding module specifications expressed in a form related to the target language.

Summary

This chapter has introduced a design technique that allows a program to be subdivided into components, or modules, that may execute in parallel. A modular design can also be realized as a sequential program. Consequently, the technique may be applied to a wide range of programming problems.

Modular design involves the identification of modules corresponding to relatively self-contained parts of a problem and the construction of an operational model of how those modules interact to fulfill the purpose of the program. Often it is useful to have modules responsible for handling operations on physical objects such as external devices, and which in some cases provide high-level interfaces to those objects. It is also useful to associate modules with each user-defined data structure in a program and to group together related program definitions. In particular, a module can group together other related modules thereby giving a hierarchical design in which the detail presented at any one level is manageable.

Further reading

The concept of a module as an 'area of responsibility' was first put forward in:
- Parnas, D.L., On the criteria to be used in decomposing systems into modules, *Comm. ACM*, Vol. 15, pp. 1053–8, 1972; reprinted in Freeman, P. and Wasserman, A.I., *Tutorial on Software Design Techniques*, 4th edn, IEEE, 1983.

The design technique that is perhaps closest in spirit to the one presented in this chapter is that of Michael Jackson, as described in:
- Jackson, M., *System Development*, Prentice Hall, 1983.

Many design techniques based on graphical notations have been proposed. Those that are relevant to the construction of concurrent programs concentrate initially on *data flow* (rather than on the method of flow). A summary of most of the common techniques can be found in:
- Peters, L.J., *Software Design: methods and techniques*, Yourdon Press, 1981.

Exercises

3.1 Give a configuration diagram and an operational model for a program to control a microprocessor-based digital stop-watch. The watch is operated by a single button. The first depression of the button clears the display, the second starts the watch running and the third stops it again.
(*Hint*: Remember that the internal clock in the watch is a *device*.)

3.2 Give a configuration diagram and an operational model for a program to control a microprocessor-based 24-hour digital alarm clock whose specification is as follows:

(a) The alarm clock can display either the current time or the alarm setting according to the position of a two-way TIME/ALARM switch; in either case the time is displayed in the form:
    hours : minutes
(b) The time setting may be altered by:
  (i) moving the TIME/ALARM switch to TIME,
  (ii) moving a two-way LOCK/UNLOCK switch to UNLOCK,
  (iii) pressing a CYCLE button to advance attention from one component of the display to another (the current component blinks),
  (iv) pressing an ADJUST button repeatedly to modify the current component value by one,
  (v) returning the LOCK/UNLOCK switch to LOCK.
(c) The alarm setting may be made in the same way by first setting the TIME/ALARM switch to ALARM.
(d) The alarm is triggered when the current time and the alarm time match and a SET/UNSET switch is in the SET position.
(e) The alarm is stopped by pressing a STOP button.

3.3 Modify the design developed in the filling station case study to deal with payment exclusively by credit card. Assume that a credit card reader is situated beside each pump and that the filling station has a telephone link over which a customer credit rating can be obtained automatically by the computer system, which will then lodge the details of each customer transaction.

3.4 Give an operational model for a concurrent text index program which, given a set of words and a document held as pages of text, will produce an index identifying the pages on which those words occur.

3.5 Suggest how the design for the concordance program, discussed on page 33, might be expressed in the programming language Pascal. Comment on how well the resulting program structure matches the design structure that was developed for it.

Four

THE REPRESENTATION OF CONCURRENT PROGRAMS

The previous chapter demonstrated how a program could be subdivided into a number of modules that might execute in parallel. The resulting program design was expressed in a diagrammatic form, supplemented by a commentary that outlined both the responsibility of the modules and the nature of the information that they exchange.

A program design in this form does not involve any particular programming language notation and so might be translated into one of a number of different target languages. This chapter considers how modular designs can be expressed in the programming language Pascal Plus, whose major features are based on proposals made by C.A.R. Hoare. Pascal Plus is fairly representative of a range of modern general-purpose languages that incorporate features to support modular concurrent programming. Other examples include Ada, Concurrent Euclid, Concurrent Pascal and Modula-2. The principal characteristics of these languages and the main differences between them are discussed in Chapter 11.

The remainder of this chapter identifies the type of language constructs that are required to represent a modular design and also discusses some of the problems and pitfalls that are often encountered in coding the interaction of concurrent program components. All of the examples given are expressed in Pascal Plus. Thus it is necessary to present and explain enough of the language to make these examples comprehensible. However, to avoid distracting the reader with an excessive amount of language detail some of the more complex aspects of Pascal Plus that are relevant to Chapter 4 have been tackled separately in a 'Question and Answer' section at the end of the chapter. Other features of the language are introduced in later chapters as and when the need arises. Those who would prefer to see a more immediate and concise description of Pascal Plus should consult its definition given in Appendix 1.

Module representation: basic requirements

The modular design technique is most effective in cases where the modules present in a design can be implemented by analogous program structures in the target language. The basic requirements are for:

(a) a module construct that enables all of the definitions and declarations associated with a module to be encapsulated;
(b) a module construct that can be executed in parallel with other similar module constructs;
(c) a mechanism that enables module constructs to communicate reliably with each other.

Requirements (b) and (c) are not met in the more traditional general purpose languages such as FORTRAN, COBOL and Pascal. However, requirement (a) is partly met by these languages. Pascal, for example, has a procedure construct that can bring together the full range of programming features available in the language, including variable declarations, constant and type definitions and further procedure definitions.

A procedure is a suitable representation for a module whose state need not be preserved from one module activation to the next. Consider, for example, the modules in the sequential version of the temperature/humidity alarm system discussed in the previous chapter. For convenience, the module diagram for this system is shown again as Figure 4.1.

Most of the modules here can be represented adequately by procedures. For example, if it is assumed that the temperature is denoted by a value of type **Integer**, then the *temperature display* module might be expressed as a procedure with a heading of the form:

```
procedure TemperatureDisplay (Temperature: Integer);
```

The details of how the temperature is displayed are all contained within this procedure and so it is an appropriate representation for the corresponding module identified in the design. The same is true of the other modules in the system, apart from the *bell* module, which has to remember previous bell operations that have been performed. Specifically:

(a) if the bell is ringing because either the temperature or humidity is out of range then it cannot be started a second time if both measurements go out of range;
(b) if both the temperature and humidity are out of range and one returns to normal the bell must still continue to ring.

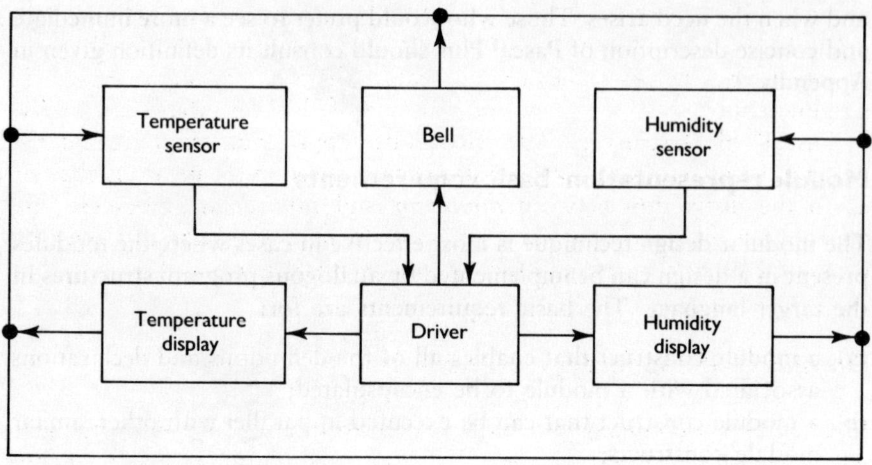

Figure 4.1 Temperature/humidity alarm system: module structure of sequential solution

These conflicts are easily resolved by keeping track of the number of requests to start the bell, using a counter declared as follows:

var BellRequests: 0 . . NumberOfUsers;

The *bell* module is thus represented by the variable BellRequests, together with two procedures which are called whenever it is required to turn the bell on or off, viz.:

```
procedure StartBell;
  begin
    BellRequests := BellRequests + 1;
    if BellRequests = 1 then {start bell}
  end {StartBell};

procedure StopBell;
  begin
    BellRequests := BellRequests − 1;
    if BellRequests = 0 then {stop bell}
  end {StopBell};
```

These procedures hide the details of how the bell is started and stopped (indicated informally) but they do not match exactly the corresponding module in the design. The difference is that the declaration of BellRequests is made outside the procedures because this value must survive successive procedure calls. As a result of this conflict with the design structure the program loses some of the clarity of the design and, more important, the data involved are now less secure since they are accessible to other modules.

In general, Pascal is not sympathetic to the implementation of our modular design technique, but several languages possessing more appropriate facilities have been derived from Pascal. In addition to the provision of concurrency facilities, the essential feature that such languages provide is a tighter control over the scope and visibility of identifiers than that defined by Pascal's block structure. Before looking at appropriate language features in detail let us return to the general question raised in the previous chapter as to the distinction between *dominant* and *subordinate* modules. The appropriate representation of each module in a program can only be decided if its role in the program is first clearly defined.

Dominant and subordinate modules

In Chapter 3 a dominant module was described as a program component which provided a motive force within the program, while a subordinate module was described as a component which provided a service for dominant modules. In languages that support modular design there are generally constructs for both types of module. In concurrent programs some or all of the modules might be deemed dominant. In the temperature/humidity warning system, for example, all five modules in the concurrent version of the design (Figure 3.3) can, in principle, run in parallel. In the programming language Ada this is indeed the most likely representation that would be used. In other languages, however, including Pascal Plus, the designer is encouraged to limit the amount of concurrency involved by representing as processes only those modules that have a clearly defined motive role.

In the temperature/humidity warning system the *temperature sensor* and *humidity sensor* modules have a motive role in that they continually take temperature and humidity measurements. The *bell* and *display* modules, however, simply respond to the information that they are given. That is, only the sensor modules need be represented as concurrently executing processes. The result, in this case, is that the two processes concerned then interact only with subordinate modules and not with each other. Interactions of this type are very efficient because no synchronization is involved, as would be the case with two communicating processes. Indeed, apart from Ada, languages supporting modular concurrent programming tend to prohibit direct interaction between concurrently executing processes. This means that if a program design suggests that two concurrent processes should interact it is necessary to introduce an intermediate subordinate module to support this interaction. Although this may represent a distortion of some designs, in many cases it is advantageous for processes to communicate in this way. In particular, it allows one process producing data for another to leave that data in a subordinate module and continue on its way, rather than wait for the receiving process to accept the data it has provided.

Chapter 7 discusses in detail how data can be communicated among concurrent processes. The next three sections look at the representation, in the programming language Pascal Plus, of processes that execute concurrently and of their subordinate modules. The concurrent processes are called *processes*, while the subordinate modules are divided into two types:

(a) *envelopes*, which are used by only one process;
(b) *monitors*, which are shared by several processes.

Unshared subordinate modules: the envelope concept

The basic subordinate module construct available in Pascal Plus is called an *envelope*. To illustrate its structure consider how the *bell* module in the sequential version of the temperature/humidity warning system might be expressed in Pascal Plus:

```
envelope module Bell;
   const NumberOfUsers = 2;
   var BellRequests: 0..NumberOfUsers;

   procedure *Start;
     begin
        BellRequests := BellRequests + 1;
        if BellRequests = 1 then {start bell}
     end {Start};

   procedure *Stop;
     begin
        BellRequests := BellRequests - 1;
        if BellRequests = 0 then {stop bell}
     end {Stop};

   begin {Bell}
     BellRequests := 0;
     ***;
     if BellRequests <> 0 then {stop bell}
   end {Bell};
```

The envelope shown here provides the required encapsulation for the data declaration and operations associated with the *bell* module.

The envelope has a similar structure to a Pascal procedure or function and may appear in the same declaration positions. As with any Pascal block the identifiers declared within an envelope block are hidden from surrounding blocks. However, those identifiers whose declarations are preceded by an asterisk may be referred to from outside the envelope. Thus they are termed *visible* (or *exported*) *attributes* of the envelope. In the example, the procedures Start and Stop are visible outside the Bell envelope while the variable BellRequests is hidden. The visible attributes define an *interface* through which other modules may interact with the envelope.

Visible attributes of an envelope may be accessed using the same notation available for record fields in Pascal. So, for example, in the surrounding block we may refer to the procedure Start using the dot notation:

    Bell.Start

or by means of a with-statement

    with Bell **do** Start

Again, like other blocks, the envelope has a statement-part. However, for an envelope this will normally consist of two parts:

(a) statements to carry out any initialization that is required in the envelope before use can be made of its visible attributes;
(b) statements to perform any finalization that is required before the termination of the envelope block.

The initialization and finalization parts are separated by the *** symbol, which is called an *inner-statement*. This inner-statement must always be present in the statement-part of an envelope, even in cases where there are no initialization or finalization statements.

Initialization in the Bell envelope involves setting the BellRequests variable to its initial value of zero and finalization involves stopping the bell, if necessary.

The lifetime of an envelope module is that of the block in which it is declared, with the initialization of the envelope preceding execution of the statement-part of that surrounding block, and the finalization following completion of execution of the statement-part of the block. Thus, the variable BellRequests is guaranteed to have been initialized properly before the surrounding block can use the Start and Stop operations. Similarly, only when the statement-part of the surrounding block has been completed will the Bell envelope attempt to turn off a still-ringing bell.

Where variables are declared as visible attributes of an envelope, access to them from outside the envelope is *read-only*, i.e. their values cannot be altered directly from outside. Hence, even if BellRequests had been preceded by an asterisk in its declaration, the surrounding program may only inspect its value, and may not attempt to change its value other than by means of a call of Start or Stop. Similarly, an envelope has read-only access to nonlocal variables declared in enclosing blocks.

The *temperature display* module might also be represented by an envelope rather than by a procedure:

    envelope module TemperatureDisplay;

        procedure *Show (Temperature: Integer); ...;

        begin ... **end** {TemperatureDisplay};

It is then possible to maintain local information about the display. For

example, the last temperature displayed might be retained so that a new
temperature would only be output if it differed from the old value by some
predefined amount.

Envelopes can also be defined in a form that allows multiple instances to
be created. This is achieved by omitting the word **module** from the block
heading and then declaring any required *instances* of the envelope, thus:

```
envelope ATemperatureDisplay;

  procedure *Show (Temperature: Integer); ...;

  begin ... end {ATemperatureDisplay};

instance
  TemperatureDisplay: ATemperatureDisplay;
```

In this case the combined envelope definition and instance declaration are
equivalent to the original envelope module definition.

Envelopes in this form may have formal parameter lists comparable to
those used for procedures and functions. For example, if the warning system
displays the temperature in more than one place then several instances of
the temperature display envelope will be required to handle the separate
displays. Each instance of the envelope can be initialized with a device
reference identifying the display with which it is associated, thus:

```
instance
  TemperatureDisplay1: ATemperatureDisplay (3);
  TemperatureDisplay2: ATemperatureDisplay (5);
```

Dominant modules: the process concept

With the notable exception of Ada, most other programming languages
supporting concurrency allow the representation of the modules of a program that execute concurrently as a procedure-like structure. This is true of
Pascal Plus. For example, the temperature sensor module in the concurrent
version of the temperature/humidity warning system might be expressed as
a Pascal Plus *process* as follows:

```
process module TemperatureSensor;
    const LowBound = ...; HighBound = ...;
    var T: Integer;
    begin
      while {system running} do
        begin
            {measure temperature T};
            TemperatureDisplay.Show (T);
            if (T < LowBound) or (T > HighBound)
            then begin
                    Bell.Start;
```

```
            repeat
               {measure temperature T};
               TemperatureDisplay.Show (T);
            until (T > Lowbound) and (T < HighBound);
            Bell.Stop
         end
      end
   end {TemperatureSensor};
```

This process executes a loop in which temperature is measured (implied informally by a comment), displayed, and its value checked against the required range. If the value is outside the permitted range the Start operation of the Bell envelope is invoked and another loop executed until the temperature returns to normal; the Stop operation of the Bell envelope is then invoked.

Pascal Plus processes, like envelopes, can be defined in a form which permits multiple instance declarations. Thus the *temperature sensor* module might have been declared in the form:

```
process ATemperatureSensor;
   . . .
   begin
   . . .
   end {ATemperatureSensor};


instance
   TemperatureSensor: ATemperatureSensor;
```

In addition, like an envelope instance, a process instance comes into being on entry to the block in which its declaration appears. The language rules for Pascal Plus have been chosen to permit a very simple model of process activation and termination but, before considering that solution, let us look at the general problem.

It might be expected from the preceding discussion in this and earlier chapters that a concurrent program would exhibit concurrent behavior at its point of activation. In practice, however, it is usually necessary to initialize the state of the program, sequentially, before any concurrent activity can occur. Thus, using most programming languages a concurrent program is implemented as a sequential process which splits into concurrent processes at some point, or points, during its execution.

One possibility is to permit the initial sequential process to activate other processes, each of which has the same capability. The pattern of behavior of the program that results can be represented as in Figure 4.2.

This *execution profile* of the program resembles a tree, each branch of which represents the lifetime of a process. The overall program thus terminates when each of its individual processes has terminated.

Another model of execution is to consider concurrency as resulting from a sequential process that separates, or *forks* temporarily into several pro-

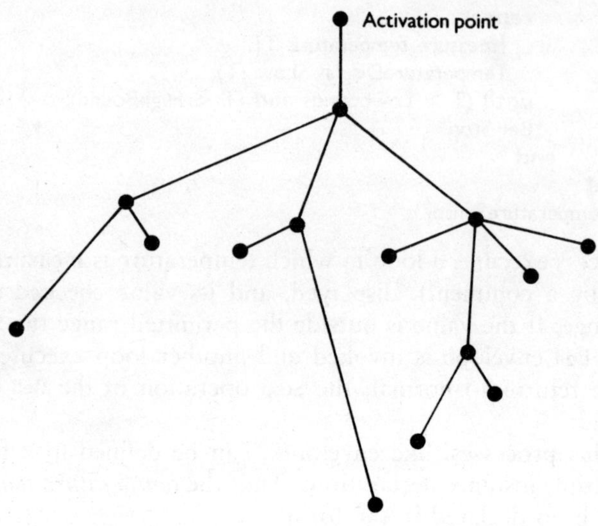

Figure 4.2 Concurrent program execution profile

cesses, each of which can fork again in the same way. Figure 4.3 shows an execution profile for a program with this pattern of behavior.

This is known as *fork-and-join* concurrency. In this model a concurrent program terminates when the initial process terminates. Pascal Plus, in effect, implements this model with the simplifying restriction that only one

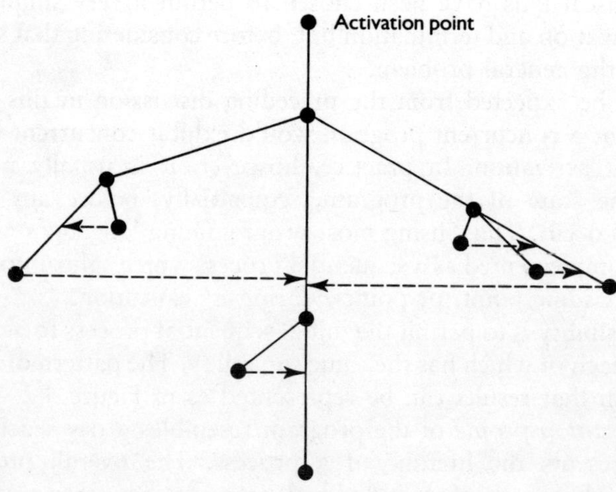

Figure 4.3 Concurrent program execution profile

fork can occur. This behavior is illustrated for a program involving five process instances, A to E, in Figure 4.4.

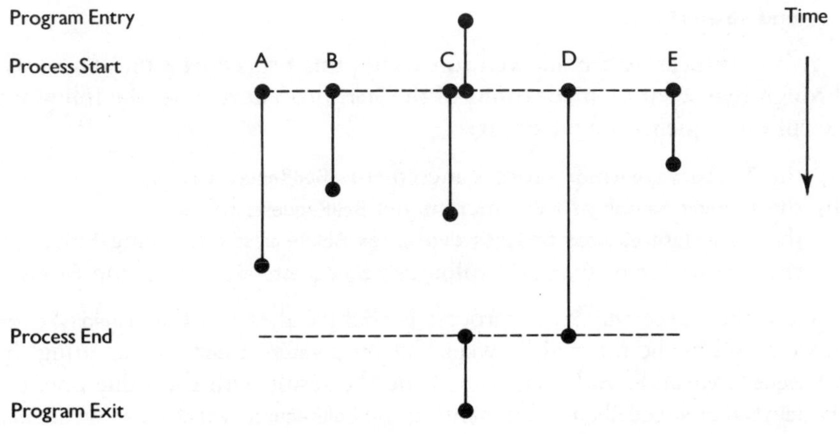

Figure 4.4 Pascal Plus program execution profile

The diagram shows a time trace of the execution of the five processes. On entry to the program there is a delay before the processes start, corresponding to the time taken to initialize the subordinate modules of the program. This delay is necessary to ensure that the initial state of the subordinate modules is established before they engage in interaction with processes. When the last process has stopped there is also a period before the program terminates in which the subordinate modules execute their finalization code. The execution time of the program is dictated by the execution time of the longest running process. Consequently, if one process goes into an infinite loop the program as a whole will not terminate.

In programming terms, all process instances exist on entry to the program with no new processes being created as the program executes. This means, for example, that processes cannot be declared within procedures or functions.

Shared subordinate modules: the monitor concept

The monitor construct of Pascal Plus is an envelope that can be accessed by several processes. To clarify why a different construct is needed consider what might happen in the temperature/humidity alarm system if both the TemperatureSensor and HumiditySensor processes attempt to ring the bell at (roughly) the same time. The bell is triggered by a call to the Start procedure of the Bell module. That procedure was implemented as follows:

```
procedure *Start;
  begin
    BellRequests := BellRequests + 1;
    if BellRequests = 1 then {start bell}
  end {Start};
```

If both processes are allowed to execute this procedure simultaneously, through two separate invocations of the Start procedure, then the following execution sequence might occur:

(a) the TemperatureSensor process increments BellRequests to 1;
(b) the HumiditySensor process increments BellRequests to 2;
(c) the TemperatureSensor process evaluates BellRequests=1, giving False;
(d) the HumiditySensor process evaluates BellRequests=1, also giving False.

Here the TemperatureSensor process is slightly ahead of the HumiditySensor process and in the interval between the TemperatureSensor incrementing the BellRequests variable and then comparing the result with the value one, the HumiditySensor succeeds in incrementing the BellRequests variable as well. As a result the alarm is not triggered at all!

The procedure Start is known as a *critical region* since it should only be executed by one process at a time, otherwise it may operate incorrectly.

The problem identified in this example can occur in general if two or more processes are allowed to manipulate the same data simultaneously. This is a particularly unpleasant type of fault because it is unlikely to occur very often, and being *time-dependent* and therefore transient, is not an error that can be detected by any systematic testing of the program.

One way to protect data accessed by several processes is to restrict access to the subordinate module, in which the data is defined, to one process at a time – that is, once any call has been made to the shared module any subsequent call is blocked (i.e. execution of the calling process is suspended) until the first operation is complete. The sequence of actions involved can be imagined as follows. When a call is made to a shared module its effect is to put up a barrier around the complete module which prevents other processes having calls accepted. When the first operation is complete the barrier is removed to allow another process to interact with the monitor. Thus, for example, if the TemperatureSensor process is the first to call the Start procedure of the Bell module, the HumiditySensor process is denied access until the TemperatureSensor process finishes. In addition, the HumiditySensor process is similarly delayed if it attempts to call procedure Stop when the TemperatureSensor process is executing procedure Start.

Such a *mutual exclusion* protection mechanism is achieved in Pascal Plus by declaring the subordinate module to be a *monitor* rather than an *envelope*. No other change to the text is necessary as the language compiler generates appropriate object code to provide the necessary protection.

The consequences of accessing shared data without mutual exclusion are considered to be so problematic that Pascal Plus permits envelope instances to be declared in a concurrent program only within process declarations. Thus, for example, even though the temperature and humidity display modules are accessed by only one process each must be declared as a monitor. In such cases the mutual exclusion protection is redundant and will not be implemented by an optimizing compiler.

The overall structure of one possible representation of the concurrent version of the temperature/humidity alarm sytem (Figure 3.3) can now be given:

```
program TemperatureHumidityAlarmSystem ;
       . . .
    monitor module Bell; . . . ;

    monitor module TemperatureDisplay; . . . ;

    process module TemperatureSensor; . . . ;

    monitor module HumidityDisplay; . . . ;

    process module HumiditySensor; . . . ;

    begin *** end {TemperatureHumidityAlarmSystem};
```

The sensor modules are implemented as processes and the bell and display modules as monitors. On entry to the program the initialization of the monitors is performed automatically. The body of the program is then executed. This contains an inner statement whose purpose is to activate all of the process instances in the program. These instances then execute in parallel.

Note that the structure of this program is very close to that given for its design. In this simple example five modules were identified in the design and these have been represented by five corresponding program blocks.

Pascal Plus provides a *library* mechanism that both aids the separate development of modules and also enables the program to be presented in a concise form. Using the library mechanism the definitions of the various modules can each be replaced by a library retrieval declaration indicating that the text of the module concerned will be found in a corresponding library file. For example:

```
process module TemperatureSensor in Library;
```

With this representation, a reader of the program text who is not interested in the details of particular modules is not distracted by the bulky text involved. If the reader does wish to see the details, then he or she simply inspects the corresponding file in the module library. When such a program is compiled, the compiler, on encountering a reference to a library module, incorporates the contents of the corresponding library file.

The module retrieved by a library declaration may be free-standing, in that its meaning is independent of the program environment in which it is retrieved, or it may depend on certain global definitions which the environment must provide. This flexibility is provided to allow modules to be defined in a general form, where possible. For example, the Bell monitor contains a definition of the number of using processes – a value which would have to be modified if, say, another temperature sensor were to be added to the system. To facilitate such a change the definition of the constant concerned can be taken outside the module definition and placed in an *environment specification* in the retrieval declaration. Thus, in the case of the Bell monitor the retrieval declaration might be given as follows:

```
monitor module Bell in Library
   (Where const NumberOfUsers = 2;);
```

In general, an environment specification defines the necessary nonlocal quantities for a library module without necessitating the use of these identifiers in the surrounding program itself. Further details of the library mechanism may be found in Appendix 1.

'Look before you leap': a synchronization problem

The monitor construct helps the programmer to avoid certain types of process interaction error by providing a mechanism that can give each process exclusive access to shared data. However, interaction errors can still occur if a process attempts two successive monitor operations under the assumption that the monitor state remains unchanged between these operations. To see how this error might occur in practice consider how a program to control access to a car park might be implemented. The main requirements of the program are as follows:

(a) The car park has one entrance and one exit.
(b) At the entrance there is a barrier which must be raised to allow a car to enter the park. The arrival of a car is detected by an underground sensor. A second sensor beyond the barrier detects when a car has entered the park, thus enabling the barrier to be lowered again. The pair of sensors must be triggered in the required order; otherwise the barrier remains down.
(c) At the exit there is a similar barrier that operates in the same way.
(d) If the car park becomes full a large *car park full* sign is illuminated at the entrance and when a car approaches the barrier it is not raised.

(Note that, as in other examples, only *some* aspects of a car park control system are considered. For example, no account has been taken of cars pulling trailers, or of the barrier and sensor equipment failing to operate. With such simplifications we can concentrate on the synchronization problems which the example is intended to illustrate.)

A configuration diagram and a first-level modular design for the car park control might be given as in Figures 4.5 and 4.6.

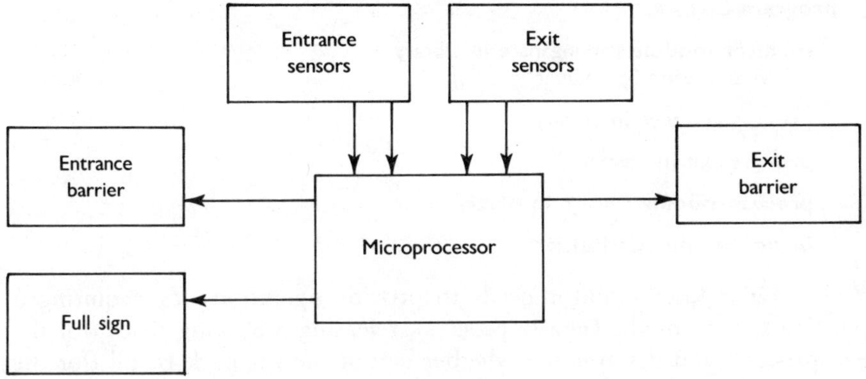

Figure 4.5 Car park configuration diagram

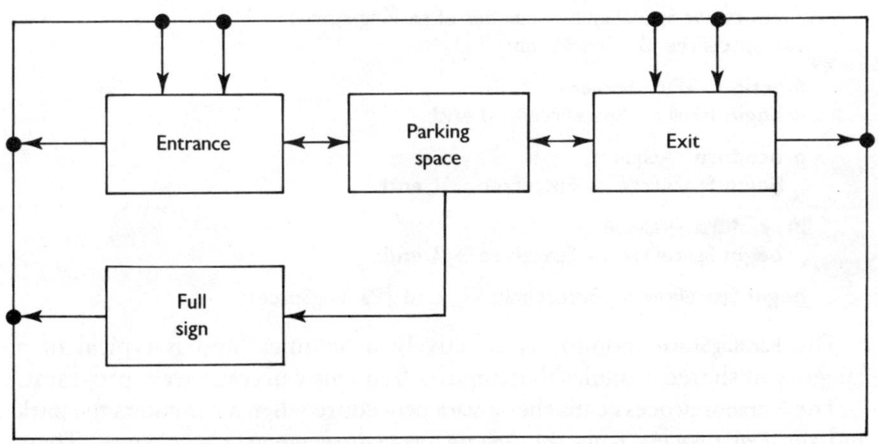

Figure 4.6 Car park control program: module structure

The *parking space* module maintains a record of the number of free spaces available in the car park and the *entrance* and *exit* modules look after all the activities associated with cars entering and leaving the park. The *full sign* module is responsible for switching the full sign on and off when necessary, acquiring the information it needs from the *parking space* module. The *entrance* and *exit* modules each have three external connections corresponding to their links to two underground sensors and a barrier.

This description implies that the *entrance*, *exit* and *full sign* modules have motive roles and so can be represented as processes, while the *parking space* module is subordinate and so might be represented as a monitor. The overall program structure is then:

```
program CarPark;

    monitor module ParkingSpace in Library
       (Where const SpaceLimit = ...;);

    process Entrance in Library;

    process Exit in Library;

    process module FullSign in Library;

    begin *** end {CarPark};
```

The ParkingSpace monitor needs to provide operations for acquiring a parking space (for the Entrance process), releasing a parking space (for the Exit process) and determining whether or not the car park is full (for the FullSign and Entrance processes). The monitor might be implemented as follows:

```
monitor module ParkingSpace;
{assumes const SpaceLimit = number of parking space}
    var SpaceFree: 0..SpaceLimit;

    function *IsFull: Boolean;
       begin IsFull := SpaceFree = 0 end;

    procedure *Acquire;
       begin SpaceFree := SpaceFree − 1 end;

    procedure *Release;
       begin SpaceFree := SpaceFree + 1 end;

    begin SpaceFree := SpaceLimit; *** end {ParkingSpace};
```

The ParkingSpace monitor is effectively a 'counter' and is typical of a category of shared modules that appears frequently in concurrent programs.

The Entrance process calls the Acquire procedure when a car enters the park and the Exit process calls the Release procedure when a car leaves. These procedures decrement and increment, respectively, a count of the number of available parking spaces recorded by the variable SpaceFree. Before the Entrance process allows a car to enter the park it checks that there is space available using the function IsFull. The Entrance process might thus be expressed as follows:

```
process module Entrance;
    begin
       repeat
          {await arrival of car at sensor 1};
          while ParkingSpace.IsFull do {nothing};
          ParkingSpace.Acquire;
          {raise barrier};
          {await arrival of car at sensor 2}
          {lower barrier}
       until {system close-down}
    end {Entrance};
```

The sensor and barrier operations are shown informally as comments. If the Entrance process finds that the park is full it *waits* for a space to become free. The *waiting* is implemented by the Entrance process executing a loop in which it repeatedly calls the IsFull function until the value False is returned. At that point the Entrance process calls the Acquire procedure to acquire a space, and then goes through the steps required to admit the car.

The program as it stands will work correctly but its structure is not satisfactory. Its weakness can be illustrated by extending the system to handle a second entrance. This might be necessary if, for example, it is found that a long queue builds up at the entrance at certain times of the day. If the second entrance has exactly the same characteristics as the first then it might be handled in the control program by generalizing the Entrance module to a form from which multiple instances can be declared. Parameters are required to identify the entrance on which each instance operates:

```
process Entrance (Identity : . . .);
    . . .
```

Two instances of this process are then declared as follows:

```
instance
    Entrance1, Entrance2: Entrance ( . . .), ( . . .);
```

The values passed would typically be references with which the associated devices can be addressed.

This modification seems plausible but the resulting program is now incorrect. As it stands there is a possibility that the variable recording the number of free spaces will be decremented when its value is zero, and the program's subsequent behavior will be erroneous. The fault lies with the way in which the decision is taken to allow a car to enter. Each Entrance process checks that there is space in the park via the IsFull function and then calls Acquire to decrement the SpaceFree variable if the value returned by IsFull is False. In doing so, however, there is an incorrect assumption that the variable SpaceFree will not have changed between the inspection of its value in the function call and the subsequent decrement operation. In reality, the following sequence of operations might occur:

(a) Entrance1 calls IsFull finding SpaceFree at 1;
(b) Entrance2 calls IsFull finding SpaceFree at 1;
(c) Entrance1 calls Acquire which sets SpaceFree to 0;
(d) Entrance2 calls Acquire which sets SpaceFree to −1!

Both Entrance processes call the IsFull function at roughly the same time; both find the value of SpaceFree is one, and so both allow a car to enter, causing the SpaceFree variable to violate its lower bound.

Since the fault has been caused by assuming that the inspection of SpaceFree and its adjustment are indivisible actions, the solution to this synchronization problem is to ensure that the actions cannot be interrupted.

This is readily achieved by insisting that these two actions are consecutive inside the ParkingSpace monitor:

```
monitor module ParkingSpace;
   {assumes const SpaceLimit = number of parking spaces}
   var SpaceFree: 0. . SpaceLimit;

   function *IsFull: Boolean;
      begin IsFull := SpaceFree = 0 end;

   procedure *TryToAcquire {var OK: Boolean);
      begin
         OK := SpaceFree <> 0;
         if OK then SpaceFree := SpaceFree − 1
      end {TryToAcquire};

   procedure *Release;
      begin SpaceFree := SpaceFree + 1 end;

   begin
      SpaceFree := SpaceLimit;
      ***
   end {ParkingSpace};
```

(The IsFull function is still provided since it is needed by the FullSign process.)

Following this modification to the ParkingSpace monitor the Entrance process now assumes the following form:

```
process Entrance (Identity: . . .);
   var OK: Boolean ;
   begin
      repeat
         . . .
         repeat ParkingSpace.TryToAcquire (OK) until OK;
         . . .
      until {system close-down}
   end {Entrance};
```

When a car arrives at an entrance, the corresponding Entrance process calls the monitor procedure TryToAcquire in an attempt to obtain a parking space on its behalf. If a space is available, it is allocated, and the Boolean parameter OK is set to True, otherwise the parameter is set to False. This call is repeated until a True value is obtained.

Note that it would appear to be slightly tidier for the Entrance process to loop inside the monitor so that a return from the monitor would imply that a parking space had been allocated. That is, in place of the loop in the process we might instead use a single call to a new interface routine expressed as follows:

```
procedure *Acquire;
   begin
      while SpaceFree = 0 do {nothing};
```

```
        SpaceFree := SpaceFree − 1
    end {Acquire};
```

Unfortunately this representation puts the car park control program into an infinite loop whenever the car park becomes full! It is always incorrect to loop inside a monitor awaiting a change to its local data because any process capable of making that change will, by definition, be excluded for as long as the first process is executing the call of the monitor procedure concerned. Hence, any 'busy-waiting' loop inside a monitor will always lead to an erroneous program.

The general synchronization problem of inspecting shared data and then performing some action which assumes that the data has remained unchanged in the interval, tends to be a common source of error to those new to writing concurrent programs. The technique of 'inspecting and then acting' is perhaps partly encouraged by the old adage 'look before you leap' but more likely it can be attributed to a style of programming acquired when constructing sequential solutions. For example, in processing data items from a Pascal sequential file it is usual to construct a loop of the form:

```
while not Eof (InputFile) do
   begin
      Read (InputFile, DataItem);
      {process data item}
   end
```

This loop is satisfactory as part of a sequential program but, if the input file is shared by several processes in a concurrent program, the test on the state of the file and the reading of a data item must not be separated — otherwise a process may at some stage attempt to read beyond the end of the file. Thus the loop is better expressed in the form:

```
repeat
   M.TryToRead (DataItem, OK);
   if OK then {process data item}
until not OK
```

The TryToRead procedure is a visible operation of a monitor M, in which the data file is declared. The procedure can be expressed as follows:

```
procedure TryToRead (var DataItem: ItemType; var OK: Boolean);
   begin
      OK := not Eof (InputFile);
      if OK then Read (InputFile, DataItem)
   end {TryToRead};
```

In all situations where a value that is shared by two or more processes is inspected and then modified by those processes, a programmer must ensure that these operations are *indivisible*, i.e. that they are combined into a single monitor procedure.

Explicit process synchronization: the condition concept

One of the objectives of any control program is that it should treat *fairly* the processes which it administers. The various components of the car park control program, developed in the previous section, now appear to behave correctly. However, from the point of view of the users of the car park the program is still faulty. The problem no longer lies with the number of cars that are admitted, but with the order in which admissions take place. As the program stands, when a car leaves the park and there is a car waiting at both entrances it is not possible to predict which car will be allowed to proceed. Thus, there is a possibility that the longer waiting car will not be the first to enter. This unfair allocation may occur again and again and cause some rancour if the queues of waiting cars are visible to each other!

The competition among processes for shared resources (e.g. parking space) is an example of a *resource management problem* – problems of this type occur frequently in the programming of concurrent systems. Consequently, languages supporting concurrency usually need to provide some facility for explicit process queuing, i.e. a facility for suspending the further execution of a process until the condition under which it may safely progress is met. Such a facility makes the programming of resource acquisition operations less clumsy and also conserves processor power by avoiding busy-waiting loops in which processes idle until the resources they need are available.

In Pascal Plus, the suspension of a process on a queue, and the subsequent reactivation of that process, are effected through instances of a standard module named Condition, which has the following interface:

```
monitor Condition;
     {Maintains a queue of suspended process instances, partially  }
     {ordered by a priority value specified at the point of their  }
     {suspension. Processes with the same priority value are held  }
     {in their arrival order.                                      }
     {The queue is in ascending order of priority value.           }
  type NonNegative = 0..Maxint;
  procedure *PWait (P: NonNegative);
     {Suspends process on priority queue at position determined}
     {by the value of P.                                       }
  procedure *Wait;
     {Performs PWait with a default priority "Maxint div 2".    }
  procedure *Signal;
     {If the queue is empty then no effect, else the process    }
     {at the head of the queue is reactivated.                  }
  function *Empty: Boolean;
     {Returns True, if queue is empty and False otherwise.      }
  function *Length: NonNegative;
     {Returns count of process instances in queue.              }
  function *Priority: NonNegative;
     {Returns the priority value with which the process at the  }
     {head of the queue was suspended; it is an error if the    }
```

```
    {queue is empty when this operation is invoked.              }
  begin
    {initially the queue is empty}
  end {Condition};
```

The Condition module is shown as a monitor which it resembles in that only one process at a time can interact with a Condition instance. However, a Condition instance uses the exclusion mechanism of the monitor in which it is declared rather than having a separate mechanism of its own.

Associated with each instance of Condition is an ordered queue on which processes may be suspended using the PWait and Wait routines. PWait is the basic operation. When invoked it suspends the calling process on the queue at a position determined by the priority value parameter passed to the routine. By convention a high priority value indicates a low priority status so a top priority process has a priority value of zero. The suspended process is positioned in the queue behind all processes with either a lower or the same priority value. Thus, for processes of equal priority the queue ordering reflects their order of arrival. Often queuing is performed solely by order of arrival and the simpler Wait operation can be used in such cases. The Wait operation is equivalent to:

```
  PWait (DefaultPriority)
```

where the Default Priority is the midpoint of the priority range, i.e. Maxint **div** 2.

The Signal operation is used to reactivate whichever process, if any, is currently suspended at the head of a condition queue. All other processes on the queue are left suspended in the same order. A call of Signal applied to an empty queue has no effect.

The remaining three condition operations provide details of the current state of a condition queue. The Empty operation returns the value True if there are no processes on the queue and False otherwise. Length gives the number of processes currently suspended and Priority returns the queuing priority value of the process at the head of the queue.

The use of the condition mechanism can be illustrated by showing a revised version of the ParkingSpace monitor in which any Entrance process that is unable to proceed is suspended until a parking space becomes available:

```
  monitor module ParkingSpace;
  {assumes const SpaceLimit = number of parking spaces}
      var SpaceFree: 0..SpaceLimit;
      instance Queue: Condition;

      function *IsFull: Boolean;
         begin IsFull := SpaceFree = 0 end;

      procedure *Acquire;
         begin
            if SpaceFree = 0 then Queue.Wait;
            SpaceFree := SpaceFree - 1
         end {Acquire};
```

```
    procedure *Release;
      begin
        SpaceFree := SpaceFree + 1;
        Queue.Signal
      end {Release};

    begin SpaceFree := SpaceLimit; *** end {ParkingSpace};
```

The corresponding code for an Entrance process now takes the form:

```
process Entrance (Identity : . . .);
  begin
    repeat
        . . .
        ParkingSpace.Acquire;
        . . .
    until {system close-down}
  end {Entrance};
```

The request for a parking space is now a simple call to the Acquire procedure of the ParkingSpace monitor. If space is available the SpaceFree variable is decremented and the calling process is allowed to continue. However, if the park is full the calling process is suspended by means of a call of Queue.Wait. *At the same time the suspended process releases its exclusive access to the monitor in which the condition instance is declared.*

When a space is freed, through a call to the procedure Release, the SpaceFree variable is incremented, as before, and then a Queue.Signal operation invoked. If a process is suspended on the condition queue at that moment it is reactivated and continues execution immediately after its point of suspension. That is, it decrements the SpaceFree variable and proceeds to acquire the space that has just been released.

If both Entrance processes are suspended on the condition queue then their order in the queue reflects their order of arrival. Thus, the longer waiting process, and therefore the longest waiting customer, will be allowed to enter the car park first. If both entrances have queues of cars then the net effect will be to alternate entry from one entrance to the other as spaces become free – a policy that most customers will feel is fair.

Discussion of the Condition monitor concept concludes our survey of the basic range of language facilities that might be used to support the representation of concurrent programs. These facilities have only been discussed in broad terms and the details of how, in particular, monitor exclusion is handled are insufficient to enable a reader to start writing programs. The next section covers the exclusion mechanism in more depth by discussing 'typical' questions that might be posed in this area.

Monitor exclusion: further details

Concurrent Pascal, Concurrent Euclid and Modula-2 are examples of monitor-based programming languages. Consequently, all of the questions pertaining to the Pascal Plus exclusion mechanism in this section will also be pertinent when using any of the other languages. Different answers will often result and some of these are discussed in Chapter 11, in which other approaches to the representation of concurrent programs are examined. Answers to queries concerning other aspects of Pascal Plus can be found in the language definition in Appendix 1.

Question 1

Can a monitor interface procedure include a recursive call, or a call of another procedure within the same monitor? If so, does this mean that a particular client process may attempt to acquire exclusive access to the monitor a second time?

Answer

A monitor procedure can include either a recursive call or a call to another interface procedure within the same monitor, with only one attempt being made to acquire exclusive access to the monitor. This is possible because the actions of acquiring and releasing exclusion effectively bracket the first call to the monitor procedure, with no further acquisition or release taking place once the process has gained access. For example, given:

```
monitor module M;

  procedure *Proc;
    begin ... Proc; ... end;

  begin ... end {M};
```

a call from outside M to the procedure Proc generates the following sequence of actions:

```
Acquisition of access to monitor M
Execution of M.Proc
Release of access to monitor M
```

while the internal recursive call to Proc has none of these acquisition and release actions associated with it.

Question 2

If a Signal operation is applied to a process on a condition queue when, precisely, is the process reactivated? There would seem to be a possibility that the signaled process and the signaling process might both be active simultaneously in a monitor, thereby violating the exclusion principle.

Answer

In general, a condition signal is used to indicate that the monitor is in a suitable state for a suspended process to continue. That process is resumed immediately the signal is issued so that definite assumptions can be made about the state of the data held by the monitor. Meanwhile, the signaling process is itself suspended until the resumed process completes execution of the monitor, or is resuspended within the monitor.

For example, consider the ParkingSpace monitor in the car park example. When an Entrance process is reactivated it decrements the number of parking spaces available without checking that the current value is nonzero. This is only safe if it is assumed that the signal issued by the Exit process causes the suspended Entrance process to run immediately without the possibility of interference from the other Entrance process.

If a process issues a signal immediately prior to leaving a monitor, i.e. as its last action within a monitor procedure, then, as an optimization, exclusive access to the monitor may be transferred from one process to another and both processes allowed to run. However, as a general rule, when a signal is issued in the execution of a monitor procedure exclusive access to the monitor is transferred from one process to another and the signaling process is suspended until the monitor is free.

Question 3

The reply to Question 2 makes it clear that two processes are never active in a monitor in the same time but the reactivation point of a suspended signaling process is still vague. In particular, can any other process obtain access to the monitor ahead of the one that issued the signal?

Answer

If there is competition for access to a monitor between a process that is suspended because it issued a signal and a process suspended when attempting to enter the monitor through an interface procedure, the signaling process is given preference when the monitor subsequently becomes free.

Other processes may also be involved if a signaled process itself issues a signal. The rule here is that signal calls are *stacked*. That is, when a process releases exclusive access to a monitor, the right of access is transferred to the process that signaled the exiting process, if any. Thus, if process A signals process B which signals process C, then when C is finished with the monitor, right of exclusive access is transferred to process B, and when B finishes, right of exclusive access is transferred to process A.

Question 4

Can a call be made from one monitor to another and, if so, does the process involved then lose its exclusive access to the first monitor?

Answer

Calls from one monitor to another are allowed but the calling process retains exclusive access to all of the monitors through which it passes. If the process is suspended on a condition queue in one monitor its exclusive access to that monitor and all others is released. The signal operation that subsequently reactivates the process gives access to the monitor in which the process was suspended but permission to re-enter the other monitors is only obtained as the process returns to each one. Such a process has priority over any process attempting to enter a monitor through an interface procedure but has a lower priority than a process delayed because it issued a signal in that monitor.

Consider, for example, the following situation where three processes A, B and C, interact with two monitors M1 and M2. The action of each process is to enter M1, which in turn causes the process concerned to enter M2. In M2 a process is suspended if no other process is suspended, otherwise the arriving process reactivates the waiting process. M1 and M2 are as follows:

```
monitor module M2;
   instance Queue: Condition;

   procedure *Enter;
     begin
       with Queue do
         if Empty then Wait else Signal
     end {Enter};

   begin *** end {M2};

monitor module M1;

   procedure *Enter;
     begin M2.Enter end;

   begin *** end {M1};
```

The following sequence of operations may occur:

(a) Processes A, B and C all attempt to enter M1 in that order. Process A gains entry and both B and C are made to wait.

(b) Process A enters M2 by the call of M2.Enter *and is suspended on the condition queue, releasing access to both* M1 *and* M2.

(c) Process B enters M1 and then M2 and signals the condition queue.

(d) Process B is suspended and process A is given exclusive access to M2 (B still has exclusive access to M1).

(e) Process A leaves M2 but is suspended on trying to return to M1.

(f) Process B is restarted, returns to M1, and then leaves M1.

(g) Process A returns to M1 and then leaves it, allowing process C to enter M1.

(h) Process C enters M1, then enters M2 and is suspended on the condition queue.

All of this may seem rather complex but it is often the case that the precise order of events is not important. Also, most monitor operations do not usually involve calls to other monitors. Thus much of the detail given here on the transfer of monitor access need only be considered in fairly rare circumstances.

Question 5
Is a call to a Condition operation from within a monitor the same as a nested monitor call?

Answer
No. The important difference is that a Condition instance becomes part of the monitor in which it is declared and has no separate exclusion mechanism of its own.

Question 6
Can a process be declared inside a monitor and, if so, how does this affect the control of monitor exclusion?

Answer
A process can be declared in a monitor without having any effect on the way in which exclusion is controlled. If the process makes calls to routines of the enclosing monitor the effect is the same as for a process which calls those routines from outside the monitor. Thus, from the point of view of exclusion, there is no difference between the following:

(a) **monitor module** M;
```
    . . .
    procedure Proc; . . . ;
    process module P;
       begin . . . Proc; . . . end;
    begin . . . end {M};
```

and

(b) **monitor module** M;
```
    . . .
    procedure *Proc; . . . ;
    begin . . . end {M};

  process module P;
    begin . . . M.Proc; . . . end;
```

Question 7
Can a monitor have a variable in its interface? If so what happens if a process tries to modify that variable when another process is present in the monitor?

Answer

Variables can be exported by a monitor (as with envelopes). A reference to such a variable (from outside the monitor) is equivalent to an interface function call and is protected by the normal exclusion mechanism. Hence, if a process A attempts to reference the value of a variable in a monitor while another process B has exclusive access to the monitor, process A is delayed until process B leaves the monitor.

Question 8

Can a Condition instance be accessed directly by a process?

Answer

Yes. From the point of view of exclusion each operation performed on a Condition instance is equivalent to calling an interface routine of the monitor in which the Condition instance is declared.

Program termination

A concurrent program terminates if there are no processes to execute. This event will occur when every process in the program has either completed its designated task *or* is suspended while awaiting some event that will not occur. In the latter case the termination may be an indication of process deadlock. However, in practice, it is desirable to allow a program to terminate normally in this way because it is often impractical to reactivate suspended processes and arrange for their clean termination. Thus, in Pascal Plus, programs may terminate, quite correctly, with processes suspended on Condition instances.

If necessary, a check can be made for deadlock, with the help of a standard Pascal Plus Condition instance called AllWaiting. A process suspended using AllWaiting is selected for execution if there are no other processes that can run, i.e. the AllWaiting queue is 'signaled' implicitly at that point.

The AllWaiting Condition instance was developed to facilitate the representation of simulation models – a topic which is discussed in Chapter 8.

Specifying modules

The programs that were partly developed in the preceding sections, for the temperature/humidity alarm system and the car park control system, were coded directly from informal design descriptions. Such direct implementations can, in principle, be attempted for simple problems where the design and coding of the program are performed by the same person but, in general, this approach is undesirable. Instead, an attempt should be made to produce a precise specification of the program and each of its modules before attempting to code the latter. At the very least, there is usually a practical requirement that each module be defined in such a way that it can be coded independently of every other module so that a program design can be coded or maintained by a programming team.

A specification for a module must define its purpose and interaction, if any, with other modules. An interaction between any pair of modules is generally represented in a programming language by a call to a routine defined by the called module. Thus, the *interface* between two modules can generally be defined by the set of routines, and associated data definitions that the modules provide for each other. Very few programming languages permit full mutual dependency between modules and in the case of Pascal Plus no dependency whatsoever is allowed. As a consequence, for each pair of interacting modules one is a *supplier* and the other is a *user*. The facilities supplied by a module can be summarized in the form of a *module skeleton*. For example, the interface between the *exit* module and the *parking space* module in the car park control system might be given as follows:

```
monitor module ParkingSpace;
    {Handles the allocation of parking spaces}
    function *IsFull: Boolean;
    procedure *Acquire;
    procedure *Release;
    begin
        {initially, all parking spaces are available}
    end {ParkingSpace};
```

Similarly, the interface between the *bell* module and the *temperature sensor* module in the temperature/humidity alarm system can be given thus:

```
monitor module Bell;
    {Controls the activation and deactivation of the alarm bell}
    procedure *StartBell;
    procedure *StopBell;
    begin
        {Initially, the alarm bell is not ringing}
        {finally, the alarm bell is stopped if it is ringing}
    end {Bell};
```

Each module skeleton has a comment describing its purpose, one describing its initial state and possibly one describing its final state, if it is relevant. For a using module, the language definition of each interface operation must be supplemented with a description of the purpose of the operation and its method of use. For example, in the case of the interface between the *temperature sensor* and *bell* modules, this means stating that:

- StartBell is used to start the bell ringing and StopBell is used to stop it.
- Calls must be made alternately to StartBell and StopBell, with the first call being to StartBell.

From the point of view of the implementor of a supplying module which has several using modules the effect of interleaved calls from those modules must be defined. In the case of the *bell* module, for example, we need to state that:

- StartBell starts the bell ringing, unless some other module has already started it ringing.
- StopBell stops the bell ringing, unless some other module wishes it to continue ringing.

In the examples given in the remainder of this book, supplying modules are shown in a skeleton form that is suitable for an implementor of the module. Thus, for example, the *bell* module might be presented as:

```
monitor module Bell;
   {Controls the activation and deactivation of the alarm bell}
   procedure *StartBell;
      {Starts the bell ringing, unless some other module has}
      {already started it ringing.                          }
   procedure *StopBell;
      {Stops the bell ringing, unless some other module wishes}
      {it to continue ringing.                                }
   begin
      {initially, the alarm bell is not ringing}
      {finally, the alarm bell is stopped if it is ringing}
   end {Bell};
```

Summary

Modules identified in the modular decomposition of a problem fall into either dominant or subordinate categories, where the dominant modules provide a motive force in the program and the subordinate modules provide a service for the dominant modules. The subordinate modules may be further subdivided into those that are used only by a single dominant module and those that are shared by several such modules. In the latter case it is necessary to have some protection mechanism so that each dominant module can use the facilities of a subordinate module without interference from other dominant modules.

These three categories of module have corresponding constructs in monitor-based programming languages of which Pascal Plus is an example. In Pascal Plus a dominant module is represented by a *process*, a shared subordinate module by a *monitor* and an unshared subordinate module by an *envelope*.

Concurrent programs can be constructed using such facilities alone. However, it is more efficient to have an additional mechanism to enable a process to be suspended whenever what it requires is currently unavailable – rather than require the process repeatedly to execute a busy-waiting loop in which it looks for some change in the program state which will indicate that it can proceed. In monitor-based programming languages the suspension and reactivation of processes is handled explicitly. In Pascal Plus, for example, all such operations are dealt with by instances of a standard module called Condition. With a mechanism of this type the control of monitor exclusion becomes more complex. In particular, it is necessary for a process to give up its exclusive access to a monitor whenever it is suspended, and it must then reacquire that access whenever it is later reactivated.

Further reading

The implementations of the temperature/humidity and car park control systems are completed in Chapter 9 which deals with real-time programming.

Apart from this book other illustrations of the use of Pascal Plus may be found in:
- Welsh J. and McKeag, R.M., *Structured System Programming*, Prentice Hall, 1980.
- Welsh, J., Elder, J. and Bustard, D.W., *Sequential Program Structures*, Prentice Hall, 1984.
- Elder, J., *Construction of Data Processing Software*, Prentice Hall, 1984.

The language itself was first described in:
- Welsh, J. and Bustard, D.W., Pascal Plus: another language for modular multiprogramming, *Software: practice and experience*, Vol. 9, pp. 947–57, 1979.

The monitor, condition and envelope constructs of Pascal Plus are based on proposals made by C.A.R. Hoare. The monitor and condition are described in:
- Hoare, C.A.R., Monitors: an operating system structuring concept, *Comm. ACM*, Vol. 17, pp. 549–57, 1974.

While the precursor to the envelope appears in:
- Hoare, C.A.R., The structure of an operating system, in *Language Hierarchies and Interfaces*, Lecture Notes in Computer Science, No. 46, Springer, 1976.

Facilities similar to those defined in Pascal Plus may be found in the programming languages:
- Concurrent Pascal, described in: Brinch Hansen, P., *The Architecture of Concurrent Programs*, Prentice Hall, 1977.
- Concurrent Euclid, described in: Holt, R.C., *Concurrent Euclid, The UNIX System, and TUNIS*, Addison Wesley, 1983.

Exercises

4.1   Design a monitor module with a single interface procedure such that the first four processes that call the procedure are suspended and the fifth process reactivates the waiting four.

       Convert this monitor module into a form which allows multiple instances to be declared where, for each instance, the number of processes to be suspended is defined as a parameter. Suggest how a monitor of this type might be of use in a concurrent program.

4.2   The assumption made in programming the **Bell** monitor of the temperature/ humidity monitoring system was that once the bell was started it would continue to run without further assistance from the program. Suggest how the **Bell** monitor might be modified to cope with a bell that needs a sequence of signals to keep it running. The **Bell** monitor alone should be modified, allowing the other modules to interact with it in exactly the same way as in the original solution.

4.3   It was suggested that the **FullSign** process in the car park example might be implemented as a loop in which the number of free parking spaces is inspected regularly and the full sign switched on or off as necessary. How might the **ParkingSpace** monitor be modified to suspend the execution of the **FullSign** process until the car park becomes full, thus avoiding any processor power wastage?

4.4   What problems might occur if the rules for monitor exclusion in Pascal Plus were such that a process suspended on a condition queue gave up exclusive access only to the monitor in which a **Wait** operation is invoked, rather than releasing exclusion on all monitors to which the process has access?

      (*Hint*: Trace the effect of this change through the example discussed under Question 4 in the final section of this chapter.)

4.5   Suggest how the filling station control program, discussed as a case study in Chapter 3, might be expressed in Pascal Plus.

4.6   Implement the hide-and-seek simulation program discussed on page 37 in Chapter 3. It can be assumed that there is a function **RandomInteger** available, with heading:

```
function RandomInteger (Min, Max: Integer): Integer;
```

which returns a random value in the range **Min..Max**.

4.7   Design and implement a concurrent Pascal Plus program that can determine the number of occurrences of a specified word in a given file of text. Assume that the file has been written as a sequence of text line records, defined thus:

```
type Line = record
              Length: 0..80;
              Chars: packed array [1..80] of Char
            end;
```

Five

THE TESTING OF CONCURRENT PROGRAMS

This chapter presents an implementation of the concurrent sorting program discussed in the first chapter and uses it for illustrative purposes in a discussion of how concurrent programs can be tested.

A concurrent sorting program

In Chapter 1 it was suggested that a list of data items might be sorted concurrently by splitting the list up into a number of sublists, sorting the sublists in parallel and then merging them (sequentially) into a final sorted list. If it is assumed that the unsorted list is held in a file on disk, that the sorted list is returned to another file on disk and that all of the sorting is performed in main memory, then the diagram for the modular design of the program might take the form shown in Figure 5.1.

The *unsorted list* module is responsible for obtaining the data items to be sorted from the *disk* module (1) and supplying these data items to the *sort* modules (2). The *sort* modules sort the data items they receive and pass them to the *merge* module (3), where they are merged into a single sorted list which is passed to the *sorted list* module (4) for output to the *disk* module (5).

In this problem concurrency is used to reduce the overall execution time of the sorting program. This means that the solution should be tailored to take account of the environment in which the program is executed. Thus it is desirable to know, for example, how many central processors are available to execute processes in parallel, how fast disk transfers are

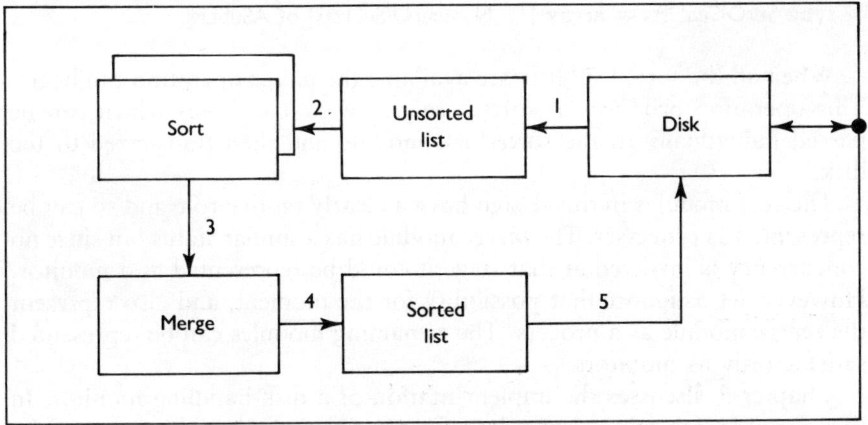

Figure 5.1 Concurrent sort program: module diagram

performed in relation to the speed of sorting, whether or not disk transfers can be performed concurrently, and so on.

Let us assume the following environment characteristics:

- there are four central processors;
- the total central processing time needed to initiate the disk transfers involved is negligible in relation to the time required to perform the sort;
- operations on the disk are performed sequentially, with only one data item being transferred either to or from the disk at a time.

Since there are four central processors, and very little power is needed for i/o operations, four sort modules can be used. The major constraint in the system is the limitation that data items can only be read individually. To keep the level of concurrent behavior high, data items read from disk can be passed to the *sort* modules as soon as possible. That is, instead of passing complete sublists to the *sort* modules for sorting, each *sort* module can accumulate the data items it receives in sorted order.

We do not know in advance how long each sublist will be so a sublist is best represented as a linked list of data items, possibly defined as follows:

```
ASublist  =  ↑  ASublistRecord;
ASubListRecord  =  record
                      Next: ASublist;
                      Item: ItemType
                   end;
```

When the end of the sequence of data items supplied by the sorted list module is encountered each *sort* module passes its sorted sublist to the *merge* module. Assuming that the number of sublists is defined by the constant NumberOfSublists, then the set of sublists might be defined as follows:

```
type SetOfSubLists = array [1..NumberOfSublists] of ASubList;
```

When all the sorted sublists are available the merge operation can begin. This operation produces a (sorted) sequence of data items which can be passed individually to the *sorted list* module and then transferred to the disk.

The *sort* modules in this design have a clearly motive role and so can be represented as processes. The *merge* module has a similar status but since no concurrency is involved at that stage it could be represented as a monitor. However, let us ignore that possibility for the moment, and also represent the *merge* module as a process. The remaining modules can be represented satisfactorily as monitors.

Chapter 9 discusses the implementation of a disk-handling monitor. In this example, for convenience, let us assume that the initial version of the program is to be executed under the control of a general-purpose operating system (as discussed in Chapter 2) and represent disk operations using the standard sequential file facilities provided by the language.

Assuming that the number of sorting processes is denoted by the constant NumberOfSorters then the complete concurrent sort program may be expressed as follows:

```
program ConcurrentSort;
    const NumberOfSorters = 4;
          NumberOfSublists = NumberOfSorters;
    type ItemType = ...;
          SorterRange = 1..NumberOfSorters;
          ASublist =    ↑ ASublistRecord;
          ASubListRecord = record
                              Next: ASublist;
                              Item: ItemType
                           end;
          SetOfSubLists = array [1..NumberOfSublists] of ASubList;

    monitor module UnsortedList in Library;

    monitor module Exchange in Library;

    process Sort in Library;
    instance Sorters: array [SorterRange] of Sort;

    monitor module SortedList in Library;

    process module Merge in Library;
    being *** end {ConcurrentSort}.
```

The *unsorted list* module supplies data items individually to a set of competing *sort* modules. Following the guideline given in the previous chapter, namely that when processes compete to obtain data items the check as to whether or not an item is present should be indivisible from the acquisition of the item, leads to a monitor definition of the form:

```
monitor module UnsortedList;
   {Reads a sequence of data items from disk and supplies them}
   {in the order read.                                         }
   procedure *TryToGetItem (var Item: ItemType; var OK: Boolean);
      {Supplies a data item in Item if one is available.}
      {If item available then OK is set to True, and I}
      {returns the data item.                         }
      {If item not available OK is set to False, and  }
      {the value of Item is not defined.              }
   begin
      {initially, prepare to supply data items}
   end {UnsortedList};
```

In monitor-based programming languages processes cannot interact directly so an intermediate monitor must be used to pass sublists between the Sort and Merge processes. This monitor might be of the form:

```
monitor module Exchange;
   {Handles the transfer of sublists between the Sort and Merge }
   {processes. Sublists are stored as they arrive from the      }
   {Sort processes and are passed on to the Merge process when}
   {the full set has been received.                          }
   procedure *DepositASubList (S: ASubList);
      {Accepts a sublist S and adds it to the set of sublists}
   procedure *GetAllSubLists (var S: SetOfSubLists);
      {Returns the complete set of sublists expected, waiting, if}
      {necessary, until they have all been deposited.           }
   begin
      {initially, the set of sublists is empty}
   end {Exchange};
```

Each **Sort** process deposits its sublist via the **DepositASubList** procedure and the **Merge** process removes the complete set of sublists by calling **GetAll-SubLists**. The assumption here is that the **Merge** process is suspended, if necessary, inside the **Exchange** monitor until all the sublists are available.

Data items are passed individually to the **SortedList** monitor as the merge operation proceeds. The form of this monitor might be as follows:

```
monitor module SortedList;
   {Accepts a sequence of data items and transfers them}
   {to the disk in the same order.                     }
   procedure *DepositAnItem (Item: ItemType);
      {Accepts a data item in Item}
   begin
      {initially, prepare to accept data items}
   end {SortedList};
```

The top-level design of the program is now complete, allowing each module block to be further developed independently. For the UnsortedList monitor the main concern is to ensure that no process is made to wait, unnecessarily, for a data item to be read. To avoid any delay a local process might be made responsible for reading ahead on the disk and a *buffer* used to hold the data items obtained. Buffering is discussed in detail in Chapter 7. For the moment let us assume that buffering and read-ahead are implemented as part of the sequential file mechanism allowing the UnsortedList monitor to be expressed as follows:

```
monitor module UnsortedList;
    var InputFile: file of ItemType;

    procedure *TryToGetItem (var Item: ItemType; var OK: Boolean);
        begin
            OK := not Eof (InputFile);
            if OK then Read (InputFile, Item)
        end {TryToGetItem};

        begin Reset (InputFile, 'UnsortedList'); *** end {UnsortedList};
```

The only point to note here is the Pascal Plus facility for associating a file variable with an external file by giving the physical name of the file as a second parameter to a call of the standard Reset procedure. This enables file variables which are bound to external files to be declared inside modules. Such files are not named in the parameter list of the program.

The Exchange monitor can be implemented as follows:

```
monitor module Exchange;
    type *SetOfSubLists = array [SorterRange] of ASubList;
    var Sublists: SetOfSubLists;
        Next: 0..NumberOfSublists;
    instance Queue: Condition;

    procedure *DepositASubList (S: ASubList);
        begin
            Next := Next + 1;
            Sublists [Next] := S;
            if Next = NumberOfSublists then Queue.Signal
        end {DepositASubList};

    procedure *GetAllSubLists (var S: SetOfSubLists);
        begin
            if Next <> NumberOfSublists then Queue.Wait;
            S := Sublists
        end {GetAllSubLists};

        begin Next := 0; *** end {Exchange};
```

The GetAllSubLists procedure delays the Merge process, until the number of sorted sublists deposited in the monitor reaches the total expected. When a Sort process calls DepositASubList the sorted sublist it supplies is placed in the array of sublists. The final Sort process to arrive signals Queue to reactivate the Merge process, if necessary.

Each Sort process places each item it receives directly into an ordered sublist. The sublists are significant data structures in the program so each Sort process might include a local module to handle sublist operations. The two operations required are:

(a) the insertion of an item into a sublist;
(b) the extraction of a copy of a sublist – used when transferring a completed sublist to the Merge process.

The sublist module can be represented by an envelope with the following structure:

```
envelope module Sublist;
   var *S: ASubList;
   procedure * Insert (Item: ItemType);
      {Inserts Item into the sublist S in sort order}
   begin
      {initially, the sublist is empty}
   end {Sublist};
```

Using this abstraction the Sort process can be expressed simply, as follows:

```
process Sort;

   envelope module Sublist in Library;

   var OneFound: Boolean;
       Item: ItemType;

   begin {Sort}
     repeat
        UnsortedList.TryToGetItem (Item, OneFound);
        if OneFound then Sublist.Insert (Item)
     until not OneFound;
     Exchange.DepositASubList (Sublist.S)
   end {Sort};
```

The more complex details of how the sublist insertion is performed are contained totally within the Sublist module. Assuming that the item type is such that values can be compared directly for ordering and that the items should be in ascending order, then the module might be implemented thus:

```
envelope module Sublist;
   var *S: ASubList;

   procedure *Insert (Item: ItemType);
      var Index, Previous, Entry: ASublist;

      function PositionFound: Boolean;
         begin
            if Index = nil
            then PositionFound := True
            else
               PositionFound := Index ↑ .Item > = Item
         end {PositionFound};

      begin {Insert}
         {prepare sublist entry}
         New (Entry);
         Entry ↑ .Item := Item;
         {find insertion position}
```

```
        Index := S;
        Previous := nil;
        while not PositionFound do
          begin
            Previous := Index;
            Index := Index ↑.Next
          end;
        Entry ↑.Next := Index;
        if Previous = nil
        then S := Entry
        else Previous ↑.Next := Entry
    end {Insert};

  begin S := nil; *** end {Sublist};
```

In a similar way the Merge process may include a data structure module to
handle operations on the set of sublists. The only operation needed is the
removal of the next smallest item in the sublists, if any, so the module can be
represented by an envelope of the form:

```
envelope module TheSetOfSublists;
  procedure *TryToRemoveSmallestItem (var Item: ItemType;
                                      var OneFound: Boolean);
    {Supplies the smallest item Item in the set of sublists,}
    {if possible.                                           }
    {If an item is available, OneFound is set to True and   }
    {the item returned in Item.                             }
    {If an item is not available, OneFound is set to False, }
    {and Item is not defined.                               }
  begin
    {initially, obtain the sublists from Exchange module}
  end {TheSetOfSublists};
```

Using this module the Merge process may be expressed as follows:

```
process module Merge;

  envelope module TheSetOfSublists in Library;

  var OneFound: Boolean;
      Item: ItemType;

  begin {Merge}
    repeat
      TheSetOfSublists.TryToRemoveSmallestItem (Item, OneFound);
      if OneFound then SortedList.DepositAnItem (Item)
    until not OneFound
  end {Merge};
```

The smallest item in the sublists can be found by inspecting the next
available item in each sublist and removing the smallest value, if any. Using
this strategy the TheSetOfSublists envelope can be implemented as follows:

```
envelope module TheSetOfSublists;
  var Sublists: SetOfSubLists;
```

```
    procedure *TryToRemoveSmallestItem (var Item: ItemType;
                                        var OneFound: Boolean);
      var Possible, Index: SorterRange;
          OldEntry: ASublist;
      begin
        OneFound := False;
        for Index := I to NumberOfSorters do
          if Sublists [Index] <> nil then {sublist not empty}
            if not OneFound
            then {first item found}
              begin
                OneFound := True;
                Possible := Index;
                Item := Sublists [Index] ↑ .Item
              end
            else {not first item – is it smaller?}
              if Sublists [Index] ↑ .Item < Item then
                begin {update smallest}
                  Possible := Index;
                  Item := Sublists [Index] ↑ .Item
                end;
        if Onefound then
          begin
            OldEntry := SubLists [Possible];
            Sublists [Possible] := Sublists [Possible] ↑ .Next;
            Dispose (OldEntry)
          end
      end {TryToRemoveSmallestItem};

    begin Exchange.GetAllSubLists (Sublists); *** end {TheSetOfSublists};
```

Note that the call to acquire the sublists from the Exchange monitor, in the initialization of the TheSetOfSublists module, may result in the 'caller' being suspended. The initialization part of an envelope or monitor is invoked (implicitly) on entry to the block in which the module is declared. So, in effect, it is the Merge process that invokes GetAllSubLists and it is therefore this process that is suspended if the sublists are not available.

The SortedList module can be implemented by writing each item it receives directly to an external file, which can be expressed as follows:

```
monitor module SortedList;
  var OutputFile: file of ItemType;
  procedure * DepositAnItem (Item: ItemType);
    begin Write (OutputFile, Item) end;
begin
  Rewrite (OutputFile, 'SortedList');
  ***
end {SortedList};
```

Once again the Pascal Plus file binding mechanism is used to associate an external file with a locally declared file variable.

The concurrent sort program is now complete. The following sections consider how concurrent programs can be tested, using the sort program to motivate the discussion.

Modular testing

At some stage in the implementation of any program it is necessary to convince oneself that the program matches its specification and is free from logical errors. This involves constructing a suitable input data set which exercises each part of the specification and which, when its elements are supplied to the program, drives it through every statement at least once.

The division of a program into a set of disjoint modules with narrow well-defined interfaces, not only eases the problem of constructing and of understanding the program, but also helps in the task of investigating its correctness. In principle, so-called *modular testing* seeks to establish the correctness of each module individually before attempting any test of the behavior of the program which they constitute. In practice, this may be achieved by:

(a) *isolated* modular testing, in which each module is tested using an artificial test harness constructed for the purpose;
(b) *incremental* modular testing, in which the modules are added one by one to the growing program framework – the behavior of the resulting unit is tested or retested at each stage.

The intended method of program testing should be considered at the program design stage since there is often a number of alternative ways to subdivide a problem into modules and some program designs are likely to be more amenable than others to isolated module development.

In some cases, the incremental approach to testing avoids the significant problems of providing an adequate test harness for each of the modules concerned. In general, incremental testing is justifiable when:

(a) the test harness required for isolated testing of the module is as complex, and hence as error prone, as the incremental program harness itself;
(b) the modules are available for testing in an appropriate incremental order;
(c) the execution behavior of the modules is determinate.

Condition (b) implies that the modules of a program are constructed, or at least tested, in an order appropriate for incremental testing. For large programs, whose development may be split into a number of modules that are allocated for implementation to independent programmers or programming teams, such constraints on the timing of module development may be inconvenient, making isolated testing the only real option, regardless of the effort involved.

From condition (c) it follows that isolated module testing is necessary in most concurrent programs since the behavior of combinations of modules is often indeterminate. In Chapter 2 it was pointed out that when a concurrent program is executed in a sequential environment (i.e. where the concurrent behavior is simulated) its behavior is determinate. However, it is still difficult to predict the single execution path in advance so in this case also isolated testing is usually desirable. The next two subsections consider what is involved in testing modules in isolation, dealing first with the traditional case where the test harness is sequential.

Isolated module testing: sequential case

When devising tests for a module it is best to consider carefully how each part of the module can be exercised rather than testing the module in a random fashion. Essentially, this involves identifying the different circumstances in which the module operations are invoked.

For example, consider what tests are appropriate for the Sublist module of the concurrent sort program if it is applied to integer values in the range 0..9. The only significant sublist operation is the insertion of an item value. The sublist is either empty or nonempty initially and, if nonempty, insertion can be at the beginning or end of the sublist, or at some intermediate point if more than one element is present.

Once the different cases have been identified a sequence of test calls can be devised. The following program tests the operation of the Sublist module following the suggestions made above:

```
program TestSublist (Output);
   const NumberOfSorters = 4;
         NumberOfSublists = NumberOfSorters;
   type ItemType = 0..9;
        SorterRange = 1..NumberOfSorters;
        ASublist = ↑ASublistRecord;
        ASubListRecord = record
                           Next: ASublist;
                           Item: ItemType
                         end;
        SetOfSubLists = array [1..NumberOfSublists] of ASubList;

   envelope module Sublist in Library;

   type String = packed array [1..5] of Char;

   procedure Check (Expected: String);
      var Index: ASublist;
      begin
         Write ('Expected ', Expected, ' Actual ');
         Index := Sublist.S;
         if Index = nil
         then Write ('Empty')
```

```
        else
          repeat
            Write (Index ↑ .Item:1);
            Index := Index ↑ .Next
          until Index = nil;
          Writeln
        end {Check};

      begin {TestSublist}
        Check ('Empty');
        Sublist.Insert (6); {empty}
        Check ('6       ');
        Sublist.Insert (3); {first}
        Check ('36      ');
        Sublist.Insert (9); {end}
        Check ('369     ');
        Sublist.Insert (5); {in between}
        Check ('3569 ')
      end {TestSublist}.
```

The output produced by this program is as follows:

```
Expected Empty   Actual Empty
Expected 6       Actual 6
Expected 36      Actual 36
Expected 369     Actual 369
Expected 3569    Actual 3569
```

Note that, in constructing the test harness for a module, it is often useful to output the state of the module after each operation, together with a description of the expected state. Any mismatch should then be obvious and should be checked automatically, where possible.

Isolated module testing: concurrent case

The main concern when testing a monitor is to examine the different ways in which processes can interact through that monitor. The correctness of the basic exclusion mechanism can be assumed so what remains to be tested are:

(a) the method of information exchange between processes;
(b) the synchronization of processes suspended and reactivated using Wait and Signal operations.

To test the Exchange monitor we first identify the different cases involved. When studying process synchronization the main concern is to identify the different process arrival orders that can occur. For the Exchange monitor there are three cases to consider:

(a) The Merge process arrives before any of the Sort processes.

(b) All of the Sort processes arrive before the Merge process.
(c) Some Sort processes arrive before the Merge process, and some after it.

Three separate programs are needed to test these cases. (A single program could be used if the Exchange monitor is extended with a reinitialization facility.) For each program the execution of the processes concerned has to be synchronized so that they invoke the Exchange monitor operations in the required order. The synchronization may be achieved in one of two ways:

(a) by suspending the processes in the required order on a condition queue and then reactivating them, one at a time, to perform their test calls;
(b) by channeling identical processes through a test harness monitor and making each process that arrives perform the next test in sequence; only one process at a time can enter a monitor so the tests will be performed individually.

Each of these techniques is now considered in turn.

Ordering processes using a condition queue

Having worked out a particular test sequence each process can be assigned an order number, allocated sequentially from zero upward (say). The following monitor provides a single procedure Join which suspends a calling process on a local condition queue using the test order number as a priority value:

```
monitor module TestSequence;
   instance Queue: Condition;

   procedure *Join (TestNumber: TestRange);
      {Suspends process on condition queue using TestNumber}
      {as a priority value.                               }
      begin Queue.PWait (TestNumber) end {Join};

   process module Sequencer;
      {Reactivates test processes one at a time}
      begin
        repeat
          AllWaiting.Wait;
          Queue.Signal
        until Queue.Empty
      end {Sequencer};

   begin *** end {TestSequence};
```

The PWait operation suspends each process at the required point in the condition queue regardless of the order of arrival. The monitor contains a local process Sequencer which reactivates the waiting processes one at a time. This process uses the Pascal Plus standard condition instance AllWaiting to achieve the desired synchronization.

Although the test processes are activated individually, some tests may result in other processes being reactivated. As a consequence, care must be

taken with the output of test results to avoid confusion. In particular, this
means that all test results should be directed to a single module for output
rather than allowing the test processes to send messages to the output
stream directly. A *state* module, as described in Chapter 3, is ideal for this
purpose. For a test of the Exchange monitor the *state* module might take the
form:

```
monitor module TestExchangeState;
    procedure *NoteTestStarted (TestNumber: TestRange;
        Description: packed array [I..J:Integer] of Char);
      {Outputs test number and description}
    procedure *NoteTestComplete (TestNumber: TestRange);
      {Outputs test number with completion indication}
    procedure *NoteSublistsFound (S: SetOfSublists);
      {Outputs set of sublists S}
    begin
      {initially, output test header}
      {finally, output test trailer  }
    end {TestExchangeState};
```

Using the TestSequence and TestSequenceState monitors, the test program
for the Exchange monitor might be expressed as follows:

```
program TestExchange (Output);
    const   NumberOfSorters = 4;
            NumberOfSublists = NumberOfSorters;
    type    ItemType = 0..9;
            SorterRange = I..NumberOfSorters;
            ASublist = ↑ ASublistRecord;
            ASubListRecord = record
                                 Next: ASublist;
                                 Item: ItemType
                             end;
            SetOfSubLists = array [I..NumberOfSublists] of ASubList;
            TestRange = 0..4;

    monitor State = TestExchangeState in Library;

    monitor module Exchange in Library;

    monitor module TestSequence in Library;

    process DoSort (TestNumber: TestRange);
        var S, Entry: ASubList;
            Index: TestRange;
        begin
          TestSequence.Join (TestNumber);
          {set up a sorted sublist}
          S := nil;
          for Index := TestNumber downto I do
            begin
                New (Entry);
                Entry ↑ .Item := Index;
                Entry ↑ .Next := S;
```

```
                    S := Entry
                end;
            State.NoteTestStarted (TestNumber, 'sublist deposited');
            Exchange.DepositASubList (S);
            State.NoteTestComplete (TestNumber)
        end {DoSort};
    instance
        SortTests: array [1..4] of DoSort [(0), (1), (3), (4)];

    process module DoMerge;
        const TestNumber = 2;
        var Lists: SetOfSubLists;
        begin
            TestSequence.Join (TestNumber);
            State.NoteTestStarted (TestNumber, 'sublists requested');
            Exchange.GetAllSubLists (Lists);
            State.NoteTestComplete (TestNumber);
            State.NoteSublistsFound (Lists)
        end {DoMerge};

    begin *** end {TestExchange}.
```

Each process is given an order number which, for a Sort process, is passed
as a parameter in its declaration. The test order selected here is:

(a) two Sort processes deposit their sublists in the Exchange monitor;

(b) the Merge process arrives to obtain the set of sublists and is suspended;

(c) two Sort processes deposit their sublists in the Exchange monitor – when
     the second of the processes has achieved this objective the Merge process
     is reactivated and returns with the full set of sublists supplied in (a) and
     (c).

When this program is executed it produces a trace of the form:

Test of Exchange Monitor

```
    Test: 0 sublist deposited
    Test: 0 complete
    Test: 1 sublist deposited
    Test: 1 complete
    Test: 2 sublists requested
    Test: 3 sublist deposited
    Test: 3 complete
    Test: 4 sublist deposited
    Test: 2 complete
    Test: 4 complete

    Sublists received:
    1: empty
    2: 1
    3: 1 2 3
    4: 1 2 3 4
```

Exchange test complete

Each test process makes a single monitor call, around which are placed' two calls to the State monitor to mark the beginning and end of a test. The output that results summarizes the effect that each monitor call has on the calling process. For processes that return immediately from a monitor call the start and stop messages are consecutive. If a process is suspended its completion message follows the start message of the test process which reactivates it. In addition to the monitor call information, data values can also be output where appropriate, or shown for the Merge process.

Ordering processes by means of the monitor exclusion mechanism

An alternative way to put the test processes into a predefined order is to insert the test statements in one procedure of a monitor and have an appropriate number of identical processes call that procedure. Each calling process is given a test order number on entry to the procedure and, using this value, the appropriate test is selected via a case-statement. So, for example, a test harness monitor for the Exchange monitor, performing the same tests as before, might be constructed as follows:

```
monitor module TestHarness;
   const TestLimit = 4;
   type TestRange = 0..TestLimit;
   var NextTestNumber: -1..TestLimit;

   procedure DoTest;
     var Index, TestNumber: TestRange;
         S, Entry: ASubList;
         Lists: SetOfSubLists;
     begin
       NextTestNumber := NextTestNumber + 1;
       TestNumber := NextTestNumber;
       case TestNumber of
       0, 1, 3, 4:
         begin
           {set up a sorted sublist}
           S := nil;
           for Index := TestNumber downto 1 do
             begin
               New (Entry);
               Entry ↑.Item := Index;
               Entry ↑.Next := S;
               S := Entry
             end;
             State.NoteTestStarted (TestNumber, 'sublist deposited');
             Exchange.DepositASubList (S);
             State.NoteTestComplete (TestNumber)
           end;
         2:
           begin
             State.NoteTestStarted (TestNumber, 'sublists requested');
             Exchange.GetAllSubLists (Lists);
```

```
          State.NoteTestComplete (TestNumber);
          State.NoteSublistsFound (Lists)
       end
     end
   end {DoTest};

 process Tester;
   begin DoTest end;
 instance Testers: array [TestRange] of Tester;

 begin NextTestNumber := −1; *** end {TestHarness};
```

Here five identical process instances are channeled through the DoTest procedure of the TestHarness monitor. Only one process at a time can execute this procedure, as a consequence of the monitor exclusion mechanism, so only one test is performed at a time. Note that:

(a) At the start of the DoTest procedure a process is assigned a test number; this is recorded within the procedure so that, if the process is suspended when it makes a call to the monitor under test, it will be able, on its resumption, to determine the test being performed.

(b) All test output could have been produced directly within the DoTest procedure; however, the State monitor has been used so that the two test methods discussed can be more easily compared.

The choice of technique for ordering test processes in test harnesses is largely a matter of taste since the amount of effort involved in each case is similar. It should be noted, however, that it is not possible to apply the second of the synchronization techniques in all monitor-based languages – a problem which is discussed further in Chapter 11. The first synchronization technique is perhaps more widely applicable than the second but it still requires a facility equivalent to the Pascal Plus AllWaiting condition.

Thorough testing of a concurrent program involves more than just testing the correctness of each module completely or even ensuring that the program as a whole produces the expected output when executed with a well-chosen set of input data. In addition, we need to check that the processes of the program work together in the *expected* manner. In particular, this involves checking that the processes are not delayed unduly while interacting. This might result in a diminution of the degree of concurrent behavior actually exhibited by the program. The next section considers how the behavior of a program can be presented in a form suitable for study by the implementor, and suggests how the relevant information can be gathered and organized.

Presenting program behavior

The test harnesses for the sort program, discussed in the previous section, presented the behavior of processes as a trace of their entry to, and exit from, monitor routines. The same technique can be used to summarize the behavior of the complete program. However, this often produces a large quantity of *trace data* from which it is difficult to extract useful information. To obtain a clear picture of how a program is behaving the programmer must decide carefully what aspects of its execution are of interest, and then work out how data appropriate to each aspect may be accumulated and presented.

When the number of processes is relatively small and short-lived their behavior can be presented in a tabular form that shows the major events in the execution of each. For example, in the sorting program we might record each data item received by a Sort process and, for the Merge process, simply record the start of the merge operation. Table 5.1 shows the output from a test run in which 21 data items are sorted.

This table has one column for each process, so the behavior of any process can be studied by scanning the entries in the appropriate column. The time sequence behavior of the processes can be deduced by looking across the columns. At the bottom of each column an appropriate summary for each process concerned is given which, in this case, identifies the number of items handled by each Sort process.

A display table of this form may be produced by a *state* module to which the processes of the program pass relevant information as they execute. For the sort program the *state* module might take the form:

```
monitor module TestSortState;
   {Produces a behavior table for the sort program}
   type *ProcessReferenceNumber = 1 . . NumberOfProcesses;
   procedure *NoteItemObtained (P: ProcessReferenceNumber);
      {Indicates that a Sort process has obtained a data item}
   procedure *NoteMergeStarted;
      {Indicates that the Merge process has obtained the set}
      {of sublists.                                        }
   begin
      {initially, outputs the table header   }
      {finally, outputs a behavior summary}
   end {TestSortState};
```

Each process which calls the *state* module must have either a unique identification number or it must enter through a routine used by only one process. In the latter case each Sort process can be given a reference number at its point of declaration by means of a parameter of the Sort process type. A Sort process calls NoteItemObtained each time it acquires an item, and the Merge process calls NoteMergeStarted whenever it has obtained the sublists.

The State monitor can be expressed as follows:

```
monitor module TestSortState;
   const IndentWidth = 4;
         NumberOfProcesses = 5;
         TableWidth = 60;
```

Table 5.1 Behavior in concurrent sort program

Sort 1	Sort 2	Sort 3	Sort 4	Merge
Has item	Has item	Has item	Has item	
Has item	Has item	Has item	Has item	
Has item	Has item	Has item	Has item	
Has item	Has item	Has item	Has item	
Has item	Has item	Has item	Has item	
			Has item	
				Started
Total 5	Total 5	Total 5	Total 6	

```pascal
      MergePosition = 5;
      ColumnWidth = 11;
type *ProcessReferenceNumber = 1..NumberOfProcesses;
     StepRange = 0..NumberOfProcesses;
     LineRange = 0..TableWidth;
var Total: array [SorterRange] of 0..Maxint;

procedure PrintLine;
  var Count: LineRange;
  begin
    Write ('   ': IndentWidth);
    for Count := 0 to TableWidth do Write ('__');
    Writeln
  end {PrintLine};

procedure Indent;
  begin Write ('   ': IndentWidth) end;

procedure TabAcross (Steps: StepRange);
  var Count: ProcessReferenceNumber;
  begin
    for Count := 1 to Steps do Write ('   ': ColumnWidth)
  end {TabAcross};
```

```
  procedure *NoteItemObtained (P: ProcessReferenceNumber);
    begin
      Indent;
      TabAcross (P − 1);
      Write (' Has item');
      TabAcross (NumberOfProcesses − P);
      Writeln;
      Total [P] := Total [P] + 1
    end {NoteItemObtained};

  procedure *NoteMergeStarted;
    begin
      Indent;
      TabAcross (MergePosition − 1);
      Writeln (' Started')
    end {NoteMergeStarted};

  procedure Initialize;
    var Index: SorterRange;
    begin
      PrintLine;
      Indent;
      for Index := 1 to NumberOfSorters do
        Write (' Sort', Index:3, ' l');
      Writeln (' Merge l');
      PrintLine;
      for Index := 1 to NumberOfSorters do
        Total [Index] := 0
    end {Initialize};

  procedure Finalize;
    var Index: SorterRange;
    begin
      PrintLine;
      Indent;
      for Index := 1 to NumberOfSorters do
        Write (' Total', Total [Index]:2, ' l');
      Writeln ('            l');
      PrintLine
    end {Finalize};

  begin Initialize; ***; Finalize end {TestSortState};
```

Such *state* modules need to be tailored to meet the needs of individual
programs. However, the suggested structure of the above State monitor can
be used as a template when developing other similar monitors. For longer
running applications, where the same behavior is repeated again and again,
it is desirable to output only part of the trace. When a larger number of
processes is involved the space available for the description of their behavior
must be reduced, but even single letters or graphic symbols can be adequate
in many cases. The activities of very large numbers of interacting processes

must be shown selectively and, perhaps, the program run several times to determine its behavior overall.

Summary

Program modules can either be tested in isolation or incrementally. Concurrent programs are difficult to test incrementally because their behavior is indeterminate. The logic of individual processes, being sequential, can be assessed in a traditional way but different techniques are required to test the interaction of processes in monitors. A monitor may be tested using a set of processes each of which is assigned a particular monitor test call. These processes are then put into a predetermined test sequence. This can be achieved either by suspending them in the required order and then allowing them to proceed individually to perform their tests, or by channeling all of them through a single monitor which allows only one process at a time to proceed, as a consequence of the monitor exclusion mechanism. Both techniques, however, rely on particular facilities being available in the implementation language used.

When the parts of a concurrent program have been tested and the program itself has been executed to produce the desired output, the behavior of the program must still be examined in detail to ensure that it conforms to the expected model of operation. Information on the significant events that occur in a program can be reported to a single *state* module which gathers this information and presents a summary in a form suitable for the application.

Further reading

A procedure for the systematic testing of monitors is described in:
- Brinch Hansen, P., Reproducible testing of monitors, *Software: practice and experience*, Vol. 8, pp. 721–9, 1978.

A technique for *proving*, rather than just testing, the correctness of monitors is given in:
  Howard, J.H, Proving monitors, *Comm. ACM*, Vol. 19, pp. 273–85, 1976.

A broader discussion of proving the correctness of monitors and other forms of concurrent program construct may be found in:
- Ben-Ari, M., *Principles of Concurrent Programming*, Prentice Hall, 1982.

Exercises

In addition to the exercises given here problems involving monitor testing may also be found at the end of Chapters 6 and 7.

5.1   Modify the concurrent sort program, developed in this chapter, to sort a file of
student records. Assume that each record holds the name of a student and a
single grade assessment, thus:

```
Student = record
            Name: packed array [1..20] of Char;
            Grade: 0..100
        end
```

Produce two versions of the program: one to sort the students by name into a
lexicographic order, and one to sort the students by grade number. Try to
minimize the differences between the programs so that retesting is also
minimized.

5.2   Modify the concurrent sort program to implement the **Merge** module as a
monitor. What effect does this change have on the testing of the program?

5.3   Modify the **TestSortState** monitor on page 90 so that it can be used in versions
of the sort program containing different numbers of **Sort** processes.

5.4   Suggest how the temperature/humidity control system, discussed in Chapters 3
and 4, might be extended with a printing device and a real-time clock so that a
trace and a summary of the temperature and humidity measurements can be
given.

Six

RESOURCE MANAGEMENT

A significant number of concurrent programs contain modules responsible for administering pools of *resources* shared by several processes. Such *resource management* modules are particularly common in general-purpose operating systems where the processes that implement user commands, for example, compete on behalf of users for a wide range of shared facilities such as data files, main and secondary memory, magnetic tape units and so on. One example of a resource module in the concurrent programs that have appeared in earlier chapters is the ParkingSpace monitor in the car park control system, discussed in Chapter 4. This monitor kept track of the number of parking spaces available and thus was able to prevent entry to the car park whenever all of the spaces were taken.

The purpose of this chapter is to consider various general strategies for handling the allocation of resources in a concurrent program and to illustrate how these strategies may be implemented by developing a range of corresponding resource management modules.

Resource management concepts

Resources may be defined *statically* or *dynamically*. Statically defined resources exist throughout the lifetime of a program, whereas dynamically defined resources may be created or destroyed as program execution proceeds. User files in an operating system are an example of resources that are created dynamically, while the disk on which the files reside is an example of a static resource.

A resource may be *sharable* in that several processes may have access to it at one time, or it may be *exclusive*, meaning that only one process at a time

. 95

may use it. For example, a file is generally sharable to processes reading its data, whereas a lineprinter is generally allocated exclusively to one process.

For the purposes of discussion we can divide resource management problems into two main groups:

(a) those in which the competing processes require access to only one resource at a time;
(b) those where each process needs access to several resources simultaneously.

The multiple resources may be of the same type, as in the multiple allocation of sectors of a shared disk. Alternatively, the resources may be different as, for example, in the case of a process transferring the contents of a disk file to a magnetic tape, where permission is needed to use both shared resources before the operation can begin.

A classification of resource management problems is shown in Table 6.1.

All of the categories listed in Table 6.1 may involve resources that are either allocated for exclusive use or are shared simultaneously by several processes. Also, with the exception of (a), the number and identity of the resources involved may be fixed or vary dynamically.

The meaning of each category is fairly obvious with the exception of (c). This can be explained by analogy with the allocation of tables in a restaurant. For some customers of the restaurant, all of the tables are identical but others may insist, for example, on sitting by a window, or away from the door. Thus, an allocation is made to customers from the group of tables that they find acceptable, i.e. from a subset of the N similar resources being administered.

The two main general problems encountered when controlling the allocation of resources are:

(a) *starvation*, also known as *indefinite postponement* or *indefinite waiting*, where a process is repeatedly denied resources because those resources becoming free are given to other (higher priority) processes;
(b) *deadlock*, where processes are mutually blocked in their attempt to obtain resources because each process holds one or more resources required by one or more of the other competing processes.

Table 6.1 Classification of resource management problems

	Single resource required	Multiple resources required
(a)	One resource defined	–
(b)	One resource from N identical resources	M resources from N identical resources
(c)	One resource from a subset of N similar resources	M resources from a subset of N similar resources
(d)	–	M resources from sets of different resources

Deadlock and starvation prevent a process obtaining the resources it seeks and, as a consequence, prevent the process making progress in its execution. Deadlock can only occur when processes need access to more than one resource at a time but starvation is possible in any resource management situation.

There are two ways of dealing with the problems of deadlock and starvation: one is to *avoid* such errors and the other is to *detect and recover* from them. As with all ills, prevention is usually better than cure, and so methods of avoiding deadlock and starvation should be considered first when implementing any concurrent program. However, the normal practical constraint on achieving this goal is that the costs involved must be 'reasonable'. The price to be paid is a combination of:

(a) the run-time overheads of maintaining a suitable resource acquisition interface;
(b) the loss of flexibility in acquiring resources which results from the restrictions imposed by the interface.

In some cases, especially database applications, the price for avoiding deadlock, in particular, is often considered to be too high. Thus, instead, a mechanism for detecting and recovering from deadlock is used. That is:

(a) resources are allocated without any attempt to exclude the possibility of deadlock, but
(b) a periodic check for deadlock is performed and, if it is discovered, some suitable recovery procedure is instigated.

Techniques for dealing with deadlock and starvation are discussed throughout this chapter when considering the various classes of resource management problem listed in Table 6.1. Before dealing with particular cases, however, let us first consider the general structure of the modules that might be used to handle the allocation of the resources involved.

Resource management modules: basic requirements

A *resource* in a concurrent program may be defined as a facility for whose use several processes compete. In that sense all of the subordinate modules shared by processes administer a *resource* in that they provide a service to which only one process at a time has access. The type of resource that is of particular interest here, however, is one whose acquisition, use and release require more than one visit to the module administering the resource, i.e. cases where the acquisition and release of the resource cannot be handled by the exclusion mechanism controlling access to the resource module. Instead, the acquisition and release operations must be programmed explicitly. For example, the ParkingSpace monitor presented in Chapter 4 was defined with two such explicit operations which may be described in general resource management terms as:

(a) A facility, Acquire, for acquiring resources, with a commitment to wait, if necessary, until those resources are available.
(b) A facility, Release, for releasing resources previously acquired.

These operations are common to most resource management problems. The ParkingSpace monitor also illustrates one of the main objectives sought in administering any collection of resources, namely to allocate the resources 'fairly'. Fairness is usually achieved by satisfying resource requests in a *first-come-first-served* order but in some circumstances a different order may be appropriate. For example, maintenance staff working on an operating system may need to sort out problems affecting all users and so should be given priority when they require access to shared resources. Conversely, some operating system activities, such as the incremental copying of disk files for security purposes, have a low priority and may be required to wait until the resources involved are not required for any other purpose. To cater for these cases we can provide an additional resource management operation PriorityAcquire that allows a process to wait with a specified priority status for resources, so that when resources are allocated they are given to processes with high priorities in preference to those with lower priorities.

Another resource management operation needed is one which permits a process to attempt the acquisition of resources without the process being delayed if those resources are unavailable. For example, in an interactive operating system a user is normally prevented from gaining access to any shared file which is currently in use. This, means that the process implementing user operations is informed that the file is unavailable rather than being delayed until the file is free. In general a tentative attempt to acquire a resource has two forms – one with a stated priority, PriorityTryToAcquire, and one that uses a default priority, TryToAcquire.

These four acquisition operations and the single release operation are adequate for most applications. Each resource module can thus be represented by a monitor of the following form:

```
monitor ResourceControl;
{assumes const PriorityLimit = limit on priority range}
    type *PriorityRange = 0..PriorityLimit;
    procedure *PriorityTryToAcquire (P: PriorityRange;
                                     var OK: Boolean ...);
        {Tries to obtain resources, using the specified priority }
        {P, returning an indication of the success, of           }
        {otherwise, of the operation in OK.                      }
        {If the resources are available, OK is set to True.      }
        {If the resources are unavailable OK is set to False.    }
    procedure *TryToAcquire (var OK: Boolean ...);
        {Tries to obtain resources, using the default priority,  }
        {'PriorityLimit div 2', returning an indication of the   }
```

```
    {success, or otherwise, of the operation in OK.          }
    {If the resources are available OK is set to True.        }
    {If the resources are unavailable OK is set to False.     }
  procedure *PriorityAcquire (P: PriorityRange ...);
    {Tries to obtain resources, using the specified priority }
    {P, waiting, if necessary, until the resources are       }
    {available.                                               }
  procedure *Acquire (...);
    {Tries to obtain resources, using the default priority   }
    {'PriorityLimit div 2', waiting, if necessary, until the }
    {resources are available.                                 }
  procedure *Release (...);
    {Release resources.                                       }
    {It is assumed that the resources have been acquired     }
  begin
    {initially, prepare for resource requests}
  end {ResourceControl};
```

The parameter list for each operation has not been shown as this will depend on the nature of the resources being administered. When allocating resources individually the PriorityTryToAcquire and TryToAcquire operations are identical.

The techniques used in allocating resources in multiple units build on those used for allocating resources individually, so we will consider this latter case first. Also, for simplicity, the allocation of statically defined resources acquired for exclusive use is dealt with before looking at the other variations.

Allocating resources individually

Deadlock cannot occur when a process holds only one resource at a time. Starvation is also unlikely but may happen if any resource is heavily used and the processes that compete to access it have different priorities. In general, starvation is possible when resources are allocated in any order other than *first-come-first-served*. It is the responsibility of the program designer to ensure that priorities are allocated appropriately. In many applications it is adequate to use the default priority for each process which then guarantees that starvation is avoided.

The allocation of resources individually involves three different cases, as identified in Table 6.1:

(a) there is only one resource to be administered;
(b) there is a group of *identical* resources to be administered, any one of which will satisfy a calling process;
(c) there is a group of *similar* resources to be administered, only some of which will satisfy a calling process.

Each of these cases is now considered in turn.

One resource defined

The simplest case of allocating resources individually is that in which there
is only one resource to be administered. In an operating system that resource
might be any single shared facility such as a single communications line into
a computer network or any single device. The control of one resource is
handled simply by recording whether or not that resource is free, which can
be expressed as follows:

```
monitor SingleResource;
{assumes const PriorityLimit = limit on priority range}


    type *PriorityRange = 0..PriorityLimit;
    var Free: Boolean;
    instance Queue: Condition;

    procedure *TryToAcquire (var OK: Boolean);
      begin
        OK := Free;
        Free := False
      end {TryToAcquire};

    procedure *PriorityAcquire (P: PriorityRange);
      begin
        if not Free then Queue.PWait (P);
        Free := False
      end {PriorityAcquire};

    procedure *Acquire;
      begin PriorityAcquire (PriorityLimit div 2) end;

    procedure *Release;
      begin
        Free := True;
        Queue.Signal
      end {Release};

begin
    Free := True;
    ***
    end {SingleResource};
```

The value of the variable Free in the monitor indicates the current allocation
state of the resource. Initially, it has the value True and thereafter switches
between False and True as the resource is acquired and released.

Note that, although the monitor is given in a form from which multiple
instances can be derived, the Pascal Plus library mechanism permits it to be
retrieved as a single instance module, as follows:

```
monitor module SingleResource in Library
   (Where const PriorityLimit = Maxint;);
```

This avoids the inconvenience of keeping two copies of the module which
differ only in their heading.

One resource from *N* identical resources

In the car park control problem the ParkingSpace monitor allocated resources that were not identified individually within the program – the monitor simply gave permission for a car to enter the park, after which the customer selected any parking space that was free. For such applications, the resource monitor can have an interface identical to that used for the SingleResource monitor. Internally, the Boolean variable becomes a resource *counter* and the acquisition and release operations are adjusted accordingly:

```
monitor OneFromN;
{assumes const PriorityLimit = limit on priority range      }
{         const ResourceLimit = count of resources available}
    type *PriorityRange = 0..PriorityLimit;
    var NumberFree: 0..ResourceLimit;
    instance Queue: Condition;

    procedure *TryToAcquire (var OK: Boolean);
      begin
        OK := NumberFree > 0;
        if OK then NumberFree := NumberFree − 1
      end {TryToAcquire};

    procedure *PriorityAcquire (P: PriorityRange);
      begin
        if NumberFree = 0 then Queue.PWait (P);
        NumberFree := NumberFree − 1
      end {PriorityAcquire};

    procedure *Acquire;
    begin PriorityAcquire (PriorityLimit div 2) end;

    procedure *Release;
      begin
        NumberFree := NumberFree + 1;
        Queue.Signal
      end {Release};

    begin NumberFree := ResourceLimit; *** end {OneFromN};
```

The counter, NumberFree, is set initially to the resource limit value and then decremented and incremented by one following each acquisition and release operation, respectively.

The number of resources administered by the module is supplied when an instance of the monitor is retrieved from the library. For example, an instance of this module to handle twenty identical resources might be retrieved from its library file as follows:

```
monitor module OneFromN in Library
    (Where const PriorityLimit = Maxint;
          const ResourceLimit = 20;);
```

This resource limit can, alternatively, be supplied as a parameter. The module heading is then defined as follows:

```
monitor ParameterizedOneFromN (ResourceLimit: Integer);
```

and the NumberFree variable declared thus:

```
var NumberFree: 0..Maxint;
```

Most of the examples that follow use the technique of giving required module definitions in an environment specification.

In many applications some means of identification must be associated with each resource administered. In such cases a resource module requires interface operations that include a parameter identifying, or *naming* the resource acquired or released. For example, if we assume that each resource is represented by a value from a positive integer subrange then the resource monitor can take the following form:

```
monitor NamedOneFromN;
{assumes const PriorityLimit = limit on priority range       }
{          const ResourceLimit = count of resources available}
    type *PriorityRange = 0..PriorityLimit;
         *Resource = 1..ResourceLimit;
    procedure *TryToAcquire (var OK: Boolean; var R: Resource);
    procedure *PriorityAcquire (P: PriorityRange; var R: Resource);
    procedure *Acquire (var R: Resource);
    procedure *Release (R: Resource);
    begin
        {initially, all resources are free}
    end {NamedOneFromN};
```

Within the NamedOneFromN monitor the pool of free resources can be maintained by a local module that adds and removes resources to and from the pool by means of the following operations:

```
monitor ResourcePool;
{assumes const ResourceLimit = count of resources available}
{          type  Resource = 1..ResourceLimit                }
    type *ResourceSet = set of Resource;
    var *Pool: ResourceSet; {set of free resources}
    procedure *SelectAnyOne (var R: Resource);
        {Selects a resource from Pool and assigns it to R.}
        {It is assumed that Pool is not empty.            }
    procedure *SelectNamedOne (R: Resource);
        {Selects the resource R from Pool.}
        {It is assumed that R is in Pool.   }
    procedure *ReturnOne (R: Resource);
        {Puts the resource R into Pool.      }
        {It is assumed that R is not in Pool.}
    begin
        {initially Pool is fully – all the resources are available}
    end {ResourcePool};
```

The operations SelectAnyOne and SelectNamedOne enable a resource to be withdrawn from the pool. In the first case any resource is acceptable while in the second the named resource is to be taken. ReturnOne enables a resource to be returned to the resource pool. Using this module the allocation of a single identifiable resource can be implemented as follows:

```
monitor NamedOneFromN;
{assumes const PriorityLimit = limit on priority range          }
{        const ResourceLimit = count of resources available}
    type *PriorityRange = 0..PriorityLimit;
          *Resource = 1..ResourceLimit;
    instance Queue: Condition;

    monitor module ResourcePool in Library;
        {Using ResourceLimit and Resource}

    procedure *TryToAcquire (var OK: Boolean; var R: Resource);
        begin
          OK := ResourcePool.Pool <> [];
          if OK then ResourcePool.SelectAnyOne (R)
        end {TryToAcquire};

    procedure *PriorityAcquire (P: PriorityRange; var R: Resource);
        begin
          if ResourcePool.Pool = [] then Queue.PWait (P);
          ResourcePool.SelectAnyOne (R)
        end {PriorityAcquire};

    procedure *Acquire (var R: Resource);
        begin PriorityAcquire (PriorityLimit div 2, R) end;

    procedure *Release (R: Resource);
        begin
          ResourcePool.ReturnOne (R);
          Queue.Signal
        end {Release};

    begin *** end {NamedOneFromN};
```

The operations of the acquisition and release routines in the NamedOne-FromN monitor are similar to those of the two earlier monitors. A process calling PriorityAcquire, for example, will receive a resource from the pool, if possible, and if not, is suspended until a resource is available. A process releasing a resource puts that resource back into the pool and signals any waiting process so that it can resume its execution and obtain the resource just freed.

The resource pool might be implemented as follows:

```
monitor ResourcePool;
{assumes const ResourceLimit = count of resources available}
{         type Resource = 1..ResourceLimit                    }

    type *ResourceSet = set of Resource;

    var *Pool: ResourceSet;

    procedure *SelectAnyOne (var R: Resource);
```

```
        begin
          R := I;
          while not (R in Pool) do R := R + I;
          Pool := Pool − [R]
        end {SelectAnyOne};

      procedure *SelectNamedOne (R: Resource);
        begin Pool := Pool − [R] end {SelectNamedOne};

      procedure *ReturnOne (R: Resource);
        begin Pool := Pool + [R] end {ReturnOne};

      begin Pool := [I..ResourceLimit]; *** end {ResourcePool};
```

It is assumed that the pool has been checked before a SelectAnyOne or
SelectNamedOne operation is attempted so that neither operation can fail,
and, by implication, no other process should be able to operate on the
resource pool in the meantime.

One resource from a subset of N similar resources

Occasionally a pool of resources of the same basic type will have differences
that are relevant to some of the using processes. Consider, for example, an
operating system which gives processes access to shared lineprinters, some
of which have a full character set and some a reduced character set, without
lower-case letters. Files containing text in the reduced character set may be
output on any printer but all other files must be directed to one of the full
character set printers.

The implementation of a resource management module to handle this
type of allocation is quite complex. As before, the general requirement is
that each released resource should be allocated to the process at the head
of the waiting queue. Now, however, processes have different resource
requirements, so a released resource may have to be given to a process further down the queue, if the topmost process cannot accept the resource just
freed. The fairest method of allocation is to inspect the requirements of each
process in waiting order looking for the first one (if any) that can accept the
released resource.

Consider, for example, a situation in the printer problem where there are
no printers available and a sequence of three processes A, B, C arrive
requesting printer types *full*, *reduced* and *full*, respectively.

If all three processes use the Acquire operation they are suspended in their
arrival order, as suggested by the diagram in Figure 6.1.

If the first printer type released is *full* then the process at the head of the
queue, process A, is reactivated. However, if a reduced printer is the first to
appear then this is of no use to process A and so the printer can be offered
fairly to process B. Process B is then reactivated leaving A and C suspended
in the same order.

A Condition instance queue can only have its topmost process activated so

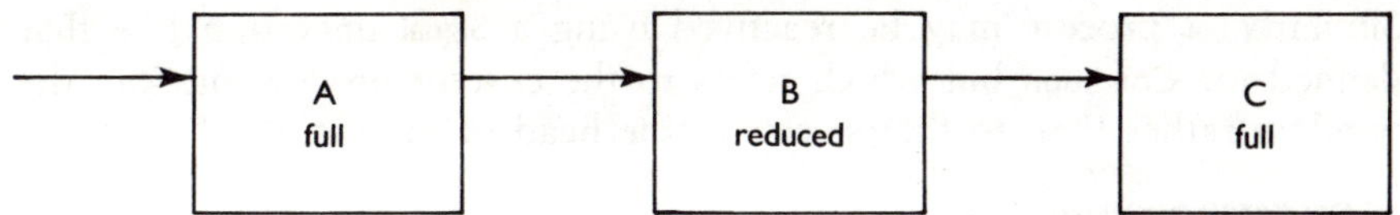

Figure 6.1 Time ordered list of processes awaiting a printer

a suitable module must be programmed explicitly to provide more selective activation. The operations defined for such a module can be based on the set of facilities offered by the standard Condition monitor, and extended with operations for manipulating the queue directly. Thus, conceptually, we need to provide a *list* rather than a queue abstraction. The module implementing this abstraction is given the name ConditionList.

The only information associated with a process on a Condition instance queue is the priority with which it is suspended. For a process suspended on the proposed condition list there must be provision for associating additional information with each suspended process so that its reasons for waiting, or *requirements*, may be inspected. In this way a process need only be reactivated when its requirements are satisfied. The requirements of a waiting process may be supplied when the process is suspended. As with a standard Condition two operations can be defined for this purpose:

procedure *Wait (Details: Requirements);
procedure *PWait (P: PriorityRange; Details: Requirements);

The complementary Signal operation may be applied to a process at any position in the list of waiting processes, where the position is determined by scanning the list from its head. This facility may be provided through a *window* mechanism that gives access to individual process entries in the list. The window can be moved to the front of the list with the operation:

procedure *Reset;

and advanced step by step down the list with the operation:

procedure *Next;

When the window is over a process entry the waiting requirements of the suspended process may be obtained through the operation:

procedure *Content (**var** Details: Requirements);

and the details changed, if required, using a replacement operation:

procedure *Replace (Details: Requirements);

The waiting priority of the process in the window may be inspected using an operation identical in form to that defined for the Condition monitor:

function *Priority: PriorityRange;

Similarly, a process may be reactivated using a Signal operation like that defined for Condition but which refers to the current process entry in the window rather than to the process at the head of the list:

procedure *Signal;

If there is no process entry in the window then Signal has no effect; otherwise the entry is deleted and the window is moved to the next entry, if any.

Length and Empty list tests can also be provided. When the list is empty the content of the window is undefined. However, it is convenient to give its position a meaningful interpretation. In general, the window can reside outside the list where this state is determined through the test:

function *InList: Boolean;

Thus InList is False when the list is empty and may also become False following a Next or Signal operation applied when the window is over the last list entry. Any attempt to advance the window explicitly when InList is False is an error, apart from the Signal operation which has been defined to have no effect in this case. The Wait and PWait operations leave the window over the first entry in the list.

The complete ConditionList abstraction may be summarized as follows:

```
monitor ConditionList;
{assumes type  PriorityRange = nonnegative integer subrange  }
{          type  Requirements = any type with := applicable     }
{          const QueueLimit = maximum length of condition list}
  {________ List Manipulation Operations ________}
  function *InList: Boolean;
    {Returns True if window is over a process entry, and}
    {False otherwise.                                   }
  procedure *Reset;
    {Sets window on first entry in list, if any.}
  procedure *Next;
    {Advances window.                        }
    {It is assumed that InList is False initially.}
  procedure *Content (var Details: Requirements);
    {Returns requirements of process entry in window.}
    {It is assumed that InList is False initially.        }
  procedure *Replace (Details: Requirements);
    {Replaces requirements of process entry in window.}
    {It is assumed that InList is False initially.        }
  {________ Condition Operations ________}
  procedure *PWait (P: PriorityRange; Details: Requirements);
    {Inserts process entry in list at position determined}
    {by P, leaving the window over the first entry.      }
  procedure *Wait (Details: Requirements);
    {Calls PWait with default priority 'Maxint div 2'.}
  procedure *Signal;
    {If InList is True then activates process whose entry is}
    {in the window, deleting the entry from the list and    }
```

```
      {advancing the window.                             }
      {If InList is False there is no effect.            }
   function *Empty: Boolean;
      {Returns True if the list is empty and False otherwise.}
   function *Length: Integer;
      {Returns the length of the list.}
   function *Priority: PriorityRange;
      {Returns the waiting priority of the process whose}
      {entry is in the window.                           }
      {It is assumed that InList is True initially.      }
   begin
      {initially the list is empty, InList is False}
   end {ConditionList};
```

Using this ConditionList monitor the implementation of a resource monitor to allocate one from a specified subset of similar resources is now quite straightforward.

In terms of the resource management abstraction, a problem of this type can be handled by extending the acquisition operations with an additional parameter specifying the set of resources that are acceptable to the calling process. So, for example, procedure Acquire might have a heading of the form:

```
   procedure *Acquire (var R: Resource; AcceptableSet: ResourceSet);
```

Thus, the 'requirements' that must be recorded for each suspended process are the set of resources acceptable to the process. The NamedOneFromSubset module may then be expressed as follows:

```
   monitor NamedOneFromSubset;
   {assumes const PriorityLimit  = limit on priority range       }
   {         const ResourceLimit = count of resources available  }
   {         const ProcessLimit  = maximum number of processes}
   {                                 using this monitor.           }
      type *PriorityRange = 0 . . PriorityLimit;
           *Resource = 1 . . ResourceLimit;
           *ResourceSet = set of Resource;
      var ResourceJustFreed: Resource;

      monitor module ConditionList in Library
        (Where const QueueLimit = ProcessLimit;
              type  Requirements = ResourceSet;);

      monitor module ResourcePool in Library;
        {Using ResourceLimit and Resource}

      procedure *TryToAcquire (var OK: Boolean; var R: Resource;
                                AcceptableSet: ResourceSet);
         begin
           OK := AcceptableSet * ResourcePool.Pool <> [];
           if OK then
             begin
               R := 1;
               while not (R in AcceptableSet * ResourcePool.Pool) do
```

```
                    R := R + I;
                ResourcePool.SelectNamedOne (R)
            end
        end {TryToAcquire};

    procedure *PriorityAcquire (P: PriorityRange; var R: Resource;
                                    AcceptableSet: ResourceSet);
        var OK: Boolean;
        begin
            TryToAcquire (OK, R, AcceptableSet);
            if not OK then
                begin
                    ConditionList.PWait (P, AcceptableSet);
                    R := ResourceJustFreed
                end
        end {PriorityAcquire};

    procedure *Acquire (var R: Resource; AcceptableSet: ResourceSet);
        begin
            PriorityAcquire (PriorityLimit div 2, R, AcceptableSet)
        end {Acquire};

    procedure *Release (R: Resource);
        var AcceptableSet: ResourceSet;
            MatchFound: Boolean;
        begin
            ConditionList.Reset;
            MatchFound := False;
            while ConditionList.InList and not MatchFound do
                begin
                ConditionList.Content (AcceptableSet);
                if R in AcceptableSet
                then begin
                        ResourceJustFreed := R;
                        ConditionList.Signal;
                        MatchFound := True
                    end
                else ConditionList.Next
                end;
            if not MatchFound then ResourcePool.ReturnOne (R)
        end {Release};

    begin *** end {NamedOneFromSubset};
```

The **Release** routine compares the identity of the resource that is being
freed with the requirements of each waiting process in turn. If any process
can accept the resource the identity of the resource is placed in the variable
ResourceJustFreed and the corresponding process entry signaled. A reactivated
process then takes the resource identity directly from ResourceJustFreed rather
than going to the resource pool to find it, which saves time.

In general, each process entry in a condition list can be represented by a
record containing:

(a) the priority of the waiting process;
(b) the details of what that process requires before it can be reactivated;
(c) a *link* to a condition queue on which the process is suspended.

The nature of the first two entries has already been discussed but the third needs some explanation. The first point to clarify is that the condition mechanism is the only facility available in Pascal Plus for suspending the execution of a process – hence each process on the condition list must be associated with a Condition instance in some way. To give sufficient control over the ordering of suspended processes it is convenient to use a separate Condition instance for each process. Pascal Plus does not permit a Condition instance to be declared as a field of a record so a more indirect (and less elegant) method has to be used. The technique is to represent (c) by an index into an array of Condition instances, declared as follows:

```
type ConditionRange = 1..QueueLimit;
instance Conditions: array [ConditionRange] of Condition;
```

The allocation of these references can be handled by an instance of the general resource pool module, retrieved thus:

```
monitor module QueuePool = ResourcePool in Library
   (Where const ResourceLimit = QueueLimit;
           type  Resource = ConditionRange;);
```

Note how the library retrieval may specify a more appropriate name for the module being retrieved.

As the number of Condition instances is fixed the list of process entries can be implemented adequately by an array, declared thus:

```
type ProcessDescriptor = record
                        P: PriorityRange;
                        Details: Requirements;
                        Queue: ConditionRange
                    end;
var List: array [ConditionRange] of ProcessDescriptor;
```

The complete ConditionList module can be expressed as follows:

```
monitor ConditionList;
{assumes type  PriorityRange = nonnegative integer subrange  }
{         type  Requirements = any type with := applicable    }
{         const QueueLimit = maximum length of condition list}
   type ConditionRange = 1..QueueLimit;
        ProcessDescriptor = record
                        P: PriorityRange;
                        Details: Requirements;
                        Queue: ConditionRange
                    end;
   var *Length: 0..QueueLimit;
       Window: 1..Maxint;
```

```
          List: array [ConditionRange] of ProcessDescriptor;
instance Conditions: array [ConditionRange] of Condition;

monitor module QueuePool = ResourcePool in Library
  (Where const ResourceLimit = QueueLimit;
         type  Resource = ConditionRange;);

function *InList: Boolean;
  begin InList := (Window <= Length) end;

procedure *Reset;
  begin Window := 1 end;

procedure *Next;
  begin Window := Window + 1 end;

procedure *Content (var Details: Requirements);
  begin Details := List[Window]. Details end;

procedure *Replace (Details: Requirements);
  begin List[Window].Details := Details end;

procedure *PWait (P : PriorityRange; Details; Requirements);
  var PositionFound: Boolean;
      Index: 1..Maxint;
      C: ConditionRange;
  begin
  {ensure window is at the beginning of the list}
   Window := 1;
  {find insertion position}
   Index := 1;
   PositionFound := False;
   repeat
     if Index <= Length then
       if List [Index].P <= P
       then Index := Index + 1
       else PositionFound := True
   until PositionFound or (Index > Length);
   {create a gap}
    Length := Length + 1;
    for C := Length downto Index + 1 do
      List [C] := List [C − 1];
   {insert list entry}
    List [Index].P := P;
    List [Index].Details := Details;
    QueuePool.SelectAnyOne (List [Index].Queue);
   {suspend process}
    Conditions [List [Index].Queue]. Wait
   end {PWait};

procedure *Wait (Details: Requirements);
  begin PWait (PriorityLimit div 2, Details) end;

procedure *Signal;
  var C: ConditionRange;
  begin
```

```
          if Window <= Length then
            with List [Window] do
              begin
                  Conditions [Queue].Signal;
                  QueuePool.ReturnOne (Queue);
                {Remove entry from list}
                  for C := Window to Length - I do
                    List [C] := List [C + I];
                  Length := Length - I
              end
      end {Signal};

  function *Empty: Boolean;
    begin Empty := (Length = 0) end;

  function *Priority: PriorityRange;
    begin Priority := List [Window].P end;

  begin Window := I; Length := 0; *** end {ConditionList};
```

The implementation of each condition list operation is straightforward apart from PWait and Signal. The action of PWait is to:

(a) inspect the priority of each waiting process in list order until either a process with a priority status lower than that specified as a parameter to PWait is found, or the end of the list is encountered;
(b) create a gap in the list, if necessary, by moving each of the entries for lower priority processes one position further down the list;
(c) insert an entry for the process being suspended, obtaining access to a Condition instance from the QueuePool module;
(d) suspend the process invoking PWait using the allocated Condition instance.

Signal reactivates a process, if any, whose descriptor is currently in the window, and deletes that descriptor from the list by moving each of the entries for lower priority processes one place towards the start of the list.

The use of the NamedOneFromSubset resource monitor may be illustrated by developing a module to allocate the full and reduced character set printers discussed earlier. Let us assume that there are three full character set printers and two reduced printers, which are identified by integer values in the range I to 3 and 4 to 5, respectively. If it is further assumed that a process obtaining a printer is also expected to release it, and that a process is always prepared to wait for a printer to become free, then the printer allocation module might be expressed in the following form:

```
monitor module LinePrinters;
  const *NumberOfPrinters = 5;
        *LineLimit = 120;
  type *PrinterType = ( *Full, *Reduced);
      *Line = record
                *Length: 0..LineLimit;
```

```
                            *Data: packed array [1..LineLimit] of Char
                    end;
        monitor module PrinterPool = NamedOneFromSubset IN Library
           (Where const PriorityLimit = Maxint;
                  const ResourceLimit = NumberOfPrinters;
                  const ProcessLimit = 20 {say};);

        envelope *PrinterInterface (Required: PrinterType);
           var P: PrinterPool.Resource;

           procedure *PrintLine (L: Line); ...;
           procedure *TakeNewPage; ...;

           begin {PrinterInterface}
              if Required = Full
              then PrinterPool.Acquire (P, [1..3])
              else PrinterPool.Acquire (P, [1..NumberOfPrinters]);
              ***;
              TakeNewPage;
              PrinterPool.Release (P)
           end {PrinterInterface};

        begin *** end {LinePrinters};
```

Note that:

(a) Each process which requires a printer requests either a Full or Reduced
printer type, providing this information as a parameter when declaring
an instance of the PrinterInterface envelope, e.g.:

```
instance MyPrinter: LinePrinters.PrinterInterface (LinePrinters.Full);
```

Internally, this request is interpreted as a request for a printer in the
corresponding ranges [1..3] or [1..NumberOfPrinters]. The identity of the
device allocated is kept within the envelope and so is not accessible to
the user process.

(b) An actual printer is acquired implicitly through the initialization action
of the PrinterInterface envelope. Two operations, PrintLine and TakeNew-
Page, are then available for sending lines of text to the printer and
advancing to a new page, respectively. These operations are implemented entirely within the envelope as the process has exclusive access to
the printer acquired.

(c) The printer is released implicitly by the finalization action of the
envelope after the last page of output has been sent to the printer.

The completion of this monitor is set as an exercise at the end of Chapter 9,
and a solution may be found in Appendix 2.

Allocating resources in multiple units

The resource management problems discussed in the previous section involved processes competing for either a single resource or one from a pool

of identical, or similar resources. The assumption made was that each process needed access to only one resource at any time. It is perhaps not immediately obvious why this assumption is necessary and, therefore, why multiple resource acquisition cannot be handled simply through a sequence of single resource requests. The distinction can be illustrated with analogies taken from interactions that 'might' occur in everyday life.

First consider the case of a group of workmen who share a single tool box. When a workman is given a job to do he goes to the tool box and selects the tools he needs. If any are missing he waits until they have been returned. One day two workmen approach the tool box together, both needing a hammer and a chisel. Both are ill-mannered and unfriendly. Being ill-mannered they rummage through the tool box at the same time, with one picking up the hammer and the other the chisel. Being unfriendly, they make no attempt to talk to each other while waiting for the appearance of the tool they lack, and so fail to appreciate that they have the same needs. At the end of the day the foreman finds them standing idly by the tool box and, being unfamiliar with the subtleties of resource management problems, fires them.

This analogy illustrates *deadlock*, which can occur when allocating multiple resources to competing processes. When processes are deadlocked in their attempt to obtain resources they may be suspended, as implied by the workmen standing idly by the tool box, or they may carry out operations without any possibility of making real progress.

Consider, again by analogy, another sad case. Two couples, whom we will refer to by the letters A and B, decide, independently, to get married on the same day in the same church and use the same hotel for their reception after the ceremony. Couple A book the church first while couple B start by booking the hotel. Couple A succeed in booking the church but then find that the hotel is not available because couple B have booked it. To recover, couple A reserve the hotel for the following day with the intention of returning to the church to adjust their booking there accordingly. Meanwhile, couple B, who have booked the hotel first, find that the church is not free on that day and so advance their church booking to the following day, hoping also to move the hotel booking forward one day. The situation is now equivalent to the initial position. If this strategy is continued it will lead to a 'wedlock deadlock' in which neither couple will succeed in marrying unless one pair give up in disgust or decide that they are becoming too old to make the step worthwhile.

These analogies illustrate how deadlock can result from the attempted acquisition of different types of resources. The same problem can also arise, however, when only one resource type is involved. For example, if four magnetic tape drives are available for general use and two processes each attempt to acquire three drives by making individual requests they may become deadlocked with each holding two drives.

There are four necessary conditions for deadlock to occur in the allocation of resources:

- processes claim exclusive control of the resources they require;
- processes hold resources already allocated to them while waiting for additional resources;
- resources cannot be removed from the processes that hold them;
- a circular chain of processes exists in which each process holds resources that are required by the next process in the chain.

As deadlock arises only when resources are acquired in a piecemeal fashion, it can be avoided by insisting that all resources are acquired at the same time. That is, a process should request all of the facilities it needs for a particular task at one time, with the guarantee that the acquisition of the resources cannot be interrupted by requests from other processes. So, in terms of the analogies, deadlock can be avoided if only one workman at a time selects tools from the tool box, or if each wedding couple makes their hotel and church bookings simultaneously using two telephones!

A second method of avoiding deadlock, when allocating resources of different types, is to restrict the allocation to a predefined order, and so avoid any circular dependency among processes awaiting resource allocations. For example, using the workmen and wedding couple analogies again, deadlock can be prevented if:

(a) the tools from the tool box can only be picked up in some specified sequence;

(b) the couples adopt a tradition of always booking the church first and only then considering where to hold the reception.

The following subsections consider the problem of deadlock in discussing how resources are allocated in multiple units. The first case treated is where the resources involved are of the same type, and where deadlock is avoided by allocating the resources simultaneously.

M resources from *N* identical resources

Following the pattern set for single resource allocation the first multiple resource module developed is one in which the identity of the resources is not recorded. Such a module might take the form:

```
monitor MFromN;
{assumes const PriorityLimit = Limit on priority range        }
{         const ResourceLimit = count of resources available}
{         const ProcessLimit = maximum number of processes}
{                         using this monitor                }
    type *PriorityRange = 0..PriorityLimit;
         *ResourceSize = 0..ResourceLimit;
    procedure *TryToAcquire (var OK: Boolean; Needed: ResourceSize);
    procedure *PriorityTryToAcquire (P: PriorityRange; var OK: Boolean;
                                  Needed: ResourceSize);
    procedure *PriorityAcquire (P: PriorityRange; Needed: ResourceSize;);
    procedure *Acquire (Needed: ResourceSize);
```

```
        procedure *Release (Given: ResourceSize);
        begin
           {initially, all resources are available}
        end {MFromN};
```

These operations follow the general resource module pattern with each now specifying the number of resources requested or freed, as appropriate. With multiple resources we use the two forms of tentative acquisition – one with and one without a priority parameter.

The number of free resources in an MFromN module can be maintained as a counter, as in the OneFromN case. The administration of the counter is now much more complex, however, as there are three additional factors to consider:

(a) a process may have to wait for several Release calls in order to accumulate sufficient resources to satisfy its needs;

(b) a single release of resources may be sufficient to satisfy several waiting processes;

(c) resources may be free even though there are processes on the waiting queue.

To handle the allocation of resources it is thus necessary to record the number of resources required by each waiting process in order to decide whether or not a process should be reactivated when resources are released. This means that the queue must be maintained using an instance of the ConditionList monitor as discussed for the NamedOneFromSubset monitor in the previous section.

The MFromN monitor can be expressed as follows:

```
monitor MFromN;
{assumes const PriorityLimit  = limit on priority range        }
{         const ResourceLimit = count of resources available   }
{         const ProcessLimit  = maximum number of processes}
{                                 using this monitor            }
    type *PriorityRange = 0..PriorityLimit;
         *ResourceSize = 0..ResourceLimit;
    var NumberFree: ResourceSize;

    monitor module ConditionList in Library
       (Where const QueueLimit = ProcessLimit;
              type Requirements = ResourceSize;);

    function TryAllowed (P: PriorityRange): Boolean;
       begin
          ConditionList.Reset;
          if ConditionList.Empty
          then TryAllowed := True
          else TryAllowed := ConditionList.Priority > P
       end {TryAllowed};

    procedure *PriorityTryToAcquire (P: PriorityRange; var OK: Boolean;
                                Needed: ResourceSize);
```

```
        begin
            OK := TryAllowed (P) and (Needed <= NumberFree);
            if OK then NumberFree := NumberFree - Needed
        end {PriorityTryToAcquire};

    procedure *TryToAcquire (var OK: Boolean; Needed: ResourceSize);
        begin
            PriorityTryToAcquire (PriorityLimit div 2, OK, Needed)
        end {TryToAcquire};

    procedure *PriorityAcquire (P: PriorityRange; Needed: ResourceSize);
        begin
            if not TryAllowed (P) or (NumberFree < Needed) then
            ConditionList.PWait (P, Needed);
            NumberFree := NumberFree - Needed
        end {PriorityAcquire};

    procedure *Acquire (Needed: ResourceSize);
        begin PriorityAcquire (PriorityLimit div 2, Needed) end;

    procedure *Release (Given: ResourceSize);
        var StillAllocating: Boolean;
            Needed: ResourceSize;
        begin
            NumberFree := NumberFree + Given;
            StillAllocating := True;
            ConditionList.Reset;
            while StillAllocating and not ConditionList.Empty do
            begin
                {attempt to acquire resources for}
                {top priority waiting process      }
                ConditionList.Content (Needed);
                if Needed <= NumberFree
                then ConditionList.Signal
                else StillAllocating := False;
            end
        end {Release};

    begin
        NumberFree := ResourceLimit;
        ***
    end {MFromN};
```

Each acquisition operation first checks to ensure that no process with the same or higher priority is currently suspended awaiting resources. If there is such a process then the calling process is either suspended or returns without any resources, according to the type of operation attempted. If an acquisition is allowed to proceed then the number of resources that the process needs is compared with the number available. For a tentative acquisition an allocation is made if the number of resources available is greater than or equal to the number needed. For the Acquire and PriorityAcquire operations a calling process must either obtain its full requirement or be suspended.

With this scheme, processes with the same priority status are allocated resources strictly in their order of arrival. The outcome is fair but may not result in the maximum utilization of the resources concerned. This follows from the fact that, whenever the process at the head of the waiting queue requires a large number of resources, these have to be accumulated, and thus left unused, before the allocation is made. For some applications the resources can be better utilized by giving priority to those processes that have small resource requirements. However, resources cannot always be allocated to those processes that can use them, regardless of arrival order, because there is then a danger that a process making a large request will never be satisfied, causing *starvation*. Thus, any scheme that gives priority to those processes with small resource requirements must, at the same time, guarantee that the needs of processes with large resource requirements are met in a 'reasonable' time.

One way to achieve this result is to associate with each process a *decaying* priority value which takes account of the number of resources that the process requires and the length of time that the process has been waiting to receive them. The simplest representation for the waiting time of a process is a number denoting its arrival order with respect to other processes attempting resource acquisitions. A waiting priority value can then be determined using the following equation:

```
process priority := specified priority + arrival number +
                weighting factor * number of resources requested
```

The degree of preference given to processes requesting small numbers of resources is adjusted through the weighting factor.

In a BiasedMFromN monitor implementing this strategy, each acquisition operation advances the arrival number by one. A request is then considered only if the waiting queue is empty or if the top process on the queue has a lower priority status than that calculated for the process making the request. The longer that a process is suspended on the queue the higher its priority status becomes in relation to new arrivals. Thus, each process request will eventually be satisfied, regardless of the number of resources involved.

In circumstances where the identity of each resource is to be made available the acquisition and release operations of a NamedMFromN multiple resource module will each require a parameter that specifies a set of resources. So, for example, procedure Acquire might take the form:

```
procedure *Acquire (var R: ResourceSet; Needed: ResourceSize);
```

Internally the strategy used to transfer resources among the processes is very similar to the case in which resource identities are not required.

M resources from a subset of N similar resources

To handle the allocation of resources that differ slightly, a NamedMFrom-Subset module will combine the strategies used in the NamedOneFromSubset monitor with those used in the MFromN monitor. However, no new techniques are involved, and so we need not discuss this case further, but leave the implementation as an exercise.

M resources from sets of different resources

In some programs, processes need exclusive access to several resources of differing types simultaneously. One general technique for allocating such resources, that avoids deadlock, is to perform the allocation in a single monitor and require each process to obtain all the resources that it needs through a single acquisition request to that monitor. Another approach, in cases where the resources can be ordered, is to allocate resources in a defined order and so prevent a *circular dependency* among competing processes, which is one of the necessary preconditions for deadlock. With this latter technique the allocation of different types of resource can be handled by separate modules. The alternative to avoiding deadlock, is to detect it when it occurs and recover from it. All of these techniques for handling deadlock are discussed in the subsections that follow, in connection with the administration of resources of mixed type.

The monolithic module approach

The allocation of resources of mixed types in a concurrent program can be administered by one module to avoid the possibility of deadlock. To illustrate what is involved consider the simplest case where the identity of the resources is not required. The resource module might then have the form:

```
monitor ResourceControl;
   procedure *PriorityTryToAcquire (P: PriorityRange;
                                    var OK: Boolean;
                                    Needed: ResourceCollection);
   procedure *TryToAcquire (var OK: Boolean;
                            Needed: ResourceCollection);
   procedure *PriorityAcquire (P: PriorityRange;
                               Needed: ResourceCollection);
   procedure *Acquire (Needed: ResourceCollection);
   procedure *Release (Given: ResourceCollection);
   begin
      {initially, all resources are available}
   end {ResourceControl};
```

This module is similar to the MFromN monitor. The main difference is that, internally, waiting processes are notionally allocated whatever resources are available. Thus, any resources that are in the free pool can be allocated to any process that arrives, regardless of whether or not other processes are waiting.

The basic strategy used for allocating resources can be summarized as follows:

> Try to take resources needed from the free pool
> **if not** all resources obtained **then**
>   try to take resources from lower priority waiting processes
> **if not** all resources obtained **then**
>   either wait or return, according to the type of operation attempted – for a tentative
>   operation any resources obtained are returned to the free pool

When resources are released the following procedure is used:

> Allocate the resources to waiting processes in their priority order
>   – **if** any reaches its complement **then** reactivate it
> Return unused resources to the free pool

This strategy for handling the allocation of resources is discussed in more detail in a later section which deals with management of resources that are defined dynamically.

The technique of obtaining all of the resources needed for an operation in one acquisition request avoids deadlock but is not always ideal for the following reasons:

(a) If processes acquire all of the resources that they will ever need at the beginning of their execution they will hold some resources for longer than necessary. This is inefficient and will tend to reduce the overall performance of the program. One way of reducing this effect, in some cases, is to split lengthy operations into a sequence of *phases* where the resources needed for each phase are acquired and released at the beginning and end of the phase, respectively.

(b) As all resource requests are handled by one module, that module will form a bottleneck in any program where resource acquisition and release operations are performed frequently.

E.W. Dijkstra has proposed a solution to problem (a) that allows processes to acquire resources only when they need them. His solution is known as the *banker's algorithm*, so named because it was first illustrated by considering how a banker might make loans and receive payments (with respect to a given source of capital).

The banker's algorithm
The banker's algorithm allows resources to be allocated in a piecemeal fashion but will only permit an allocation to take place if it is safe to do so, i.e. if it is certain that deadlock will not occur as a result of the allocation. In order to check for *potential* deadlock the allocation module must be aware of the maximum resource requirements of each process in the system and must also maintain a record of the resources currently held by each process. Thus, each process must make itself known to the allocation module initially, specifying the resources it will require. In return, the module can then assign to the process a unique reference key by which the process can identify itself each time it wishes to acquire or release resources.

The initial process identification might be performed through an operation of the form:

procedure NoteMaximumRequirement (Claim: ResourceCollection;
                                                    var Reference: Key);

As the banker module will check for deadlock on each resource request, resources can be acquired individually. So an Acquire operation, for example, might be defined thus:

procedure Acquire (Reference: Key; R: Resource);

To clarify the circumstances in which a resource request is refused let us consider the simple case where:

(a) the only resource type is a magnetic tape drive of which there are four in total;
(b) there are two processes, A and B, each of which has a maximum requirement of three drives.

Assume that each process initially obtains one drive. As there are then two drives available the situation is clearly safe because either process can complete its allocation. If process A now attempts to acquire a drive it can be allowed to proceed. The situation is still safe because A can complete its allocation and so return one or more drives in due course to allow B to finish. The position is as follows:

Tapes free: 1

                                Process A   Process B
Tapes allocated: 2   1

If process B now attempts to acquire a drive the allocation is prevented because deadlock will occur if either process returns for its third drive.

The algorithm that is used to avoid deadlock simulates the allocation of the resource requests that are outstanding to ensure that there is at least one way in which all of the waiting processes can obtain their full quota of resources, and so complete their execution. When the full claim for any process is met its resources are notionally released and these are used to complete the allocation of other processes in the same way. A situation is then safe if all process requests can be satisfied.

The banker's algorithm is seldom used in practice because the checking involved tends to be time-consuming. Also the technique is difficult to apply effectively because it is not satisfactory for each process to identify, initially, every resource that it might ever use during its execution. What matters is the combination of resources that are required at any one time. If the using processes are not so specific then resource allocations may be refused in situations where deadlock cannot occur. For example, if a process needs a lineprinter and a magnetic tape during its execution but does not require them simultaneously then the allocation of one or other of these resources

may be denied in situations that are safe. Thus, to make best use of resources, processes are obliged to consider their use of resources in phases
and indicate their maximum use of resources for each phase independently.

Resource allocation in a fixed order
If resources can be ordered then deadlock can be avoided by allocating those
resources in that order. The implications of this technique are:

(a) Resources may be acquired separately as long as they are requested in
     the prescribed order.
(b) If a process requires a resource R of a type lower in the sequence than
     resources which it already holds it must release the higher order
     resources held before attempting to acquire R, after which the released
     resources are reacquired again in order.
(c) If a process requires a resource of type T and already holds one or more
     resources of that type then it must release those resources and acquire
     all that are needed in one operation.

As an illustration of this technique let us consider the allocation of tools
from a tool box, where the tools available are:

4 screwdrivers, 1 hammer, 1 chisel, 2 saws, 1 drill, 1 tape measure

If the allocation sequence is defined to follow the order in which the tools
are named above, then a workman who already has a screwdriver and a saw
may obtain the drill directly. If he then finds that he needs a second saw,
however, he must first release the drill *and* the one saw that he holds. He
may then attempt to acquire two saws (in a single operation), followed by
the drill, in that order.

With this technique the management of different resource types can be
handled by separate allocation modules, which leads to a more acceptable
program structure. Also, the solution avoids deadlock without incurring
any appreciable execution overhead. Its main disadvantages are that it is
applicable only to resources that can be released and reacquired without any
ill effect and to resources where an adequate resource order can be imposed.
The first condition is not met, for example, by a shared graph plotter because it is unacceptable for a process to release and reacquire this resource is
in the middle of using it.

Ordered resource acquisition can often be used in simulation programs.
Consider, for example, how a simulation model of workmen using a tool
box might be expressed. The rules for acquiring and releasing tools in the
prescribed order can be implemented by an envelope of the following form:

```
envelope ToolAccess;
   procedure * Acquire (T: Tool);
      {Acquires a tool T, releasing and reacquiring any tools}
      {of the same or higher order.                         }
   procedure * Release (T: Tool);
```

```
    {Releases a tool T — it is assumed that T has been}
    {acquired previously.                             }
begin
    {initially, no tools are held}
    {finally, any tools still held are released}
end {ToolAccess};
```

Here tools may be acquired and released individually, where the tool type is defined, thus:

```
type Tool = (Screwdriver, Hammer, Chisel, Saw, Drill, TapeMeasure);
```

A workman requiring a hammer and chisel might be represented by a process expressed as follows:

```
process module Fred;
    instance ToolBox: ToolAccess;
    begin
        ToolBox.Acquire (Hammer);
        ToolBox.Acquire (Chisel);
                . . .
    end {Fred};
```

Each envelope instance must keep track of the resources held by the associated workman process. With this information the envelope can release resources and reacquire them, where necessary, to preserve the expected acquisition order.

If a version of the MFromN module is used which takes the number of resources administered as a parameter thus:

```
monitor ParameterizedMFromN (ResourceLimit: Integer);
```

then the allocation of the tools can be handled by an array of these monitors declared as follows:

```
instance ToolSet: array [Tool] of ParameterizedMFromN
                [(4), (1), (1), (2), (1), (1)];
```

The complete implementation of the ToolAccess envelope can be expressed thus:

```
envelope ToolAccess;
    var MyTools: array [Tool] of 0..Maxint;

    procedure * Acquire (T: Tool);
        var Index: Tool;
        begin
        {release same and higher order tools}
            for Index := T to TapeMeasure do
                if Mytools [Index] <> 0 then
                    ToolSet [Index].Release (MyTools [Index]);
        {update tools held}
            MyTools [T] := MyTools [T] + 1;
```

```
      {acquire tools needed}
        for Index := T to TapeMeasure do
          if MyTools [Index] <> 0 then
              ToolSet [Index].Acquire (MyTools [Index])
      end {Acquire};

    procedure * Release (T: Tool);
      begin
        ToolSet [T].Release (1);
        MyTools [T] := MyTools [T] - 1
      end {Release};

    procedure Initialize;
      var Index: Tool;
      begin
        for Index := ScrewDriver to TapeMeasure do
          MyTools [Index] := 0
      end {Initialize};

    procedure Finalize;
      var Index: Tool;
      begin
        for Index := ScrewDriver to TapeMeasure do
          if MyTools [Index] <> 0 then
              ToolSet [Index].Release (MyTools [Index])
      end {Finalize};

    begin Initialize; ***; Finalize end {ToolAccess};
```

This module prevents deadlock and also ensures that each process releases
any resources that are not returned explicitly.

Detecting and recovering from deadlock

It is desirable to construct all concurrent systems in such a way that the
possibility of deadlock is avoided. However, in applications where this requirement is impractical the alternative approach of detecting and recovering from deadlock can be used. This may be necessary, for example, in an
operating system where user programs are permitted to acquire access to a
sequence of files individually.

When deadlock occurs in a concurrent system it may result in all of the
processes present being suspended – a situation which is easy to detect.
However, it is not adequate to respond to this situation alone since deadlock
may involve as few as two processes. Also, it is not sufficient to look for
under-utilization of the processors executing the processes since competition for processors may be such that the processors are fully utilized
anyway.

The only satisfactory technique is to investigate the interdependency of
waiting processes. This involves:

(a) noting those resources that are in use;

(b) for each process either using resources or waiting to use them, recording the identity of the resources concerned.

This information can be expressed in the form of a *resource dependency graph*. The graph has two sets of nodes: one set for those resourcs in use and one set for the processes that are either using or waiting to use resources. Arcs join the resource and process nodes to denote their interdependency. Consider, for example, a situation in the tool box problem where two workmen, Fred and Bert, await resources as follows:

> Fred: holds a saw and a chisel, and is awaiting a hammer;
> Bert: holds a screwdriver and a hammer, and is awaiting a saw.

A third workman, Joe, holds a saw and the tape measure. The resource dependency graph representing this situation might be drawn as shown in Figure 6.2.

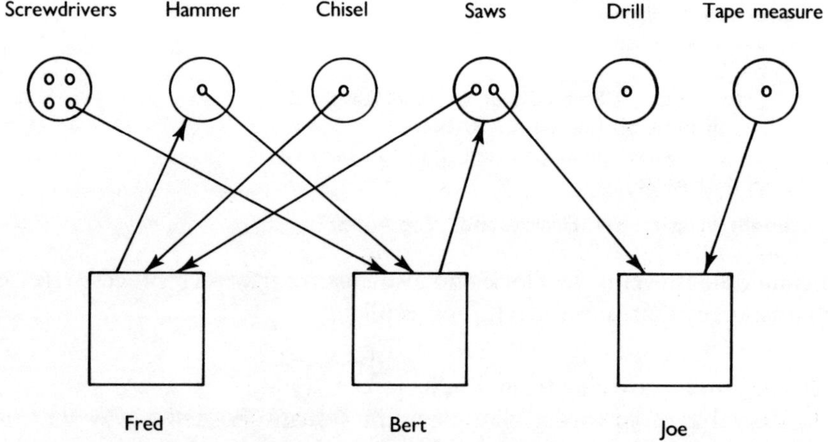

Figure 6.2 Resource dependency graph

To check for deadlock a technique similar to that outlined earlier for the banker's algorithm is used. In this case, however, we are only trying to identify some acquisition and release sequence that will allow the present process requirements to be satisfied; deadlock may still occur at some point in the future if a different sequence is followed. The test for *current* deadlock is performed by first releasing (notionally) all of the resources held by any process that is not delayed awaiting resources, and removing those resource connections from the graph. The freed resources are then allocated (notionally) to any of the waiting processes that require them. If any one of those processes is then able to proceed, its resource allocation is released and distributed to other waiting processes in the same way. At each stage the graph is *reduced* and the system is then declared *deadlock-free* if the graph can be *completely reduced*.

In the example, Joe has no waiting dependency and so his resources, a saw and the tape measure, may be released reducing the graph to the form shown in Figure 6.3.

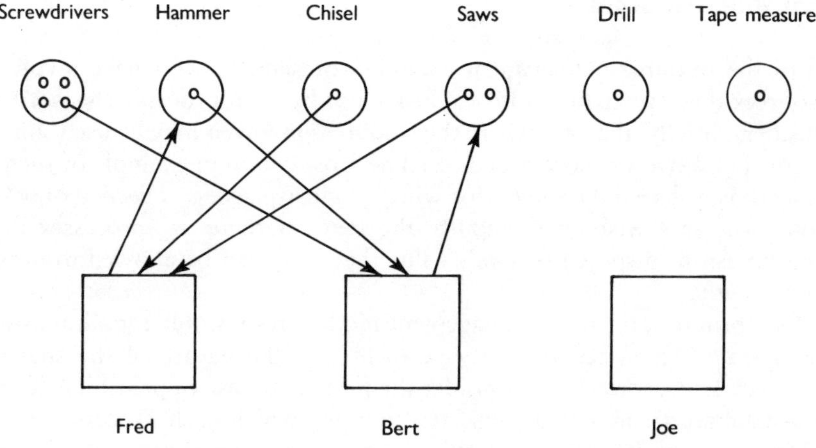

Figure 6.3 Partially reduced dependency graph

Bert can then be given the saw that he needs. This completes the resources he requires, thereby allowing all of his tools to be freed and the resource graph to be reduced accordingly. Finally Fred can then obtain the hammer that he requires, so completing his allocation and allowing the graph to be *completely reduced*.

In circumstances where deadlock is allowed to occur, a recovery procedure must be defined. That procedure may simply involve activating waiting processes and informing them that their attempt to obtain resources has failed. Depending on the situation the process may then try again later or abandon the operation involved. Another method of recovery is to take resources from one or more processes and give them to other processes. However, this approach is often impractical. In particular, the technique implies that if a resource is transferred from a process A to a process B then any effect that A has had on the resource, from the time that it acquired it, is undone.

Dynamically defined resources

In situations where resources are created and destroyed dynamically their administration is very similar to that described already for statically defined resources. That is, essentially the same logic is used, the only difference being that a mechanism must be provided for introducing new resources to the resource manager and for indicating that others no longer exist. An

example of the administration of a dynamically defined resource is given in
the next section that deals with sharable resources.

Sharable resources

All of the resource management examples presented so far have involved
resources that are acquired for exclusive use by each process. This section
considers, briefly, the case where the resources involved may be used simultaneously by two or more processes. The most common example of such a
resource is a shared data item, for which exclusive access is needed only by
those processes wishing to modify the item. If there are processes that
simply wish to inspect the item's value then they can be allowed to do so
concurrently.

The form of a resource management module responsible for administering sharable resources will vary according to the nature of the sharing
involved. To fix ideas let us consider the particular case of providing access
to a database treated as a single resource for which each process obtains
either *read* or *write* access as required, and where several processes may be
allowed to read simultaneously. The form of the corresponding resource
management module might be as follows:

```
monitor DatabaseAccess;
   type *AccessMode = ( *Read, *Write);
   procedure *PriorityTryToAcquire (P: PriorityRange;
                                    var OK: Boolean;
                                    AccessRequired: AccessMode);
   procedure *TryToAcquire (var OK: Boolean;
                            AccessRequired: AccessMode);
   procedure *PriorityAcquire (P: PriorityRange;
                               AccessRequired: AccessMode);
   procedure *Acquire (AccessRequired: AccessMode;
   procedure *Release;
   begin
      {initially, the database is free}
   end {DatabaseAccess};
```

If a process requests *read* access to the database then permission to read
can be given if:

(a) there are no processes using the database;
(b) other processes currently have *read* access to the database *but* there are
    no processes with the same or a higher priority waiting to write to it;
    this qualification is just the normal rule that ensures that processes with
    the same priority gain access to the resource in their order of arrival.

Internally, the module must record the current mode of access, if any,
together with details of any processes that are either currently using the
database or waiting to use it.

If a reading process releases its access to the database then the number of current readers is decremented by one. If there are other current readers then no further action is taken; otherwise the first process on the waiting queue, if any, is reactivated. That process must be one wishing to write to the database as other readers would not have been delayed.

When a writing process releases access to the database the first process on the waiting queue may either be one wishing to read or one wishing to write. If it is a reader then there may be a sequence of such processes on the queue, all of which can be activated. As usual, the reactivations follow the priority order in which the processes are queued. A complete implementation of the database access module might be expressed as follows:

```
monitor DatabaseAccess;
{assumes const PriorityLimit  = limit on priority range          }
{         const ResourceLimit = count of resources available     }
{         const ProcessLimit  = maximum number of processes}
{                              using this monitor                }
    type *PriorityRange = 0..PriorityLimit;
         *AccessMode = ( *Read, *Write, None);
    var CurrentAccessMode: AccessMode;
        Readers: 0..Maxint;

    monitor module ConditionList in Library
      Where const QueueLimit = ProcessLimit;
            type  Requirements = AccessMode;);

    procedure *PriorityTryToAcquire (P: PriorityRange; var OK: Boolean;
                                     AccessRequired: AccessMode);

      function TryAllowed (P: PriorityRange): Boolean;
        begin
          ConditionList.Reset;
          if ConditionList.Empty
          then TryAllowed := True
          else TryAllowed := ConditionList.Priority > P
        end {TryAllowed};

      begin {PriorityTryToAcquire}
        OK := False;
        if TryAllowed (P) then
        case CurrentAccessMode of
          None: begin
                  OK := True;
                  CurrentAccessMode := AccessRequired;
                  if AccessRequired = Read then Readers := 1
                end;
          Read: if AccessRequired = Read then
                  begin
                    OK := True;
                    Readers := Readers + 1
                  end;
          Write: ;
```

```pascal
        end
    end {PriorityTryToAcquire};

procedure*TryToAcquire (var OK: Boolean;
                            AccessRequired: AccessMode);
  begin
    PriorityTryToAcquire (PriorityLimit div 2, OK, AccessRequired)
  end {TryToAcquire};

procedure *PriorityAcquire (P: PriorityRange; AccessRequired: AccessMode);
  var OK: Boolean;
  begin
    PriorityTryToAcquire (P, OK, AccessRequired);
    if not OK then ConditionList.PWait (P, AccessRequired)
  end {PriorityAcquire};

procedure *Acquire (AccessRequired: AccessMode);
  begin
    PriorityAcquire (PriorityLimit div 2, AccessRequired)
  end {Acquire};

procedure *Release;
  var SwitchPossible: Boolean;
      AccessRequired: AccessMode;
  begin
    if ConcurrentAccessMode = Read
    then begin
            Readers := Readers − 1;
            SwitchPossible := Readers = 0
         end
    else SwitchPossible := True;
    if SwitchPossible then
      if ConditionList.Empty
      then CurrentAccessMode := None
      else
        begin
          ConditionList.Reset;
          ConditionList.Content (CurrentAccessMode);
          if CurrentAccessMode = Read
          then {Awaken sequence of readers}
            repeat
              Readers := Readers + 1;
              ConditionList.Signal;
              if not ConditionList.Empty then
                ConditionList.Content (AccessRequired);
            until (AccessRequired <> Read) or ConditionList.Empty
          else {awaken writer}
            ConditionList.Signal
        end
    end {Release};

begin {DatabaseAccess}
  CurrentAccessMode := None;
```

```
    Readers := 0;
    ***
end {DatabaseAccess};
```

This solution is consistent with the techniques used throughout this chapter but a different and simpler monitor solution is often presented for this problem. The more common method uses two waiting queues: one for processes wishing to write to the database and one for processes wishing to read from it. This separation makes queuing simpler because there is no need to associate any further information with the waiting processes. Thus waiting processes can be held on basic condition queues. However, by using two queues, knowledge of the relative arrival order of processes is lost and hence some adjustment is needed to make the allocation fair once more. This is usually achieved by alternating access to the database between readers and writers.

The form of the solution that is given most frequently assumes that all processes have the same priority and are prepared to wait to use the database. In addition, it is normal to provide separate acquire and release operations for each type of access, thus:

```
monitor ClassicDataBaseAccess;
    var Readers: 0..Maxint;
        InUseByWriter: Boolean;
    instance ReadingAllowed, WritingAllowed: Condition;

    procedure *StartRead;
        begin
            if InUseByWriter or not WritingAllowed.Empty then
                ReadingAllowed.Wait;
            Readers := Readers + 1
        end {StartRead};

    procedure *StartWrite;
        begin
            if (Readers <> 0) or InUseByWriter then
                WritingAllowed.Wait;
            InUseByWriter := True
        end {StartWrite};

    procedure *EndRead;
        begin
            Readers := Readers - 1;
            if Readers = 0 then WritingAllowed.Signal
        end {EndRead};

    procedure *EndWrite;
        begin
            InUseByWriter := False;
            if ReadingAllowed.Empty
            then WritingAllowed.Signal
```

```
        else repeat
                ReadingAllowed.Signal
            until ReadingAllowed.Empty
      end {EndWrite};

    begin {ClassicDataBaseAccess}
      InUseByWriter := False; Readers := 0; ***
    end {ClassicDataBaseAccess};
```

The operation of this monitor may be summarized as follows:

(a) A reader is given access to the database if there are no current or waiting writers.

(b) A writer is given access to the database if there are no current readers or writers.

(c) A reader releasing access to the database allows a writer to proceed if there are then no current readers.

(d) A writer releasing access to the database allows all waiting readers, if any, to proceed – otherwise a waiting writer, if any, is activated.

This allocation scheme is adequate in practice but may not always be fair. For example, consider the case where three processes A, B and C arrive requesting *write*, *write* and *read* access, respectively. If the database is free initially, then process A will proceed while B and C are made to wait. When A finishes, process C proceeds rather than process B, which has been waiting longer. It is perhaps desirable that the method of access to all resources should not just avoid starvation or deadlock but also guarantee that processes of equal status are treated identically. In this way the performance of the program concerned is likely to be more predictable.

The technique of treating a database as a single unit of shared data is satisfactory whenever the processes handling user access to the database are not delayed unduly, i.e. whenever competition for exclusive access to the database does not often result in processes being suspended. This will tend to be the case, for example, if most of the users are readers, or if each database operation is short, or if there are few concurrent users of the system. In applications where any attempted access to the database results in appreciable delays, the speed of access can be improved by splitting the data up into a number of separate items and controlling access to each item individually. The choice of item size will vary from one application to another but, in general, the smaller the data item the greater the potential for concurrency in the system. However, as the item size decreases the number of data items for which access is required before an operation can be performed increases. As a result the additional processing involved may offset the advantage resulting from concurrent access. Thus, for each application a suitable item size must be chosen to give the best overall effect.

The general problem of controlling access to groups of data items appears to be very similar to the problem of allocating resources of mixed types, discussed earlier, but there are three important differences:

(a) each data item is distinct so, in effect, there is only one item of each type to control;
(b) the number of data items involved may be very large;
(c) data items are created and destroyed dynamically so the pool of resources is not fixed as it was in the other resource management problems that we have considered so far.

Point (a) rather suggests that each data item might be administered separately, but given (b), it is usually preferable to use a single allocation module. From (c) it follows that the module concerned must have a means of recording details of data items in a flexible way to allow for data items being created or destroyed. In addition, point (b) suggests that only resources that are currently in use should be maintained by the module to save space.

To illustrate how the resulting module might operate let us first simplify the problem by assuming that all processes have the same priority and that each data item is acquired for exclusive use by a process even if the process wishes only to inspect the item concerned. This second assumption is quite reasonable if reading and writing are both equally likely.

A data item in the resource pool can be represented by a unique reference (e.g. a storage address). For each data item there may also be an associated list of processes that are currently waiting to obtain access to that item. As a process may be waiting for several data items this suggests that the waiting lists must be linked in some way. One scheme is to have a single descriptor for each waiting process and have the entries in the waiting lists for data items reference these descriptors. Also the number of data items still needed by each process can be recorded in its descriptor so that when this value reaches zero the process is reactivated.

Consider, for example, a situation in which there are four data items in use: R1, R2, R3 and R4, and that four processes, A, B, C and D then request access to the data items as follows:

Process	Data items needed
A	R1
B	R1, R4
C	R1
D	R2, R4

As the data items are all in use at that time the four processes are suspended. The links between the waiting processes and the data items they require are set up as shown in Figure 6.4.

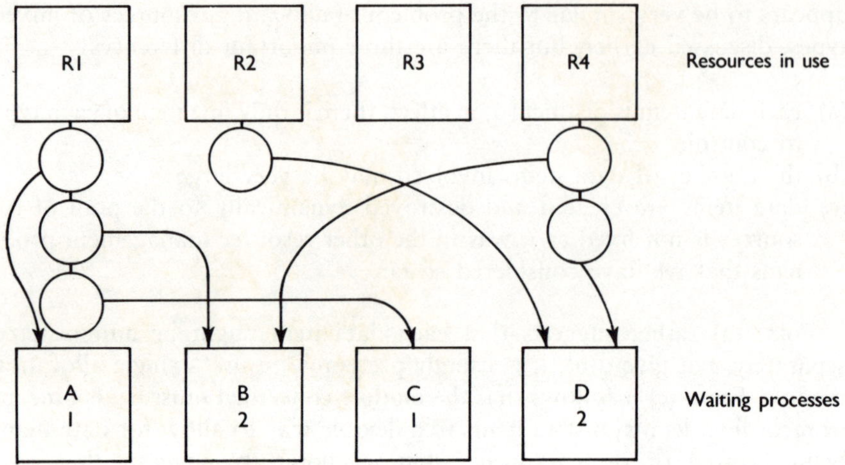

Figure 6.4 Data item/waiting process linking scheme

The effect of trying to acquire access to a group of data items may be summarized as follows:

```
for each item needed do
    if the item is not in the resource pool
    then
        add the item to the pool
    else
        begin
            if this process is not awaiting other items then
                create a process waiting record
            increment the count in the waiting record by one
            add a process link to the list of links attached to that item
        end
    if this process requires access to any items then suspend it
```

The effect of releasing a collection of resources can be described in a similar way:

```
for each item released do
    if its process waiting list is empty
    then
        delete the item from the pool
    else
        begin
            remove the link to the process at the head of the waiting list
            decrement the count in the corresponding process record by one
            if the count is zero then
                reactivate that process and delete its waiting record
        end
```

The implementation of a module following this strategy is set as an exercise at the end of this chapter.

Virtual resources

The sharing of resources in a concurrent program should be avoided where possible so that the chance of processes being delayed is minimized; thus making the performance of the program more predictable. In some cases the resources can be supplied in such numbers that each process is almost certain to obtain what it requires without delay. However, while some resources, such as disk space, are usually present in large quantities others are, of necessity, not so freely available. For example, it would be unreasonable to suggest that a multi-user computer system should provide twenty lineprinters to cope with peak demand when one printer would be adequate if the total user output is distributed throughout the day. Nevertheless, in some cases, it is still possible to give users the impression that such resources are much more freely available by 'simulating' them in some appropriate way. For example, in the case of a printer, the use of this device can be simulated by directing user output to intermediate files that are subsequently transferred to the real printer by a process dedicated to that task, as implied in Figure 6.5. Thus, for each process, the lineprinter becomes a *virtual* resource that can generally be obtained at any time.

It should be noted, that some operating systems expect the print files to reside in the user's file space. Hence, if the user issues a command such as:

PRINT MyFile

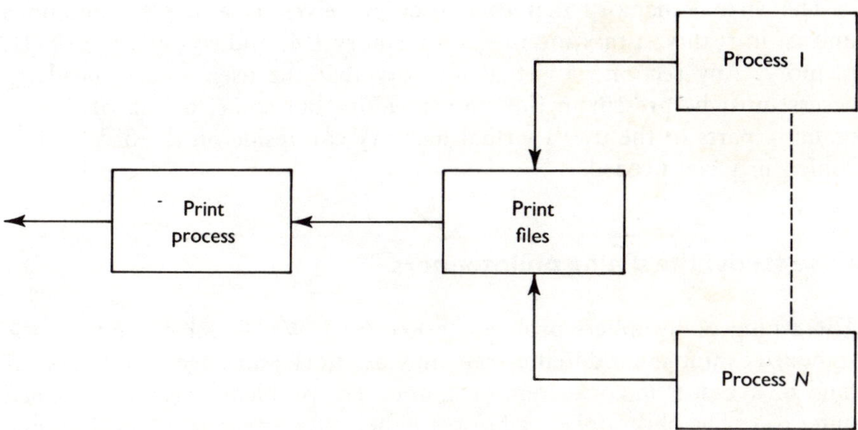

Figure 6.5 Virtual lineprinter

the system merely notes the print request but does not take a copy of the file MyFile. Consequently, the user is expected to preserve the file intact until a listing appears.

Many shared physical devices can be made virtual in this way, including magnetic tapes, graph plotters and card readers. For each input device a process is required to move the information from the device to disk before the data can be accessed and this operation must clearly be planned in advance if the user is not to be delayed.

The virtual resource most commonly discussed in the literature is main memory. *Virtual memory* is presented to each user as a sequence of memory *pages*, or *segments*, as illustrated in Figure 6.6.

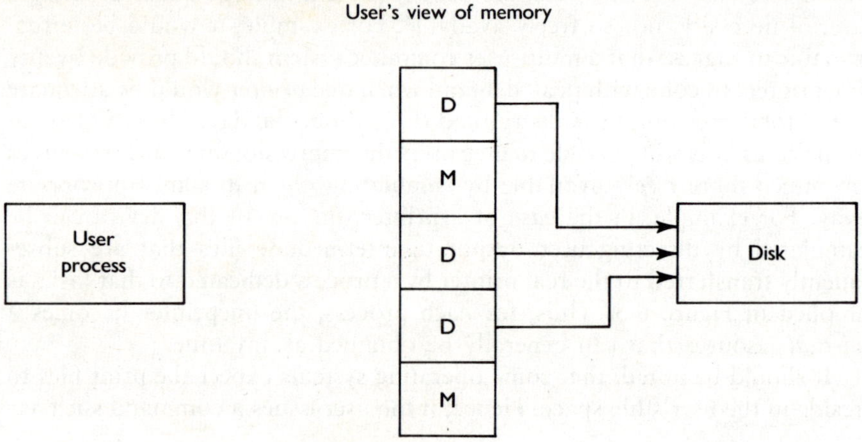

User's view of memory

User process

D

M

D

D

M

Disk

Figure 6.6 Virtual memory

The virtual memory that each user perceives as a single contiguous unit is, in reality, a mixture of main memory (M) and secondary disk (D) memory. Any section of virtual memory that the user process needs to access must be present in the main memory but some, or all, of the remaining parts of the user's virtual memory can reside on the disk and be copied in when needed.

Case study: the dining philosophers

The dining philosophers problem (posed by E.W. Dijkstra) is one of the standard examples used to illustrate how deadlock and starvation can occur (and be avoided) in concurrent programs. The problem is usually specified in terms of five philosophers who spend their time either eating or thinking. They eat at a single communal table where each has a reserved place. The table is laid out as shown in Figure 6.7.

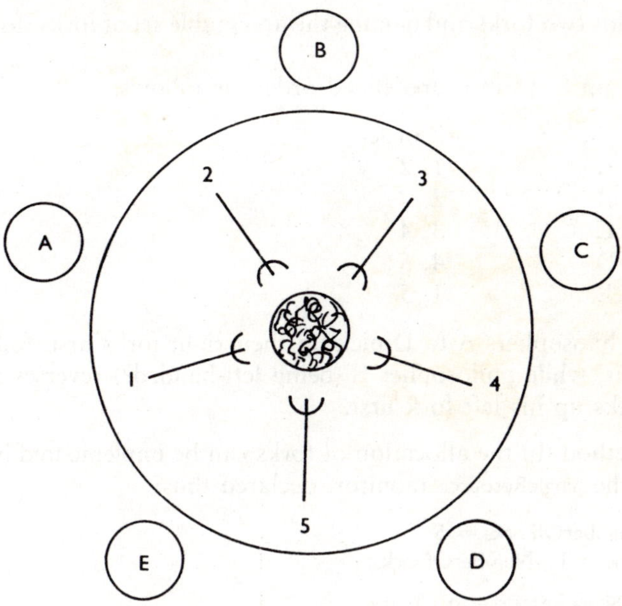

Figure 6.7 Philosophers' table setting

Spaghetti is the only type of food provided and it is so knotted that two forks are needed to eat it. In all, five forks are available but each philosopher is only permitted to pick up the forks on either side of his seat. Thus, for example, philosopher A must eat with forks 1 and 2.

The problem set is to devise an allocation scheme for the forks so that deadlock and starvation are prevented. In this problem the starvation is literal. If the philosophers pick up forks one at a time there is a danger that all five philosophers will attempt to pick up their left forks simultaneously, causing deadlock, and so starve to death waiting for their right forks to appear. Alternatively, if a philosopher is permitted only to pick up the forks he needs when both are available then he may still starve if his neighbors eat alternately without interruption, since the two forks he needs are never available simultaneously.

The key to solving this problem, in terms of the techniques that have been discussed in this chapter, is to recognize that each fork is unique and so the problem is one which involves the administration of five different resources. With this insight the allocation of the forks can be handled by:

(a) acquiring the forks through a suitable NamedMFromSubset monitor, where each philosopher names the set of forks that he is prepared to receive; thus, philosopher A might acquire resources through a call of the form:

```
Acquire (2, [1, 2], SetGiven)
```

asking for two forks and naming the acceptable set of forks (forks 1 and 2); or

(b) picking up forks in a predefined order, as follows:

Philosopher	Fork order
A	1, 2
B	2, 3
C	3, 4
D	4, 5
E	1, 5

Thus, philosophers A to D pick up their right forks first, followed by their left, while philosopher E (being left-handed?) reverses the order and picks up his left fork first.

Using method (b) the allocation of forks can be implemented by five instances of the SingleResource monitor, declared thus:

```
const *NumberOfForks = 5;
type *Fork = 1..NumberOfForks;

monitor SingleResource in Library;
instance ForkAccess: array [Fork] of SingleResource;
```

Philosopher A, for example, might then be represented by a process of the following form:

```
process module PhilosopherA;
   ...
   begin
   ...
   ForkAccess [1].Acquire;
   ForkAccess [2].Acquire;
   Eat;
   ForkAccess [2].Release;
   ForkAccess [1].Release;
   ...
   end {PhilosopherA};
```

We shall return to the dining philosophers in Chapter 8 and consider how their eating and sleeping habits might also be represented in a concurrent program that simulates their behavior.

Summary

One of the main circumstances in which processes interact in a concurrent program is when they compete for access to resources that they share. A process may require one or more resources at the same time and those resources may be of the same or different types. The resources may be defined statically within the program or created and destroyed as it executes. Also, some may be acquired for exclusive use by one process or may be sharable by several processes. This chapter has attempted to classify the different resource management situations that can occur and to explain what is involved in administering resources in each case. One of the main concerns has been to consider the problem of deadlock in detail and to present strategies for either avoiding deadlock or detecting and recovering from it. The problem of starvation in the allocation of resources was also discussed.

Further reading

Resource management modules are used extensively in the implementation of operating systems. Monitor-based examples can be found in:
- Brinch Hansen, P., *The Architecture of Concurrent Process*, Prentice Hall, 1977.
- Welsh, J. and McKeag, R.M., *Structured System Programming*, Prentice Hall, 1980.
- Joseph M., Prasad V.R. and Natarajan N., *A Multiprocessor Operating System*, Prentice Hall, 1984.

More information on virtual resources, particularly virtual memory, can be found in:
- Lister, A.M., *Fundamentals of Operating Systems*, Macmillan, 1985.
- Deitel, M.D., *An Introduction to Operating Systems*, Addison Wesley, 1984.

The management of concurrent access to data items is discussed in most database texts. For example, see Chapter 11 of:
- Ullmann, J., *Principles of Database Systems*, Computer Science Press, 1983.

Exercises

6.1   Devise suitable tests for the **NamedOneFromN**, **MFromN**, and **DatabaseAccess** modules presented in this chapter.

6.2   Implement the **BiasedMFromN** module discussed on page 117. The solution outlined there uses an order numbering scheme for processes that involve a value which increases steadily as acquisition calls are made. How can the module be implemented to take account of the possibility that the calculated priority might overflow the integer limit of the machine?

6.3   Implement the **NamedMFromN** module discussed on page 117.

6.4   Implement the **NamedMFromSubset** module discussed on page 118. (Note that this monitor can be used to implement the first strategy suggested for allocating forks to the philosophers in the dining philosophers problem discussed on page 136.)

6.5   Implement the banker's algorithm discussed on page 119, assuming that each resource is represented by a unique integer.

6.6　Implement the strategy for controlling access to data items discussed on pages 131–133, assuming that each item is identified by a unique integer, that all processes have the same priority, and that each process is prepared to wait, if necessary, for the data items which it requires to become free.

Seven

COMMUNICATION MANAGEMENT

The direct interaction of concurrent processes is not permitted in most monitor-based programming languages. In cases where a program design indicates that two processes need to interact, their communication must be performed through an intermediate subordinate module. This chapter considers how such communication modules may be implemented using the two basic mechanisms that are available.

(a) *synchronized* communication, where the execution of two processes is aligned (in the communication module) to allow the transfer of data from one process to the other to take place;
(b) *buffered* communication, where a process sending data is allowed to leave it in the communication module for subsequent collection by a receiving process.

Both types of communication module can have the same general form. This form is outlined in the following section and subsequent sections discuss possible implementations.

Communications modules: basic requirements

For both synchronized and buffered communication the two basic operations required of a communications module are those of accepting data from a *producer* process and supplying data to a *consumer* process. For synchronized communication there is exactly one *producer* and one *consumer*, whereas with buffered communication there may, in principle, be any number of both *producers* and *consumers* involved.

The send and receive operations, for either buffered or synchronized

communication, may be *committed* or *tentative*. With a committed operation the process involved waits, if necessary, until the operation it attempts
is complete. That is, a *producer* waits, if necessary, for its data to be
accepted and a *consumer* waits, if necessary, for data to be supplied to it.
With a tentative operation the process involved does not wait but returns
with an indication of the success or otherwise of the operation. Note that,
with synchronized communication, the communication can only occur if
either the *producer* or *consumer*, or both, perform a committed operation.

These four operations support a simple form of one-way communication.
In addition, it may be desirable to have operations that permit a *consumer*
to send an acknowledgement for the data it has received to the *producer*
concerned, or to allow the *producer* and *consumer* to switch roles. Communication modules to support these various types of behavior generally
need to be tailored to each application. Here we will consider only the
simple case of one-way communication, although it should be noted that in
some circumstances a *dialog* between processes can be implemented by
using two one-way communication channels.

The four operations defined for one-way communication can be represented as exported procedures of a OneWayChannel monitor of the form:

```
monitor OneWayChannel;
{assumes type ItemType with := applicable}
    procedure * Send (Item: ItemType);
        {Accepts a data item in Item, making the sender wait,}
        {if necessary, until the operation can be completed.   }
    procedure * Receive (var Item: ItemType);
        {Supplies a data item in Item, making the receiver}
        {wait, if necessary, until an item is available.        }
    procedure * TryToSend (Item: ItemType; var OK: Boolean);
        {Accepts a data item in Item if one is available.        }
        {If the data item is accepted OK is set to True.         }
        {If the data item cannot be accepted OK is set to False.}
    procedure * TryToReceive (var Item: ItemType; var OK: Boolean);
        {Supplies a data item in Item if one is available.    }
        {If a data item is available then OK is set to True}
        {and the value is returned in Item.                     }
        {If a data item is not available then OK is set to }
        {False and Item is not defined.                         }
    begin
        {initially, the channel is empty}
    end {OneWayChannel};
```

The type of data transmitted through the channel is specified when an
instance of this module is retrieved from the library. For example, if integer
values are being transmitted, then an instance of the OneWayChannel module
can be retrieved as follows:

```
monitor module IntegerChannel = OneWayChannel in Library
    (Where type ItemType = Integer;);
```

The next two sections present implementations of this general module for both synchronized and buffered communications.

Synchronized communication

Synchronized communication between two concurrent processes requires each process to issue matching Send and Receive operations which are then synchronized to enable one process to transfer data directly to another. In operational terms the first process that attempts the transfer is made to wait until the other is ready.

Synchronized communication can be simulated by a monitor of the following form:

```
monitor SynchronizedChannel;
{assumes type ItemType with := applicable}

    var Data: ItemType;
    instance Rendezvous: Condition;

    procedure *Send (Item: ItemType);
      begin
        Data := Item;
        if Rendezvous.Empty
        then Rendezvous.Wait else Rendezvous.Signal
      end {Send};

    procedure *Receive (var Item: ItemType);
      begin
        if Rendezvous.Empty
        then Rendezvous.Wait else Rendezvous.Signal;
        Item := Data
      end {Receive};

    procedure *TryToSend (Item: ItemType; var OK: Boolean);
      begin
        OK := not Rendezvous.Empty;
        if OK then {receiver ready}
          begin
            Data := Item;
            Rendezvous.Signal
          end
      end {TryToSend};

    procedure *TryToReceive (var Item: ItemType; var OK: Boolean);
      begin
        OK := not Rendezvous.Empty;
        if OK then {sender ready}
          begin
            Rendezvous.Signal;
            Item := Data
          end
```

```
      end {TryToReceive};

   begin *** end {SynchronizedChannel};
```

This monitor assumes that there is exactly one process sending data and one process receiving it. The transfer occurs only when both processes have indicated to the monitor that they are ready. A data item is then passed from one to the other through the local variable Data of the monitor.

Consider how two processes might perform a synchronized transfer using the Send and Receive operations. The first process to arrive is suspended using the local Condition instance Rendezvous. The data item supplied by the sending process is assigned to the local variable Data and the Rendezvous queue is inspected. If the queue is empty the sender is placed on it, otherwise the queue is signaled to reactivate the waiting receiver. Similarly, the receiving process on arrival is suspended if the queue is empty, otherwise the waiting sender is reactivated. When the rendezvous is completed by the arrival of the second process the receiving process obtains the data item it seeks from the variable Data and the two processes continue their executions independently.

An example: pass-the-parcel simulation

As an illustration of the use of the SynchronizedChannel monitor consider how a simulation model of the children's game of pass-the-parcel might be constructed. In this game, children seated in a circle pass a present, wrapped in several layers of paper, from one to another. Music is played as the parcel is circulated and each time the music stops the child holding the parcel removes one wrapper. This procedure is repeated until the final wrapper is removed. The child who removes that wrapper may then keep the present.

The only information about a parcel that needs to be modeled is the number of layers of paper that it contains. The parcel can therefore be represented satisfactorily by a variable defined over a nonnegative integer subrange. Each child can be represented by a process and the communication of the parcel controlled by instances of the SynchronizedChannel monitor. For N children we require N instances – each handling the transfer of the parcel between an adjacent pair of children. Figure 7.1 gives a graphical representation of the communication scheme for four children.

The parcel communication channels can be declared as follows:

```
type Parcel = 0..Maxint;
     ChildRange = 1..NumberOfChildren;

monitor SynchronizedChannel in Library
   (Where type ItemType = Parcel;);
instance Channel: array [ChildRange] of SynchronizedChannel;
```

Assuming that the parcel is passed in a clockwise direction, each child process must be initialized with the identities of:

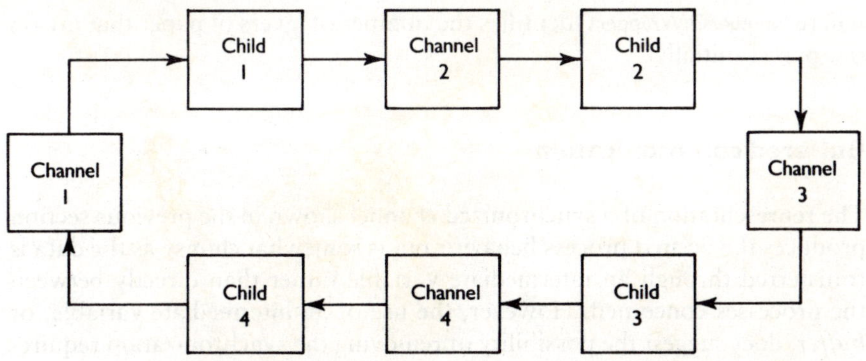

Figure 7.1 Pass-the-parcel: a graphical representation

(a) the *right* channel through which it receives the parcel;
(b) the *left* channel through which it passes on the parcel.

Using these values to index the array of SynchronizedChannel monitors, the
behavior of a child can then be represented as:

```
process Child (Left, Right: ChildRange);
   var P: Parcel;
   begin
      repeat
         Channel[Right].Receive (P);
         if not Music.Playing then
            begin
               P := P − 1;
               if P > 0 then Music.Start
            end;
         if P > 0 then Channel[Left].Send (P)
      until P = 0
   end {Child};
```

The parcel descriptor P is received from the right channel and passed to
the left channel if the music is playing. If the music has stopped a wrapper
is removed. The music is then restarted if any wrappers remain and the
parcel passed on.

It is assumed that the music is modeled by a module that provides:

(a) a Boolean variable Playing which indicates whether or not music is
     currently playing;
(b) a procedure Start which is used to restart the music, if necessary, after a
     wrapper has been removed.

To introduce the parcel into the circle we might use a Dad process that passes
the parcel to a child by means of the call:

```
Channel[1].Send (NumberofWrappers)
```

where NumberOfWrappers identifies the number of layers of paper that are on the parcel initially.

Buffered communication

The representation of a synchronized channel shown in the previous section produces the desired process behavior but is somewhat clumsy as the data is transferred through an intermediate variable rather than directly between the processes concerned. However, the use of an intermediate variable, or *buffer*, does suggest the possibility of removing the synchronization requirement and allowing the sending process to continue its execution rather than waiting, unnecessarily, for the receiving process to arrive.

Buffered communication breaks the direct connection between communicating processes and thereby reduces the possibility of their execution being delayed unduly. If the buffer is empty a sending process may deposit its data and continue to execute. If the receiving process removes the data before the sender returns again, the interaction will have taken place without either process being delayed. In other words, as far as both individual processes are concerned communication will have been immediate. However, if the receiving process enters the monitor first then clearly it must be suspended until the sending process arrives. So, in effect, the processes behave as they did in the synchronized case. The communication is also effectively synchronized if the sending process is consistently faster than the receiver and so finds the buffer full each time it attempts to send data.

One advantage of buffered communication is that it enables both sides of any interaction to be performed tentatively. With synchronized communication either the sender or receiver, or both, must make a commitment to wait for the other to arrive because communication between them can only occur if one or other is suspended awaiting interaction. This point can be illustrated by considering, for example, a variation of the pass-the-parcel problem in which two parcels are circulated in opposite directions. At first glance it may seem that the situation can be modeled by introducing a second set of synchronized channel monitors to represent the second direction of communication. However, such a solution is inadequate because a child must be able to accept a parcel in either direction and so cannot wait for one particular parcel to arrive – as is required with synchronized communication. The two-parcel situation can be modeled with a buffered channel and a solution of this type will be presented shortly.

Another advantage of buffered communication is that it is not restricted to only one sender and one receiver. In general, multiple senders and receivers can interact through the same module and, usually, without any account being taken of the number of processes involved.

The remainder of this section considers how single and multiple item buffers can be implemented.

Single item buffer

The simplest buffer holds exactly one data item. Such a buffer may be expressed as follows:

```
monitor SingleItemBuffer;
{assumes type ItemType with := applicable}
    var Data: record
                    case Present: Boolean of
                        True: (Item: ItemType);
                        False: ( )
                    end;
    instance DataAvailable, SpaceAvailable: Condition;

    procedure *Send (Item: ItemType);
      begin
        if Data.Present then SpaceAvailable.Wait;
        Data.Present := True;
        Data.Item := Item;
        DataAvailable.Signal
      end {Send};

    procedure *Receive (var Item: ItemType);
      begin
        if not Data.Present then DataAvailable.Wait;
        Item := Data.Item;
        Data.Present := False;
        SpaceAvailable.Signal
      end {Receive};

    procedure *TryToSend (Item: ItemType; var OK: Boolean);
      begin
        OK := not Data.Present;
        if OK then begin
                    Data.Present := True;
                    Data.Item := Item;
                    DataAvailable.Signal
                end
      end {TryToSend};

    procedure *TryToReceive (var Item: ItemType; var OK: Boolean);
      begin
        OK := Data.Present;
        if OK then begin
                    Item := Data.Item;
                    Data.Present := False;
                    SpaceAvailable.Signal
                end
      end {TryToReceive};

  begin Data.Present := False; *** end {SingleItemBuffer};
```

The buffered data item is held in a variant record. In the Synchronized-Channel monitor a receiving process could tell whether or not any data item was available by checking the rendezvous queue. As the sending process is no longer obliged to wait, the Boolean variable Present has been introduced to identify the buffer state. If a process calls Send when the buffer is full the process is suspended on the SpaceAvailable condition queue. Similarly, if a process calls Receive when the buffer is empty, it is suspended on the complementary DataAvailable queue. Each time the buffer state is changed the process making the change signals the corresponding condition queue. Thus:

(a) A sending process, on placing a data item into the buffer, signals the DataAvailable condition in case a receiving process is waiting to obtain a data item.

(b) A receiving process, on extracting a data item from the buffer, signals the SpaceAvailable condition in case a sending process is waiting to deposit a data item.

The same technique can be used for a multiple item buffer.

Multiple item buffer

The number of data items held in a buffer is dictated by the relative production and consumption rates of the processes using the buffer. In general there are three cases to consider:

(a) If the consumer process is faster than the producer process then the data provided by the producer will be consumed as soon as it is available and so single item buffer communication is perfectly adequate.

(b) If the producer process is faster than the consumer process then the consumer is never delayed and so a single item buffer is again adequate. A multiple item buffer may be used in this case, however, in applications where it is desirable to free the producer process at the earliest possible opportunity.

(c) If the producer and consumer processes generate and consume data at similar rates then their behavior needs to be looked at more closely before deciding on a suitable buffer size. If both processes operate steadily then a single element buffer is adequate. However, if the operating speed of either process is irregular then the buffer size should be sufficiently large to avoid the other process being affected, if possible. For example, consider the case where a producer process reads a sequence of large data records from a disk file and subdivides them into a stream of smaller data items for use within a program. Let us assume that:

   (i) The small data items are placed in a multiple item communication buffer.

   (ii) The time taken to read a large data record is much greater than the time taken to prepare a small data item and place it in the buffer.

(iii) The rate at which small data items enter the buffer is faster than the rate at which they can be consumed.

In such circumstances data items will accumulate in the buffer during the subdivision of the large data record and then be consumed during the delay on moving from one data record to another. Consequently, the receiving process should not be aware of the file reading delay.

The role of a multiple item buffer is to smooth out temporary mismatches in the rate at which data is produced and consumed. In practice buffer sizes are not critical and rough size estimates are usually adequate. However, in cases where memory constraints are tight it is better to keep buffer sizes small initially and then expand them, where necessary, to improve performance.

Now consider how a multiple item buffer might be implemented. The main constraint to be observed is that buffered items are expected to emerge from the buffer in the order in which they entered it. This means that the data items must be kept in a *queue* within the buffer. The queue can be represented as a separate data structure of the form:

```
envelope Queue;
{assumes const MaxItems = number of items in queue}
{        type  ItemType with := applicable           }
    function *Empty: Boolean;
        {Returns True if the queue is empty and False}
        {otherwise.                                  }
    function *Full: Boolean;
        {Returns False if there is space for at least one more   }
        {item to be appended to the queue and True otherwise.}
    function *Length: Integer;
        {Returns the number of items in the queue.}
    procedure *Append (X: ItemType);
        {Appends the value of X to the queue; it is assumed}
        {that Full is False when this operation is invoked.   }
    procedure *Remove (var X: ItemType);
        {Removes the first data item in the queue and returns it     }
        {in X; it is assumed that Empty is False when this operation is}
        {invoked.                                                }
    begin
        {initially queue is empty, and Full is false}
    end {Queue};
```

A multiple item buffer will have the same structure as that shown for the single item case but each data operation is now implemented by means of queue operations, thus:

```
monitor MultipleItemBuffer;
{assumes const MaxItems = number of items in buffer}
{        type  ItemType with := applicable          }

    monitor module Queue in Library;
        {using MaxItems and ItemType}
```

```
instance DataAvailable, SpaceAvailable: Condition;

procedure *Send (Item: ItemType);
  begin
    if Queue.Full then SpaceAvailable.Wait;
    Queue.Append (Item);
    DataAvailable.Signal
  end {Send};

procedure *Receive (var Item: ItemType);
  begin
    if Queue.Empty then DataAvailable.Wait;
    Queue.Remove (Item);
    SpaceAvailable.Signal
  end {Receive};

procedure *TryToSend (Item: ItemType; var OK: Boolean);
  begin
    OK := not Queue.Full;
    if OK then begin
                Queue.Append (Item);
                DataAvailable.Signal
              end
  end {TryToSend};

procedure *TryToReceive (var Item: ItemType: var OK: Boolean);
  begin
    OK := not Queue.Empty;
    if OK then begin
                Queue.Remove (Item);
                SpaceAvailable.Signal
              end
  end {TryToReceive};

begin *** end {MultipleItemBuffer};
```

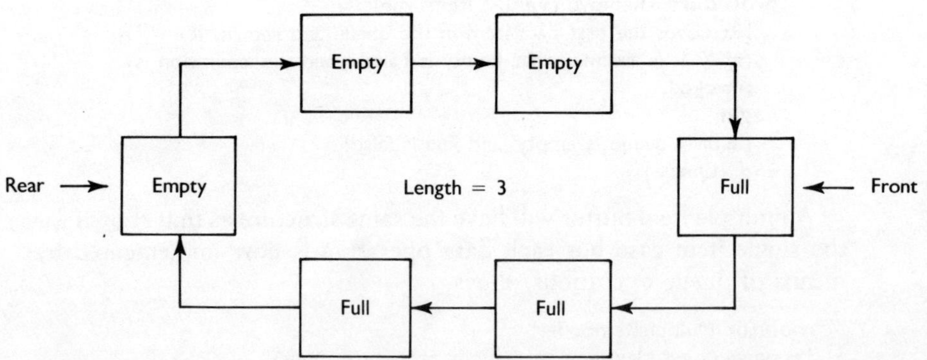

Figure 7.2 Cyclic buffer

One common implementation of a finite queue uses a ring structure as illustrated in Figure 7.2.

Such a ring, or *cyclic buffer* is maintained using two markers, Rear and Front, indicating the beginning and end of the queue, respectively, together with a Length value recording the current length of the queue. If there is space in the buffer a new item may be added to the end of the queue at the Rear position, and the Rear marker advanced one position clockwise. Similarly, if the buffer is not empty the item at the head of the queue can be removed from the Front position, and the Front marker advanced one position clockwise. If the Rear and Front markers coincide then the buffer is either full or empty as distinguished using the Length count.

A cyclic buffer may be implemented using an array as follows:

```
envelope Queue;
{assumes const MaxItems = maximum number of items in queue}
{        type ItemType = type of items in queue             }
    var  Buffer: array [I..MaxItems] of ItemType;
         Front, Rear: I..MaxItems;
         *Length: 0..MaxItems;

    function *Empty: Boolean;
      begin Empty := (Length = 0) end;

    function *Full: Boolean;
      begin Full := (Length = MaxItems) end;

    procedure *Append (X: ItemType);
      begin
        Buffer [Rear] := X;
        Rear := Rear mod MaxItems + I;
        Length := Length + I
      end {Append};

    procedure *Remove (var X: ItemType);
      begin
        X := Buffer [Front];
        Front := Front mod MaxItems + I;
        Length := Length - I
      end {Remove};

    begin Length := 0; Front := I; Rear := I; *** end {Queue};
```

The Front and Rear markers are index values into the array. The sequence of array elements can be seen to correspond to the entries in the ring by considering the first element of the array to follow the last.

Alternative implementations of this Queue module might employ a chained representation in which records to hold the queue items are allocated dynamically, and are linked together by pointers. Thus, an upper bound does not have to be placed on the number of items in the queue.

An example: pass-the-parcel with two parcels

In the variation of the pass-the-parcel game in which two parcels are circulated in opposite directions we might use two buffered channels between each child to model the communication involved. That is, we picture each child as looking left and right, repeatedly, waiting for a parcel to arrive. However, an alternative, simpler model, is to picture the parcels being transferred from one child's lap to another's. A lap can then be represented as a single element buffer:

```
instance
    Laps: array [ChildRange] of SingleElementBuffer;
```

With two parcels in circulation some means of distinguishing them is required. This might be achieved by representing a parcel as follows:

```
type LayerRange = 0..Maxint;
     Directions = (Clockwise, Anticlockwise);
     Parcel = record
                  Direction: Directions;
                  Layers: LayerRange
              end;
```

We also have a further synchronization problem to consider as the music can only start when both parcels have been unwrapped. The situation is relatively complex because some account must be taken of the possibilities that:

(a) the present in one parcel may be found ahead of the other, leaving a single parcel to circulate towards the end of the game;
(b) one child may have to unwrap two parcels.

In the single parcel case each Child process informed a Music module after it had removed a layer of paper. When two parcels are involved, the call to the Music monitor must include details of the number of parcels that that child has unwrapped and also indicate the number of parcels that are being passed on. That is, the Music monitor must now take the form:

```
monitor module Music;
    var *Playing: Boolean;
    procedure *Start (ParcelsUnWrapped, ParcelsPassed: ParcelCount);
        {Notes start request and starts the music if all the parcels   }
        {left in the game have had one layer of paper removed and       }
        {there is at least one parcel with layers remaining.            }
        {If 'ParcelsPassed − ParcelsPassed <> 0' then the number of}
        {parcels in circulation has been reduced by the difference.     }
        {It is assumed that this operation is invoked only when the     }
        {music is not playing.                                          }
    begin
        {initially, music is playing}
    end {Music};
```

The behavior of each child can then be described thus:

```
process Child (Me, Left, Right: ChildRange);
    var P1, P2: Parcel;
        ParcelsPassed: 0..2;
        SecondParcel: Boolean;

    procedure PassIfNecessary (P: Parcel);
      begin
        if P.Layers > 0 then
          if P.Direction = Clockwise
          then Laps [Left].Send (P)
          else Laps [Right].Send (P)
      end {PassIfNecessary};

    begin {Child}
      repeat
        Laps [Me].Receive (P1);
        if not Music.Playing then
          begin
            {take a layer of paper off the parcel}
            P1.Layers := P1.Layers − 1;
            if P1.Layers > 0
            then ParcelsPassed := 1
            else ParcelsPassed := 0;
            {look for a second parcel}
            Laps [Me].TryToReceive (P2, SecondParcel);
            if SecondParcel
            then
              begin
                P2.Layers := P2.Layers − 1;
                if P2.Layers > 0 then
                  ParcelsPassed := ParcelsPassed + 1;
                Music.Start (2, ParcelsPassed);
                PassIfNecessary (P2)
              end
            else Music.Start (1, ParcelsPassed)
          end;
        PassIfNecessary (P1);
      until False
    end {Child};
```

Each Child process waits until a parcel arrives and if the music has
stopped, a layer of paper is removed. A second parcel is then sought (tentatively) and if one is present a layer of paper is removed from it. The Music
monitor is then informed of the number of parcels that have been unwrapped and the number that are being passed on. Any parcel with layers
remaining is then transferred to the left or right child according to the direction of circulation specified for the parcel.

A full version of the single parcel game simulation is developed in
Chapter 8, with the two parcel case left as an exercise.

The sort program revisited

To further illustrate the use of buffered communication let us return to the
concurrent sort program for which a solution was developed in Chapter 5.
In this program a number of identical Sort processes prepared sorted sublists
in parallel. When each Sort process was finished it passed its sublist to an Exchange module. A Merge process collected all the sublists from the Exchange
module and combined them into a final sorted list. The Merge process was
made to wait by the Exchange module until all the sublists had arrived.

In place of the special-purpose Exchange monitor we can now use an
instance of one of the buffer modules. A single item buffer is adequate
because there is no disadvantage in making some of the Sort processes wait
when they arrive at the same time:

```
monitor Exchange = SingleItemBuffer in Library
   (Where type ItemType = ASublist;);
```

The Sort process definition is then adjusted to call the Send procedure of the
buffer monitor in place of the original call to DepositASublist.

In the Merge process the sublists are now obtained individually rather
than all at once. This change affects only the call of GetAllSubLists which can
be replaced by the loop:

```
for Index := 1 to NumberOfSublists do
   Exchange.Receive (Sublists [Index])
```

The remainder of the sort program is unaffected.

The Exchange monitor is not the only place in the sort program where a
communications buffer might be used. In general, the buffering the technique is also applicable to the transfer of data to and from peripheral
devices, since a device is in effect a process which has been implemented in
hardware. In the sort program this means that the modules that deal with
the input of the unsorted list and the output of the sorted list might include:

(a) buffers to hold data items;
(b) device handling processes responsible for transferring data between the
     buffers and the devices involved.

This technique is considered in detail in Chapter 9.

Summary

Concurrent processes in a program can either pass data to each other
directly, by synchronizing their execution, or indirectly, by transferring the
data through an intermediate buffer. In monitor-based programming languages this latter form of communication alone is supported.

Buffered communication often enables processes to pass data to each
other more efficiently because the sending process is not made to wait until

the receiving process is ready. Also the same module can handle data sent or received by several processes and allows both sides of an interaction to be tentative.

The number of items held in a buffer changes according to variations in the rate at which data items are produced in relation to variations in the rate at which they are consumed. In general, the objective is to select a buffer size so that neither producers nor consumers are delayed unnecessarily.

Most process intercommunication in a concurrent program can be handled by a module providing a simple range of data transfer operations and this chapter has shown how several modules of this type can be implemented.

Exercises

7.1   Devise suitable tests for the SynchronizedChannel, SingleItemBuffer and Multiple-ItemBuffer modules presented in this chapter.

7.2   Develop a version of the temperature/humidity control program (presented in Chapter 4) that implements the five main modules as processes and uses appropriate communication modules to handle the transfer of data between the processes.

7.3   Design and implement a multiple item buffer monitor through which processes can exchange messages. Assume that each process is identified by a unique value in a small integer subrange and that a message is defined as follows:

```
ProcessIdentification = 1..N;
Message = record
            Sender, Receiver: ProcessIdentification;
            Text: packed array [1..80] of Char
          end;
```

Eight

DISCRETE EVENT SIMULATION

This is the first of three chapters that consider the use of concurrency in specific application areas. The areas covered are *discrete event simulation*, *real-time programming* and *operating systems*, in that order. For each area the relevance of the techniques presented in earlier chapters is shown and some new technical problems are discussed.

Simulation models: basic concepts

Several simulation programs were presented, briefly, in earlier chapters as a means of illustrating general aspects of concurrent program design and representation. Two of the programs concerned the simulation of a game played by children; in Chapter 3, the game was hide-and-seek and in Chapter 7, it was pass-the-parcel. Both simulation programs are considered here in more detail.

A basic modular design of the form shown in Figure 8.1 was suggested for the hide-and-seek simulation program.

In the hide-and-seek game, one child is nominated as the 'seeker'. The 'seeker' allows the other children to find hiding places and then goes off in search of them. Each child who is discovered becomes a 'seeker' and the game ends when the last child hiding has been located.

In the simulation program, modules representing the hiding children and the seeker keep a *state* module informed of their progress which enables the terminating condition for the program (i.e. all children found) to be detected.

A program can be constructed from this design, and was set as an exercise at the end of Chapter 4. However, what results is not a useful simulation

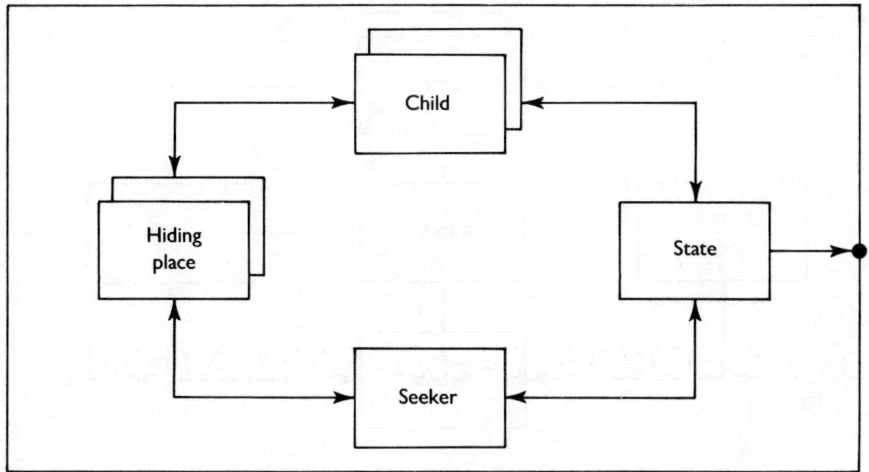

Figure 8.1 Hide-and-seek simulation program: basic structure

model in that the concept of *time* is missing. For a simulation model to serve its purpose it must model the passage of time so that the relative time order of activities is portrayed. For example, in the hide-and-seek case we may wish to obtain answers to such crucial questions as:

> If there are forty hiding places and ten children, including the 'seeker', how long will a game last if it takes each child twenty seconds to inspect a hiding place (to hide or seek), assuming that the hiding places are selected randomly with equal probability?

In terms of the modular diagram for the hide-and-seek problem the administration of time can be handled by a *clock* module, whose connection with the other modules is shown in Figure 8.2. There are two types of connection to the *clock* module.

(a) The *clock* module provides the *state* module with the *current* time (1), when required. The *state* module is then able to present a chronological log of the behavior of the model by combining time information with any activities that are reported to it by the *child* and *seeker* modules. Note that 'time', in this context, is completely independent of the execution time of the program implementing the model.

(b) The *child* and *seeker* modules also report their activities to the *clock* module (2, 3) to enable it to arrange for these activities to be pursued in the required time order. More specifically, the *clock* module is required to synchronize the various activities involved, which it can achieve by causing the modules that identify the activities to be executed in an appropriate sequence.

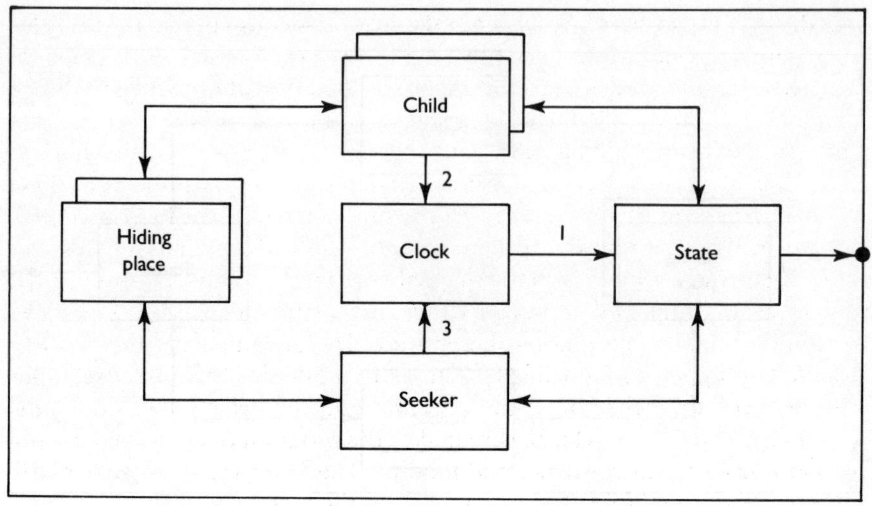

Figure 8.2 Hide-and-seek simulation program with clock

The roles of the *state* and *clock* modules, and their implementation, are topics discussed in more detail later in this chapter. So, also, is the question of how *random* behavior can be modeled. Before that, however, the next section gives a definition of some of the simulation terms that are used.

Simulation models: some definitions

A *simulation program* may be defined as a representation, or *model*, of some *system* that is under investigation. A system may be defined, in general terms, as a collection of interdependent elements, or *entities*, that operate together to achieve some specified goal. For example, in the hide-and-seek simulation the system is the *game* and the entities are the *children* and the *hiding places*. The *dynamic entities* in a model are entities that engage in activities. Dynamic entities can change the *system state* which is represented by *state variables*. A Boolean flag indicating whether or not a hiding place is occupied is an example of a state variable.

A *stochastic* model is one in which one or more state variables take on values in accordance with a *probability distribution*. Such stochastic variables are generally introduced to take account of *uncertainty* in the model. For example, in the hide-and-seek model the next hiding place to be examined by a 'seeker' is uncertain, or *random*.

The system state changes with *time*. A *continuous system simulation* is one in which one or more state variables change continuously with time. A *discrete system simulation* is one in which the state variables change only at specified points in time. An *event* is the instantaneous change in the value of a state variable. More generally, the term *event* is used to describe an occurrence in the model which has an associated time. In the hide-and-seek simulation, for example, the discrete events of interest are the start and end of each search of a hiding place and the start and end of a child hiding.

This chapter considers only discrete system simulation problems as these can be modeled using processes to represent the dynamic entities concerned. Such processes are referred to here as *entity processes*. Continuous simulations generally require a mathematical treatment, where the state of the system at any time is determined from a set of time-dependent equations defining a relationship among the entities. The advantage of the *process-oriented* approach to modeling is that it often establishes a direct relationship between the behavior of the program and the behavior of the model that it represents. This relationship makes the program easier to understand and so it is easier to construct and modify. The latter factor is particularly important as simulation programs are modified frequently when experimenting with variations to the model.

Operationally, discrete simulation involves the administration of a collection of events that are identified as the simulation program is executed. Each event has an associated *event time*. Within a model, time can either be advanced in fixed length increments – the *unit advance* approach – or, more commonly, advanced from one event to the next – the *event driven*, or *discrete event*, approach. The remainder of this chapter considers the representation of discrete event simulation programs.

Simulated time

Dynamic entities in a simulation model engage in activities. Some activities take a known length of time to complete while the duration of others will depend on the behavior of various dynamic entities in the model. For example, in the hide-and-seek model the time taken to inspect a hiding place is known but the time that each child spends hiding will depend on the behavior of the 'seeker' that finds the child.

In programming terms, a dynamic entity can be represented by a process. The engagement of a dynamic entity in an activity of known duration can then be implemented by delaying the execution of the entity process using the *clock* module for the time taken to complete the activity being modeled, i.e. by suspending the process concerned until the value of simulated time, or *pseudotime*, within the model matches the completion time of the activity. For activities whose duration is not known, the process modeling the entity concerned is suspended by a mechanism separate from that of the *clock* module. For example, a child hiding can be represented by suspending the process modeling the child, in the module modeling the hiding place. Such a process is reactivated by the entity process (or processes) in the model on whose behavior the duration of the activity depends. For example, the waiting time of a child depends on the behavior of the 'seeker' that finds the child. Thus, in the model it is the process modeling the 'seeker' which is responsible for reactivating the process modeling the hiding child.

The preceding discussion suggests that a *clock* module must provide at least two operations:

(a) to supply the current value of pseudotime;
(b) to suspend an entity process engaged in a specific activity until pseudo-
     time can be advanced to the completion time of that activity.

The basic form of such a module might be as follows:

```
monitor module Clock;
{assumes const TimeLimit = maximum duration of simulation  }
{         const EntityLimit = total number of entity processes}
{         type  TimeType = type of values representing time  }
    type *TimeScale = TimeType;
    var *Pseudotime: TimeScale; {current value of simulated time}
    procedure *Hold (Period: TimeScale);
        {Suspends the calling process for the length of simulated}
        {time specified by Period.                               }
    begin
        {initially, Pseudotime is zero}
    end {Clock};
```

The variable Pseudotime gives the current value of simulated time, which starts at zero. The procedure Hold suspends an entity process for a specified period of time. Thus, the reactivation time for an entity process is the sum of Period and the value of Pseudotime at the point of suspension. The module assumes a value TimeLimit defining the maximum duration of the simulation. This value is used, if necessary, as a cut-off point beyond which the Clock monitor will no longer reactivate entity processes. That is, a time beyond which no further events will occur.

The time unit defined for a simulation model will vary from one applica-tion to another. In one case it might be microseconds and in another days or years. The time unit is not represented explicitly but there is a requirement that all parts of the model assume the same unit, i.e. a requirement that all dynamic entities in the model use the same clock, as this is their common means of synchronization. Time itself may be represented in several ways. The most common representation is as values of type Real, but values of type Integer, or some subrange of Integer are also used.

The Clock monitor, as defined, places a limit, EntityLimit, on the number of entity processes that it can accept for suspension via calls to procedure Hold. This limit is imposed for implementation reasons.

Processes are suspended in their reactivation time order on an *event queue* defined within the Clock monitor. Time advances by reactivating the first entity process, if any, on the event queue and setting Pseudotime to the reactivation time of the process concerned. The necessary precondition for such an event is that all of the entity processes be suspended, either in the Clock monitor or on a condition queue in some other monitor. In practice there is also a practical requirement that any other processes in the program should also be suspended at that point. The processes may be on any program defined condition queue but may not be on the standard AllWaiting queue. This latter restriction is necessary as the AllWaiting facility is used to implement the Clock monitor. This point is considered further when details of an implementation are presented.

To help clarify the basic clock mechanism and to illustrate the use of the Clock monitor let us consider the operation of a trivial example – that of a program to simulate a person laundering clothes by putting them through a washing machine and then a dryer. In this problem there is only one entity process, that modeling the launderer, and this process is suspended only within the Clock monitor. Let us assume that the only activities that need to be modeled are the use of the two pieces of equipment, which run for thirty and forty minutes respectively (say). With these assumptions a program to model the laundry system might be expressed as follows:

```
program SoloLaundrySimulation (Output);
{Time unit is MINUTES}
   const WashingTime = 30; DryingTime = 40;

   monitor module Clock in Library
      (Where const TimeLimit = Maxint;
             const EntityLimit = 1;
             type  TimeType = Integer;);

   monitor module State in Library;

   process module Launderer;
      begin
         Clock.Hold (WashingTime);
         Clock.Hold (DryingTime)
      end {Launderer};

 begin *** end {SoloLaundrySimulation}.
```

The washing and drying operations are represented by calls to the Hold procedure of the Clock monitor. Each call specifies the time required to complete the associated activity and results in the calling entity process being suspended.

The general requirement for a simulated clock to advance from one event time to the next is that all the entity processes in the program are suspended. In this example there is only one such process so an event is triggered by each of its calls to the Clock monitor. An event causes the value of Pseudotime to be advanced to the corresponding event time and the entity process awaiting that event is then reactivated. Thus, the Launderer process returns immediately from both of its calls to Hold with the only outcome being that

Pseudotime advances first to thirty and then to seventy. At that point the execution of the Launderer process is complete and the simulation as a whole terminates.

The State monitor in this example might serve simply to report the value of pseudotime at the point of termination:

```
monitor module State;
  begin
    ***;
    Writeln ('Laundry completion time:   ', Clock.Pseudotime: 2, '  MINUTES')
  end {State};
```

To illustrate the case where entity processes are suspended outside the Clock monitor consider the situation where two people do their laundry using the same washing machine and dryer, with one person arriving twenty-five minutes after the other. The corresponding simulation program might be expressed as follows:

```
program DuoLaundrySimulation (Output);
{Time unit is MINUTES}
    const Washing Time = 30; Drying Time = 40;

    monitor module Clock in Library
       (Where const TimeLimit = Maxint;
              const EntityLimit = 2;
              type  TimeType = Integer;);

    monitor module State in Library;

    monitor SingleResource in Library
       (Where const PriorityLimit = Maxint;);
    instance Washer, Dryer: SingleResource;

    process Launderer (StartTime: Clock.TimeScale);
       begin
          Clock.Hold (StartTime);
          Washer.Acquire;
          Clock.Hold (WashingTime);
          Washer.Release;
          Dryer.Acquire;
          Clock.Hold (DryingTime);
          Dryer.Release
       end {Launderer};
    instance Launderer1, Launderer2: Launderer (0), (25);

    begin *** end {DuoLaundrySimulation}.
```

Access to the washing machine and dryer is controlled by two instances of a SingleResource monitor (as developed in Chapter 6). Initially both Launderer processes call Hold to await their entry to the situation being simulated. The start times are specified as parameters to the corresponding process instances. For Launderer1 there is no delay but Launderer2 is suspended for twenty-five (simulated) minutes. Launderer1 starts by obtaining immediate access to the washing machine and is then suspended for the specified washing time of thirty minutes.

At this point in the simulation there are two events recorded: the entry of Launderer2 at time twenty-five and the completion of the wash by Launderer1 at time thirty. As both entity processes are suspended the simulation proceeds to the first event. Pseudotime becomes twenty-five and the Launderer2 process is reactivated. However, it is quickly suspended again when attempting to acquire access to the washing machine because Launderer2 is still using it. Once again both entity processes are suspended so the simulation moves on to the next event (the only one recorded) which is the completion of the wash by Launderer1. Pseudotime becomes thirty and Launderer1 is reactivated. Launderer1 then releases access to the washing machine, thus allowing Launderer2 to run. And so it goes on, until both entity processes have completed their execution.

An implementation of the clock monitor

The basic behavior of the Clock monitor bears some resemblance to the operation of the TestSequence monitor discussed in Chapter 5, and is implemented in a similar way. (This seems appropriate as testing can be regarded as a simulation of the program under test.)

The basic structure of the Clock monitor might be expressed as follows:

```
monitor module Clock;
{assumes const TimeLimit = maximum duration of simulation  }
{         const EntityLimit = total number of entity processes}
{         type  TimeType = type of values representing time  }
  type *TimeScale = TimeType;
  var *Pseudotime: TimeScale;

  monitor module ClockQueue in Library;

  procedure *Hold (Period: TimeScale);
     begin ClockQueue.Join (Pseudotime + Period) end;

  procedure Alarm (var Activation: Boolean); . . . ;

  process module Tick;
     var Activation: Boolean;
     begin
       repeat
         AllWaiting.PWait (Maxint);
         Alarm (Activation)
       until not Activation
     end {Tick};

  begin Pseudotime := 0; *** end {Clock};
```

Event times are maintained by a local monitor ClockQueue. Entity processes are suspended in the ClockQueue monitor following calls to procedure

Hold. The progression from one event to the next is controlled by the process Tick. Tick waits until all the entity processes are suspended and then invokes procedure Alarm. Process Tick uses the standard AllWaiting condition instance to delay itself until all entity processes have been suspended. The situation is potentially unsafe in that other (nonentity) processes in the program may also use AllWaiting. To reduce the risk of conflict, Tick is suspended with the lowest possible priority value, i.e. Maxint. The situation is then safe as long as this extreme priority is not used in any call to AllWaiting.PWait elsewhere in the simulation program. In practice, the use of AllWaiting in other circumstances is not likely to involve calls to PWait anyway so the security risk imposes no significant constraint on the construction of simulation programs.

The action of procedure Alarm in the Clock monitor is to advance Pseudo-time to the event time of the entity process at the head of the event queue and to reactivate all entity processes with the same event time. No activation occurs if the event queue is empty or if the reactivation time of the topmost process is beyond the specified value of TimeLimit.

The monitor ClockQueue might be defined as follows:

```
monitor module ClockQueue;
    {Maintains a queue of suspended process instances}
    {in ascending event time order.                  }
    function *Empty: Boolean;
        {Returns True if queue is empty and False otherwise.}
    procedure *Join (Time: TimeScale);
        {Suspends process on event queue at position determined}
        {by the value of Time.                                 }
    procedure *Signal;
        {Reactivates the process at the head of the queue.   }
        {It is assumed that the queue is not empty when this}
        {operation is invoked.                               }
    function *EventTime: TimeScale:
        {Returns the event time with which the process at the   }
        {head of the queue was suspended. It is assumed that the}
        {queue is not empty when this operation is invoked.     }
    begin
        {initially, the event queue is empty}
    end {ClockQueue};
```

The Join operation is used to suspend an entity process. For a process at the head of the queue the function EventTime returns its reactivation time and Signal reactivates it. Both the EventTime and Signal operations require that the queue be nonempty, which can be checked via the function Empty. Given this definition of ClockQueue, the Alarm procedure can be expressed as follows:

```
procedure Alarm (var Activation: Boolean);

    function AllRequiredAwake: Boolean;
    begin
```

```
            if ClockQueue.Empty
            then AllRequiredAwake := True
            else  AllRequiredAwake := ClockQueue.EventTime > Pseudotime
         end {AllRequiredAwake};

      begin {Alarm}
        if ClockQueue.Empty {no events recorded}
        then Activation := False
        else
           if ClockQueue.EventTime > TimeLimit {time limit exceeded}
           then Activation := False
           else
              begin
                Activation := True;
                Pseudotime := ClockQueue.EventTime;
                repeat ClockQueue.Signal until AllRequiredAwake
              end
      end {Alarm};
```

No activation occurs if the event queue is empty or if the reactivation time of the entity process at the head of the queue is beyond the defined time limit. If an activation can proceed the value of Pseudotime is set to the reactivation time of the entity process at the head of the queue and all entity processes awaiting that event time are reactivated.

Note that in the special case where the time scale used is defined over the nonnegative interger subrange the clock queue can be represented by an instance of Condition. Event times are then used as 'priority values to suspend the entity processes via PWait calls.

Presenting model behavior

A process-oriented approach to modeling often has the advantage that there is a direct relationship between the behavior of a simulation program and that of the model that it represents. This relationship aids understanding of the program and also makes the task of presenting the behavior of the model more straightforward. A model's behavior can be output by a *state* module to which entity processes pass relevant state information as the simulation proceeds. The *state* module can present a representation of the model's behavior during the execution of the simulation program or summarize that behavior when the simulation is complete, or both. The basic objective is to provide output which captures the model's behavior adequately. The most desirable form is, perhaps, as a cartoon or *animation* that depicts the entities present and their interaction in terms of the system being modeled. In general, such a representation will involve a substantial amount of programming effort so other, simpler forms of output must be considered. One approach is to implement an *observer* process to inspect the state of the model periodically and present a snapshot of that state.

Alternatively, since the state of a discrete event simulation model only changes at event times, its state can be presented when events occur. For example, the behavior of two people washing and drying clothes might be presented as in Table 8.1.

Table 8.1 Behavior in laundry simulation

Time (mins)	Launderer 1	Launderer 2
0	Arrives	
.	Seeks washing machine	
.	Starts washing machine	
.	.	.
25	.	Arrives
.	.	Seeks washing machine
.	.	.
30	Washing complete	Starts washing machine
.	Seeks dryer	
.	Starts dryer	
.	.	.
60	.	Washing complete
.	.	Seeks dryer
.	.	.
70	Drying complete	Starts dryer
.	Leaves	
.	.	.
110	.	Drying complete
.	.	Leaves
.	.	.

Table 8.1 shows the activity of the dynamic entities at each event time. The behavior of the entities at any particular time can be determined by locating the required time in the left-hand column and then inspecting the entries across the table at that point. The behavior of a particular entity can be studied by scanning the appropriate column. A dot in any column indicates that an activity which started earlier is still in progress. Thus, for example, at time fifty, Launderer1 is using the dryer (started at time thirty) and Launderer2 is using the washing machine (also started at time thirty).

To construct such a table the *state* module must be informed of each change in the state of an entity that the modeler wishes to observe. For the laundry problem this information can be supplied through a single interface procedure that identifies the entity and its current activity, thus:

```
monitor module LaundryState;
    type *Action = ...;
        *EntityReferenceNumber = 1..NumberOfEntities;
    procedure *NoteAction (A: Action;
                            E: EntityReferenceNumber);
    {Records the action A for entity E}
```

```
  begin
    {initially, output table header}
    {finally, complete table and output summary, if any}
  end {LaundryState};
```

For the laundry simulation the activities of interest are the arrival and departure of the customers, their acquisition and release of the washing machine and dryer, and their use of this equipment. These significant activities can be represented by values of an enumerated type as follows:

```
type *Action = ( *Arrival, *Departure,
                 *SeekWasher, *StartWasher, *StopWasher,
                 *SeekDryer, *StartDryer, *StopDryer);
```

Each Launderer process then reports the activities, thus:

```
process Launderer (StartTime: Clock.TimeScale;
                   P: State.EntityReferenceNumber);

  procedure Note (A: State.Action);
    begin State.NoteAction (A, P) end;

  begin
    Clock.Hold (StartTime);
    with State do
      begin
        Note (Arrival);
        Note (SeekWasher);
        Washer.Acquire;
        Note (StartWasher);
        Clock.Hold (WashingTime);
        Washer.Release;
        Note (StopWasher);
        Note (SeekDryer);
        Dryer.Acquire;
        Note (StartDryer);
        Clock.Hold (DryingTime);
        Dryer.Release;
        Note (StopDryer);
        Note (Departure)
      end
  end {Launderer};
```

The entity actions that are reported to the *state* module are accumulated until an event occurs (indicated by the advance of Pseudotime). At that point the activity information is displayed.

There may be several separate pieces of activity information to output for each entity process and the information must follow the order in which it was reported. The activity information associated with each process is therefore held on a separate queue associated with the process, and this might be represented as follows:

```
monitor Queue in Library
  (Where type ItemType = Action;);
```

```
instance Activities: array [EntityReferenceNumber] of Queue;
```

The implementation of the NoteAction procedure can then be expressed thus:

```
procedure *NoteAction (A: Action; E: EntityReferenceNumber);
  begin
    if LastEventTimeRecorded < Clock.Pseudotime then
      DisplayRecordedActivities;
    Activities [E].Append (A)
  end {NoteAction};
```

Before recording an action a check is made to see if an event has occurred since the last recording. This is indicated if the last event time noted is less than the current value of simulated time. If an event has occurred, a description of the actions that have been reported since the last event is output.

The full *state* module for the laundry simulation might be expressed as follows:

```
monitor module LaundryState;
  const NumberOfEntities = 2;
        TextLimit = 24;
        HalfText = 12;
        TimeSize = 4;
        LineLimit = 60;
        TimeUnit = 'Minutes';
  type *Action = ( *Arrival, *Departure,
                   *SeekWasher, *StartWasher, *StopWasher,
                   *SeekDryer, *StartDryer, *StopDryer);
       *EntityReferenceNumber = 1..NumberOfEntities;
       TextRange = 1..TextLimit;
       EntryText = packed array [TextRange] of Char;
  var Description: array [Action] of EntryText;
      EntityName: array [EntityReferenceNumber] of EntryText;
      LastEventTimeRecorded: Clock.TimeScale;

  monitor Queue in Library
    (Where type ItemType = Action;);
  instance Activities: array [EntityReferenceNumber] of Queue;

  procedure DisplayRecordedActivities;
    var ActionReported: Boolean;
        E: EntityReferenceNumber;

    procedure DisplayAction (Entity: EntityReferenceNumber;
                             var ActionReported: Boolean);
      var A: Action;
      begin
        if Activities [Entity].Empty
        then
          Write ('   ', '.': HalfText, '  ': HalfText, '  ')
```

```
        else
          begin
            ActionReported := True;
            Activities [Entity].Remove (A);
            Write (' ', Description [A], ' ')
          end
      end {DisplayAction};

  begin
    Write (' ', LastEventTimeRecorded: TimeSize, ' ');
    ActionReported := False;
    for E: = I to NumberOfEntities do
      DisplayAction (E, ActionReported);
    Writeln;
    while ActionReported do
      begin
        ActionReported := False;
        Write (' ', '.': TimeSize, ' ');
        for E := I to NumberOfEntities do
          DisplayAction (E, ActionReported);
        Writeln
      end;
    LastEventTimeRecorded := Clock.Pseudotime
  end {DisplayRecordedActivities};

procedure *NoteAction (A: Action; E: EntityReferenceNumber);
  begin
    if LastEventTimeRecorded < Clock.Pseudotime then
      DisplayRecordedActivities;
    Activities [E].Append (A)
  end {NoteAction};

procedure PrintLine;
  var L: I . . LineLimit;
  begin
    Write (' ');
    FOR L: = I to LineLimit do Write ('__');
    Writeln
  end {PrintLine};

procedure Initialize;

  procedure DisplayHeader;
    var E: EntityReferenceNumber;
    begin
      PrintLine;
      Write (' ', 'Time': TimeSize, ' ');
      for E := I to NumberOfEntities do
        Write (' ', EntityName [E], ' ');
      Writeln;
      PrintLine
    end {DisplayHeader};
```

```
        begin
          EntityName [1] := 'Launderer 1              ';
          EntityName [2] := 'Launderer 2              ';
          DisplayHeader;
          {initialize activity descriptions}
          Description [Arrival]      := 'Arrives                   ';
          Description [Departure]    := 'Leaves                    ';
          Description [SeekWasher] := 'Seeks washing machine ';
          Description [SeekDryer]    := 'Seeks dryer               ';
          Description [StartWasher] := 'Starts washing machine ';
          Description [StopWasher] := 'Washing complete      ';
          Description [StartDryer]   := 'Starts dryer              ';
          Description [StopDryer]    := 'Drying complete        ';
          LastEventTimeRecorded := 0
        end {Initialize};

      procedure Finalize;
        begin
          DisplayRecordedActivities;
          PrintLine
        end {Finalize};

    begin Initialize; ***; Finalize end {LaundryState};
```

Table 8.1 shows the output produced by this module. In addition to the
table, it is usually desirable to summarize selected aspects of the behavior of
each entity. In particular, it is often convenient to have information on those
entities that have been unable to perform certain operations immediately
and to obtain details of how long the entities were delayed as a result. For
the laundry simulation the summary might typically report any delays resulting from competition to use the washing machine and dryer, thus:

Launderer 1
    uses washing machine immediately
    uses dryer immediately

Launderer 2
    wait 5 minutes for washing machine
    waits 10 minutes for dryer

A summary of this form can be obtained by noting the start times of each
action in the NoteAction procedure. The summary is then output as one of
the finalization actions of the *state* module. The additions needed to the
LaundryState monitor are as follows:

```
    monitor module LaundryState;
                . . .
      var EntityDetails:
```

```
                    array [EntityReferenceNumber] of
                       record
                          Time: array [Action] of Clock.TimeScale
                       end;
                    . . .
        procedure *NoteAction (A: Action: E: EntityReferenceNumber);
          begin
             EntityDetails [E].Time [A] := Clock.PseudoTime;
                  . . .
          end {NoteAction};

        procedure Finalize;

           procedure ProduceSummary;
              var E: EntityReferenceNumber;
                  WasherDelay, DryerDelay: Clock.TimeScale;
              begin
                 Writeln; Writeln;
                  for E := 1 to NumberOfEntities do
                  with EntityDetails [E] do
                    begin
                       Writeln (EntityName [E]);
                       WasherDelay := Time [StartWasher] − Time [SeekWasher];
                       if WasherDelay = 0
                       then Writeln (' uses washing machine immediately')
                       else Writeln ('  waits', WasherDelay:1, '  ', TimeUnit,
                                      ' for washing machine');
                       DryerDelay := Time [StartDryer] − Time [SeekDryer];
                       if DryerDelay = 0
                       then Writeln ('  uses dryer immediately')
                       else Writeln ('  waits ', DryerDelay:1, '  ', TimeUnit,
                                      ' for dryer');
                       Writeln
                    end
              end {ProduceSummary};

           begin
             . . .
             ProduceSummary
           end {Finalize};

        begin . . . end {LaundryState};
```

When the number of entity processes in a simulation program is small an identifying reference for each entity can be passed as a parameter to the process instance modeling that entity. However, if the number of such entity processes is substantial as, for example, in the case of entity processes representing customers using a launderette, then it is usually better for the identifying references to be allocated by a module defined for that purpose. That is, the first action of each entity process would be to obtain its reference, thus:

```
monitor module EntityReferences;

  type *ReferenceRange = 0..Maxint {say};
  var Next: ReferenceRange;

  procedure *GetReference (var Identity: ReferenceRange);
    begin
      Identity := Next;
      Next := Next + I
    end {GetReference};

  begin
    Next := 0;
    ***
  end {EntityReferences};
        . . .
process Entity;
      . . .
  var Identity: EntityReferences.ReferenceRange;
        . . .
  begin
    EntityReferences.GetReference (Identity);
        . . .
  end {Entity};
```

In applications where the number of entities is very large it may also be
desirable to reuse the entity processes to simulate several entities in the
model. This can be achieved by expressing the entity processes concerned in
the form of a loop in which entity details are acquired dynamically, i.e. each
entity process is used to simulate a sequence of similar entities. Consider,
for example, an entity process used to simulate the behavior of a customer
in a launderette. Assuming that customer arrival times are supplied by a
Times monitor (discussed later) then a customer process might be expressed
as follows:

```
process Customer;
      . . .
  begin
    repeat
      CustomerReferences.GetReference (Identity);
      ArrivalTime := Times.NextArrival;
      Clock.Hold (ArrivalTime − Clock.Pseudotime);
          . . .
    until False
  end {Customer};
```

Each instance of this entity process executes indefinitely; the assumption
being that the simulation terminates as a result of a time limit imposed on
the Clock monitor. At the beginning of the loop a customer reference is
obtained followed by an arrival time for that customer, i.e. the time at
which the customer enters the launderette. The entity process is then suspended to await that time.

This reuse of entity processes is possible because it is only those customers who have actually arrived at the launderette, and are trying to use its facilities, that have to be modeled.

The number of Customer processes instances declared must be sufficient to represent the maximum number of customers who may be present in the launderette at any one time. If insufficient process instances are created a Customer process will be given a start time which is behind the current value of simulated time. Should this occur the program will fail. To avoid such problems it is preferable to use a separate process for each entity, initially, and to consider the optimization of reusing processes only if the performance of the program is unsatisfactory.

Stochastic models

Most simulation models are *stochastic*, meaning that the behavior of the entities in the system being modeled is not known exactly, or, more specifically that the outcome of certain operations, or the times of certain events, is not known precisely. This uncertainly is modeled by one or more state variables taking on values in accordance with a probability distribution; that is, taking values each of which has a corresponding *probability*, or likelihood, of occurrence. For example, in the pass-the-parcel simulation it may be found from observation that the duration of the music varies from five seconds to fifty seconds (say) with an average, or *mean*, playing time of twenty-five seconds.

The range of possible values and their probability estimates are generally given in the form of a probability distribution graph, as illustrated in Figure 8.3 for the distribution of observed playing times for the pass-the-parcel game.

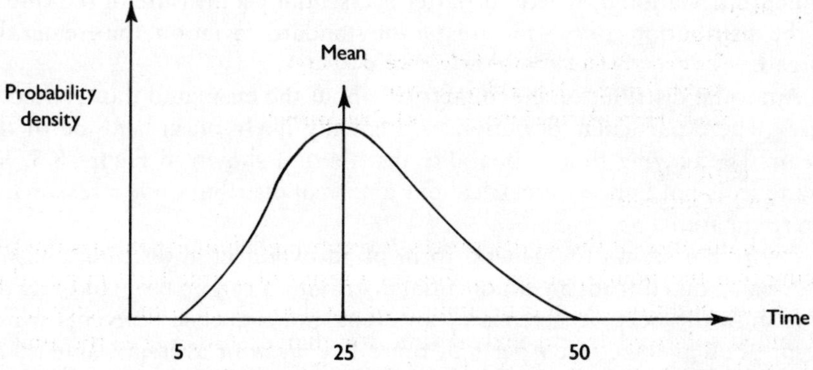

Figure 8.3 Probability distribution: an example

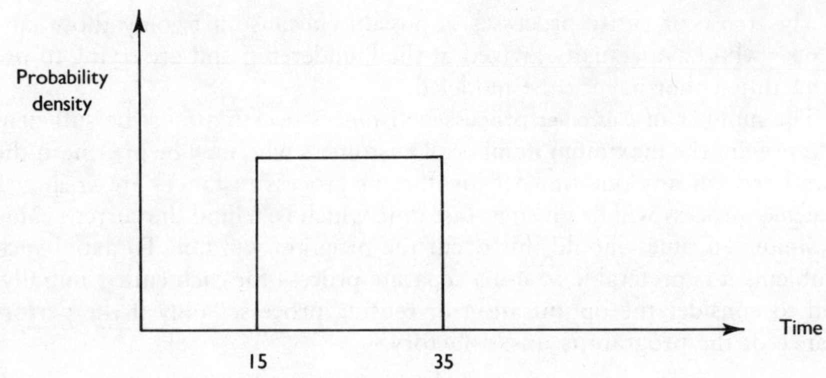

Figure 8.4 A uniform probability distribution

Selecting values from a given probability distribution tends to be one of the more time-consuming aspects of a simulation program. To reduce costs it is common practice to fit a standard distribution function to the actual distribution so that values may be selected more easily. For example, in the pass-the-parcel model it might be considered adequate to chop off the tails of the distribution curve and assume that all times between fifteen and thirty-five seconds (say) are equally likely. That is, to assume that the playing times are distributed *uniformly* over the defined range, as implied in Figure 8.4.

For a more accurate fit we might consider trying to match the observed distribution to one of a standard set of distribution functions. Only two such functions are considered here: one is for a *normal* distribution and one is for an *exponential* (or *negative exponential*) distribution. The general shape of a normal distribution is shown in Figure 8.5.

A normal distribution is characterized by two quantities: a mean m and a standard deviation d, where the latter is essentially a measure of the spread of the distribution curve – the greater the standard deviation, the greater the spread.

A normal distribution is symmetrical about the mean and thus is used in cases where particular deviations are equally likely on either side of the mean. The playing time probability distribution shown in Figure 8.3, for example, is not quite symmetrical but a normal distribution is a reasonable approximation.

Figure 8.6 shows the general form of an exponential distribution.

A value taken from an exponential distribution can be thought of as the time until the next occurrence of an event in a sequence of events which occur at an average rate r per unit time. The *mean* or average value is $1/r$. The arrival of customers at a launderette, for example, might be modeled by

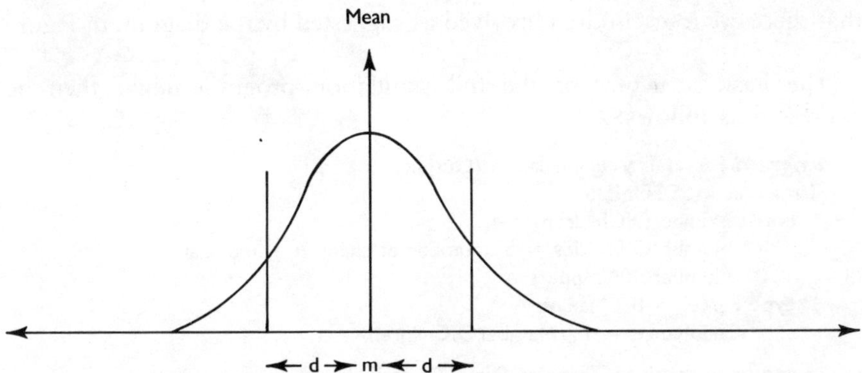

Figure 8.5 Normal distribution curve

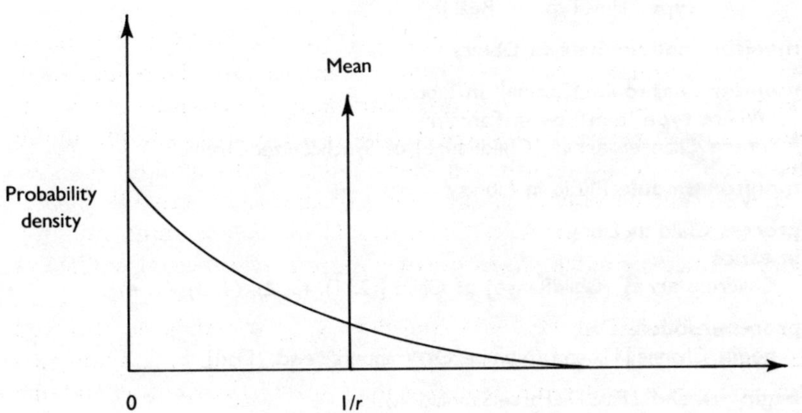

Figure 8.6 Exponential distribution

an exponential distribution assuming an average rate of ten customers per hour (say).

As an illustration of how times selected from distribution functions may be administered in a simulation program let us consider a full implementation of the pass-the-parcel game, for one parcel. Here, a number of children sitting in a circle pass a wrapped parcel from one to another while music plays. When the music stops the child holding the parcel removes a layer of paper. The music then starts again and the parcel is passed on. This procedure is repeated until the present at the center of the parcel has been uncovered.

In the simulation program the transfer of the parcel between children is performed via an instance of a SynchronizedChannel monitor. Let us assume that there are four children involved as suggested by the diagram in Figure 8.7.

The basic structure of the full simulation program might then be expressed as follows:

```
program PassTheParcelSimulation (Output);
{Time unit is SECONDS}
    const NumberOfChildren = 4;
          NumberOfEntities = 5 {number of children + musician};
          NumberOfWrappers = ...;
    type Parcel = 0..Maxint;
         ChildRange = 1..NumberOfChildren;

    monitor module Times = ParcelTimes in Library;

    monitor module Clock in Library
      (Where const TimeLimit = Times.SimulationPeriod;
             const EntityLimit = NumberOfEntities;
             type  TimeType = Real;);

    monitor module State in Library;

    monitor SynchronizedChannel in Library
      (Where type ItemType = Parcel;);
    instance Channel: array [ChildRange] of SynchronizedChannel;

    monitor module Music in Library;

    process Child in Library;
    instance
      Children: array [ChildRange] of Child [(2, 1), (3, 2), (4, 3), (1, 4)];

    process module Dad;
      begin Channel[1].Send (NumberOfWrappers) end {Dad};

    begin *** end {PassTheParcelSimulation}.
```

The TimeType for the Clock monitor is given as Real in this case as some of the times will be sampled from distribution functions which return values of

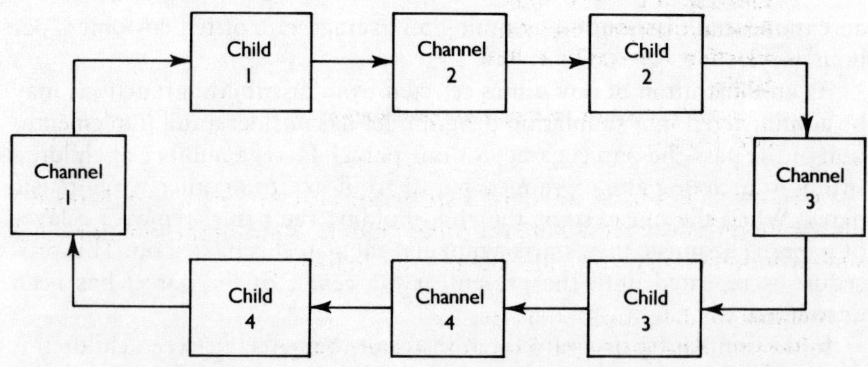

Figure 8.7 Pass-the-parcel: a graphical representation

that type. The event queue limit has been set at one greater than the number of children in order to take account of events associated with the playing of music. There is generally no time limit on the execution of the program as the simulation should stop when the parcel has been unwrapped completely.

The time unit in the program is 'seconds'. The times for the various activities in the model are supplied by a *times* module. A module of this type can be used in most simulation programs to hide the details of how the various activity or event times are determined. Such values are usually generated dynamically but, in some cases, they might be determined in advance. One possibility is for the times to be produced as part of the initialization action of the *times* module. Alternatively, the times might be taken from a file prepared separately by another program. The latter approach is convenient if the simulation program is executed frequently with the same data and the preparation time of the data is substantial.

For the pass-the-parcel model the *times* module is required to provide three types of value:

(a) the time taken to pass the parcel from one child to another, which might be given as a constant time of two seconds (say);

(b) the duration of the music which controls the time spent passing the parcel before a layer of paper is removed; this might be represented by values sampled from a normal distribution with a mean of twenty-five seconds and a standard deviation of six seconds (say);

(c) the time taken to remove a layer of paper; this might be represented by values sampled from a normal distribution with a mean of eight seconds and a standard deviation of two seconds (say).

To a user of the *times* module all three times can be presented as functions:

```
monitor module ParcelTimes;
   {Time unit is SECONDS}
      function *PassParcel: Real;
      function *PlayingTime: Real;
      function *UnwrapTime: Real;
      begin
         {initially, prepare to supply sampled values}
      end {Times};
```

Selecting values from standard distributions can be performed through a library module declared within the *times* module. Some of the functions that such a module might provide include the following:

```
monitor module BasicDistributions;
   function *UniformInteger (Min, Max: Integer): Integer;
      {Returns an integer value in the range Min to    }
      {Max inclusive, selected uniformly over the range.}
```

```
function *UniformReal (Min, Max: Real): Real;
   {Returns a real value in the range Min to Max,    }
   {excluding the limit values, selected uniformly over}
   {the range.                                        }
function *Exponential (Rate: Real): Real;
   {Returns a value selected from an exponential}
   {distribution defined by the Rate value.      }
function *Normal (Mean, StandardDeviation: Real): Real;
   {Returns a value selected from a normal distribution}
   {defined by the Mean and StandardDeviation values. }
begin
   {initially, prepare to supply values}
end {BasicDistributions};
```

This module makes available four functions which return values from
uniform, exponential and normal distributions, as discussed previously.

The PlayingTime and UnwrapTime functions in the Times monitor can be
implemented using the Normal function. The *times* module thus takes the
form:

```
monitor module ParcelTimes;
{Time unit is SECONDS}

   monitor module BasicDistributions in Library;

   const *SimulationPeriod = Maxint; {no limit}
         *PassParcel = 2;
          MusicMean = 25;
          MusicDeviation = 6;
          UnwrapMean = 8;
          UnwrapDeviation = 2;
   var    TotalPlayingTime: Real;
          PlayingSessions: 0..Maxint;
                 . . .
   function *PlayingTime: Real;
      {Returns the next playing time sampled from a}
      {normal distribution.                        }
      var Time : Real;
      begin
        Time := BasicDistributions.Normal (MusicMean, MusicDeviation);
        if Time < 0.0 then PlayingTime := 0.0
        else PlayingTime := Time;
        TotalPlayingTime := TotalPlayingTime + Time;
        PlayingSessions := PlayingSessions + 1
      end {PlayingTime};

   function *UnwrapTime: Real;
      {Returns the next playing time sampled from a}
      {normal distribution.                        }
         . . .
   begin
     TotalPlayingTime := 0.0;
```

```
        PlayingSessions := 0;
            . . .

    ***;
    if PlaySessions > 0 then
        State.NoteMean ('playing time', TotalPlayingTime/PlayingSessions);
            . . .
    end {ParcelTimes};
```

The implementation of the UnwrapTime function is similar to that shown for the PlayingTime function and so has not been given in full. It should be noted that:

- Values sampled from a normal distribution may be negative which in some models may have no meaning. Here, for example, the playing time may go negative. In such cases a zero time can be returned by the sampling function but care must be taken to ensure that the mean is not affected as a result.

- Times sampled from any distribution will only have the desired mean if sufficient values are taken. As a check, a running total should be kept of the times returned by any function and the means calculated when the simulation is complete. The actual means might be reported to the *state* module for output, as shown in the ParcelTimes monitor. Alternatively, each actual mean and its expected value might be compared in the *times* module and a fault reported if the magnitude of the difference is outside some program defined limit.

- When deriving arrival times from an exponential distribution, as in the case of customers arriving at a launderette, it is necessary to keep track of the previous time returned as the exponential function only gives the length of time to the next arrival. That is, the basic form of an arrival function is as follows:

```
function *NextArrival: Real;
    var Time: Real;
    begin
        Time := BasicDistributions.Exponential (ArrivalRate);
        LastArrival := LastArrival + Time;
        NextArrival := LastArrival
    end {NextArrival};
```

Here it is assumed that NextArrival is initialized to zero (for convenience, details of the accumulated times allocated have been omitted).

An explanation of how the BasicDistributions module can be implemented is given later after the remainder of the pass-the-parcel simulation program has been discussed.

The basic structure of the Music module is as follows:

```
monitor module Music;
    var *Playing: Boolean;
    procedure *Start; . . .;
```

```
process module Musician; ...;
begin
   Playing := True;
   ...
end {Music};
```

The Music monitor provides access to a variable Playing which indicates whether or not music is currently playing. Playing is initially True but is set to False by a local Musician process. The Musician is restarted by calls to the procedure Start.

The complete implementation of the Music monitor is as follows:

```
monitor module Music;
   var *Playing: Boolean;
   instance MusicianQueue: Condition;

   procedure *Start;
      begin
         Playing := True;
         MusicianQueue.Signal {activate musician}
      end {Start};

   procedure Stop;
      begin
         Playing := False;
         MusicianQueue.Wait
      end {Stop};

   process module Musician;
      begin
         repeat
            Clock.Hold (Times.PlayingTime);
            Stop
         until False
      end {Musician};

   begin Playing := True; *** end {Music};
```

The synchronization between the Musician process and the processes representing the children is achieved by suspending the Musician process at the end of a playing interval and reactivating that process again when a call is made to Start.

The implementation of the Child process follows the general outline given in Chapter 7:

```
process Child (Left, Right: ChildRange);
   var P: Parcel;
   begin
      repeat
         Channel[Right].Receive (P) ;
         if not Music.Playing then
            begin
{*}            Clock.Hold (Times.UnwrapTime);
```

```
                 P := P − I;
                 if P > 0 then Music.Start
              end;
          if P > 0 then
            begin
{*}             Clock.Hold (Times.PassParcel);
                Channel[Left].Send (P)
            end
        until P = 0
      end {Child};
```

The main change that has been made is to add statements (marked {*}) to model the time taken to complete each activity.

Random number generators

To implement the functions that select values from the various probability distributions discussed in the previous section it is necessary to have available a *random number generator* that supplies a stream of random values. Truly random numbers are difficult to generate, so a *pseudorandom* number generator is usually employed. Such a generator produces a fixed sequence of values for a given initial state denoted by one or more *seed* values. The pseudorandom values are calculated using a numerical algorithm. The algorithm is deterministic but the values are deemed to be *random* if they pass certain statistical tests of randomness. (Further details may be obtained from the simulation texts cited at the end of this chapter.)

A basic pseudorandom number generator supplies values of type Real uniformly distributed in the range 0.0 to 1.0 exclusive. The following module implements an algorithm, suggested by Wichmann and Hill, that generates such values.

```
monitor module BasicGenerator;
   type *SeedRange = I .. 30000;
   var SeedI, Seed2, Seed3: Integer;

   function *NextValue: Real;
     var X: Real;
     begin
        SeedI := 171*SeedI mod 30269;
        Seed2 := 172*Seed2 mod 30307;
        Seed3 := 170*Seed3 mod 30323;
        X := SeedI/30269 + Seed2/30307 + Seed3/30323;
        NextValue := X − Trunc(X)
     end {NextValue};

   procedure *SetSeeds (SI, S2, S3: SeedRange);
     begin
        SeedI := SI; Seed2 := S2; Seed3 := S3
     end {SetSeeds};
```

```
begin
  {Set defaults}
  Seed1 := 42; Seed2 := 2691; Seed3 := 19032; {say}
  ***
end {BasicGenerator};
```

Details of the inner workings of this module will not be discussed here. From the user's point of view, the module supplies a stream of random numbers via the function NextValue. Different streams may be obtained by adjusting the values of the three seeds from which the stream is derived. The adjustment is made by a call to the procedure SetSeeds supplying three values in the range 1..30000.

With such a basic generator the BasicDistributions module may be implemented as follows:

```
monitor module BasicDistributions;
  monitor module BasicGenerator in Library;
  type *SeedRange = BasicGenerator.SeedRange;

  procedure *SetSeeds = BasicGenerator.SetSeeds;

  function *UniformInteger (Min, Max: Integer): Integer;
    {Returns an integer value in the range Min to Max}
    {inclusive, selected uniformly over the range.      }
    begin
      UniformInteger :=
        Trunc ((Max - Min + 1) * BasicGenerator.NextValue) + Min
    end {UniformInteger};

  function *UniformReal (Min, Max: Real): Real;
    {Returns a real value in the range Min to Max,}
    {excluding the limit values, selected uniformly }
    {over the range.                               }
    begin
      UniformReal := (Max - Min) * BasicGenerator.NextValue + Min
    end {UniformReal};

  function *Exponential (Rate: Real): Real;
    {Returns a value selected from an exponential}
    {distribution defined by the Rate value.     }
    begin
      Exponential := -(1/Rate) * Ln(BasicGenerator.NextValue)
    end {Exponential};

  function *Normal (Mean, StandardDeviation: Real): Real;
    {Returns a value selected from a normal distribution}
    {defined by the Mean and StandardDeviation values. }
    const C0 = 2.515517; C1 = 0.802853; C2 = 0.010328;
          D1 = 1.432788; D2 = 0.189269; D3 = 0.001308;
    var T1, T2, T3, P, Xp: Real;
        InversionNeeded: Boolean;
    begin
      P := BasicGenerator.NextValue;
      InversionNeeded := P > 0.5;
```

```
         if InversionNeeded then P := 1.0 - P;
         T1 := Sqrt (Ln (1/Sqr(P)));
         T2 := Sqr (T1);
         T3 := T1 *T2;
         Xp := T1 - (C0 + C1*T1 + C2*T2) /
                     (1.0 + D1*T1 + D2*T2 + D3*T3);
         if InversionNeeded then Xp := - Xp;
         Normal := Mean + StandardDeviation * Xp
      end {Normal};

   begin *** end {BasicDistributions};
```

All four functions are implemented by transforming the basic stream of random values which lie in the interval [0, 1].

The procedure SetSeeds of the local BasicGenerator module is also incorporated in the BasicDistributions module to allow different pseudorandom streams to be produced.

The dining philosophers: a simulation model

The final section of Chapter 6 considered the dining philosophers problem, which is a classic case study in resource management. This chapter concludes with a brief discussion of how the behavior of the philosophers might be represented in a simulation program.

The basic structure of the simulation model is as follows:

```
program DiningPhilosophersSimulation (Output);
{Time unit is MINUTES}
   const NumberOfForks = 5;
         NumberOfPhilosophers = 5;
   type Fork = 1..NumberOfForks;
        PhilosopherRange = 1..NumberOfPhilosophers;

   monitor module Times = PhilosopherTimes in Library;

   monitor module Clock in Library
      (Where const TimeLimit = Times.SimulationPeriod;
             const EntityLimit = NumberOfPhilosophers;
             type  TimeType = Real;);

   monitor module State in Library;

   monitor SingleResource in Library
      (Where const PriorityLimit = Maxint;);
   instance ForkAccess: array [Fork] of SingleResource;

   process APhilosopher in Library;
   instance
      Philosopher: array [PhilosopherRange] of APhilosopher
         [(1, 1, 2), (2, 2, 3), (3, 3, 4), (4, 4, 5), (5, 1, 5)];

   begin *** end {DiningPhilosophersSimulation}.
```

The philosophers spend their time either eating or thinking although, traditionally, most attention is given to their eating habits. For the purposes of simulation we might assume that:

- The time unit for the simulation is *minutes*.
- Each philosopher thinks on average for three hours before eating, with a standard deviation of fifteen minutes.
- Each philosopher eats, on average, for one hour, with a standard deviation of fifteen minutes.
- The model is simulated over a period of one week.

As in the pass-the-parcel simulation the times associated with the various operations are supplied by a *times* module based on the definitions given above.

Each philosopher process is initialized with the identities of the forks that the philosopher concerned must use. The order of the parameters defines the acquisition order of the forks. Thus, the basic behavior of each philosopher may be expressed as follows:

```
process APhilosopher (Me: PhilosopherRange;
                       FirstFork, SecondFork: Fork);
  begin
    repeat
      Clock.Hold (Times.ThinkingTime);
      ForkAccess [FirstFork].Acquire;
      ForkAccess [SecondFork].Acquire;
      Clock.Hold (Times.EatingTime);
      ForkAccess [SecondFork].Release;
      ForkAccess [FirstFork].Release
    until False
  end {APhilosopher};
```

In addition, we can add calls to the *state* module to identify the points of interest in the simulation.

With such a simulation model it can be demonstrated that the method of allocating forks does indeed avoid deadlock by observing the result of all five philosophers arriving at the same time. In the same way the model can be used to demonstrate how deadlock and starvation might occur if the forks are allocated differently.

Summary

This chapter has introduced the topic of discrete event simulation modeling by identifying the basic requirements of this application area and discussing the representation of a few simple models.

Discrete event simulation models can be implemented conveniently in any language that contains an appropriate set of concurrency primitives. Specifically, processes can be used to represent the dynamic entities in a system and the operations performed by those entities can be represented by suspending the entity processes for a corresponding period of simulated time. The passage of time, and the triggering of events that are required to occur at defined times, can be administered by a single *clock* module.

The behavior of a simulation model can be summarized if all the relevant information on its entities is passed to, and maintained by, a *state* module. In particular, this module can then show the activities performed by the dynamic entities with respect to the passage of simulated time in the model.

The outcome of some of the operations performed by an entity is uncertain, which can be modeled by taking values from a probability distribution defining the likelihood of all possible outcomes of those operations. A wide range of distribution functions is available for use in different situations. Three of the most common cases are uniform, exponential and normal distributions. Functions can provide sample values in accordance with such distributions if a basic pseudorandom number generator is available that supplies a stream of values in the interval [0, 1].

Further reading

For a review of the various approaches to the representation of simulation models, and an introduction to the languages involved, see:
- Kreutzer, W., *System Simulation Programming Styles and Languages*, Addison Wesley, 1986.

Simula is one of the principal languages that supports a *process-oriented* approach to simulation, and its design has influenced that of Pascal Plus. A presentation of discrete event simulation modeling through a series of examples expressed in Simula is given in:
- Birtwistle, G.M., *Discrete Event Modeling in Simula*, Macmillan, 1979.

For a more mathematical treatment of discrete event simulation, see:
- Mitrani, I., *Simulation Techniques for Discrete Event Systems*, Cambridge University Press, 1982.

The random number generator discussed in this chapter was based on one described in:
- Wichmann, B.A. and Hill, I.D., An efficient and portable pseudo-random number generator, *Applied Statistics*, Vol. 31, pp. 188–90, 1982.

Exercises

8.1 Suggest how the behavior of the philosophers in the dining philosophers simulation model might be presented and describe in detail how such a presentation might be generated?

8.2 Construct a simulation model for the variation of the pass-the-parcel game in which two parcels are circulated in opposite directions, as described in Chapter 7.

8.3 Construct a simulation model for a car wash where the time taken to wash a car is four minutes and where cars arrive at a rate of ten per hour. Simulate the car wash over a twelve hour period and measure the maximum queue length that forms in that time.

8.4 Construct a simulation model for customers queuing for service at four checkouts at a supermarket. Assume that:

- The service times follow a normal distribution with a mean of four minutes and a standard deviation of one and a half minutes.
- The arrival times follow an exponential distribution with an arrival rate of forty customers per hour.

Simulate the following two queuing schemes:

(a) Each customer that arrives joins the shortest queue.
(b) Customers are put into one queue and taken in order as the checkouts become free.

Evaluate these strategies by comparing the observed maximum and average times taken for customers to be served in each case.

8.5 Construct a simulation model for a bar where alcoholic drinks are served and consumed as follows:

(a) all customers have the same drink which is served by the glass;
(b) each customer queues for a drink which is poured by a barmaid;
(c) a customer who has finished a drink may return for another one by bringing back the empty glass;
(d) the barmaid always uses clean glasses and places any dirty glasses received in a sink for later washing;
(e) the barmaid washes the glasses when there are no customers to serve, or if the supply of clean glasses is exhausted;
(f) customers who have finished drinking leave their glasses on the table at which they were sitting;
(g) a bar manager collects empty glasses periodically and deposits them in the sink.

The relevant model details are:

- The model should be observed for a period of two hours.
- The customer arrival rate is twenty per hour, with an exponential distribution.
- Each customer has between one and six drinks, each number in the range being equally likely.
- The barmaid takes one minute to pour a drink.
- The time taken to consume a drink follows a normal distribution with a mean of twenty minutes and a standard deviation of five minutes.
- The barmaid takes exactly thirty seconds to wash a glass.
- The bar manager collects glasses every fifteen minutes with the first collection occurring fifteen minutes into the simulation.

- The bar manager takes three minutes to collect glasses.
- There are twenty glasses in total, all of which are clean initially.

The simulation program should determine:

(a) the total idle time of barmaid;
(b) the total, maximum and average waiting time of the customers;
(c) the time saved by refilling the glasses when customers return for another drink.

8.6   On the first day of December each year the eight teaching staff (of a typical Computer Science department) prepare Christmas cards to send to each other. The cards are posted at a central mail-box from which they are collected and distributed by a porter. Unfortunately the porter always starts celebrating early and makes some mistakes during each delivery. Specifically, instead of delivering the cards according to the office number on each envelope he unloads a bundle of cards at random in each office. On reaching the final office he 'completes' his delivery by leaving all the cards that remain.

    The offices are laid out in a rectangle with a surrounding corridor as shown in the following diagram.

2	3	4	5
1	8	7	6

    The porter always follows the corridor in a clockwise direction starting his delivery at office number 1.

    Some cards by chance reach their correct destination but most are returned to the central mail-box for redistribution. All returns are made before the porter's next delivery.

    If the state of the porter does not improve is it likely that all the cards will be delivered by Christmas, assuming that he makes four deliveries per day for eighteen working days?

    Is the result different if he staggers at the junction in the corridor so that some deliveries are made in an anticlockwise direction?

Nine

REAL-TIME SYSTEMS

In general terms, a *real-time* program may be defined as a program that is used to control one or more pieces of equipment. If the program is executed by a computer which is an integral part of that equipment then the resultant system is often referred to as an *embedded system*.

More specifically, most real-time programs are characterized by having the following principal requirements:

(a) the need to interact with a wide range of physical devices – both conventional input and output devices (e.g. VDUs) and special-purpose devices (e.g. temperature sensors);
(b) the need to respond to external events that occur concurrently;
(c) the need to respond to some external events within a specified time.

Requirement (b) means that real-time programs are inherently concurrent and so all of the material presented in earlier chapters of this book is relevant to their construction. Techniques for meeting requirements (a) and (c) are discussed in this chapter, together with a description of how real-time programs can be developed in a simulated environment.

Typical examples of real-time systems include automatic telephone exchanges, control systems for factory processes and, on a smaller scale, controllers for individual devices, such as radar scanners. Interactive database and operating systems are also real-time systems in that they perform, in parallel, operations triggered by external events and are subject to time constraints. However, in database and operating systems most of the time constraints are concerned with ensuring that users obtain a satisfactory service, while in real-time systems the time constraints are often limits that have to be met if the system is to give the correct results. For example, although it is important for an airline reservation system to reply to a seat allocation request in seconds rather than minutes, to avoid customers becoming restless, a radar scanner must keep up with the input data supplied to it if it is to maintain a correct picture on the radar screen.

Environment interaction

Most general-purpose high-level programming languages provide notations that allow most of the operations expressed in a program to be represented in a machine-independent form, so that the resulting program is portable. In Pascal, for example, all standard input/output operations are represented by operations on sequential files. Such abstract file operations are implemented as appropriate actions on physical devices in the operating environment. Thus, for example, an output statement of the form:

```
Write (User, 'Hello')
```

might cause the characters in the string to be transmitted to a VDU screen, a printing device, or buffered for subsequent output to a disk or a magnetic tape.

In real-time applications the range of devices with which a program may interact is large and varied – so much so that it is impossible to define an acceptably small set of standard abstract operations to represent interaction with them all. Each language is, therefore, forced to be selective and provide high-level support for only the most common types of external communication. In some cases input/output constructs are omitted entirely from a language definition, leaving the operations to be defined by, and tailored to, the environment to which the implementation is directed. This is the approach taken in Algol 60 and in many languages designed specifically for real-time applications, including Jovial, RTL/2, Coral 66, and, more recently, Modula-2 and Ada. With such languages environment operations are usually performed through locally defined routines (or modules) implemented using some convenient *system* language – often an assembly language. This technique gives access to the full set of facilities available in the execution environment but is not as convenient, secure, or portable as strictly defined language operations for the same purpose.

Environment operations are performed at two logical levels:

(a) a *user level* where interaction is expressed in terms of user-oriented abstract operations;

(b) an *environment level* where the method of interaction is dictated by the way in which the environment facilities are defined; for example, the definition may be that of:

    (i) an operating system interface, if the program executes on top of an operating system, or

(ii) a machine hardware interface if the program is executing on a bare machine.

The representation of each of these levels is considered in turn.

User level interaction

Any language that includes a module construct provides the capability to give access to an environment facility in a form that is convenient for general users of that facility. For example, interaction with a graph plotter might be implemented by a module of the following form:

```
envelope module SimpleGraphPlotter;
    const *Xmax = 999;
          *Ymax = 999;
    type *Xcoordinate = 0..Xmax;
         *Ycoordinate = 0..Ymax;
    procedure *GetPenPosition (var X: Xcoordinate;
                               var Y: Ycoordinate);
    procedure *LiftPenFromPaper;
    procedure *LowerPenToPaper;
    procedure *MovePenTo (X: Xcoordinate; Y: Ycoordinate);
    begin
        {initially pen is at [0, 0] and up from paper}
    end {SimpleGraphPlotter};
```

This module supports interaction with a graph plotter through a small set of abstract operations. This abstraction avoids the need for the user to know how each operation is actually implemented and also makes programs using the graph plotter more portable as the specific characteristics of the graph plotter and the method of driving it are isolated.

It is neither practical nor desirable to build environment interface modules, like the graph plotter, into a programming language. Clearly, it is impractical to consider including such descriptions for all devices in a language, but in practice the approach is even problematic for very common devices, like a VDU. One difficulty is that the range of operations that a module might provide for any specific device is not easily standardized. Some VDUs, for example, do not have cursor control, while others provide exotic features such as protected screen areas, color facilities and special graphic symbols.

In any languages it is more important to have adequate facilities for constructing modules that allow interaction with the execution environment rather than defining such modules as an integral part of the language. This is the approach that has been taken in the design of most modern programming languages such as Modula-2 and Ada. Pascal Plus adopts a similar philosophy but, being an extension of Pascal, also includes the standard file facilities of that language.

Environment level interaction

In general, languages that support direct environment interaction tend to fall into one of three groups:

(a) those that permit mixed language programming, thereby allowing a program to link to program components expressed in a lower level language and which provide a user interface to the environment;
(b) those that extend the high-level language definition with facilities normally only found in an assembly language permitting, for example, a program to refer directly to memory locations;
(c) those that define an abstract *channel* (or channels) through which environment operations may be performed with most of the convenience and security that is normally associated with a high-level programming language.

Regardless of the language used it is good practice to restrict operations that interact with the environment to particular modules, as suggested earlier for the graph plotter. In this way the portability of the resulting program is improved and it is also easier to maintain.

Modula-2 is an example of a language in group (b) while Pascal Plus is an example of a language in group (c). Precise details of these mechanisms have little relevance to concurrent program behavior, the main concern of this book. However, some descriptions of the Pascal Plus facilities are presented, briefly, to complete the development of some of the real-time programs that were discussed in earlier chapters.

In Pascal Plus all nonstandard environment interaction is handled by a single standard procedure, Perform, which takes one parameter:

```
procedure Perform (var Op: Operation);
```

The parameter Op is a record identifying the required environment operation and the data associated with that operation. The execution of the specified operation is carried out by support code that is attached to the user code. The relationship between the user code, the support code and the program environment is suggested in Figure 9.1.

The execution of a Perform operation in a user program transfers control to a routine in the support code which interprets the operation. In some cases the operation may be carried out directly on a bare machine, or the operation may be handled as a further call to an underlying operating system that implements the operation on behalf of the user program.

As an example of the use of the Perform mechanism consider the implementation of the environment operations needed in the temperature/humidity monitoring system discussed in Chapter 4. In this problem two processes measure the temperature and humidity in a room, display the current values

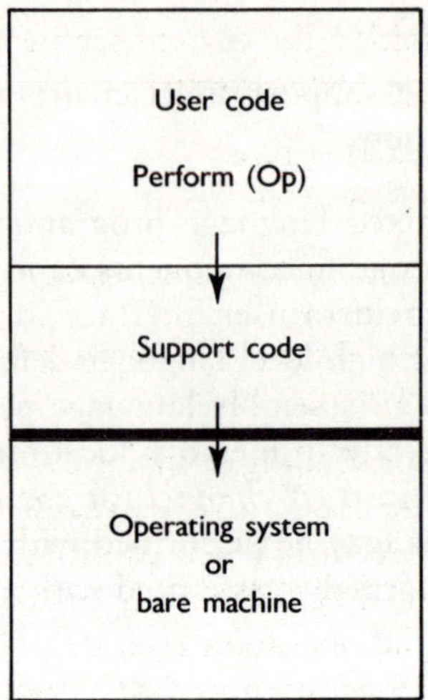

Figure 9.1 Real-time program layers

of each, and ring a bell if either value exceeds some predefined limits. The
control program communicates with five devices: a temperature sensor,
a temperature display, a humidity sensor, a humidity display and a bell.
The external connections may, therefore, be identified by five values in an
enumerated-type, thus:

```
type ExternalConnections = (TemperatureSensor, TemperatureDisplay,
                            HumiditySensor, HumidityDisplay, Bell);
```

Assuming that temperature and humidity are represented as values of
type Integer then the environment operations may be defined as a variant
record:

```
type Operation = record
                    case Facility: ExternalConnections of
                    TemperatureSensor, TemperatureDisplay:
                        (Temperature: Integer);
                    HumiditySensor, HumidityDisplay:
                        (Humidity: Integer);
                    Bell: (Switch: BellOperation)
                end;
```

where

```
type BellOperation = (On, Off);
```

The tag field identifies the required facility and the fields associated with
each tag value define the data items that are supplied or returned when an
operation is performed on that facility.

Using this record definition the current temperature, for example, might be obtained by a function of the form:

```
function CurrentTemperature: Integer;
   var TemperatureInput: Operation;
   begin
      TemperatureInput.Facility := TemperatureSensor;
      Perform (TemperatureInput);
      CurrentTemperature := TemperatureInput.Temperature
   end {CurrentTemperature};
```

The temperature sensor reading is made by setting the tag field of the operation record TemperatureInput to TemperatureSensor and then applying the Perform operation to that record. When control is returned from the call of Perform the temperature reading will have been taken and the value placed in the Temperature field of the operation record.

The definition of the operation record is not part of the Pascal Plus language. This is achieved by allowing the Perform procedure to take any record as a parameter. The mechanism is, therefore, potentially insecure but the risk of error may be reduced by providing the operation record definition in a library module. For example, the environment module for the temperature/humidity monitoring system might be given in the following form:

```
monitor module Environment;
   const EnvironmentReference = 42 {say};
   type *ExternalConnections = (ExternalIdentification,
                                *TemperatureSensor,
                                *TemperatureDisplay,
                                *HumiditySensor,
                                *HumidityDisplay,
                                *Bell);
        *BellOperation = ( *On, *Off);
        *Operation = record
                        case *Facility: ExternalConnections of
                        ExternalIdentification:
                           (Number: Integer);
                        TemperatureSensor, TemperatureDisplay:
                           ( *Temperature: Integer);
                        HumiditySensor, HumidityDisplay:
                           ( *Humidity: Integer);
                        Bell: ( *Switch: BellOperation)
                     end;
   procedure Initialize;
      var StartUp: Operation;
      begin
         StartUp.Facility := ExternalIdentification;
         StartUp.Number := EnvironmentReference;
         Perform (StartUp)
```

    end {Initialize};

    begin Initialize; *** **end** {Environment};

This module, in addition to defining the environment available for the temperature/humidity monitoring system, also checks that the user program and the underlying support code are working with the same definition of Operation. This is implemented as an initialization action in which an identification reference for the interface definition assumed by the Environment module is reported to the support code using the Perform mechanism. If there is a mismatch then the support code will abort the user program and issue a suitable error message.

Using the Environment module the complete temperature/humidity monitoring program takes the form:

```
program TemperatureHumidityControlSystem (Output);

  monitor module Environment in Library;

  monitor module Bell in Library
    (Where const NumberOfRequests = 2;);

  monitor module TemperatureDisplay in Library;

  process module TemperatureSensor in Library;

  monitor module HumidityDisplay in Library;

  process module HumiditySensor in Library;

  begin *** end {TemperatureHumidityControlSystem}.
```

The Bell module may be implemented as follows:

```
monitor module Bell;
  var BellRequests: 0..NumberOfRequests;
      BellOn, BellOff: Environment.Operation;

  procedure *Start;
    begin
      BellRequests := BellRequests + 1;
      if BellRequests = 1 then Perform (BellOn)
    end {Start};

  procedure *Stop;
    begin
      BellRequests := BellRequests - 1;
      if BellRequests = 0 then Perform (BellOff)
    end {Stop};

  begin {Bell}
    BellRequests := 0;
    BellOn.Facility := Environment.Bell;
    BellOn.Switch := Environment.On;
    BellOff.Facility := Environment.Bell;
    BellOff.Switch := Environment.Off;
    ***;
```

```
      if BellRequests <> 0 then Perform (BellOff)
   end {Bell};
```

Operation records to switch the bell on and off are set up as part of the initialization of the monitor. Switching the bell on and off then simply requires a call to Perform with the appropriate record.

Completed versions of the temperature display and sensor modules may be expressed thus:

```
monitor module TemperatureDisplay;
   var TemperatureOutput: Environment.Operation;

   procedure *Show (Temperature: Integer);
     begin
        TemperatureOutput.Temperature := Temperature;
        Perform (TemperatureOutput)
     end {Show};

begin
   TemperatureOutput.Facility := Environment.TemperatureDisplay;
   ***
end {TemperatureDisplay};


process module TemperatureSensor;
   const LowBound = ...; HighBound = ...;
   var T: Integer;
       TemperatureInput: Environment.Operation;

   function CurrentTemperature: Integer;
     begin
        Perform (TemperatureInput);
        CurrentTemperature := TemperatureInput.Temperature
     end {CurrentTemperature};

   begin {TemperatureSensor}
      TemperatureInput.Facility := Environment.TemperatureSensor;
      while True do
        begin
           T := CurrentTemperature;
           TemperatureDisplay.Show (T);
           if (T < LowBound) or (T > HighBound) then
             begin
                Bell.Start;
                repeat
                   T := CurrentTemperature;
                   TemperatureDisplay.Show (T);
                until (T > LowBound) and (T < HighBound);
                Bell.Stop
             end
        end
   end {TemperatureSensor};
```

Again the operation records are set up in advance, as far as is possible, thereby simplifying the work involved in triggering each operation.

The humidity sensor and display modules are identical in form to those shown for temperature monitoring.

Time constraints on the response to external events

In most of the problems considered in earlier chapters the execution time of the programs involved was relatively unimportant. It was assumed, of course, that the programs would be constructed in an adequate form but there were no explicit performance requirements mentioned in any of the problem specifications. The omission of time constraints from a specification usually implies that each input data item is *static* – that is, the data items exists on entry to the program and are read into main memory whenever the program is ready to process the data. In real-time systems the input data items are presented to the program dynamically and it is the responsibility of the system to deal with those items as they arrive. If this requirement cannot be met then, in some instances, the data will be lost and the program fails or behaves in some unsatisfactory way as a result.

Consider, for example, a program that is required to handle keyboard input from a VDU operating in *full-duplex* mode. In *half-duplex* mode all characters typed on the keyboard are sent directly to the VDU screen. In full duplex mode there is no direct connection between the keyboard and screen, as implied in Figure 9.2.

Characters typed on the keyboard are transmitted to the program which then sends back a response to the VDU screen. That response might be to echo back the same character or to return a bell character indicating that the character typed is not one of the set of characters expected at that point.

The time taken for the program to accept one character, respond to it, and return for the next character must be such that the program is always ready to receive each character that arrives, otherwise a character may be missed.

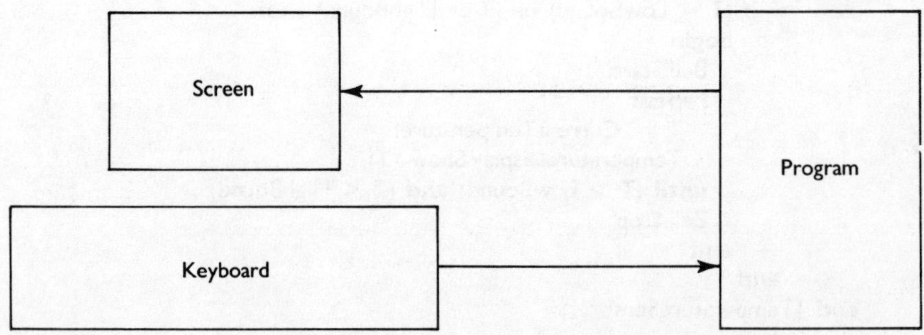

Figure 9.2 VDU operating in full duplex mode

One way to reduce the cycle time is to break the direct connection between the parts of the program that process the characters and the part that reads them. In general this can be achieved for most devices by associating a *device driver* process with the device connection and making the driver communicate with other parts of the program through a suitably defined buffer, using the techniques outlined in Chapter 7. Thus, for example, a keyboard driver might be responsible for reading characters from the keyboard and putting them into a buffer, using a loop of the form:

```
repeat
    accept a typed character;
    put character into buffer
until end of program
```

Input characters will then be lost only if the cycle time for the loop is still too slow, or if the buffer becomes full. (In the latter case it is common practice to issue an audible tone to warn the user that the last character typed has been ignored.)

The number of operations executed in the driver loop of a device process can be minimized through careful programming. However, the 'actual' speed of execution of any process is affected by competition for processing power from other processes in the program, as discussed in Chapter 2. The underlying support code should attempt to share the available processor power as fairly as possible among the active processes but in cases where it is wished to favor particular processes they can be given a high priority. In Pascal Plus, for example, each process has an initial default priority of Maxint DIV 2 which can be modified through a call of a standard procedure, Set-Priority, thus:

```
SetPriority (2)
```

With this facility, processes whose execution speeds are critical can be given a higher priority status (i.e. a low priority value!) than central processor-bound processes so that they are then more likely to obtain a central processor whenever they require it. The strategy for allocating processes to processors is discussed in Chapter 2.

Case study: management of interaction with a VDU

This section continues the development of the low-level VDU handler discussed in the preceding section and shows how modules providing higher level facilities can be built on top of that basic handler.

Basic VDU Handler

A basic VDU handler module provides access to a stream of characters from a VDU keyboard and accepts a stream of characters for output to the VDU screen. As a VDU is effectively two devices in one the internal structure of the VDU handler module might include a separate module for the keyboard and screen, thus:

```
monitor module VDUHandler;

   monitor module ScreenHandler;
      procedure *Write (Ch: Char);
         {Sends character Ch to screen returning when}
         {the character has been accepted for output.  }
      begin
         {initially, prepare to write characters: the    }
         {screen is cleared and the cursor is placed at}
         {the top left hand corner                       }
      end {ScreenHandler};

   monitor module KeyboardHandler;
      procedure *Read (var Ch: Char);
         {Receives a character from the keyboard returning}
         {when a character is available.                  }
      begin
         {initially, prepare to read characters}
      end {KeyboardHandler};

   {Interface Operations}
   procedure *Read = KeyboardHandler.Read;
   procedure *Write = ScreenHandler.Write;

   begin {initially, prepare to read and write} end {VDUHandler};
```

This VDUHandler module provides two interface operations: one to read a single character from the keyboard and the other to write a single character to the screen. These operations are equated with the corresponding operations provided by the local keyboard and screen handler modules.

As discussed already, both input from the keyboard and output to the screen are buffered. If we consider the screen and keyboard to be two separate devices then an expanded module diagram for the VDUHandler might take the form shown in Figure 9.3.

The keyboard input rate is unpredictable, but relatively slow, so a buffer size of forty characters (say) is normally adequate for most applications. The buffer can be declared as an instance of the MultipleItemBuffer of Chapter 7, thus:

```
monitor module KeyboardBuffer = MultipleItemBuffer in Library
   (Where const MaxItems = 40; type ItemType = Char;);
```

Output to the screen is also buffered. Screen output tends to occur in bursts in which characters are produced faster than they can be displayed. Thus, a screen buffer serves to smooth out the mismatch in speed between the unpredictable production rate and the fixed display rate. The buffer size will vary from one application to another, but in general it should be large enough to hold at least a few lines of output, say 200 characters:

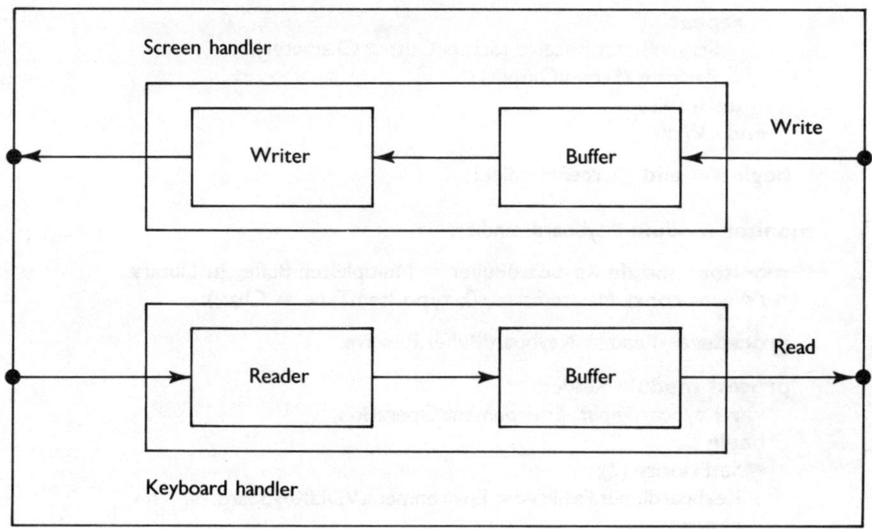

Figure 9.3 VDUHandler module structure

```
monitor module ScreenBuffer = MultipleItemBuffer in Library
  (Where const MaxItems = 200; type ItemType = Char;);
```

If we now assume that VDU operations are performed using records of
the form:

```
type Operation = record
              case *Facility: ExternalConnections of
                . . .
              VDUScreen, VDUKeyboard;
              ( *Character: Char);
                . . .
          end;
```

a complete implementation of the VDUHandler module might be expressed as
follows:

```
monitor module VDUHandler;

  monitor module ScreenHandler;

    monitor module ScreenBuffer = MultipleItemBuffer in Library
      (Where const MaxItems = 200; type ItemType = Char;);

    procedure *Write = ScreenBuffer.Send;

    process module Writer;
      var ScreenOutput: Environment.Operation;
      begin
        SetPriority (2);
        ScreenOutput.Facility := Environment.VDUScreen;
```

```
        repeat
          ScreenBuffer.Receive (ScreenOutput.Character);
          Perform (ScreenOutput)
        until False
      end {Writer};

    begin *** end {ScreenHandler};

  monitor module KeyboardHandler;

    monitor module KeyboardBuffer = MultipleItemBuffer in Library
      (Where const MaxItems = 40; type ItemType = Char;);

    procedure *Read = KeyboardBuffer.Receive;

    process module Reader;
      var KeyboardInput: Environment.Operation;
      begin
        SetPriority (2);
        KeyboardInput.Facility := Environment.VDUKeyboard;
        repeat
          Perform (KeyboardInput);
          KeyboardBuffer.Send (KeyboardInput.Character)
        until False
      end {Reader};

    begin *** end {KeyboardHandler};

  {Interface Operations}
  procedure *Read = KeyboardHandler.Read;
  procedure *Write = ScreenHandler.Write;

begin *** end {VDUHandler};
```

Note that:

(a) Pascal Plus permits the Read and Write operations of the keyboard and
    screen handler modules to be equated directly with operations on the
    respective buffers, thereby avoiding the overhead that would result
    from successive procedure calls.

(b) The device handling processes have been given a high priority to help
    ensure that no characters are missed on input and that the output rate to
    the screen is as smooth and fast as possible.

(c) When the keyboard buffer becomes full the Reader process simply waits
    until space is available. Consequently some of the characters typed may
    be lost without the user being informed of this error. Modifying the
    VDUHandler module to deal with the loss of characters in a satisfactory
    way is rather awkward because the output of a warning bell character
    must be integrated with the activity of the ScreenHandler module. One
    solution is to introduce an Arbiter module to handle screen output at the
    lowest level, as shown in Figure 9.4.

The *arbiter* module can be expressed simply as follows:

```
monitor module Arbiter;
  var ScreenOutput: Environment.Operation;

  procedure *DoScreenOutput (Character: Char);
    begin
      ScreenOutput.Character := Character;
      Perform (ScreenOutput)
    end {DoScreenOutput};

  begin
    ScreenOutput.Facility := Environment.VDUScreen; ***
  end {Arbiter};
```

The Writer process then calls this procedure to display characters and the
repeat loop in the body of the Reader process is re-expressed as follows:

```
repeat
  Perform (KeyboardInput);
  KeyboardBuffer.TryToSend (KeyboardInput.Character, OK);
  if not OK then Arbiter.DoScreenOutput (Chr (Bell))
until False
```

A higher level terminal handler

The VDUHandler module provides simple character input and output operations that can be used for almost any type of terminal, including tele-

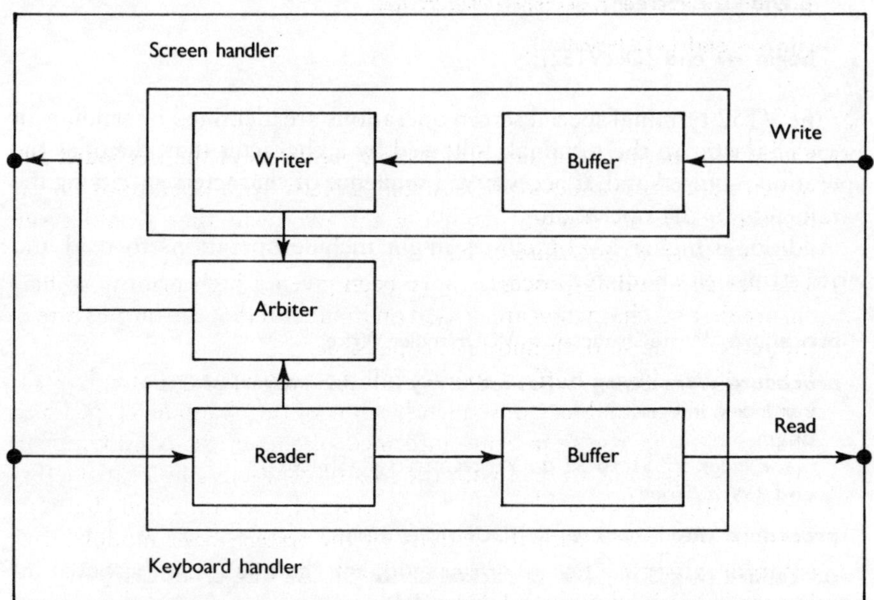

Figure 9.4 Modified VDUHandler module structure

typewriters. Modules defining interfaces for specific terminals may then be constructed on top of this basic handler. For example, operations to move the screen cursor and clear the screen might be implemented for a Dec VT52 terminal as follows:

```
envelope DecVT52;
   const *Xlimit = 79; *Ylimit = 23;
          Bell = 7;
          Return = 13;
          Escape = 27;
          CursorControl = 32;
             . . .
   type *Xcoordinate = 0..Xlimit; *Ycoordinate = 0..Ylimit;

   procedure *SetCursor (X: Xcoordinate; Y: Ycoordinate);
      begin
        VDUHandler.Write (Chr (Escape));
        VDUHandler.Write ('Y');
        VDUHandler.Write (Chr(CursorControl + Y));
        VDUHandler.Write (Chr(CursorControl + X))
      end {SetCursor};

   procedure *ClearScreen;
      begin
        SetCursor (0, 0);
        VDUHandler.Write (Chr (Escape));
        VDUHandler.Write ('J')
      end {ClearScreen};
             . . .
   begin *** end {DecVT52};
```

For the VT52 terminal special screen operations are identified by sending an Escape character to the terminal, followed by a character that identifies the operation required and, if necessary, a sequence of characters specifying the parameters to the operation.

Additional higher level facilities might include operations to read and write strings of characters, thus:

```
procedure *WriteCharacter = VDUHandler.Write;

procedure *WriteString (S: packed array [S1..S2: Integer] of Char);
   var Index: Integer;
   begin
     for Index := S1 to S2 do WriteCharacter (S[Index])
   end {WriteString};

procedure *ReadCharacter = VDUHandler.Read;

procedure *ReadString (var S: packed array [S1..S2: Integer] of Char;
                        var Length: Integer);
   var Index: Integer;
       Ch: Char;
```

```
  begin
    Index := 0;
    repeat
      ReadCharacter (Ch);
      if Ch = Chr (RubOut)
      then {delete last character typed − if any}
        begin
          if Index = 0
          then {output string is empty − issue warning}
            WriteCharacter (Chr (Bell))
          else {delete character from screen and input string}
            begin
              {move cursor back one position}
              WriteCharacter (Chr (Escape));
              WriteCharacter ('D');
              {clear character at that position}
              WriteCharacter ('  ');
              {move cursor back again}
              WriteCharacter (Chr (Escape));
              WriteCharacter ('D');
              Index := Index − 1
            end
        end
      else
        if Ch <> Chr (Return) then
          if Index = S2
          then {output string is full − issue warning}
            WriteCharacter (Chr (Bell))
          else {echo and save character}
            begin
              WriteCharacter (Ch);
              Index := Index + 1;
              S[Index] := Ch
            end
    until Ch = Chr (Return);
    Length := Index
  end {ReadString};
```

The value of S1 in the conformant array parameter to ReadString is
assumed to be 1 (as for all Pascal strings). This routine reads characters and
builds up a message string until the Return key is pressed. If the input string
exceeds the defined string limit the user is warned by the VDU bell and the
character typed is ignored. Characters in the input string may be deleted
from the current cursor position backwards using the RubOut key. Each
depression of this key moves the string index pointer back one position, if
possible, and adjusts the screen display accordingly.

The DecVT52 module illustrates how a module might be developed for a
specific type of terminal. It should be noted, however, that as an aid to portability it is usually preferable not to build such terminal-specific details into
a program. A better approach is to keep terminal descriptions on disk and

then read in the appropriate description when the user has identified his terminal type. For most terminals a description can be given as the sequence of control characters needed to perform each of the main terminal operations, such as clearing the screen and moving the cursor.

Real-time program simulation

Many real-time programs cannot be developed in the environment in which they are intended to run. It is clearly undesirable, for example, for a program controlling the guidance of a missile or the operation of a nuclear power station to be tested *in situ* as any faults in the logic of the programs concerned are likely to have a serious effect on their operating environment. Real-time programs of this type must first be tested in an environment that simulates each external operation in some appropriate way. The host environment can also be used to investigate the likely performance characteristics of such programs by means of the discrete event simulation techniques discussed in Chapter 8, i.e. by representing the performance of each environment operation as a corresponding delay of the process that instigated the operation, and then studying the overall effect.

It is important to note, however, that the time taken to execute the program statements should also be taken into account. In practice, this cannot be predicted accurately but, in some cases, it can be ignored if the statement execution time is insignificant in relation to the time taken by environment operations.

As an illustration of this real-time program simulation technique we shall develop a simulation model for the car park control program discussed in Chapter 4. Here, the physical effect of logical errors in the program is less severe than in a missile or nuclear power station but development in a simulation environment is still advantageous.

As a reminder, the basic operation of the car park is as follows:

(a) The car park has two entrances and one exit.
(b) At each entrance there is a barrier which must be raised to allow a car to enter the park. The arrival of a car is detected by an underground sensor. A second sensor beyond the barrier recognizes when a car has entered the park, thus enabling the barrier to be lowered again. The pair of sensors must be triggered in the expected order otherwise the barrier remains down.
(c) At the exit there is a similar barrier that operates in the same way.
(d) If the car park becomes full a large *car park full* sign is illuminated (visible at both entrances) and when a car approaches an entrance its barrier remains down.

The operation record defining the environment operations available in this case takes the following form:

```
type Operation = record
                    case Facility: ExternalConnections of
                    ExternalIdentification:
                        (Number: Integer);
                    Entrance1, Entrance2, Exit:
                        (Stage: BarrierOperation);
                    FullSign:
                        (Switch: SignOperation)
              end;
```

where

```
type ExternalConnections = (ExternalIdentification,
                            Entrance1, Entrance2, Exit, FullSign);
     BarrierOperation = (Raise, Lower,
                         AwaitCarAtSensor1, AwaitCarAtSensor2);
     SignOperation = (On, Off);
```

This definition provides a means of switching the full sign on and off and
for controlling the operations performed at each barrier. As before, an
initialization facility is also provided which confirms that the operation
definition is that expected by the environment.

The complete top-level implementation of the car park control program
is as follows:

```
program CarPark;

  monitor module Environment in Library;

  monitor module ParkingSpace in Library
    (Where const SpaceLimit = ...;);

  process Entrance in Library;
  instance Entrance1: Entrance (Environment.Entrance1);
           Entrance2: Entrance (Environment.Entrance2);

  process module Exit in Library;

  process module FullSign in Library;

  begin *** end {CarPark}.
```

If it is assumed that the ParkingSpace module enables the FullSign process to
await the car park becoming full and then nonfull, the ParkingSpace module
can be expressed thus:

```
monitor module ParkingSpace;
  var SpaceFree: 0..SpaceLimit;
  instance NonEmpty, Full, NonFull: Condition;

  procedure *Acquire;
    begin
      if SpaceFree = 0 then NonEmpty.Wait;
      SpaceFree := SpaceFree - 1;
      if SpaceFree = 0 then Full.Signal
    end {Acquire};
```

```
  procedure *Release;
    begin
      if SpaceFree = 0 then NonFull.Signal;
      SpaceFree := SpaceFree + 1;
      NonEmpty.Signal
    end {Release};

  procedure *AwaitFull;
    begin
      if SpaceFree > 0 then Full.Wait
    end {AwaitFull};

  procedure *AwaitNonFull;
    begin
      if SpaceFree = 0 then NonFull.Wait
    end {AwaitNonFull};

  begin SpaceFree := SpaceLimit; *** end {ParkingSpace};
```

while the FullSign process takes the form:

```
  process module FullSign;
    var SignOn, SignOff: Environment.Operation;
    begin
      SignOn.Facility := Environment.FullSign;
      SignOn.Switch := Environment.On;
      SignOff.Facility := Environment.FullSign;
      SignOff.Switch := Environment.Off;
      repeat
        ParkingSpace.AwaitFull;
        Perform (SignOn);
        ParkingSpace.AwaitNonFull;
        Perform (SignOff)
      until False
    end {FullSign};
```

The FullSign process is suspended on the Full queue until all the parking
spaces are exhausted. This is detected in the Acquire procedure. After
switching on the full sign the FullSign process calls AwaitNonFull and is suspended on the NonFull queue from where it is reactivated following the
release of a parking space.

As in earlier examples the operation records in the FullSign process are set
up initially so that each environment operation can be triggered simply by
applying Perform to the appropriate record.

The Entrance and Exit processes follow a similar pattern:

```
  process Entrance (Identity: Environment.ExternalConnections);
    var AwaitCarAtSensor1, AwaitCarAtSensor2,
        RaiseBarrier, LowerBarrier: Environment.Operation;
    begin
    {initialize environment records}
        . . .
```

```
            repeat
                Perform (AwaitCarAtSensor1);
                ParkingSpace.Acquire;
                Perform (RaiseBarrier);
                Perform (AwaitCarAtSensor2);
                Perform (LowerBarrier)
            until False
        end (Entrance);

    process module Exit;
        var AwaitCarAtSensor1, AwaitCarAtSensor2,
            RaiseBarrier, LowerBarrier: Environment.Operation;
        begin
        {initialize environment records}
            . . .
            repeat
                Perform (AwaitCarAtSensor1);
                ParkingSpace.Release;
                Perform (RaiseBarrier);
                Perform (AwaitCarAtSensor2);
                Perform (LowerBarrier)
            until False
        end {Exit};
```

To simulate the execution of this program each of the environment
operations must be simulated. This is achieved by including an explicit
Perform procedure in the program to interpret each perform call appropriately, together with the usual Times and Clock monitors:

```
    program CarParkSimulation (Output);

        monitor module Environment in Library;

        monitor module Times in Library;

        monitor module Clock in Library
            (Where const TimeLimit = Times.SimulationPeriod;
                   const EntityLimit = 4 {number of processes};
                     type TimeType = Real;);

        monitor module State in Library;

        procedure Perform in Library;
            . . .
        begin *** end {CarParkSimulation};
```

The following characteristics of the system are assumed:

(a) the car park holds one hundred cars;
(b) on average, sixty cars arrive per hour (exponential distribution);
(c) on average, a car stays for one hour with a standard deviation of
     twenty-five minutes (normal distribution);
(d) a barrier is raised and lowered in three seconds;

(e) the time taken for a car to pass through a barrier is ten seconds with a standard deviation of two seconds (normal distribution);

(f) the time taken to switch the *car park full* sign on and off is negligible.

A simulation version of the Perform procedure might be expressed as follows:

```
procedure Perform (var Op: Environment.Operation);
  begin
    with Op, Environment, Clock do
    case Facility of
      Entrance1, Entrace2, Exit:
        case Stage of
          AwaitCarAtSensor1:
            if Facility = Exit
            then Hold (Times.TextDeparture − PseudoTime)
            else Hold (Times.NextArrival − PseudoTime);
          AwaitCarAtSensor2:
            Hold (Times.BarrierTraversal);
          Raise, Lower:
            Hold (Times.BarrierUpOrDown);
        end;
      FullSign:;
    end
  end {Perform};
```

where the Times module is implemented thus:

```
monitor module Times;
  const * SimulationPeriod = 43200;   {12 hours}
        * BarrierUpOrDown = 3;
          ArrivalMean = 60;             {one car per minute}
          StayMean = 3600;              {one hour}
          StayDeviation = 1500;         {25 minutes}
          TraversalMean = 10;
          TraversalDeviation = 2;
          NumberOfCars = 1000; {must be > expected mean of 720}

  monitor module BasicDistributions in Library;

  monitor module Arrivals = Queue in Library
    (Where type ItemType = Real;);

  monitor module Departures = OrderedQueue in Library
    (Where type ItemType = Real;);

  function *NextArrival: Real;
    var Arrival: Real;
    begin
      Arrivals.Remove (Arrival);
      NextArrival := Arrival
    end {NextArrival};

  function *NextDeparture: Real;
    var Departure: Real;
```

```
      begin
         Departures.Remove (Departure);
         NextDeparture := Departure
      end {NextDeparture};

   function *BarrierTraversal: Real;
      var Traversal: Real;
      begin
         Traversal := BasicDistributions.Normal
            (TraversalMean, TraversalDeviation);
         if Traversal < 0
         then BarrierTraversal := 0
         else BarrierTraversal := Traversal
      end {BarrierTraversal};

   procedure Initialize;
      var C: 1..NumberOfCars;
            Arrival, Departure, LastArrival: Real;
      begin
         LastArrival := 0.0;
         with BasicDistributions do
         for C := 1 to NumberOfCars do
            begin
               Arrival := LastArrival + Exponential (1/ArrivalMean);
               LastArrival := Arrival;
               Arrivals.Append (Arrival);
               Departure := Normal (StayMean, StayDeviation);
               if Departure < 0.0 then Departure := 0.0;
               Departures.Enter (Arrival + Departure)
            end
      end {Initialize};

   begin Initialize; *** end {Times};
```

The arrival and departure times are generated as part of the initialization
of the Times module. The arrival times are generated in sequence, by sampling values from an exponential distribution. These values are held in a
simple queue. The departure times are derived from the arrival times and are
also put into a queue, ordered by departure time.

Note that in this application it may be beneficial to determine the arrival
and departure times separately and save the results in two files for repeated
use in successive runs of the simulation program, rather than calculating
these values each time the program is executed.

Summary

This chapter has discussed various aspects of concurrent program development that are particularly relevant to the application area of real-time programming.

Real-time programs are concurrent because they need to handle external events that occur unpredictably. Often it is necessary to react to such events quickly otherwise the events may go undetected. To avoid such errors processes are dedicated to handling device interaction and are often given high priorities so that they are more likely to be executed when they are ready to run. Also communication with external devices is generally buffered.

Real-time programs are often required to deal with many different types of physical device. For the general user, access to each device can be provided by a module that supplies suitable abstract operations for manipulating the device. Such device modules must be written with additional care since environment operations cannot be implemented entirely in a high-level language.

Real-time programs are usually developed in a simulated environment where they can be tested and evaluated more conveniently.

Further reading

Young, S.J. *Real-time Languages: design and development*, Ellis Horwood, 1982.

Exercises

9.1 Modify the VDU handler module developed in this chapter to meet the following requirements:

   (a) Screen output should be suspended if Control/S is pressed on the keyboard, and continued again if Control/S is pressed a second time.
   (b) A mechanism should be provided for clearing the contents of the screen buffer if an operation (to which the output relates) is canceled, following the user pressing Control/Y. For example, if the user asks for the contents of a text file to be displayed and then presses Control/Y, the output should be abandoned quickly even if there is a large amount of text in the screen buffer.

9.2 Complete the LinePrinters module that was partly developed in Chapter 6, by defining suitable low-level operations to drive the printers.

9.3 Develop a module that enables processes to set and inspect the current value of real-time, and also to delay their further execution, either up to a specified time, or for a specified period of time.

9.4 Implement the filling station control program (discussed in Chapter 3) in a form suitable for development in a simulated environment.

Ten

GENERAL-PURPOSE
OPERATING SYSTEMS

A general-purpose operating system manages the resources of a computing facility on behalf of the users of that facility. Typically, such resources include main and secondary memory, peripheral devices, processor power and network links to other computing facilities. The operating system is required to administer such resources *effectively*. For the first computers available commercially 'effectively' meant ensuring that the best use was made of (what was then) a very expensive piece of equipment. For the operating system, this meant sharing scarce resources among a large number of competing users and being hampered by a requirement that it should make minimal use of those resources! Today, computers are relatively cheap and can be found amongst the many electrical devices that are present in most homes. Modern computers generally have substantial amounts of both main memory and processor power. As a consequence, modern operating systems can be designed to provide a good service for users without worrying unduly about the resources that are needed to implement that service.

The purpose of this chapter is to clarify the responsibilities of an operating system and to discuss, briefly, the structure and representation of the software concerned. Most emphasis is placed on the concurrency aspects of operating system design.

From an implementation point of view, there is very little distinction between a real-time system and an operating system. Both, for example, involve concurrent behavior, both involve a substantial amount of interaction with external devices and both may have time constraints on their interaction with those devices. Because of these similarities much of the material presented in Chapter 9, on real-time systems, applies equally to operating systems and will not be repeated here.

The main distinguishing characteristic of a *general-purpose* operating system is that it supports software development, which means that it must be capable of loading and supervising the execution of user software.

Two types of operating system are discussed in this chapter:

(a) those for traditional computer architectures comprising one or more central processors sharing the same main memory;
(b) those for computing systems in which processing nodes are connected together in a network fashion.

Both types of architecture were described in Chapter 2.

Operating systems for traditional computing facilities

An operating system gives its users access to computing facilities. The use of those facilities is requested via *commands*, expressed in a *command language*. Commands may be given individually or combined as *command procedures*. Commands are presented to an operating system via an input device, such as an interactive terminal, a cardreader or a paper tape reader. A sequence of related commands (and possibly accompanying program code and data) supplied noninteractively is called a *job*. The commands are then said to be expressed in a *job description* or *job control language*. (The terms used here have many variations but the concepts are general. The main point to appreciate is that an operating system receives commands to which it must respond in some appropriate manner.)

Commands may be processed by an operating system in one of two ways:

(a) they may be processed as they are received, with the input of further commands delayed until the processing of the current command is complete, or
(b) they may be processed independently of, and possibly in parallel with, the input of further commands.

Technique (a) is often referred to as *foreground* processing and is only applicable to commands issued interactively via terminals. Technique (b) is known as *background* processing and may be used regardless of the means of command input.

A general configuration diagram for a traditional computing facility is shown in Figure 10.1, and a corresponding (simplified) first-level module diagram for an operating system suitable for such a facility is given in Figure 10.2.

The *interactive interface* modules in the module diagram are responsible for accepting commands issued interactively at the terminals. These

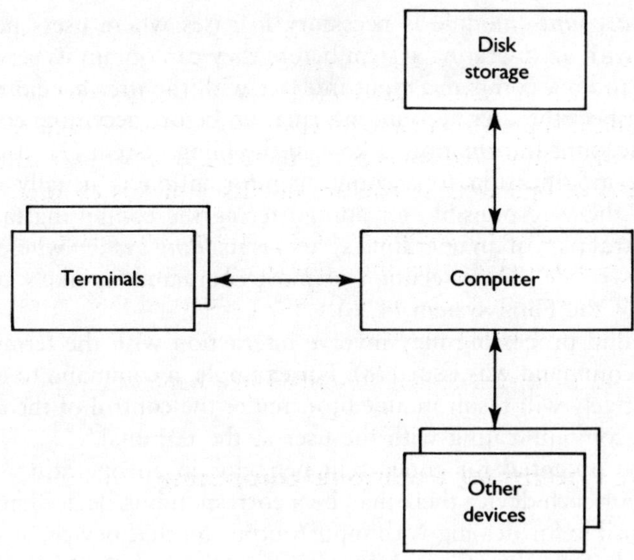

Figure 10.1 Traditional computing facility: configuration diagram

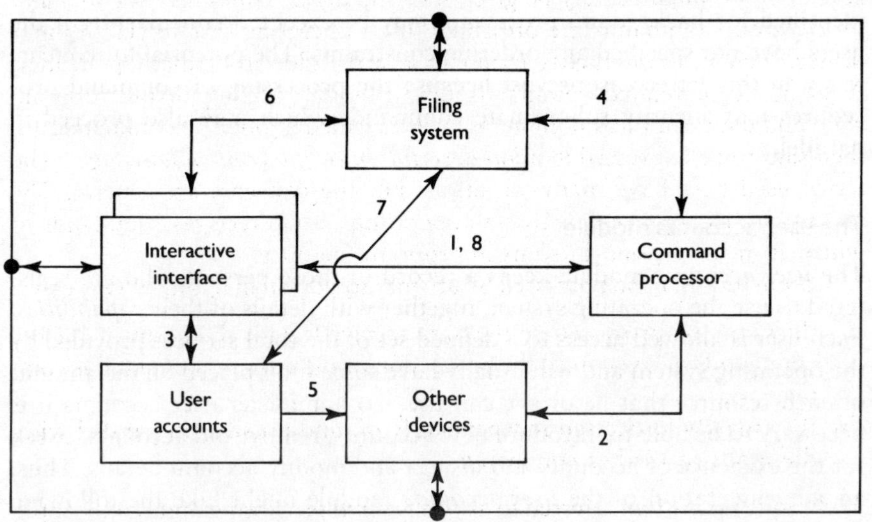

Figure 10.2 Traditional computing facility: operating system top level module structure

modules either respond directly to the commands that they receive or pass them to the *command processor* module (1) for its attention. The *command processor* may also receive commands from other input devices (2). The *other devices* module also handles operations on lineprinters, magnetic tape units, etc.

A *user accounts* module is necessary in cases where users need to be registered with an operating system before they can obtain its services. The modules handling command input interact with the *user accounts* module (3, 5) to inspect the user account information before accepting commands. The user account information is kept in the filing system (7). It should be noted that modification to accounting information is usually only performed by those responsible for administering the computing facility.

The central part of an operating system is its *filing system* where user and system files reside. The execution of most commands is likely to involve some use of the filing system (4, 6).

Foreground processing may involve interaction with the terminal from which the command was issued (8). For example, a command to edit a text file interactively will result in an editor, under the control of the *command processor*, communicating with the user at the terminal.

Note the potential for concurrent behavior in an operating system of this type. For each device there may be a corresponding device handler process responsible for dealing with input/output on that device, as described in Chapter 9. For each terminal there may also be a higher level process for managing the dialog with a user, to reflect the fact that such users interact with the operating system concurrently. In addition, the set of commands identified for background processing may be executed concurrently if the users have not specified any ordering constraints. The potential for concurrency in this latter case is vast because the processing of command procedures may identify subordinate commands which may also proceed in parallel.

The user accounts module

The *user accounts* module keeps a record of those persons who are registered to use the operating system, together with details of their *capabilities*. Each user is allowed access to a defined set of the total services provided by the operating system and will usually have some limit placed on the amount of each resource that he or she can use. To administer user accounts it is necessary to be able to introduce new accounts, remove old accounts, check for the existence of accounts and inspect and modify account details. Thus, an implementation of the *user accounts* module might take the following form:

```
monitor module UserAccounts;
  type
      *UserIdentification = ...;
      *String = ...;
      *Account = record
                    *UserNumber: UserIdentification;
                    *Password: String;
```

```
                        *SystemRights: ...;
                        *ResourceLimits: ...;
                            ...
                    end;
        procedure *Check (UserNumber: UserIdentification;
                          Password: String;
                          var Found: Boolean;
                          var User: Account);
          {If UserNumber exists then Found is set to True and the}
          {associated user account details are returned in User.   }
          {If UserNumber is not known then Found is set to False }
          {and the value of User is undefined.                    }
        procedure *Create (var User: UserAccount);
          {Creates an account and returns default user account}
          {details in User.                                   }
        procedure *Delete (UserNumber: UserIdentification;
                          var Accepted: Boolean);
          {If UserNumber is known then Accepted is set to True and }
          {the user account entry is deleted.                      }
          {If UserNumber is not known then Accepted is set to False.}
        procedure *SetPassword (UserNumber: UserIdentification;
                          NewPassword: String;
                          var Accepted: Boolean);
          {If UserNumber is known then Accepted is set True and the}
          {user's password is set to NewPassword.                  }
          {If UserNumber is not known then Accepted is set to False.}

        {Other procedures and functions to adjust system}
        {rights and resource limits                      }
                        ...

    begin
        {initially, prepare for account operations}
    end {UserAccounts};
```

Details of each user are kept in a Account record. A sample of the procedures that might be defined for inspecting and modifying user accounts is shown and the accompanying comments describe their purpose.

The interactive interface module

A possible modular representation for an *interactive interface* module is shown in Figure 10.3.

The *terminal manager* module is responsible for handling terminal input/output. This module can be based around the *VDU handler* module discussed in the previous chapter. In addition to low-level input/output it may be responsible for higher level operations such as the management of windows (on VDUs) or the basic validation of keyboard input.

The *command input* module is responsible for reading user commands

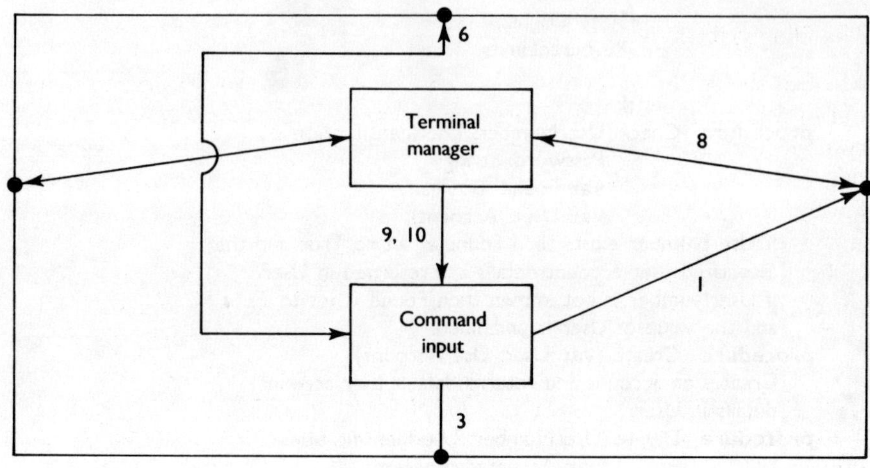

Figure 10.3 Interactive interface: module structure

(9) and either responding to them directly (10) or passing them to the *command processor* module for it to process (1).

The basic behavior of a *command input* module might be summarized as follows:

```
process CommandInput (T: Terminal);
   . . .
  begin
    repeat
     {await arrival of user at terminal T}
     {do log-in sequence to obtain UserNumber and Password}
      UserAccounts.Check (UserNumber, Password, UserKnown, User);
      if not UserKnown
      then {report authorization failure}
      else
        repeat
           {read command}
           {deal with command or pass it to the command processor}
        until {log-out command received}
      until False
    end {CommandInput};
```

Each instance of this CommandInput process deals with those users who interact with the operating system through a particular terminal T. Each user first 'logs in' by supplying (say) a user number and a password. If the user is known to the operating system the CommandInput process reads and acts upon the commands that the user makes, up to and including a command to 'log out'.

The filing system module

Most of the commands issued by a user involve the transfer of data in and out of a filing system that manages the secondary memory on disk. A filing system gives access to disk storage through a set of high-level operations that refer to storage areas by means of *logical* names. Such storage areas are known as *files*. Files are often arranged in a hierarchical tree structure, as suggested by Figure 10.4.

Each node in the tree is a file. The nonterminal nodes, known as *directories*, are files that contain descriptions of groups of other files.

The operating system users, in the scheme shown, each have a separate 'main' directory within which they may create local directories or other types of file. In general, there is no limit on the depth to which a user's file store tree can extend, subject to any disk space constraints imposed on that user.

Each file in the filing system is identified uniquely by the name of the directory in which it appears, together with the name by which the file is known within that directory. This combination defines a *path name*. Thus, in general, a file is named by the path taken from the root of the tree to its position in the tree. For example, the path name of File-2 in Figure 10.4 is:

Root-directory.User-2-directory.Local-directory-1.File-2

A file is described by an entry in the directory in which it is defined. Apart from the name of the file the directory entry will hold, typically, the physical

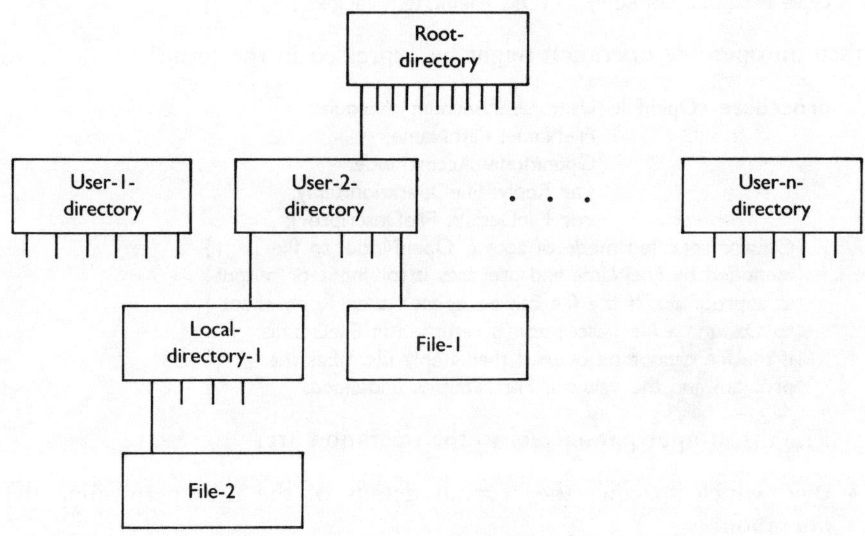

Figure 10.4 Hierarchical filing system structure

location of the file on disk, the space occupied by the file and an indication of its type (e.g. text, directory). In many operating systems a file is treated as a sequence of fixed-length data records, or *blocks* which may be accessed sequentially or directly, depending on the file type.

A filing system will generally provide a very large number of operations for file manipulation. In particular, a set of operations is often defined for each distinct type of file processed. Thus, for example, there may be operations defined for text files and others for the manipulation of directories. What all user files generally have in common, however, is that each must be *opened* before any data is either written to it or read from it, and then *closed* when the processing of its data is complete. From the point of view of concurrent processing, the significant actions associated with each open and close operation are the corresponding acquisition and release of *access* to the file concerned. As described in Chapter 6, processes writing to a file generally require exclusive access to that file while any process inspecting the contents of the file may do so concurrently with other reading processes.

If access to a file is obtained then an attempt is made to locate the file on disk, which may involve opening and searching through a sequence of directories. For an output file that does not exist a directory entry for the file is created. An existing file is made ready for input. If a file cannot be opened for any reason then access to it is released.

If we assume that the possible responses to a file operation may include an indication that the file does not exist or is currently in use, as implied by the following definition:

```
type FileOperationReply = (OK, FileInUse, FileUnknown, ...)
```

then an open file operation might be expressed in the form:

```
procedure *OpenFile (User: UserAccounts.Account;
                     FileName: PathName;
                     OpenMode: AccessMode;
                     var Reply: FileOperationReply;
                     var FileDetails: FileDescriptor);
   {Obtains specified mode of access, OpenMode, to file        }
   {Identified by FileName and prepares it for input or output}
   {as appropriate. If the file can be opened then Reply is set }
   {to OK and a file description is returned in FileDetails.     }
   {If the file cannot be opened then Reply identifies the       }
   {problem and the value of FileDetails is undefined.           }
```

The three input parameters to the operation are:

- User, which specifies the account details of the user performing the operation.
- FileName, which specifies the full path name of the file to be opened.
- OpenMode, which specifies the required opening mode.

If the file can be opened then a descriptor for that file is returned. This descriptor is then quoted in each subsequent operation performed on the file. For example, the operation to close the file may take the form:

```
procedure *CloseFile (var ThisFile: FileDetails;
                      var Reply: FileOperationReply);
```

The operations that can be applied to a file, once opened, are dictated by the acquired access mode, namely:

(a) 'read' access means that data can only be read from the file, whereas,
(b) 'write' access means that existing file data can be read, or deleted, or overwritten and that the file can be extended with new data.

In some operating systems files have to be created explicitly before they can be manipulated. In others, a file that does not exist is created automatically as a consequence of trying to open it for output.

A possible modular design for the *filing system* module is shown in Figure 10.5. The *disk space manager* module administers the space available on disk, the *disk handler* module deals with the transfer of data to and from disk and the *file access manager* module controls shared access to files.

The disk space manager module

The *disk space manager* module can be based on a reduced version of the NamedMFromN resource allocation module which was discussed in Chapter 6. Assuming that disk space is administered as a set of physical disk blocks of fixed size then the *disk space manager* module might take the form:

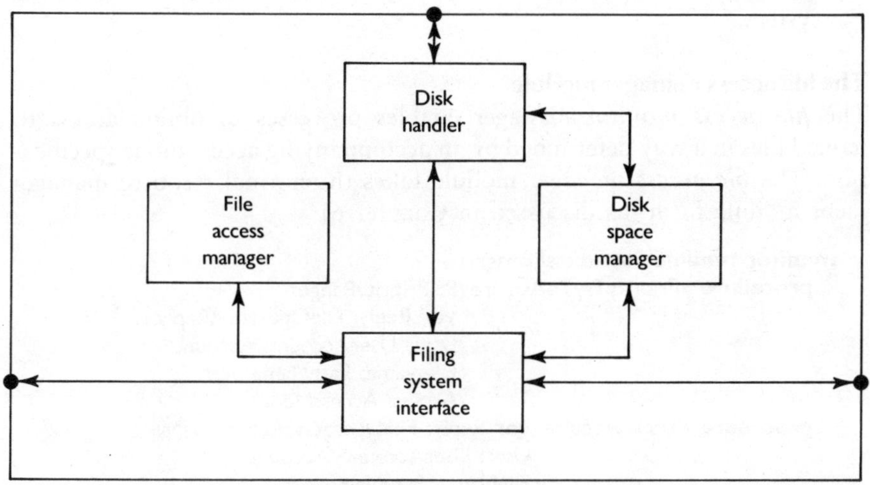

Figure 10.5 Filing system: module structure

```
monitor module DiskSpaceManager;
  procedure *TryToAcquire (var Allocation: SetOfBlocks;
                                  Needed: Integer;
                                  var Given: Boolean);
    {Tries to acquire access to the number of disk blocks    }
    {specified by Needed.                                     }
    {If the allocation can be made then Given is set to True}
    {and the identity of the disk blocks is returned in       }
    {Allocation.                                              }
    {If the allocation cannot be made then Given is set to    }
    {False and the value of Allocation is undefined.          }
  procedure *Release (Allocation: SetOfBlocks);
    {Release access to the set of disk blocks identified by}
    {Allocation.                                           }
begin
    {initially, read disk space allocation details from disk}
  end {DiskSpaceManager};
```

Calls of the procedure TryToAcquire enable a specified number of disk
blocks to be obtained. Control is returned immediately to the *filing system
interface* module reporting the result of the operation. Procedure Release
enables space that was previously allocated to be returned. (Note that the
SetOfBlocks type can be implemented as a linked list of disk addresses.)

There are no facilities to enable processes to wait for disk space to
become free. The reasons for this limitation are:

(a) waiting might result in deadlock because users must be able to acquire
    disk space incrementally;
(b) disk space should always be available anyway since any shortage will
    result in a serious degradation of the performance of the operating
    system.

The file access manager module

The *file access monitor* manager enables processes to obtain access to
named files in a way determined by an accompanying access mode specification. The *file access manager* module takes the normal resource management module form (as discussed in Chapter 6):

```
monitor module FileAccessManager;
  procedure *PriorityTryToAcquire (P: PriorityRange;
                                 var Reply: FileOperationReply;
                                 User: UserAccounts.Account;
                                 FileName: PathName;
                                 Access: AccessMode);
  procedure *TryToAcquire (var Reply: FileOperationReply;
                               User: UserAccounts.Account;
                               FileName: PathName;
                               Access: AccessMode);
  procedure *PriorityAcquire (P: PriorityRange;
```

```
                              var Reply: FileOperationReply;
                                  User: UserAccounts.Account;
                                  FileName: PathName;
                                  Access: AccessMode);
        procedure *Acquire (User: UserAccounts.Account;
                                  var Reply: FileOperationReply;
                                  FileName: PathName;
                                  Access: AccessMode);
        procedure *Release (FileName: PathName;
                                  Access: AccessMode);
        begin
            {initially, all files are free}
        end {FileAccessManager};
```

Users generally need to be able to obtain access to files incrementally, so there is potential for deadlock here. One way to deal with the problem is to use only the tentative acquisition operations and so avoid waiting. Thus, any user operation involving files to which access cannot be granted immediately may have to be abandoned if those files are in use.

Another approach is to detect and recover from deadlock by using the strategy outlined in Chapter 6. The form of the operations defined for the FileAccessManager monitor allows for this possibility. That is, the identity of each user is specified thereby enabling a resource dependency graph to be formed. In addition, the operations committed to waiting for access to file include a Reply parameter enabling a failure reply to be returned. A test for deadlock might be performed in this case by a local process which attempts, periodically (say every five minutes), to reduce the resource-dependency graph. If the graph cannot be reduced then deadlock is present. A recovery can be made by reactivating one or more processes present in the reduced graph to permit it to be fully reduced. Each process reactivated then returns from the FileAccessManager monitor with a failure message.

The disk handler module

The *disk handler* module might take the following form:

```
        monitor module DiskHandler;
        procedure *Transfer (Location: DiskAddress;
                                  Direction: TransferDirection;
                                  var Data: DataBlock;
                                  var Reply: DiskOperationReply);
            {Attempts to transfer the data identified by Data}
            {either to or from the disk, at address Location,   }
            {according to the value of Direction. The value     }
            {of Reply indicates the result of the operation.}

                        . . .

        begin
            {initially, prepare for disk operations}
        end {DiskHandler};
```

The only operation shown is Transfer, which enables data blocks to be written to or read from disk. There may also be operations to inspect the status of the disk or perform some maintenance check. Each data transfer operation specifies a disk address and the direction of transfer. For an output operation the data to be transferred is also defined. The parameter Reply is used to indicate the result of each operation.

The data that reside on disk may be interpreted in different ways in different parts of the operating system. This means that it is necessary to be able to change dynamically the type associated with the data. One possibility is to provide a language facility for declaring a 'weak type', values of which can be assigned to variables of a 'compatible' type. Two types are considered to be compatible if their values have the same storage requirement. Thus, for example, if the DataBlock type is defined as:

```
type
   Byte = 0..255;
   DataBlock = weak packed array [1..512] of Byte;
```

then values of type DataBlock are compatible with values of type CharacterBlock:

```
type CharacterBlock = array [1..512] of Char;
```

provided that values of types Char and Byte occupy the same volume of main memory (say eight bits).

An alternative means of converting a value from one type to another is to use a type transfer function, similar to the Ord and Chr functions of Pascal. That is, a function whose name identifies the desired target type and whose value is a variable or expression of a compatible type. For example, a call to procedure Transfer of the DiskHandler monitor to read a block of characters might be expressed thus:

```
DiskHandler.Transfer (Location, Direction, DataBlock(Data), Reply);
```

where the variable Data is declared as follows:

```
var Data: CharacterBlock;
```

Internally, the DiskHandler monitor is organized to ensure that disk transfers are performed efficiently. In a multi-user operating system this is particularly important as the disk is a heavily used resource. Because of its importance, the structure of the DiskHandler monitor is now discussed in more detail.

The disk handler monitor

A magnetic disk has one or more surfaces of magnetic material on which data can be stored. The disk rotates at a fixed speed and data is transferred to and from the disk via read/write heads that hover a short distance above the rotating surface(s). Sometimes the heads are fixed in one position but more usually they are attached to an arm that can move across the disk surface(s) on a radial path.

Information is stored in concentric *tracks* on a disk surface, where a track is usually made up of a fixed number of data blocks, or *sectors*, each of which holds the same volume of data.

Disk storage may be provided as a set of individual *disk units* or as collections of disk units connected to the computer through one or more *disk controllers*. Disk transfers may, in practice, be performed in terms of individual disk blocks, or sequences of blocks, or sequences of records or even sequences of words or bytes. For illustration purposes, let us consider the very simple case of a single-surface disk that enables exactly one sector of data to be read or written in each transfer operation. A disk address may then be represented thus:

```
type DiskAddress = record
                Track: TrackRange;
                Sector: SectorRange
            end;
```

As the disk is shared by many processes it is necessary for each process to obtain exclusive access to the device before a transfer is attempted. A process can be assured of a reasonably fast response to a disk transfer request if the disk is held exclusively by each process only for the duration of one transfer. That is, each process acquires access to the disk before initiating a transfer and releases access immediately afterwards.

Often a disk unit will be busy to the extent that processes are regularly required to wait for access. This allows some optimization to be made because the amount of head movement can be reduced if the transfer requests are ordered in some suitable way. One approach is to always give access to the process that wishes to make a transfer closest to the current head position. However, with this *nearest track next* scheme there is a danger that processes attempting data transfers on the outer tracks of the disk will be starved of service. An alternative technique is to move the read/write head back and forth across the disk dealing only with transfer requests in the direction of the sweep. When all requests in one direction have been processed, the direction of sweep is reversed and the same procedure followed. This is known as the *scan*, or *escalator* algorithm.

For example, consider the situation where, at a particular instant, the read/write head is sitting at track 0 and is about to handle three requests for transfers on tracks 5, 24 and 68, respectively, as implied in Figure 10.6.

The first transfer attempted is the one on track 5. The sweep direction is set to Up and the head movement is initiated. At that point the processes requiring transfers on tracks 24 and 68 are suspended awaiting their turn to perform a transfer.

Two queues are maintained: one for each direction of sweep. Both of the

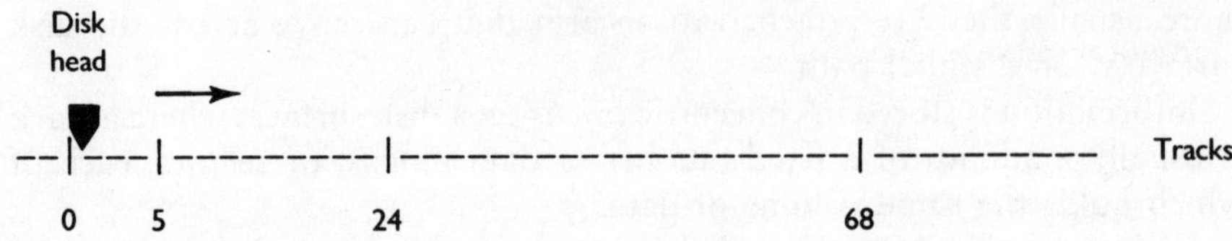

Figure 10.6 Scan algorithm: initial position

waiting processes are held on the Up queue as they will be taken in the current sweep of the disk:

SweepQueue [Up] → 24 → 68
SweepQueue [Down] → Nil

Assume that, as the head sets out for track 5, a group of three more processes arrive wishing to transfer data on tracks 50, 2 and 5, respectively. The tracks on which transfers are required are then as shown in Figure 10.7:

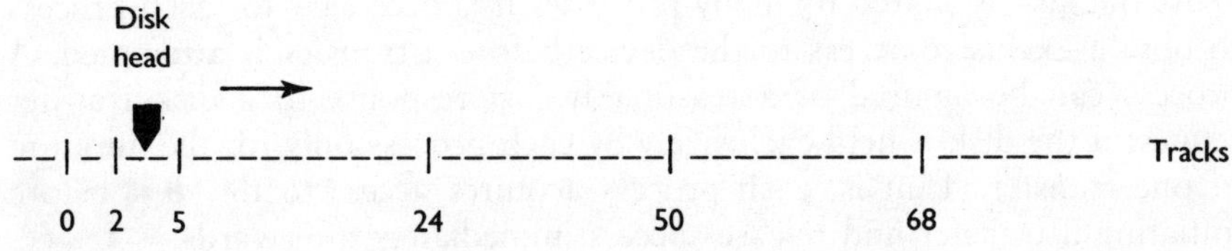

Figure 10.7 Scan algorithm: second position

The arriving processes are placed on the sweep queues as follows:

SweepQueue [Up] → 24 → 50 → 68
SweepQueue [Down] → 5 → 2

The first process (50) is suspended on the Up queue, ahead of the request for track 68. The second process (2) is placed on the Down queue, as the head will be beyond this position when it finally stops at track 5. Thus, the transfer on track 2 will only be attempted after all transfers in the current direction of sweep have been processed, together with any that are then between the head and track 2 when the head sweeps back down the disk. The third process (5) is also placed on the Down queue even though it too wishes to perform a transfer on the current destination track. This apparently harsh treatment is necessary to ensure that the head continues to make progress. Without such a restriction it is possible for starvation to occur as a result of some processes repeatedly performing transfers on the same track.

The following variation of the single resource monitor implements the scan algorithm for giving permission to a process to use the disk:

```
monitor module DiskAccess;
    {assumes type Range = nonnegative Integer subrange}
    {         const Limit = upper limit of Range         }
    type HeadDirection = (Up, Down);
    instance SweepQueue: array [HeadDirection] of Condition;
    var Sweep: HeadDirection;
        Busy: Boolean;
        Position: Range;

    procedure *Acquire (Target: Range);
      begin
        if Busy then {suspend process}
          if (Sweep = Up) and (Position < Target)
             or (Sweep = Down) and (Position <= Target)
          then SweepQueue [Up].PWait (Target)
          else SweepQueue [Down].PWait (Limit-Target);
        Busy := True;
        Position := Target
      end {Acquire};

    procedure *Release;
      begin
        {Change sweep direction if necessary}
        if SweepQueue [Sweep].Empty then
          if Sweep = Up
            then Sweep := Down
            else Sweep := Up;
        Busy := False;
        SweepQueue [Sweep].Signal
      end {Release};

    begin {DiskAccess}
      Sweep := Up;
      Busy := False;
      Position := 0;
      ***
    end {DiskAccess};
```

The Acquire procedure suspends a calling process on either the Up or Down queue using the Target track as a priority value. It is assumed that each process will move the head to the target track that is specified and so the recorded current position is adjusted to this value.

If it is assumed that the actual disk transfer is initiated using the Perform operation, as discussed in Chapter 9, then the entry in the external operation record might take the form:

```
type FileOperationReply = ( *OK, *ReadFail, *WriteFail, ... );
     Operation = record
                     case Facility: Externational Connections of
                         . . .
                     DiskIO:
                         (DiskBlock: DiskAddress;
```

```
                      Direction: TransferDirection;
                      Data: DataBlock;
                      Result: FileOperationReply);
                           . . .
              end;
```

If the DataBlock type is defined as an array of bytes, each data block will
have to be copied in and out of the Data field of an operation record on each
transfer. To avoid this overhead it is normal to pass the data by *reference*,
which can be achieved in Pascal by declaring DataBlock as a pointer type:

```
type Block = packed array [1..SizeOfBlock] of Byte;
     DataBlock = ↑ Block;
```

The complete DiskHandler module can now be expressed as:

```
monitor module DiskHandler;
   monitor module DiskAccess IN Library
      (Where const Limit = NumberOfTracks;
              type  Range = TrackRange;);

   procedure *Transfer (Location: DiskAddress;
                        Direction: TransferDirection;
                        var Data: DataBlock;
                        var Reply: FileOperationReply);
   const MaximumAttempts = 3 {say};
   var ATransfer: Operation;
       Attempts: 0..MaximumAttempts;
   begin {Transfer}
     Attempts := 0;
     ATransfer.Facility := DiskIO;
     ATransfer.DiskBlock := Location;
     ATransfer.Direction := Direction;
     ATransfer.Data := Data;
     repeat
       DiskAccess.Acquire (Location.Track);
       Perform (ATransfer);
       DiskAccess.Release;
       Attempts := Attempts + 1
     until (ATransfer.Result = OK) or (Attempts = MaximumAttempts);
     Reply := ATransfer.Result
   end {Transfer};

   begin *** end {DiskHandler};
```

Disk transfer failures are often transient and may succeed if the transfer is
attempted again. Thus the Transfer procedure has been expressed in such a
way as to take account of this possibility by repeating any failed transfer
several times and only then reporting a fault.

Note that the DiskHandler monitor as defined is actually incorrect. In its
present form there is no possibility of any process being delayed in the
DiskAccess monitor. Any execution of Transfer will result in other processes
being excluded until either a transfer has been completed or the operation

has failed. Concurrent access to Transfer can be enabled by defining it within an envelope, thus:

```
monitor module DiskHandler;
      . . .
    procedure *Transfer ( . . . ); . . . ;

    envelope *DiskInterface;
      procedure *Transfer ( . . . ); . . . ;
      begin *** end {DiskInterface};

    begin *** end {DiskHandler};
```

Access to the Transfer procedure is then obtained by declaring an instance of DiskInterface in a process or other envelope. To allow disk transfers to be instigated from a monitor a copy of the Transfer procedure might also be provided directly in the DiskHandler, as before. This correct form is messy which explains why it was not presented initially!

The command processor module

The *command processor* module is required to execute commands, either in the foreground or the background. Foreground execution means that the command specified is executed immediately whereas background execution means that commands are *buffered* and subsequently executed when a command processor is available. This suggests that the *command processor* module might take the following form:

```
monitor module CommandProcessor;
  type *CommandDescription = . . . ;
       *CommandRecord = record
                            *User: UserAccounts.Account;
                            *Command: CommandDescription
                        end
       *CommandReply = . . . ;

  monitor module CommandBuffer = MultipleItemBuffer in Library
    (Where type  ItemType = CommandRecord;
           const MaxItems = . . . ;);

  procedure ExecuteCommand (C: CommandRecord;
                            Reply: CommandReply); . . . ;

  procedure DoForegroundCommand = ExecuteCommand;

  procedure DoBackgroundCommand = CommandBuffer.Send;

  process Processor;
    var C: CommandRecord; Reply: CommandReply;
    begin
      repeat
        CommandBuffer.Receive (C);
        ExecuteCommand (C, Reply);
        {report result of execution}
```

```
        until False
    end {Processor};

instance Processors: array [I . . N] of Processor;

begin *** end {CommandProcessor};
```

The execution of a command is performed by a procedure Execute-Command. This procedure is called directly to execute a command in the foreground, identified by a call to DoForegroundCommand. A multiple item buffer is defined to hold commands for background processing. Such commands are placed in the buffer by calls to DoBackgroundCommand. The execution of these commands is then performed by instances of the process Processor which acquire commands and then execute them using the procedure ExecuteCommand.

In many operating systems there may also be a mechanism for dealing with commands in a priority order. In the simplest case this may be achieved by maintaining several distinct queues of commands, each with a different priority status. Commands may be segregated, for example, according to the amount of processor power that they require for execution. They might also be segregated if they use resources that require personal intervention such as magnetic tape units and graphplotters.

The ExecuteCommand procedure examines the type of command that it is given and takes appropriate action. The only command which we will consider here is the one which triggers the execution of a user program. If it is assumed that this command is handled by a procedure RunUserProgram, then that procedure can be pictured as shown in Figure 10.8.

Handling the execution of a user program in an operating system generally involves:

(a) acquiring main memory for the program;
(b) loading the program into main memory;
(c) starting the execution of the program;
(d) handling requests from the user program for operating system services, and
(e) coping with any mistakes that the program may make.

Most of these operations cannot be expressed easily in a high-level programming language. One particular problem is that the operating system must be able to communicate with programs expressed in a range of languages (often different from its own implementation language). This requirement makes it necessary to define the interface between the operating system and user programs in terms of the machine representation of the data involved. Such low-level detail will not be considered here. Instead, the handling of user programs is discussed in general terms, dealing with each of the five aspects of user program execution (identified above) in turn.

procedure RunUserProgram;

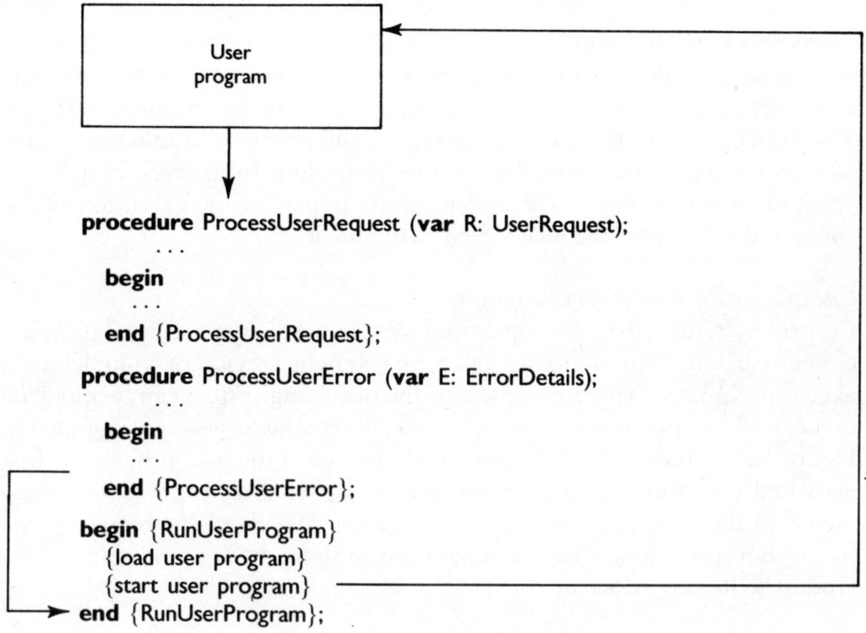

Figure 10.8 Executing user programs

Acquiring main memory

An operating system manages the main memory of the computer on which it executes. On some computers, memory is allocated as a contiguous sequence of words or bytes, whereas on other (larger) computers main memory is provided as a *virtual* resource, as discussed in Chapter 6.

On a virtual memory system a user program is loaded incrementally as it is executed. The program is divided into fixed length *pages* or variable length *segments*, each of which is loaded on *demand*, i.e. when a reference is made to the page or segment concerned during the execution of the program. Thus, main memory is acquired *dynamically*. The operating system will also have some strategy for deallocating memory dynamically. One possibility is to keep track of those pages, or segments, that have been referenced least and release them for use elsewhere when space be needed.

In a system without virtual memory it is normal to acquire a fixed amount of main memory for a user program and free that space when the program terminates.

Loading user programs

User programs are usually kept on disk. To the operating system such programs look little different from a file of data and are loaded into main memory, like data, by using block transfer operations.

Activating user programs

Having loaded all of a user program into main memory (or the first part when virtual memory is used) the execution of the program can be initiated. This is achieved by transferring control to the program in much the same way as control is transferred from one procedure to another in a Pascal program. Thus, in effect, the user program is part of the execution of the command processor instance which activates it.

Communicating with user programs

Control is returned to the operating system whenever the user program either issues a request for an operating system service or completes its execution. A user program request to the operating system can be modeled as a call to an operating system procedure ProcessUserRequest, as suggested in Figure 10.8. Indeed, it can be imagined that when the user program is first activated the ProcessUserRequest procedure is passed as a 'procedure parameter' in the invocation of the user program. Details of the request made by a user are passed to the operating system as a parameter to the ProcessUserRequest procedure.

Coping with user program errors

An operating system must validate each user request thoroughly to ensure that any error made by one user program does not affect the correct functioning of either the operating system or any other user program. For example, if a user program asks for a file block to be read into main memory then the operating system must ensure that the area of main memory that the user program identifies lies wholly within the space allocated to it.

Errors in a 'call' to the operating system from a user program are relatively easy to handle because the operating system is in control at that point. The same is not true of errors that are generated when a user program executes an illegal operation in its own area. For example, the user program may attempt to access a memory location outside its allocated area or perform a calculation that causes arithmetic overflow. Each error of this type is generally detected by the hardware of the computer and causes control to be transferred to a specific location in main memory. From there it is desirable to redirect control to an error routine, HandleUserError, in the RunUserProgram procedure, where all of the information associated with the program that has failed is held. The execution of the program is then terminated and a suitable error report passed to the user concerned.

Sometimes user programs fail by entering an infinite loop. If the loop involves a call into the operating system then the operating system can stop the program whenever it notices the faulty behavior. However, if the user program loops entirely within itself then its execution must be interrupted in some way. This can be achieved by using real-time clock interrupts. If a user program is executing when a clock interrupt occurs it is assumed that the program has been running since the last interrupt and this *time slice* is added to the program's *account*. If the program has any time allocation remaining it is allowed to continue; otherwise its execution is terminated.

Distributed operating systems

Most modern computers, of even modest size, have facilities for communicating with other computers. When computers are connected they are said to form a *data communications network*. Computers within the same vicinity form a *local area network* (or LAN for short) while computers that are more physically remote constitute a *wide area network* (WAN). Computers can also be connected via the public telephone system to form a *public switched data network* (PSDN). These various types of network and their interconnection are illustrated in Figure 10.9.

The International Standards Organization, ISO, has defined a *Reference Model* which suggests how the software responsible for handling the communication between computers can be structured into a hierarchy of seven layers. The nature and purpose of these layers will not be discussed here, except to point out that concurrency is involved in any implementation

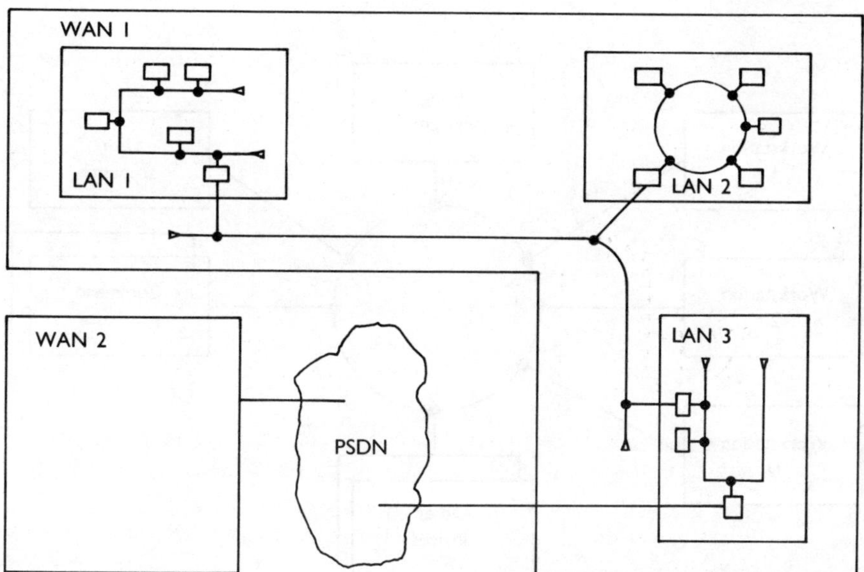

Figure 10.9 Computer networks

of the Reference Model because it allows for multiple communication channels.

Local area networks can be used to provide a general-purpose program development environment. In essence, this is achieved by *distributing* the responsibilities of a more traditional monolithic operating system over a number of nodes in a network. More specifically, nodes might be associated with each of the modules shown in Figure 10.2, as indicated in Figure 10.10.

Figure 10.10 shows the computer nodes connected using a communications ring but other forms of interconnection may be used.

The *interactive interface* modules in Figure 10.2 are the *workstation* nodes in Figure 10.10. Each workstation is a computer with its own main memory. Normally, workstations also have some form of local secondary memory in addition to the usual allocation of space in the general filing system. A filing system node is referred to in this context as a *file server*. Each workstation has sufficient power to carry out many of the commands issued by users. In particular, file editing is usually performed locally on the workstation. Commands that cannot be handled by the workstation are passed to an appropriate *command processor* node.

For a distributed computing facility of this type we might consider that a single operating system is distributed over the computer nodes. An alternative view is to assume that there is a separate operating system running on each node and they simply share knowledge of how to communicate with each other, through a defined *protocol*. This latter view reflects the practical

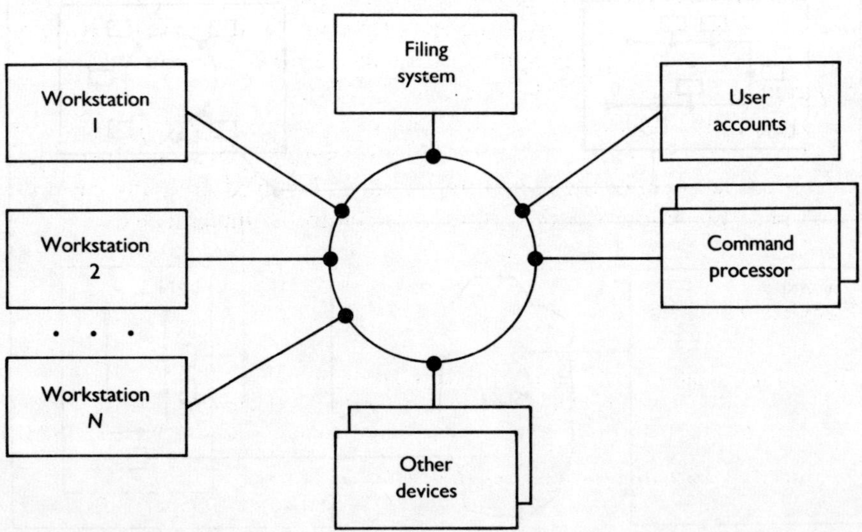

Figure 10.10 Distributed program development facility

requirement that distributed systems are formed from workstations and other device handling nodes that are supplied by a range of manufacturers – businessmen who are unlikely to collaborate in the production of a 'single' coherent operating system!

Thus, on each workstation there is an operating system of the traditional type, as described in preceding sections, and *special-purpose* operating systems on the other nodes. In the latter case the operating systems might also be described as real-time systems.

In a distributed operating system only very large files in the filing system are manipulated in an *open*, *read*, *write* or *close* sequence of operations. Normally complete files are copied in and out of the filing system from and to the nodes that wish to use them. This makes file access simpler, in many respects, but the data communications hardware can become a bottleneck. Also, modifying files is more difficult, when copies exist, since it is a major undertaking to ensure that the copies stay consistent.

Summary

An operating system has many of the characteristics of a real-time program and, in particular, is required to perform a substantial amount of device handling efficiently. The central resource in an operating system is disk storage. The use of such storage is usually handled through a filing system. A filing system must control the allocation of space on disk, control shared access to disk files and perform disk transfers efficiently.

An operating system must also be able to load and supervise the execution of user programs. Many of the operations involved are not easily represented in a high-level programming language because the nature of the user program is not known to the operating system.

An operating system may reside on one computer or be distributed across a network. In either case, the role of the operating system is to provide a service to the users of the computing facilities involved. In many cases the users need not know where or how that service is implemented.

Further reading

General information on operating systems can be found in:
- Lister, A.M., *Fundamentals of Operating Systems*, Macmillan, 1985.
- Deitel, M.D., *An Introduction to Operating Systems*, Addison Wesley, 1984.

For further information on distributed systems see:
- Sloman, M. and Kramer, J., *Distributed Systems and Computer Networks*, Prentice Hall, 1986.

Examples of the implementation of operating systems in a monitor-based programming language may be found in:

- Brinch Hansen, P., *The Architecture of Concurrent Processes*, Prentice Hall, 1977.
- Welsh, J. and McKeag, R.M., *Structured System Programming*, Prentice Hall, 1980.
- Joseph, M., Prasad, V.R. and Natajaran N., *A Multiprocessor Operating System*, Prentice Hall, 1984.

Exercises

It is clearly unreasonable to suggest that an operating system be constructed as an exercise since the amount of software involved is substantial. However, the reader may care to complete some of the modules that have been discussed in this chapter. An enthusiastic reader might even consider implementing one of the simpler nodes of a distributed operating system. One possibility is a *printer server* which accepts text files for output to one or more local lineprinters. Files awaiting output are buffered on local disk storage.

Eleven

THE REPRESENTATION OF PROCESS INTERACTION

Other approaches

Chapter 4 discussed a monitor-based representation for concurrent programs designed in a modular fashion. Concurrent programs can be structured in other ways however, and even when a modular design technique is followed, it is possible to choose other representations for the modules concerned. This chapter considers some of these alternatives. The intention is not to provide a critical assessment of the linguistic notations that are involved although some advantages and disadvantages of each are given. The main objectives are, firstly, to identify the alternative notations, then to give some illustration of their form and, finally, to suggest how such notations have arisen. All of the notations are *adequate* in the sense that any one of them can be used to construct a correctly functioning concurrent program.

The discussion is divided into four sections which deal with:

(a) the handling of process synchronization using *Boolean variables*, *semaphores* and *conditional critical regions*;
(b) synchronization rules in monitor-based languages other than Pascal Plus — specifically the languages Concurrent Euclid and Concurrent Pascal;
(c) the representation of concurrency in Modula-2 — a language which defines only low-level mechanisms for process interaction;
(d) the representation of concurrency in languages that allow processes to interact directly — in particular, Ada.

The material treated in (a) has been designed so that it can be read or presented before Chapter 4. For anyone who has already studied Chapter 4 the early part of (a) can be read fairly quickly. Also, such a person should be warned that the 'process' notation shown in (a) is not meant to be the same as that of Pascal Plus, examples of which appear in Chapter 4 and in later chapters.

Boolean variables, semaphores and conditional critical regions

In programming terms, processes interact when they access shared variables. While one process is inspecting or modifying a group of shared variables it is generally required that all other processes should be prevented from accessing the same group of variables until the first process has finished. This can be achieved by considering each section of program that references a particular group of variables as a *critical section* and allowing only one process at a time to execute such a section.

Consider the simple case of two processes **A** and **B** which increment the value of the same variable, as suggested by the following program fragment:

```
program Example1;
  {Free access to a shared variable}
  var Count: Integer;

  process A;
  begin
    ...
    Count := Count + 1;
    ...
  end {A};

  process B;
  begin
    ...
    Count := Count + 1;
    ...
  end {B};

  begin ... end {Example1}.
```

Our experience of real-world interactions suggests that if two people attempt the same operation at the same time, such as walking through the same doorway, problems will result. Thus, intuitively, when two processes attempt to modify the same variable at the same time we feel that this operation is 'dangerous'. To clarify the danger consider how the increment operation might be implemented at the machine level.

On some machines the increment statement translates into a single machine instruction, such as, for example,

```
increment Count
```

In such cases there is usually no possibility of Count being modified in an unpredictable way because most computers provide a *memory interlock* facility which allows only one processor at a time to access any particular memory location. Thus the incrementing of the Count variable will always yield the correct result because two processes can never access the variable's memory location at exactly the same time.

On other machines the increment statement may translate into several machine instructions, say:

```
push   Count        {move Count onto stack            }
push   1            {move 1 onto stack                }
add                 {add values leaving sum on stack}
pop    Count        {move sum from stack to Count}
```

Here the incrementing statement is implemented by four instructions that perform the addition on an *evaluation stack*. A separate evaluation stack is provided for each process. When several machine instructions are involved there is a possibility that when two processes execute the increment statement at the same time the value of Count may not always increase by two, as expected. Figure 11.1 illustrates how an error can occur.

Figure 11.1 shows a trace of processes A and B executing the increment statement. Process A is exactly one instruction ahead of process B and the initial value of Count is 12. Both processes move a copy of this value onto the evaluation stack, increment that copy and move the same new value, 13, back to Count – rather than the correct value of 14. Figure 11.2 shows the two stacks at the intermediate point marked by a star in Figure 11.1

This error can also occur on a single processor machine if a process is interrupted in the middle of its execution of the increment statement, as suggested in Figure 11.3.

On a single processor machine the processor is allotted periodically to different processes in an attempt to allocate the available processor power fairly (as described in Chapter 2). If the switch can occur at any point then the variables operated on by one process may change their values midway through a calculation, thereby invalidating any intermediate values that are held. In this example the processor is switched after process A has taken a

<table>
<tr><td colspan="3" align="center">process A</td><td colspan="3" align="center">process B</td></tr>
<tr><td colspan="3" align="center">. . .</td><td colspan="3"></td></tr>
<tr><td>push</td><td>Count</td><td>(12)</td><td colspan="3" align="center">. . .</td></tr>
<tr><td>push</td><td>1</td><td>(1)</td><td>push</td><td>Count</td><td>(12)</td></tr>
<tr><td>*   add</td><td></td><td>(13)</td><td>push</td><td>1</td><td>(1)</td></tr>
<tr><td>pop</td><td>Count</td><td>(13)</td><td>add</td><td></td><td>(13)</td></tr>
<tr><td colspan="3" align="center">. . .</td><td>pop</td><td>Count</td><td>(13)</td></tr>
</table>

Figure 11.1   Process interference on a multiprocessor

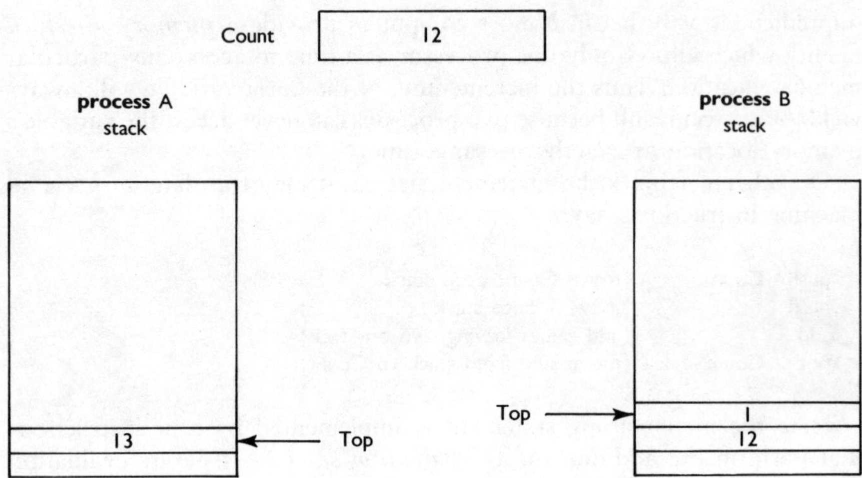

Figure 11.2 Snapshot of parallel execution of increment statement

process A			process B		
	. . .			. . .	
push	Count	(12)		suspended	
push	I	(I)		. . .	
	suspended ——————————————→ activated				
	. . .		push	Count	(12)
	. . .		push	I	(I)
	. . .		add		(13)
	. . .		pop	Count	(13)
				. . .	
	activated ←—————————————— suspended				
add		(13)		. . .	
pop	Count	(13)		. . .	
	. . .				

Figure 11.3 Process interference on a uniprocessor

copy of the variable Count which process B then modifies before control is
returned to process A.

If each increment statement is to achieve the desired effect, regardless of
the underlying machine architecture, then the statement must be protected
so that only one process at a time can execute it. That is, each process must
obtain *exclusive access* to this critical section of code so that parallel access
is prevented, as suggested by the execution trace in Figure 11.4.

Process A is the first to arrive at the increment statement and is given

process A	process B
. . .	. . .
seek permission to increment	. . .
get permission to increment	seek permission to increment
push Count (12)	. . .
push I (1)	. . .
add (13)	. . .
pop Count (13)	. . .
indicate increment complete	get permission to increment
. . .	push Count (13)
. . .	push I (1)
. . .	add (14)
. . .	pop Count (14)
. . .	indicate increment complete
. . .	. . .

Figure 11.4 An execution trace of process exclusion

permission to continue. Process B must be made to wait at its increment statement until process A indicates that it has finished.

In general, the simplest way to provide such protection is through the use of a Boolean variable which denotes whether or not a critical section of code is occupied. The following program fragment illustrates how access to a shared variable might be controlled:

```
program Example2;
    {Exclusive access to a shared variable – using a Boolean access variable}
    var Count: Integer;
        CountInUse: Boolean; {initially False}

    process A;
        var WasSet: Boolean;
        begin
            . . .
            repeat
                TestAndSet (CountInUse, WasSet)
            until not WasSet;
            Count := Count + 1;
            CountInUse := False;
            . . .
        end {A};

    process B;
        var WasSet: Boolean;
        begin
            . . .
            repeat
                TestAndSet (CountInUse, WasSet)
            until not WasSet;
```

```
            Count  :=  Count  +  1;
            CountInUse  :=  False;
               . . .

         end  {B};

      begin  . . .  end  {Example2}.
```

The value of the variable CountInUse indicates whether or not the increment statement can be executed. Any process finding CountInUse True must wait until it is False and is then permitted to continue. That process then makes CountInUse True, executes the increment statement and resets CountInUse to False. As the CountInUse variable is itself shared a special TestAndSet operation is required to ensure that CountInUse can be *both* inspected *and* assigned a value as an indivisible action.

The TestAndSet operation is normally available as a single machine instruction whose effect is equivalent to executing the following procedure:

```
procedure TestAndSet (var CountInUse, WasSet: Boolean);
   begin
      WasSet  :=  CountInUse;
      CountInUse  :=  True
   end  {TestAndSet};
```

Thus, if WasSet returns the value False the executing process has made CountInUse true and so may continue into the critical section.

The main disadvantage of using Boolean variables to protect critical sections of code is that processor power is wasted in the idling loops that repeatedly inspect the values of these variables. In the late 1960s E.W. Dijkstra proposed a *semaphore* mechanism which improves on the Boolean variable scheme by enabling processes to be suspended, if necessary, until the critical sections they wish to enter become free.

A semaphore is a nonnegative integer variable for which two operations P and V are defined. P and V are the first letters of two Dutch words: *passeren*, which means *to pass*, and *vrygeven*, which means *to release*. These operations are usually interpreted as *wait if necessary* and *signal*.

$P(s)$: for a semaphore s, any process invoking $P(s)$ is suspended if $s = 0$; otherwise s is decremented by one;

$V(s)$: if a process is suspended as a result of a P operation on a semaphore s, then $V(s)$ reactivates that process; otherwise s is incremented by one.

P and V operations on the same semaphore are mutually exclusive and each operation is atomic, i.e. neither operation can be interrupted.

It is generally assumed that the P operation is *fair*, in the sense that if several processes are suspended they are later reactivated in their suspension order.

A *binary*, or *Boolean* semaphore has an initial value of one. A semaphore that can take any nonnegative value is known as a *general*, or *counting* semaphore. (A general semaphore is used in the allocation of multiple resources of the same type and its initial value is the total number of resources available.)

The following program shows the use of a binary semaphore to control access to a shared variable:

```
program Example3;
   {Exclusive access to a shared variable – using a binary semaphore}
   var AccessToCount: BinarySemaphore;
       Count: Integer;

   process A;
     begin
       . . .
       P (AccessToCount);
       Count := Count + 1;
       V (AccessToCount);
       . . .
     end {A};
   process B;
     begin
       . . .
       P (AccessToCount);
       Count := Count + 1;
       V (AccessToCount);
       . . .
     end {B};
   begin . . . end {Example3}.
```

The AccessToCount semaphore is automatically initialized to one on entry to the program. The first process to invoke the P operation proceeds to execute the increment statement, having set the semaphore to zero. The second process, finding the semaphore with a value of zero, is suspended until the first process executes a V operation. The waiting process is then reactivated. In this way no processor power need be wasted. Also, the representation of the access protection is considerably clearer than in the equivalent Boolean variable solution.

As a second, more complex, example of the use of semaphores consider how a process A can pass a sequence of data items to a process B through a shared variable, Data:

```
program Example4;
   {Data communication – using semaphores}
   var Data: ItemType;
       AccessToSpace,          {permission to send an item;   }
       AccessToItem:           {permission to receive an item;}
         BinarySemaphore;

   process A;
     var X: ItemType;
     begin
```

```
    . . .
        repeat
            {send a data item}
            P (AccessToSpace);
            Data := X;
            V (AccessToItem);
            . . .
        until · · ·
        . . .
    end {A};

    process B;
        var Y: ItemType;
        begin
            . . .
            repeat
                {receive a data item}
                P (AccessToItem);
                Y := Data;
                V (AccessToSpace);
                . . .
            until . . .
            . . .
        end {B};

begin . . . end {Example4};
```

The semaphore AccessToSpace is used to suspend process A if Data contains
an item which has not been collected and the AccessToItem semaphore is used
to suspend process B if Data does not hold an item for collection. The semaphore AccessToSpace is initialized to one but AccessToItem is set initially to
zero as Data does not hold an item at that point.

Each process performs a V operation when it changes the state of the
communication variable Data. That is, process A performs V(AccessToItem)
after it places an item in Data and process B performs V(AccessToSpace) after it
removes an item from Data.

P and V operations need not necessarily be matched in the same program
sections, as illustrated in the second example, so a compiler has no means of
checking that the operations are performed correctly. Also there is no
obvious link between the shared variables, the semaphores that control
access to them and the critical sections of code where the variables are
referenced. The *conditional critical region* concept proposed by C.A.R.
Hoare and P. Brinch Hansen in the early 1970s, provides a higher level
mechanism for controlling access to shared variables and avoids many of
the inherent insecurities associated with semaphores. Shared variables are
placed explicitly into groups, called *resources* and exclusive access to each
resource is obtained implicitly by any process that indicates that it wishes to
enter a *region* that uses the resource. A *resource* and *region* are defined syn-
tactically as follows:

```
resource = "resource" resource-name ":" variable-list ";".
region = "region" resource-name ["when" Boolean-expression]
            "do" statement-list "end".
```

A resource declaration introduces a resource-name and a list of shared variables. A *region* identifies the shared variables that it uses by naming the resource in which they are declared. Optionally, each *region* can include a Boolean expression which defines a precondition that must be satisfied before the statement-list of the *region* is executed.

The following example illustrates the use of conditional critical regions to control access to a shared variable:

```
program Example5;
    {Exclusive access to a shared variable – using the critical region mechanism.}
    var Count: Integer;

    resource CountInUse: Count;

    process A;
      begin
        . . .
        region CountInUse do Count := Count + 1; end
        . . .
      end {A};

    process B;
      begin
        . . .
        region CountInUse do Count := Count + 1; end
        . . .
      end {B};

    begin ... end {Example5}.
```

A variable defined in a *resource* may not appear in any other resource and such a variable may only be accessed within a region that names that resource. Hence, the variable Count named in the CountInUse resource may only appear in the *statement-list* parts of the two regions in processes A and B. Because of these restrictions on conditional critical regions most of the errors that might occur in the use of semaphores are detectable at compile time. The resulting program is also easier to express and more readable than the equivalent semaphore representation since the critical sections are clearly delimited.

As an illustration of the use of a precondition for entry to a region consider the following implementation of Example 4:

```
program Example6;
    {Data communication – using conditional critical regions.}
    var Data: ItemType;
        DataPresent: Boolean; {Initially False}

    resource Channel: Data, DataPresent;
```

```
      process A;
        var X: ItemType;
        begin
          ...
          repeat
            {send a data item}
            region Channel when not DataPresent do
              Data := X;
              DataPresent := True;
            end;
            ...
          until  ...
          ...
        end {A};
      process B;
        var Y: ItemType;
        begin
          ...
          repeat
            {receive a data item}
            region Channel when DataPresent do
              Y := Data;
              DataPresent := False;
            end;
            ...
          until ...
          ...
        end {B};

      begin ... end {Example6};
```

An auxiliary variable DataPresent has been introduced to indicate whether or not Data contains a value. Process A waits until DataPresent is False and process B waits until DataPresent is True.

Note that there are two variables in the resource Channel.

The *monitor* concept quickly followed the conditional critical region proposals and was again the inspiration of P. Brinch Hansen and C.A.R. Hoare. It improves on the conditional critical region concept by bringing regions that use the same resource together into one program block. However, a monitor is less convenient for users since the associated mechanism for suspending and reactivating processes is made explicit. This backward step was considered desirable at that time because the conditional critical region mechanism was relatively expensive to implement. Today, such costs are much less important and the conditional region concept has been revived in the programming language Ada.

For monitors, Hoare proposed a *condition* mechanism for explicit process suspension and reactivation, while Brinch Hansen suggested a lower-level *queue* facility. Details of how these concepts have been realized in specific programming languages are discussed briefly in the next section.

Monitor-based programming languages

The discussion of concurrent program construction from Chapter 4 on-
wards has been illustrated by examples expressed in the programming language Pascal Plus. Pascal Plus is typical of a range of languages, including
Concurrent Euclid and Concurrent Pascal, which support the same monitor
concept, viz. a module which holds shared data to which only one process
at a time has access. The differences in the various representations of a
monitor are largely superficial. For example, a monitor to control access to
a single variable might be expressed as follows in Pascal Plus, Concurrent
Euclid and Concurrent Pascal, respectively:

Pascal Plus

```
monitor module CountAccess;

   var *Count: 0..Maxint;

   procedure *Increment;
      begin Count := Count + 1 end {Increment};

   begin
      Count := 0;
      ***
   end {CountAccess};
```

Concurrent Euclid

```
var CountAccess:
   monitor
      exports (Count, Increment)

      var Count: UnsignedInt

      procedure Increment =
         imports (var Count)
         begin Count := Count + 1 end Increment

      initially
         imports (var Count)
         begin Count := 0 end

   end {CountAccess} monitor
```

Concurrent Pascal

```
var CountAccess:
   monitor;

      var entry Count: 0..Maxint;

      procedure entry Increment;
         begin Count := Count + 1 end;

      begin Count := 0 end "CountAccess";
```

Each monitor has the same form: a block, containing a variable declaration, a mechanism for initializing that variable and a procedure which increments it. The main features of each notation are summarized below:

(a) Each language guarantees that only one process at a time can execute a particular monitor instance and hence be in a position to modify its local variables.

(b) All three languages provide an initialization mechanism that enables the state of each monitor instance to be established before any process can interact with it. Only Pascal Plus has a finalization mechanism. Monitor instances are initialized automatically in Pascal Plus and Concurrent Euclid but an explicit initialization statement is required in Concurrent Pascal:

      init CountAccess;

(c) In each case a monitor is a block containing definitions and declarations, some of which are private to the block and some of which are visible outside the block. In Pascal Plus and Concurrent Pascal a prefix ('*' and **entry**, respectively) identify the visible attributes of the monitor. In Concurrent Euclid the names of the visible attributes are enumerated in an *export* list at the head of the monitor block.

The *condition* of Concurrent Euclid and Pascal Plus, and the *queue* of Concurrent Pascal each enable processes to be suspended and reactivated through two explicit and complementary operations (Wait and Signal in Pascal Plus and Concurrent Euclid, Delay and Continue in Concurrent Pascal). However, at most one process may be suspended on a *queue* whereas any number of processes, in principle, can be suspended on a *condition*. In Concurrent Pascal if two or more processes need to be queued then a 'multi-queue' is programmed explicitly using an array of queues. The technique is similar to that described for the *condition list* of Pascal Plus in Chapter 6.

The languages differ most significantly in their rules for the transfer of exclusive monitor access from one process to another when a process is suspended or reactivated. The following points should be noted:

(a) In all three languages a signaled process is reactivated immediately.

(b) In Concurrent Pascal a Continue operation must be the last performed in an entry routine since it causes the invoking process to leave the monitor.

(c) In Pascal Plus and Concurrent Euclid a signaling process is suspended until the monitor is no longer occupied. Pascal Plus insists that signals obey a last-in first-out discipline so that, if the signaled process leaves the monitor, control is returned to the signaling process. Concurrent Euclid allows other processes to enter the monitor before the signaling process is reactivated and so, in general, the programmer can make few assumptions about the state of the monitor variables immediately after a signal operation.

(d) In Pascal Plus a process which makes a nested monitor call, and is then suspended, releases access to each monitor through which it has passed. When it is subsequently reactivated it reacquires access to each monitor individually as it returns to it. This mechanism can be expensive to implement. Concurrent Euclid and Concurrent Pascal use a less expensive, but more restrictive discipline within which access is released only to the monitor in which a process is suspended. In practice, nested monitor calls are not needed very often. In this book, for instance, there is only one example of a nested monitor call: the TestHarness monitor, discussed in Chapter 5 (which uses the Pascal Plus monitor exclusion rules to order process calls to a monitor under test). With this exception, all of the other examples can be translated mechanically into Concurrent Pascal or Concurrent Euclid. The translation of examples that use the Pascal Plus AllWaiting standard Condition instance is rather messy, however, but it can be handled in general by a module which keeps track of the processes that are active:

```
monitor module AllWaiting;
  const NumberOfProcesses = ...;
  type Nonnegative = 0..Maxint;
  var NumberActive: 0..NumberOfProcesses;
  instance Queue: Condition;

  procedure *PWait (P: Nonnegative);
    begin
      NumberActive := NumberActive - 1;
      Queue.PWait (P)
    end {PWait};

  procedure *NoteSuspension;
    begin
      NumberActive := NumberActive - 1;
      if NumberActive = 0 then Queue.Signal
    end {NoteSuspension};

  procedure *NoteActivation;
    begin NumberActive := NumberActive + 1 end;

  begin
    NumberActive = NumberOfProcesses;
    ***
  end {AllWaiting};
```

Calls to NoteSuspension and NoteActivation must be placed around each wait operation in the program. Any process which calls AllWaiting.PWait is suspended on the Condition instance Queue until all processes are inactive, as indicated by the value of the variable NumberActive. At that point Queue is signaled to allow the topmost process to proceed. (Note that for completeness the AllWaiting monitor might also include Wait, Empty, Length and Priority operations.)

Modula-2

The programming language Modula provides process and monitor constructs similar to those defined for Pascal Plus. Its successor Modula-2 also has a monitor construct but its facilities for explicit process synchronization are at a lower level than most other monitor-based languages. However, these lower level facilities make it possible to produce a Modula-2 program that provides concurrency primitives in the style of the other monitor-based languages. Such primitives are generally supplied through a user-defined module or an implementation-defined library module. Consider, for example, the implementation of a program containing two processes, one of which passes a single character to the other through a single item buffer. In Pascal Plus this program would be expressed as follows:

```
program Example7;
   {Single character transfer between two processes}

   monitor module Buffer = SingleItemBuffer in Library
      (Where type ItemType = Char;);

   process module Sender;
      begin Buffer.Send ('X') end;

   process module Receiver;
      var Ch: Char;
      begin Buffer.Receive (Ch) end;

   begin *** end.
```

To represent this program (and concurrent programs in general) in Modula-2 a support module is required that enables:

(a) processes to be defined;
(b) condition instances to be defined and initialized;
(c) the execution of processes to be started;
(d) Wait and Signal operations to be performed by processes on condition instances.

These facilities (and others) might be provided by a module with the following interface:

```
definition module Primitives;
   export qualified
      InitializeProcess, StartProcesses,
      Condition, InitializeCondition, Wait, Signal, . . .;
   type Condition;
   procedure InitializeProcess (Process: PROC; WorkSpace: CARDINAL);
   procedure StartProcesses;
```

```
    procedure InitializeCondition var C: Condition);
    procedure Wait (var C: Condition);
    procedure Signal (var C: Condition);
            . . .
    end Primitives.
```

Primitives is a Modula-2 *definition-module* for which a corresponding *implementation-module* is required. The definition-module exports a set of procedures and the type Condition by naming them in the module heading (as in Concurrent Euclid). Note that the definition of the Condition type does not make its structure visible (in the nomenclature of Modula-2 Condition is an *opaque type*).

Processes are defined as parameterless procedures (i.e. values of the Modula-2 standard type PROC). A process is initialized by means of a call of the procedure InitializeProcess which is supplied with the identity of the process (i.e. the corresponding procedure-identifier) and a Cardinal value (i.e. a nonnegative integer) defining an upper limit on the amount of main memory to be used for execution of the process.

Using the Primitives module the single character buffer might be expressed in Modula-2 as follows:

```
module Buffer [1];
    from Primitives import
        Condition, InitializeCondition, Wait, Signal;

    export qualified Send, Receive; (* exported attributes *)

    var Data: ItemType;
        DataPresent: BOOLEAN;
        DataAvailable, SpaceAvailable: Condition;

    procedure Send (Item: ItemType);
      begin
        if DataPresent then Primitives.Wait (SpaceAvailable) end;
        DataPresent := TRUE;
        Data := Item;
        Primitives.Signal (DataAvailable)
      end Send;

    procedure Receive (var Item: ItemType);
      begin
        if not DataPresent then Primitives.Wait (DataAvailable) end;
        DataPresent := FALSE;
        Item := Data;
        Primitives.Signal (SpaceAvailable)
      end Receive;

    begin (* Buffer *)
        Primitives.InitializeCondition (DataAvailable);
        Primitives.InitializeCondition (SpaceAvailable);
        DataPresent := FALSE
    end Buffer;
```

The **Buffer** module has the same form as the equivalent Pascal Plus monitor discussed in Chapter 7, except that:

(a) The module is identified as a monitor by the presence of a *priority* value in square brackets after the module name. The introduction of a priority status enables the execution of a monitor to be interrupted for the servicing of an interrupt from a peripheral device by some other higher priority monitor. This facility can be useful in time-critical real-time systems.

(b) The initialization of the local condition instances is explicit in a Modula-2 monitor since they are user-defined data structures. However, the statement-part of the module itself is executed automatically on entry to the program, thus giving some measure of security.

The complete character transfer program can be expressed in Modula-2 as follows:

```
module SingleCharacterTransfer;
  from Primitives import
     InitializeProcess, StartProcesses,
     Condition, InitializeCondition, Wait, Signal;
  from Buffer import Send, Receive;
  const WorkSpaceSize = ... ;

  procedure Sender;
     begin Buffer.Send ('X') end Sender;

  procedure Receiver;
     var Ch: Char;
     begin Buffer.Receive (Ch) end Receiver;

  begin (* SingleCharacterTransfer *)
     Primitives.InitializeProcess (Sender,   WorkSpaceSize);
     Primitives.InitializeProcess (Receiver, WorkSpaceSize);
     Primitives.StartProcesses
  end SingleCharacterTransfer.
```

The two processes are represented here by the procedures **Sender** and **Receiver** and are identified as processes by the **InitializeProcess** calls in the statement-part of the main program. The call of **StartProcesses** then commences the execution of either **Sender** or **Receiver**.

An implementation of the **Primitives** module will involve the use of 'process descriptors', each of which records the current execution point of a process. The various process queues that form, such as the queue of processes that are ready to execute and the condition queues, are then constructed as lists of process descriptors. The transfer of control from one process to another is implemented by:

- mapping the processes onto Modula-2 *co-routines* (a standard operation is provided for this purpose), and

- using another standard co-routine transfer operation that restarts a named process at its last recorded execution point; this operation saves the current execution address of the process that invokes the transfer, i.e. the address of the instruction after the transfer operation.

The main points to note about the Modula-2 language support for the representation of concurrent programs are:

(a) The Modula-2 facilities are low-level compared with those provided in the monitor-based languages. This means that these facilities are easy to implement and the language easy to transport but the need for library support for common low-level modules is greatly increased.

(b) Modula-2 allows the form and effect of the synchronization operations to be defined by the programmer thus permitting programmers to define their own concurrency primitives. However, without library support some standards are clearly necessary to facilitate the maintenance of the resulting programs.

(c) The transfer of control from one process to another is explicit in Modula-2. Consequently, it is not possible to share the processor 'fairly' so as to give the impression of parallel execution. Such an effect can be achieved by adding an explicit switching operation to the module supporting the concurrency abstraction. The price to be paid, however, is an increased complexity in the resulting programs.

Directly communicating processes

Chapter 4 suggested that the translation of a program design into a programming notation required a distinction to be made between the 'dominant' modules that provide a motive force in the program and the 'subordinate' modules that provide a service for the dominant modules. However, making such a distinction may not always be easy. This difficulty, coupled with a desire to remove the operators that control the explicit delay and activation of processes in monitor-based languages, led C.A.R. Hoare to propose a notation that involves only processes which interact directly. The notation, known as *Communicating Sequential Processes* or, more commonly, CSP has had a strong influence on the design of the facilities provided for concurrency in the programming languages Ada and occam.

Allowing processes to interact directly removes the need for both monitors and conditions. This simplification is offset, however, by the need to have additional facilities for interprocess communication, namely, the means for a process to:

(a) refer directly to another process;
(b) specify how other processes can communicate with it;

and mechanisms to enable a process to:

(c) engage in interactions with another process;
(d) select one interaction from a set of possible interactions;
(e) delay an interaction until some condition is satisfied.

Each of these requirements is considered in turn in the sections that follow.

Basic process communication

In Pascal Plus a process instance name is little more than a documentation
aid and appears only in the declaration of the instance. If one process wishes
to communicate directly with another then it must be able to name that
process. For example, in Ada the transfer of a character between two
processes can be represented as follows:

```
task Receiver is
  entry Transfer (Ch: in Character);
end;

task body Receiver is
    . . .
end Receiver ;

task Sender is
end Sender;

task body Sender is
begin Receiver.Transfer ('X'); end Sender;
```

A process in Ada is known as a *task*. Each task consists of two parts: a
specification that defines the interactions supported by the task and a *body*
that defines how the task is implemented. The Receiver task shown here
supports the transfer of a character to it through the defined entry Transfer.
An *entry* is invoked like a procedure call to a monitor, as shown.

Accepting interaction

Task interaction involves two tasks agreeing to communicate, with one task
instigating the interaction and the other accepting it. An interaction is
instigated by an *entry-call* which the receiving task accepts explicitly. The
acceptance of a call in the receiving task names the called *entry*. For
example, the implementation part of the Receiver task might be expressed as
follows:

```
task body Receiver is
  begin
    accept Transfer (Ch: in Character) do
        . . .
    end Transfer;
      . . .
  end Receiver;
```

In Ada the interaction between two tasks is known as a *rendezvous*. Two tasks are unlikely to be ready to communicate at exactly the same time so, inevitably, one task is obliged to wait until the other arrives. A rendezvous occurs in this example when the Sender task has invoked the Transfer entry and the Receiver task is ready to execute the *accept-statement*.

The 'extent' of the rendezvous is defined by the statements between the **do** of the accept-statement and the matching **end**. Once the execution of the accept-statement is complete the two tasks separate: the Receiver task to execute the statements following the accept-statement and the Sender task to execute the statements following its call of Transfer.

A task may be willing to interact with other tasks through one of several entries, in a predetermined order. For example, if the communication of data items between two tasks is buffered then an intermediate buffer task might be defined as follows:

```
task SingleItemBuffer is
   entry Send (Item: in ItemType);
   entry Receive (Item: out ItemType);
end;

task body SingleItemBuffer is
   Data: ItemType;
   begin
      loop
         accept Send (Item: in ItemType) do Data := Item;
         end Send;
         accept Receive (Item: out ItemType) do Item := Data;
         end Receive;
      end loop;
   end Buffer;
```

From the point of view of the communicating tasks this solution is now very close to the equivalent monitor form but the representation of the SingleItemBuffer task is simpler than its monitor counterpart. The advantages of the Ada approach are:

(a) An Ada task can define the order in which interactions will occur so, for example, with the single item buffer there is no need to have a Boolean variable to indicate whether or not data is present.

(b) Tasks are queued implicitly while awaiting interaction with other tasks so no explicit task suspension and reactivation is necessary.

Note that the outer loop-statement causes the task to run indefinitely.

Selecting one from a set of possible interactions

In many applications a task may be willing to take part in any one of a set of possible interactions. For example, if the operations on a shared counter variable are controlled by a task that allows the value of the variable to be

either incremented by one or inspected then the order of acceptable interactions is not predetermined. This situation is catered for in Ada by the use
of a *select-statement* whose form is illustrated in the following implementation of the shared counter example:

```
task SharedCounter is
   entry Increment;
   entry Value (V: out Integer);
end;

task body SharedCounter is
   Count: Integer;
   begin
      Count := 0;
      loop
         select
            accept Increment do Count := Count + 1;
            end Increment;
         or
            accept Value (V: out Integer) do V := Count;
            end Value;
         end select;
      end loop;
   end SharedCounter;
```

The SharedCounter task makes a nondeterministic selection between the
two interactions appearing in the select-statement. Only one interaction is
accepted at a time.

Guarded selection

Ada does not provide a mechanism for suspending the execution of a task
other than by making it wait for interaction through a task entry. This
means that some accept statements have a precondition for interaction. For
example, in a multiple item buffer, Send may only be accepted if the buffer
is not full and Receive accepted only when the buffer is not empty. This is
achieved by 'guarding' the accept-statement with a *when-clause*, thus:

```
loop
   select
      when NumberOfSpaces > 0 =>
         accept Send (Item: in ItemType) do ... end;
   or
      when NumberOfSpaces < BufferSize =>
         accept Receive (Item: out ItemType) do ... end;
   end select;
end loop;
```

Each when-clause contains a precondition which, if it is satisfied when
a task is awaiting entry, enables the associated accept-statement to be
executed.

An accept statement bears a strong resemblance to a *conditional critical region*. The 'condition' that has to be satisfied is that a task has invoked the entry identified by the accept statement, and any attached when-clause evaluates to True. Note, however, that an accept statement is only executed by the task in which it is defined.

Directly communicating processes versus monitor-based communication

This subsection gives an evaluation of the *direct* and *indirect* notations for representing process interaction in terms of a list of points. Points (a) to (e) cover 'user convenience' and (f) to (i) cover 'implementation considerations'.

(a) *Simplicity*
The use of only one type of building block, the task, for the construction of concurrent systems is appealing. However, although Ada succeeds in removing monitors and conditions, their replacement by accept-statements, select-statements and when-clauses means that no real simplification is achieved.

(b) *Sequence control and termination*
Using tasks in place of monitors means that the allowed sequence of interface calls can be controlled more easily and, in some cases, results in a dramatic simplification of the communication protocol (as shown earlier for a single item buffer).

However, these advantages are lost if a task has to be constructed in a form that allows it to terminate. This requires a special *terminate* limb to be added to a select-statement. The *terminate* limb is selected if no other interaction is possible. For example, the general form of a single item buffer is then as follows:

```
task body SingleItemBuffer is
   Data: ItemType;
   DataPresent: Boolean;
begin
   loop
     select
       when DataPresent =>
         accept Receive (Item: out ItemType) do
           Item := Data;
           DataPresent := False;
         end Receive;
     or
       when not DataPresent =>
         accept Send (Item: in ItemType) do
           Data := Item;
           DataPresent := True;
         end Send;
```

```
        or
            Terminate;
        end select;
      end loop;
    end SingleItemBuffer;
```

The complexity of the resulting task is now similar to that of the corresponding monitor solution.

(c) *Waiting queue order*

Removing explicit Wait and Signal operations by delaying process interaction
is again an appealing simplification but, in practice, turns out to be at an
unacceptably high level for applications in which tasks need to be delayed in
an order other than their order of arrival. Implementing the priority allocation of a single resource, for example, has a very complex general solution; even a specific solution allowing for only three levels of priority is
complicated. The specific solution is achieved by providing, in effect, three
separate entry calls. In Ada these are defined as a *family*, or array of entries,
thus:

```
    task SingleResource is
      entry Acquire (Priority);
      entry Release;
    end;
```

If Priority is defined as follows:

```
    type Priority = (Urgent, Normal, Low);
```

then the body of the task can be expressed thus:

```
    task body SingleResource is
      begin
        loop
          select
            accept Acquire (Urgent) do end;
          or
              when Acquire (Urgent)'Count = 0 =>
              accept Acquire (Normal) do end;
          or
              when Acquire (Urgent)'Count = 0 and
                    Acquire (Normal)'Count = 0 =>
              accept Acquire (Low) do end;
          end select;
          accept Release do end;
        end loop;
      end SingleResource;
```

The body of the SingleResource task repeatedly accepts a sequence of
Acquire and Release entry calls, where the Acquire calls are taken in priority
order. The 'Count *attribute enquiry* denotes the number of tasks waiting to

interact through a particular entry so the task body above indicates that the lowest priority calling task is only accepted if there are no tasks attempting to interact through either of the two higher priority entries.

(d) *Buffered versus synchronized communication*
The use of monitor-based communication is clumsy in applications where the design suggests that processes should interact directly. However, in practice, buffered communication often results in a better overall program performance (as discussed in Chapter 7). Thus, in practice, this form of communication is used much more frequently than synchronized communication.

(e) *Use of library modules*
Using a monitor in those cases where direct process interaction is required is not particularly inconvenient for a programmer since the required monitor can simply be copied from a software library of standard modules.

(f) *Shared memory limitation for monitors*
The monitor-based concurrency model relies on the use of a common memory in which all monitor variables reside and to which all processes have direct access. Chapter 2 discussed how a use of a shared memory limits the potential for concurrent behavior because of memory contention. However, at present this is by far the most common type of memory architecture available. Thus, monitor-based concurrency is likely to be the best solution available in the foreseeable future.

(g) *Implicit synchronization costs*
Monitor calls are very efficient. On a shared memory machine process interaction with a monitor is considerably faster than direct interaction between two tasks. For Ada tasks there is an overhead in the handling of task synchronization, whereas, for monitors a simple check is all that is required to ensure that the called monitor is not occupied. After that the code of the monitor may be executed directly by the calling process.

(h) *Explicit synchronization costs*
In tasks that accept one of several possible interactions there are often guarded accept statements all of whose preconditions must be evaluated after each interaction. Any process making a change to the state of a monitor instance deals explicitly with the reactivation of any process awaiting that change, which is usually more efficient than guarded accept-statements.

(i) *Scheduling costs*
An Ada program contains more processes than the equivalent monitor-based program and thus more effort is required to share the available processor power among those processes.

Summary

Notations proposed for the representation of process interaction in programming languages have tended to move to higher and higher levels of abstraction. This chapter has reviewed a range of notations for process interaction in an attempt to place the monitor-based concurrency model in context.

The control of process interaction is essentially the control of exclusive access to shared data. The simplest exclusion mechanism is one that uses Boolean variables or semaphores to control entry to critical regions of code that make reference to or modify shared data. Semaphores are preferable because they avoid busy-waiting loops that waste processor power. However, both mechanisms are unsatisfactory, in general, because they do not identify the critical regions involved and so their correct use cannot be checked by a compiler.

The conditional critical region notation overcomes many of the insecurities associated with semaphores and Boolean access variables. The monitor notation improves on conditional critical regions by combining the regions that use the same data.

The monitor notation has been implemented in many programming languages including Concurrent Pascal, Concurrent Euclid and Pascal Plus. Modula also embodies the same approach but Modula-2 has little direct support for the representation of concurrent programs. It provides a monitor facility but the administration of process creation and the control of process interaction are not defined by the language. The usual technique is to supply the additional concurrency primitives through a user-defined or implementation-defined module.

CSP is a notation that attempts to reduce concurrent programs to a set of processes that interact directly. The programming language Ada has adopted this model of concurrent behavior but, although some improvements over the monitor concept have been achieved, other language constructs have had to be introduced. However, programs with directly communicating processes do have the advantage that they can be executed on machines which do not have a shared memory.

Further reading

The two classic papers on semaphores are:
- Dijkstra, E.W., The structure of the THE multiprogramming system, *Comm. ACM*, Vol. II, pp. 341–6, 1968.
- Dijkstra, E.W., Cooperating sequential processes, in Genuys, F. (ed.), *Programming Languages*, Academic Press, 1968.

The conditional critical region concept is described in:
- Hoare, C.A.R., Towards a theory of parallel programming, in Hoare, C.A.R. and

Perrott, R.H. (eds), *Operating Systems Techniques*, Academic Press, 1972.
* Brinch Hansen, P., *Operating Systems Principles*, Prentice Hall, 1973.

For details of the programming languages Concurrent Pascal, Concurrent Euclid, and Modula-2, see:
* Brinch Hansen, P., *The Architecture of Concurrent Programs*, Prentice Hall, 1977.
* Holt, R.C., *Concurrent Euclid, the UNIX System, and TUNIS*, Addison Wesley, 1983.
* Wirth, N., *Programming in Modula-2* (3rd edn), Springer Verlag, Berlin, 1985.

The Ada task communication mechanism is based on CSP which is described in:
* Hoare, C.A.R., *Communicating Sequential Processes*, Prentice Hall, 1985.

Details of Ada itself may be found in:
* Watt, D.A., Wichmann, B.A. and Findlay, W., *Ada Language and Methodology*, Prentice Hall, 1987.

The programming language occam which also embodies the CSP methodology is defined in:
* INMOS Ltd, *occam Programming Manual*, Prentice Hall, 1984.

Further references to various other aspects of concurrent programming may be found in:
* Andrews, G.R. and Schneider, F.B., Concepts and notations for concurrent programming, *ACM Computing Surveys*, Vol. 15, pp. 3–44, 1983.

Exercises

A large number of monitors have been presented in this book. Some (or all!) of them can be translated into the notations discussed in this chapter as exercises.

Appendix I

PASCAL PLUS DEFINITION

The language Pascal Plus is used throughout this book to illustrate and reinforce the style of programming advocated. Pascal Plus is a well-defined superset of ISO standard Pascal, providing facilities for modular and concurrent programming. Details of the available implementations of Pascal Plus may be obtained from the Department of Computer Science, Queen's University, Belfast, BT7 1NN. A Tutorial Guide to the language is also available from the same source.

This appendix gives a concise definition of Pascal Plus. All language features referenced but not defined explicitly have the same definition as in ISO standard Pascal.

1. Blocks

The syntax of a Pascal Plus block is:

```
block = declaration-part statement-part.
```

where declaration-part has the definition:

```
declaration-part =
{label-declaration-part |
 constant-definition-part |
 type-definition-part |
 variable-declaration-part |
 procedure-or-function-declaration ";" |
 envelope-definition ";" |
 monitor-definition ";" |
 process-definition ";" |
 instance-declaration-part }.
```

The component parts of a declaration-part may appear in any order, subject to the normal declare-before-use requirement for identifiers. Each kind of component part (label-, constant-, type-, etc.) may occur zero or more times.

2. Procedure and function declarations

In Pascal Plus new procedure or function identifiers may be defined to denote existing program-defined procedures and functions. A procedure or function declaration may also be held in a system library and included in a program by using a retrieval declaration.

The syntax of a function-declaration is:

```
function-declaration =
    function-heading ";" directive |
    function-identification ";" function-block |
    function-heading ";" function-block |
    function-equivalence-declaration |
    function-retrieval-declaration.
```

The syntax of a function-equivalence-declaration is:

```
function-equivalence-declaration =
    "function" identifier "=" function-identifier.
```

The function-equivalence-declaration

```
function A = B;
```

defines A as a function identifier. The function which A denotes has:

(a) a parameter list congruous with the parameter list of the function denoted by B;
(b) the same result-type as the function denoted by B;
(c) an effect which is identical to that of the function denoted by B as determined on entry to the block that contains the equivalence declaration.

The required (i.e. standard) procedures and functions of the language may not be renamed or equivalenced in this way.

The syntax of a function-retrieval-declaration is:

```
function-retrieval-declaration =
    "function" identifier ["=" library-identifier]
    "in" [library-path-name "in"] "library"
    [environment-specification].
```

A function-retrieval-declaration is equivalent to its replacement by a function-declaration retrieved from a library of such declarations.

A resultant function is denoted in the block that contains the function-retrieval-declaration by the identifier that immediately follows the word function in the function-retrieval-declaration. This identifier is thus defined as a function-identifier in the block containing the retrieval-declaration.

The identifier that appears in the function-heading of the function-declaration in the library is called its library-identifier. If it differs from the function-identifier being defined it must be cited as the library-identifier in the function-retrieval-declaration, where:

```
library-identifier = identifier.
```

If no library-identifier appears in a function-retrieval-declaration the library-identifier of the retrieved function must be the same as the function-identifier defined by the function-retrieval-declaration.

The function-declaration to be retrieved from the library is selected in an implementation-defined manner. A library-path-name, which is a string of implementation-defined form, may be used to specify a particular selection:

library-path-name = string.

If no library-path-name is specified the selection is based on the library-identifier if one is specified. If neither a library-path-name nor a library-identifier is specified the selection is based on the function-identifier cited in the function-retrieval-declaration.

The identifier that appears in the function-heading of the function-declaration retrieved from the library may be used to denote (recursive references to) the function within itself.

Since a function-retrieval-declaration is equivalent to the inclusion of the retrieved function-declaration at the same point, the latter may refer to identifiers whose scope encloses the function-retrieval-declaration. In addition, however, the retrieved function-declaration may refer to identifiers defined in the environment-specification, if any, of the function-retrieval-declaration:

    environment-specification =
      "(" "where" environment-section {environment-section}")".

    environment-section =
      {constant-definition-part |
        type-definition-part |
        function-equivalence-declaration |
        procedure-equivalence-declaration}.

The scope of the constant-, type, function- and procedure-identifiers defined in the environment-specification is the environment-specification itself and the function-declaration retrieved from the system library.

The extensions to the definition of a procedure-declaration for Pascal Plus are identical to those given above for function-declaration, with the word **function** replaced by the word **procedure** throughout, and with item (b) in the definition of function-equivalence-declaration omitted.

3. Envelope definitions

An envelope is a set of definitions and declarations defined by the envelope-block of an envelope-definition.

An envelope instance is the set of variables, procedures and functions that result from instantiation of an envelope.

The syntax of an envelope-definition is:

envelope-definition =
    envelope-heading ";" envelope-block |
    envelope-retrieval-declaration.

envelope-heading = envelope-type-heading | envelope-module-heading.

envelope-type-heading = "**envelope**" identifier [formal-parameter-list].

envelope-module-heading = "**envelope**" "**module**" identifier.

envelope-identifier = identifier.

envelope-instance-identifier = identifier.

envelope-block = block.

The identifier in an envelope-type-heading is defined as an envelope-identifier. Instances of the envelope it denotes may be declared as explained in Section 6, with properties which are determined by the associated envelope-block, as explained in Sections 8 and 10.

The identifier in an envelope-module-heading is defined as an envelope-instance-identifier. It denotes the only instance of an envelope whose properties are determined by an associated envelope-block.

The envelope-block must not contain any references to the envelope-identifier or envelope-instance-identifier defined by the envelope-heading, i.e. an envelope must not refer to itself.

The syntax of an envelope-retrieval-declaration is:

```
envelope-retrieval-declaration =
    "envelope" [ "module" ] identifier [ "=" library-identifier ]
        "in" [ library-path-name "in" ] "library" [ environment-specification ].
```

An envelope-retrieval-declaration is equivalent to its replacement by an envelope-definition retrieved from a library of such definitions.

If the word **module** is absent from the envelope-retrieval-declaration the retrieved envelope-definition must have an envelope-type-heading. In this case, the identifier following the word **envelope** in the envelope-retrieval declaration is defined as an envelope-identifier, and denotes the envelope defined by the retrieved envelope-definition.

If the word **module** is present in the envelope-retrieval-declaration the retrieved envelope-definition may have either an envelope-module-heading or an envelope-type-heading without a formal-parameter-list. In this case the identifier following the word **module** in the envelope-retrieval-declaration is defined as an envelope-instance-identifier, and denotes the only instance of an anonymous envelope defined by the envelope-block of the retrieved envelope-definition.

Other aspects of an envelope-retrieval-declaration are identical to those of a procedure-retrieval-declaration.

4. Monitor definitions

A monitor is a set of definitions and declarations defined by the monitor-block of a monitor-definition.

A monitor instance is the set of variables, procedures and functions that result from instantiation of a monitor.

The syntax definition of a monitor-definition is identical to that of an envelope-definition given in Section 3, with the word **envelope** replaced by the word **monitor** throughout.

A monitor is an envelope which guarantees that at most one process instance is executing any procedure or function of, or accessing any variable of, a given instance of the monitor at any time.

The following additional restriction applies to a monitor-definition:

- A monitor-definition may occur only within a monitor-block, or within the program-block of a Pascal Plus program.
- The procedures and functions of a monitor instance may be passed as parameters only to procedures and functions of the same monitor instance.

5. Process definitions

A process is a set of definitions and declarations defined by the process-block of a process-definition.

A process instance is the set of variables, and the execution sequence that results from instantiation of a process.

The rate of progress of the execution of a process instance is independent of the progress of other process instances in the program except as determined by their use of monitor instances.

The definition of a process-definition is identical to that of an envelope-definition given in Section 3, with the word **envelope** replaced by the word **process** throughout. The following additional restriction applies to process-definitions:

- A process-definition may occur only within a monitor-block, or within the program-block of a Pascal Plus program.

6. Instance declarations

Envelope, monitor and process instances are declared in an instance-declaration-part, the syntax of which is:

```
instance-declaration-part =
    "instance" instance-declaration ";" { instance-declaration ";" }.

instance-declaration =
    envelope-instance-declaration |
    monitor-instance-declaration |
    process-instance-declaration.
```

The syntax of an envelope-instance-declaration is:

```
envelope-instance-declaration =
    simple-envelope-declaration | envelope-array-declaration.
```

A simple-envelope-declaration declares one or more envelope-instance-identifiers, each of which denotes one instance of the specified envelope:

```
simple-envelope-declaration = identifier-list ":" envelope-specification.

envelope-specification = envelope-identifier [ instance-parameter-lists ].

instance-parameter-lists = actual-parameter-list { "," actual-parameter-list }.
```

Each identifier in the identifier-list of a simple-envelope-declaration is defined as an envelope-instance-identifier, and denotes a corresponding instance of the envelope denoted by the envelope-identifier:

```
envelope-instance-identifier = identifier.
```

If that envelope is defined without a formal-parameter-list the envelope-specification must not contain an actual-parameter-list. If the envelope is defined with a formal-parameter-list the envelope-specification must contain exactly one actual-parameter-list for each identifier in the identifier-list. Each actual-parameter-list must correspond to the formal-parameter-list of the envelope, as defined for an actual-parameter-list of a procedure or a function in Pascal. Each actual-parameter-list is used in the instantiation of the corresponding envelope instance as explained in Section 10.

An envelope-array-declaration declares one or more envelope instance array identifiers, each of which denotes an array of instances of the specified envelope:

```
envelope-array-declaration = identifier-list ":" envelope-array-specification.

envelope-array-specification =
    "array" "[" "index-type" "]" "of" envelope-identifier [ instance-array-parameter-lists ].
```

instance-array-parameter-lists =
  instance-array-parameter-list { "," instance-array-parameter-list }.

instance-array-parameter-list = "["instance-parameter-lists"]".

Each identifier in the identifier-list of an envelope-array-declaration is defined as an envelope-instance-array-identifier and denotes a corresponding array of instances of the envelope denoted by the envelope-identifier:

envelope-instance-array-identifier = identifier.

If the envelope is defined without a formal-parameter-list the envelope-array-specification must not contain an actual-parameter-list. If the envelope is defined with a formal-parameter-list the envelope-array-specification must contain exactly one instance-array-parameter-list for each identifier in the indentifier-list. Each instance-array-parameter-list must contain one actual-parameter-list for each value of the index-type of the array. Each actual-parameter-list must correspond to the formal-parameter-list of the envelope, as defined for an actual-parameter-list of a procedure or function in Pascal. Each actual-parameter-list is used in the instantiation of the corresponding envelope instance as explained in Section 10.

The definition of a monitor- or process-instance-declaration is identical to that of an envelope-instance-declaration, with the word **monitor** or the word **process**, respectively, substituted for the word **envelope** throughout.

A monitor- or process-instance-declaration may appear only in a monitor-block or in the program-block of a Pascal Plus program.

Use of an envelope or monitor instance is denoted by an envelope-or-monitor-access:

envelope-or-monitor-access = envelope-access | monitor access.

envelope-access = envelope-instance-identifier | indexed-envelope.

indexed-envelope = envelope-array-identifier "["index-express"]".

The index-expression of an indexed-envelope must be assignment-compatible with the index-type of the envelope-array-specification used to declare the envelope-instance-array-identifier.

The definition of a monitor-access is identical to that of an envelope-access with the word **monitor** substituted for the word **envelope** throughout.

7. Instances as parameters

Envelope or monitor instances may be passed as parameters to other blocks. The extension to formal-parameter-list is:

formal-parameter-section =
  value-parameter-specificiation |
  variable-parameter-specification |
  procedural-parameter-specification |
  functional-parameter-specification |
  conformant-array-parameter-specification |
  envelope-parameter-specification |
  monitor-parameter-specification.

The syntax of an envelope-parameter-specification is:

envelope-parameter-specification = **"instance"** identifier-list ":" envelope-identifier.

Each identifier in the identifier-list of an envelope-parameter-specification is defined as an envelope-instance-identifier in the block, if any, of which it is a formal parameter. The corresponding actual parameter must be an envelope-access to an instance of the same envelope.

The definition of a monitor-parameter-specification is identical to that of an envelope-parameter-specification, with the word **envelope** replaced by the word **monitor** throughout.

The syntax of actual-parameter in Pascal Plus is:

```
actual-parameter =
    expression | variable-access | procedure-identifier |
    function-identifier | envelope-or-monitor-access.
```

Envelope or monitor instances are passed by reference. The actual parameter is accessed before activation of the block to which it is passed. The corresponding formal parameter denotes the accessed envelope or monitor instance during the activation.

8. Envelope and monitor interfaces

An identifier defined within an envelope- or monitor-block may be made visible outside the block by prefixing the identifier by a star ("*") in its declaration or definition.

Such identifiers are referenced outside the block using the dot or with notation applied to Pascal records. To integrate these starring and access conventions into the existing definition of Pascal a distinction must be made between the roles played by identifier occurrences, which in the standard definition of Pascal are classified as either *defining* or *applied* occurrences. As the names imply, a defining occurrence is where an identifier is defined and an applied occurrence is where it is used.

In the definition of Pascal, defining occurrences are represented in the syntax by the direct use of the meta-identifier identifier, as in these examples:

```
type-definition = identifier "=" type-denoter.
```

```
procedure-heading = "procedure" identifier [ formal-parameter-list ].
```

For these occurrences of identifier the appropriate definition in Pascal Plus is:

```
identifier = [ "*" ] letter { letter | digit }.
```

where the optional star applies only to defining occurrences within an envelope- or monitor-block.

A starred identifier is one which has been declared with a star in this way. It is visible to other blocks, and can have applied occurrences outside the block in which it is declared. In the definition of Pascal all applied occurrences of identifiers are denoted by meta-identifiers which specify the role of the identifier, such as variable-identifier. Such meta-identifiers all have trivial syntax definitions such as:

```
variable-identifier = identifier.
```

In Pascal Plus, however, a variable-identifier may either be an identifier whose declaration as a variable is currently in scope, or it may be a reference to a starred-variable-identifier declared in an envelope- or monitor-block of which an instance is currently in scope. In that case the envelope or monitor instance concerned must be specified as part of the variable-identifier, thus:

```
variable-identifier =
    identifier | envelope-or-monitor-access "." starred-variable-identifier.
```

```
starred-variable-identifier = variable-identifier.
```

The above rules apply not just to variable identifiers. In general they apply anywhere that the Pascal syntax refers to an identifier of a specific variety (variable-identifier, type-identifier, function-identifier etc.) Thus, using the term x-identifier to refer to any one of these possibilities, the general rules are:

```
x-identifier =
    identifier | envelope-or-monitor-access "." starred-x-identifier.

starred-x-identifier = x-identifier.
```

where the x specified must be the same on both sides of any production in which it appears.

A starred-x-identifier referenced in this way may be used in any way appropriate to an x-identifier, with the single restriction that starred variables are *read-only* to external blocks. That is, a starred variable may be inspected by other blocks, but it may only be assigned a value, or passed as a variable parameter, by the code of the envelope or monitor in which it is declared.

Conversely an envelope, monitor or process may use the variables declared in blocks which enclose its definition, by the normal rules of scope, but may not directly assign values to such global variables or pass them as variable parameters.

9. Simple statements

Pascal Plus introduces an additional simple statement, the inner-statement, with the following syntax:

```
simple-statement = empty-statement |
                   assignment-statement |
                   procedure-statement |
                   goto-statement |
                   inner-statement.
inner-statement = "***".
```

The executable effect of an inner-statement is explained in Section 10.

Pascal Plus imposes two restrictions on the use of goto-statements, which are as follows:

- An envelope-, monitor- or process-block must not contain a goto-statement that refers to a label defined in a block enclosing the envelope-, monitor- or process-block.
- If execution of a goto-statement within the execution of an inner-statement (as defined in Section 10) causes the execution of the inner-statement to be interrupted, an error occurs.

10. Activations, instantiations and inner statements

A Pascal Plus program is executed by the activation of its program-block. The activation of a block B is defined as follows:

(a) If block B contains no defining points for instance-identifiers or instance-array-identifiers the activation of block B is the activation of the statement-part of B; otherwise the activation of B is the instantiation of the instance of instance array denoted by the first instance-identifier or instance-array-identifier defined in B.

(b) Instantiation of an instance-array is the instantiation of the first instance contained by the array. Instances contained by an envelope or monitor array are ordered according to the corresponding values of the index-type. Instances contained by a process array are ordered in an implementation-dependent manner.

(c) Instantiation of an envelope, monitor or process instance involves the evaluation of the corresponding actual-parameter-list, if any, followed by the activation of the corresponding envelope-, monitor- or process-block.

(d) Activation of the statement-part of a program-, procedure-, function-, envelope- or monitor-block involves the immediate execution of the compound-statement that forms the statement-part, as defined for Pascal, but subject to the definition of the execution of inner-statements, which follows as (f) to (h).

(e) Activation of the statement-part of a process-block causes execution of the compound-statement that forms the statement-part of a block to be delayed, pending resumption as defined in (g) below.

(f) The execution of an inner-statement contained by the statement-part of an envelope- or monitor-block E, which has been activated by instantiation of an instance I within the activation of a block B, is defined as follows:

If I is an element of an instance array then the next element contained by that array, if any, is instantiated; otherwise the instance or instance array denoted by the next instance-identifier or instance-array-identifier defined in B, if any, is instantiated; otherwise the statement-part of B is executed.

(g) The execution of an inner-statement contained by the statement-part of a program-block causes all executions of the statement-parts of process-blocks which have been suspended as defined in (e) above, to be resumed simultaneously, and the execution of the statement-part of the program-block to be suspended.

(h) The execution of the statement-part of the program-block is resumed either when the execution of the statement-parts of the process-blocks is complete or when the execution of the process instances involved is suspended, as defined in Section 11.

11. Monitor exclusion and conditions

A process execution is the pattern of execution that results from the instantiation of a process.

At most one process execution may involve execution of any procedure or function of, or access to any variable of, a given monitor instance at any time. The process execution is said to *enter* the monitor instance concerned when such an execution or access begins, and to *leave* it when the execution or access is complete. In the course of such an execution or access the process execution is said to have *exclusion* on the monitor instance concerned.

A process execution which attempts to enter a monitor instance when another process execution has exclusion on it is suspended until exclusion on the monitor instance is available.

A process which enters a second monitor instance while holding exclusion on a first retains exclusion on both monitor instances while execution within the second monitor instance proceeds.

Process executions may suspend themselves on condition queues. A condition queue is an instance of the monitor, denoted by the predefined identifier Condition, which provides the operations:

```
monitor Condition;
  type NonNegative = 0..Maxint;
  procedure *PWait (P: NonNegative);
  procedure *Wait;
```

```
        procedure *Signal;
        function *Empty: Boolean;
        function *Length: NonNegative;
        function *Priority: NonNegative;
        begin
           {initially queue is empty}
        end {Condition}
```

The process executions suspended on a condition queue at any moment form an ordered queue. This order determines the order in which they are resumed, and is determined by the order in which they suspend themselves, and by the priority number with which they are suspended. A process execution P in a condition queue is resumed before any process execution on the same queue with a priority number greater than that of P, and before any process execution on the same queue with the same priority number which suspended itself after P.

For a Condition instance C, execution of the statement C.PWait (N) by a process execution P suspends P on the queue associated with condition C with priority number N, and releases exclusion on all monitor instances currently held by P. Execution of the statement C.Wait is equivalent to execution of the statement C.PWait (Maxint **div** 2).

Execution of the statement C.Signal by a process execution P causes resumption of the process execution Q, if any, at the front of the queue associated with C. If no process executions are suspended on the queue the statement has no effect. Resumption of Q involves the re-acquisition by Q of exclusion on the monitor instance in which Q was suspended, followed by the resumption of its execution. If P and Q require exclusion on the same monitor instance to continue, P is suspended until Q leaves the monitor instance concerned.

The statements C.PWait (N), C.Wait and C. Signal may only be executed by a process execution.

The function C.Empty returns True if no process executions are suspended on the queue associated with C; otherwise it returns False.

The function C.Length returns the number of process executions suspended on the queue associated with C.

The function C.Priority returns the priority number of the process execution suspended at the front of the queue associated with C. If no process executions are suspended on the queue an error occurs.

Process executions acquire exclusion on a monitor instance I, with a local condition queue C, in the order:

(a) Those that have been suspended as a result of executing a C.Signal statement.
(b) Those that have been suspended on attempting to return to the monitor instance I after leaving some other monitor instance entered from I.
(c) Those that have been suspended on attempting to enter monitor instance I.

Process executions in groups (b) and (c) are resumed in their order of suspension. Process executions in group (a) are resumed in their reverse order of suspension.

12. Other facilities

Predefined identifiers

Pascal Plus defines the following predefined identifiers in addition to those predefined in standard Pascal:

Terminate

The identifier Terminate is predefined as a procedure-identifier which denotes a parameterless procedure. Execution of this procedure by a program causes its execution
to be complete.

Perform

The identifier Perform is predefined as a procedure-identifier which denotes a procedure
which takes a single reference parameter of any record type. The effect of executing
the procedure is implementation-defined.

SetPriority

The identifier SetPriority is predefined as a procedure-identifier which denotes a
procedure which takes a single value parameter in the range 0..Maxint. Execution of
the statement SetPriority (N) by a process execution causes the priority number of
that process execution to be set to the number N. The priority number of process
executions which have not executed such a statement is defined to be Maxint **DIV** 2. In
the event that all process executions not suspended cannot proceed simultaneously,
a process execution with a lower priority number takes precedence over one with a
higher priority number.

   The statement SetPriority (N) may only be executed by a process execution.

AllWaiting

The identifier AllWaiting is predefined as a monitor-instance-identifier and denotes an
instance of the predefined monitor Condition. Processes may apply all operations
defined by the Condition monitor except the operation Signal to the instance AllWaiting
with the normal effect. An implicit signal operation is applied to the instance All-
Waiting when all process executions within a program execution are suspended.

SizeOf

The identifier SizeOf is predefined as a function-identifier which denotes a function
which takes a type-identifier as a parameter and returns the number of storage units
that are occupied by a variable of that type. The storage unit type is implementation-
defined.

   Like the New procedure of Pascal there are two forms of the SizeOf function:

```
SizeOf (T)
SizeOf (T, Cl, ..., Cn)
```

For variant record types the type-identifier may, optionally, be followed by case
constants Cl..Cn corresponding in order to increasingly nested variants of the
record. Any variant not specified must be at a deeper level of nesting than that
specified by Cn.

AddressOf

The identifier AddressOf is predefined as a function-identifier which denotes a function
which takes a single variable parameter and returns the storage address of that
variable. The storage address type is implementation-defined.

Type transfer mechanism

A variable or expression of any type may be recast as a variable or expression of
another type whose storage requirement is identical. The syntaxes of variable-access
and expression become:

```
variable-access =
   type-identifier "( "variable-access" )" |
   entire-variable | component-variable |
   identified-variable | buffered-variable.
expression =
   type-identifier "( "expression" )" |
   simple-expression [ relation-operator simple-expression ].
```

File binding

The standard Pascal procedures Reset and Rewrite may take a second parameter of type string:

```
Reset (F, B)
Rewrite (F, B)
```

If B is present in either procedure it will result in the binding of the file-variable F to an entity that is external to the program, where the binding is implementation-defined. A file binding, once established, remains effective through subsequent Reset or Rewrite calls to the same *file-variable* in which no binding is specified. If a binding is specified for a file that is already bound the new binding supersedes the existing binding.

Appendix 2

SOLUTIONS TO EXERCISES

1. An introduction to concurrency

1.1 Parallel search for a data item

The search for a data item in a list of such items can be performed by first dividing the list up into a number of disjoint parts and then analyzing the parts in parallel with separate processes.

The result of the search might be reported either by:

(a) each process reporting the success or otherwise of its search directly to the output stream, or
(b) by each process reporting the result of its search to an intermediate program module which then produces a summary when all of the processes have finished.

In general, technique (b) is the preferred approach. Its main advantage is that it allows the output results to be presented in a predetermined form, whereas with technique (a) the order of output is indeterminate.

The program will terminate if either the data item is found or if the search is complete. In the former case the process that finds the data item might cause the program to stop by invoking some explicit *terminate* operation. Alternatively, termination might be indicated by the state of a Boolean variable to which all of the searching processes have access. This variable is initially set to indicate that the search is in progress and is cleared by any process finding the data item sought. Each process must inspect the state of the Boolean variable periodically to see whether it should continue searching or stop.

General techniques for handling concurrent program output are presented in Chapter 5, and program termination is discussed in Chapter 4.

1.2 Parallel maze search

A maze can be searched concurrently by processes that explore separate paths. Initially, there is one path, at the entrance, but as that is explored others are identified.

If there is a limitless supply of searcher processes then one can be assigned to each path that is identified. If the number of processes is fixed then a current set of unexplored paths can be maintained and the processes obtain and search one path after another until the entrance is found.

Each path that is explored is marked in some way to ensure that it is not explored twice. Any searcher encountering a dead-end either terminates or searches a different path, depending on the method of search being used.

Note that if a separate searcher is used for each path the number of searchers needed will increase with the size of the maze.

Another case that might be considered is where the search starts simultaneously at both the entrance and the 'exit'.

2. The execution of concurrent programs

2.1 Nondeterministic behavior in a sequential environment

A concurrent program that is executed in a sequential environment can behave in a nondeterministic way if a random number generator is used to decide whether or not each potential processor switch should occur.

Note that, in general, such a mechanism may consume a relatively large amount of processor power in relation to that used by the concurrent program itself.

2.2 Regular process switching in a sequential environment

Switching from one process to another on block entry or exit will result in a fair allocation of processor power unless one or more blocks involve a substantial amount of processing. To allow for this case switching might be performed immediately before each backward jump executed by any process, under the assumption that all substantial processing will involve a loop of some sort. This will result in a fair allocation of processor power but is expensive to operate.

2.3 Printing a file in an asynchronous i/o environment

A program to transfer the contents of a text file to a printer might contain two processes that execute in parallel: one responsible for reading text from the file and the other for writing text to the printer, as suggested by the following diagram:

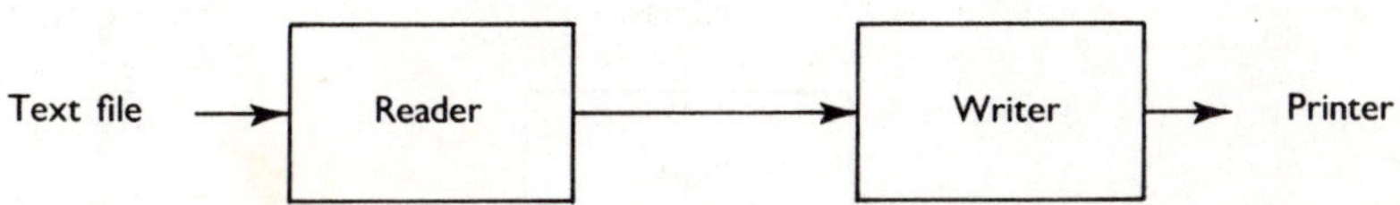

On a computer with one central processor the *Reader* can be executed in parallel with the transfer of text to the printer *or* the *Writer* can be executed in parallel with the transfer of text from the text file. If it is required that *both* devices operate in parallel with the central processor then the text has to be transferred from the *Reader* to the *Writer* through an intermediate *buffer*.

Buffering techniques are considered in Chapter 7 and device handling is discussed in Chapter 9.

2.4 Noninterrupting device transfers

If a machine has a real-time clock then this can be used to control the suspension time of processes that initiate i/o operations on devices that do not generate an interrupt. Specifically this involves:

(a) suspending such processes on a *time* queue, ordered by the expected completion time of each device operation;

(b) updating the current time on each interrupt from the real-time clock and comparing the resulting time with the completion time of the process at the head of the *time* queue; if the times match then that process is allowed to run;

(c) ensuring that the transfer is indeed complete; this involves checking the status of the device concerned, repeatedly, until the status indicates that the transfer has finished.

Note that in (c) it is not worthwhile returning the process to the *time* queue because the completion of the transfer should be imminent.

2.5 Concurrent sorting program in a multiprocessor environment

On a tightly coupled multiprocessor the full unsorted list and sorted sublists would reside in the common memory. It is desirable to have at least four processing units to sort the four sublists in parallel. When this phase is complete one of the processors can then be used to merge the sorted sublists.

On a loosely coupled multiprocessor it is more convenient to use five processing units. The additional unit would be responsible for distributing the sublists to the other four processing units (that sort the sublists in parallel), and for performing the final merge.

A full implementation of the concurrent sort program is developed in Chapter 5.

3. The design of concurrent programs

3.1 Stop-watch example

Configuration diagram

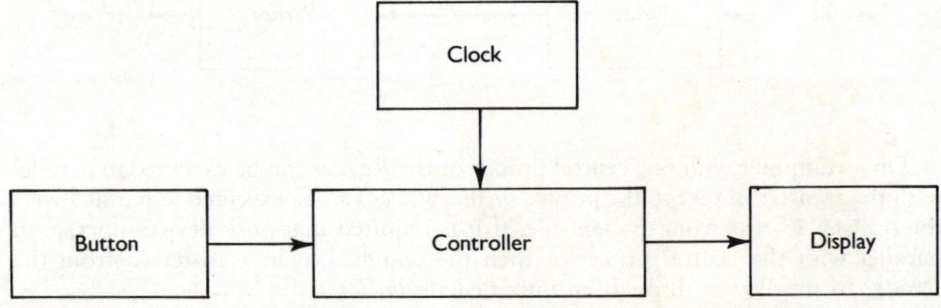

Operational model: module diagram

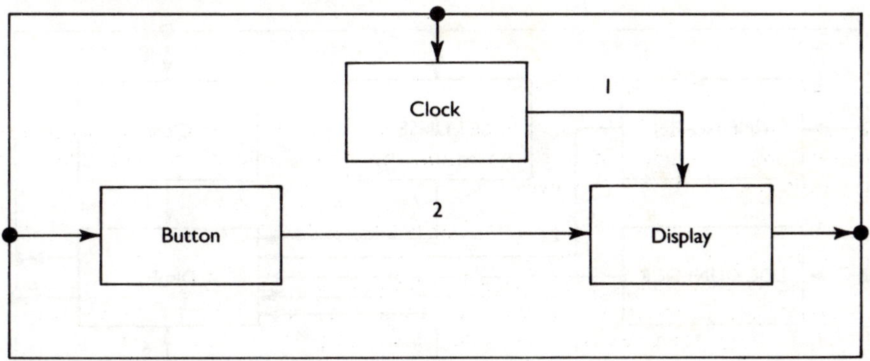

Module descriptions

There are three modules: one associated with each external device. The *clock* module receives clock pulses which it retransmits to the *display* module (1). Whenever the stop-watch button is pressed the *button* module receives a signal which it passes on to the *display* module (2). The *display* module adjusts the time display in a cycle of three phases as button signals are received: first the display is set to zero, then a dynamic display of advancing time is shown and then the display is frozen.

3.2 24-hour digital alarm clock

Configuration diagram

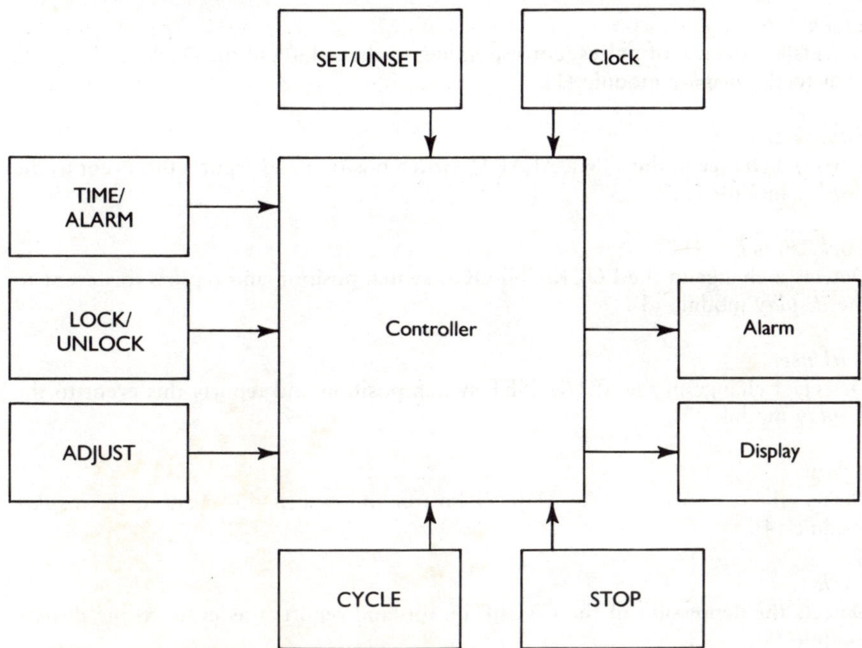

Operational model: module diagram

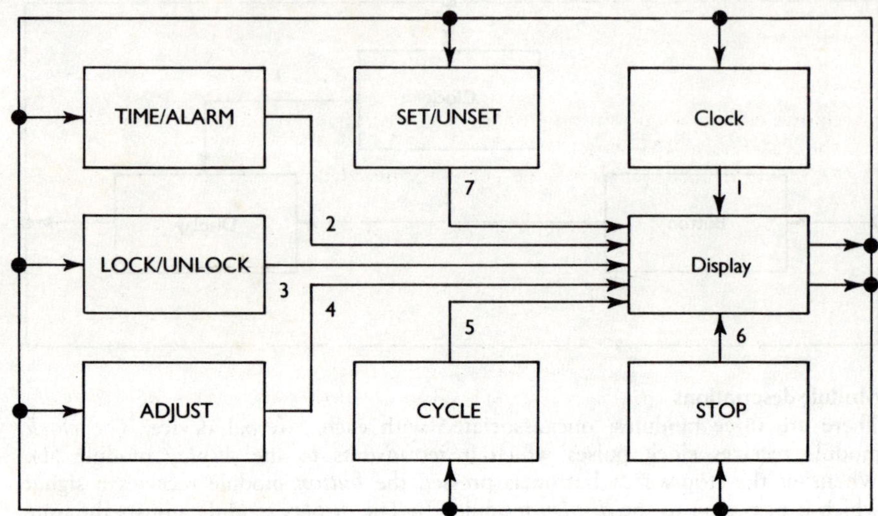

Summary of module behavior
There are eight modules, all of which are concerned with device handling. Most of the work is done by the *display* module to which information is passed from the other modules.

Module descriptions

Clock
Detects a sequence of pulses (corresponding to the ticking of the clock) and reports each to the *display* module (1).

Time/Alarm
Detects a change in the TIME/ALARM switch position and reports this event to the *display* module (2).

Lock/Unlock
Detects a change in the LOCK/UNLOCK switch position and reports this event to the *display* module (3).

Set/Unset
Detects a change in the SET/UNSET switch position and reports this event to the *display* module (7).

Adjust
Detects the depression of the ADJUST button and reports this event to the *display* module (4).

Cycle
Detects the depression of the CYCLE button and reports this event to the *display* module (5).

Stop
Detects the depression of the STOP button and reports this event to the *display* module (6).

Display
(a) Shows either the current time or the alarm setting depending on the position of the TIME/ALARM switch (2).
(b) In the TIME setting, shows the current time advancing based on signals sents from the *clock* module (1).
(c) Freezes the display and blinks the hours value if the LOCK/UNLOCK switch is put into the UNLOCK position (3).
(d) Following (c), allows the blinking value to be incremented by one on receipt of each signal from the *adjust* module (4). After 60 the value displayed is 00.
(e) Following (c), allows the blinking value to be switched between hours and minutes on receipt of each signal from the *cycle* module (5).
(f) Triggers the alarm if the alarm and time settings are the same *and* the SET/UNSET switch is in the SET position.
(g) Stops the alarm on receipt of a signal from the *stop* module (6) or after one minute has elapsed (i.e. the time setting has changed).

3.3 Credit card at the filling station

Operational model: top level module diagram

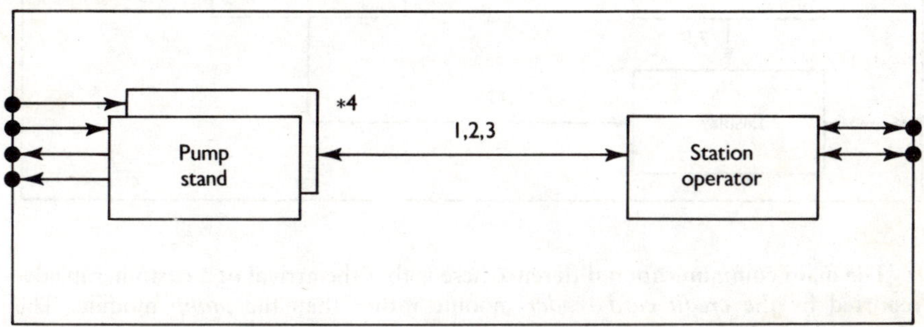

The *pump stand* module is extended with an external connection for the credit card reader. The *station operator* module has two external connections: one is to a telephone link and the other is to a printing device on which each transaction is recorded. There might also be a VDU, as before, but each transaction no longer needs a human operator to be present.

Module descriptions

Pump stand
As before, except that a customer's arrival is detected when a credit card is inserted into the reader. The credit card number is then sent to the station operator (1).

Station operator
(a) Receives notification of the arrival of a customer (1), checks the customer's credit rating over the telephone link and if satisfactory sends permission to start

the appropriate pump to the *pump stand* module (2).

(b) Receives details of a customer transaction from the *pump stand* module (3), then processes the credit transaction over the telephone link and prints a transaction record.

Pump stand module

Module diagram
The *pump stand* module will contain an extra module to handle the credit card reader.

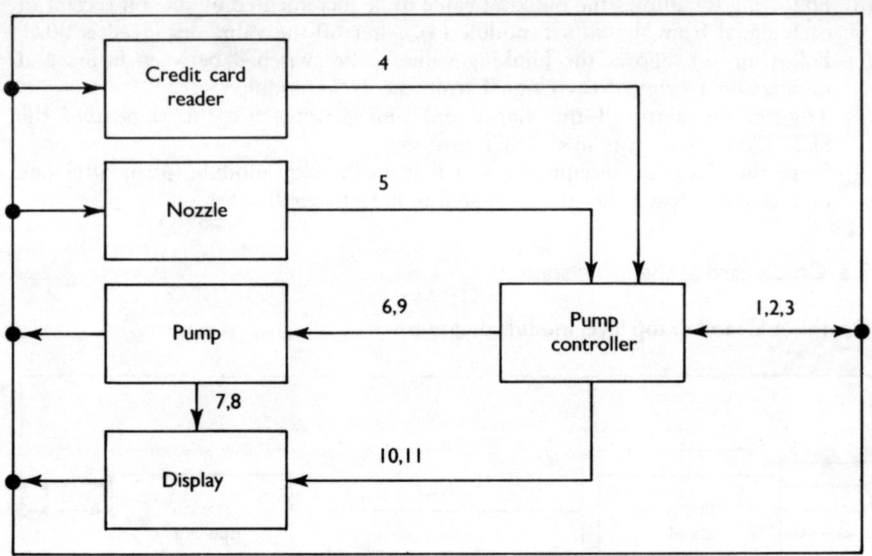

The main communication difference here is that the arrival of a customer is now reported by the *credit card reader* module rather than the *pump* module. The customer's credit card number is passed to the *pump controller* (4) and then on to the *station operator* module (1).

Station operator module structure

Module diagram
The *station operator* module can be subdivided into three modules as shown in the next diagram.

Module descriptions

Pump stands interface
(a) Receives a credit card number (1) from a *pump controller* module and sends it on to the *telephone link* module (12).
(b) After (a), receives a report from the *telephone link* module (13) indicating whether or not the customer's credit rating is satisfactory.

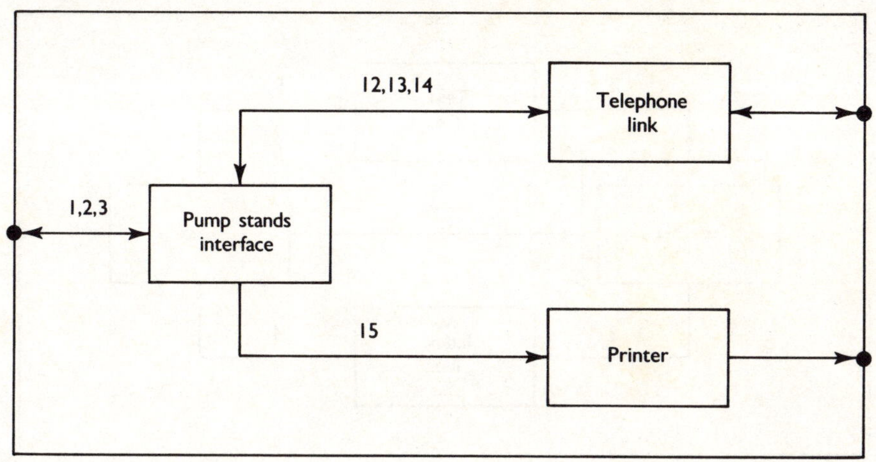

(c) After (b), indicates to the *pump controller* whether or not the pump should be started (2).
(d) Receives transaction details from a *pump controller* module (3) and passes it to the *telephone link* (14) and *printer* modules (15).

Telephone link
(a) Receives a credit card number from the *pump stands interface* module (12), checks the customer's credit rating by telephone and reports the result to the *pump stands interface* module (13).
(b) Receives transaction details from the *pump stands interface* module (14) and processes the credit transaction by telephone.

Printer
Receives transaction details from the *pump stands interface* module (15) and prints them.

3.4 Text index program

Module diagram

As shown in the next diagram the *text file* module provides pages of text from the input document (2) for a set of *searcher* modules that operate in parallel. Each word is compared with the set of index words expected and any that are found are passed to the *index file* module (3) which generates and sends an appropriate index to a disk file (4). The index words and input text are obtained from disk files (1, 5).

3.5 Concordance program in Pascal

In Pascal, the *disk* module operations would be implemented by the standard sequential file operations defined for the language. The three remaining modules can be represented as procedures leading to a program of the form:

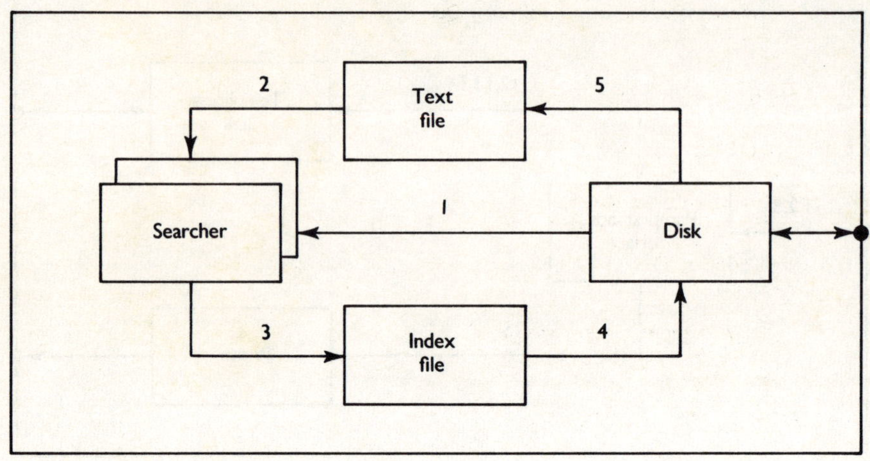


```
program Concordance (InputText, OutputReport);
    ...
  var InputText, OutputReport: Text;

  procedure ReadTextWord (var Word: ...); ...;

  procedure WriteResultWord (Word: ...); ...;

  procedure ProduceConcordance; ...;

begin
  Reset (InputText);
  Rewrite (OutputReport);
  ProduceConcordance
end {Concordance}.
```

The resulting program bears some resemblance to the design structure discussed in Chapter 3 but the data which outlives successive procedure calls, like the InputText and Report files, is less secure than implied by the program design because the variables holding such data must be declared outside the procedures implementing those modules. In the case of the InputText and Report files these data are accessible throughout the program.

Chapter 4 considers program structures that provide better support for the modular design technique.

4. The representation of concurrent programs

4.1 Synchronization monitor

The monitor described in this question can be used to synchronize the activity of a set of processes. The first form is as follows:

```
monitor module Synchronize;
  instance Queue: Condition;

  procedure *Align;
    begin
      if Queue.Length = 4
```

```
            then repeat Queue.Signal until Queue.Empty
            else Queue.Wait
        end {Align};

    begin *** end {Synchronize};
```

The general form is then:

```
    monitor Synchronize (Limit: Integer);
      instance Queue: Condition;

      procedure *Align;
        begin
          if Queue.Length = Limit
          then repeat Queue.Signal until Queue.Empty
          else Queue.Wait
        end {Align};

      begin *** end {Synchronize};
```

with instances declared accordingly:

```
      instance
        FourWaySynchronization: Synchronize (4);
```

4.2 Temperature/humidity warning system with a different bell

```
    monitor module Bell;
      var BellRequests: 0..NumberOfUsers;

      process module Ringer;
        begin
          while {system running} do
            if BellRequests > 0 then {send bell signal}
        end {Ringer};

      procedure *Start;
        begin
          BellRequests := BellRequests + 1
        end {Start};

      procedure *Stop;
        begin
          BellRequests := BellRequests - 1
        end {Stop};

      begin {Bell}
        BellRequests := 0;
        ***
      end {Bell};
```

The interface procedures now simply adjust the value of the BellRequests variable.
A local process Ringer is responsible for sending a succession of signals to ring the bell
whenever BellRequests is nonzero. Note also that there is now no need to have any
finalization code for the Bell module.

4.3 Modified parking space monitor

The solution to this problem may be found in Chapter 9.

4.4 Modified exclusion rules

With respect to the example given in Question 4 of this chapter, if exclusion is only released for the monitor in which a process is suspended then after process A has been suspended in M2, in step (b), no further progress can be made since processes B and C will still be unable to enter MI. The processes involved are then deadlocked. These exclusion rules are used in the programming languages Concurrent Euclid and Concurrent Pascal which are discussed briefly in Chapter 11.

4.5 Filling station program in Pascal Plus

The top-level modules in the design can be represented by monitor instances as shown in the following program skeleton. The reference numbers given in the skeleton correspond to the module interactions identified in the design.

```
program FillingStation;
  type PumpRange = 1..4;
       Transaction = record Volume, Cost: Integer {say} end;

  monitor module StationOperator;
    procedure *NoteArrival (At: PumpRange);
      {Reports customer arrival (1) – a return implies customer accepted (2)}
    procedure *NoteTransaction (T: Transaction);
      {Reports volume and cost of fuel for a customer (3)}
    begin
      {initially, no arrivals are recorded}
    end {StationOperator};

  monitor PumpStand (P: PumpRange);
  instance PumpStands: array [PumpRange] of PumpStand
                  [(1), (2), (3), (4)];

  begin *** end {FillingStation}.
```

The structure of the PumpStand monitor might be as follows:

```
  monitor PumpStand (P: RumpRange);

  monitor module Display;
    procedure *Reset;
      {Clears pump stand display (7)}
    procedure *NextUnitIssued;
      {Updates display for unit of fuel issued (8)}
    procedure *GetTransaction (var T: Transaction);
      {Supplies details of fuel issued and its cost (10, 11)}
    begin
      {initially, display is clear}
    end {Display};

  monitor module Pump;
    procedure *Start;
      {Switches on the pump (6)}
    procedure *Stop;
      {Switches off the pump (9)}
    begin
      {initially, the pump is off}
    end {Pump};

  monitor module Nozzle;
    procedure *AwaitCustomer;
      {Waits until the nozzle is lifted (4)}
    procedure *AwaitCompletion;
```

```
        {Waits until the nozzle is returned to its holder (5)}
      begin
        {initially, the nozzle is in its holder}
      end {Nozzle};

   process module PumpController;
      var T: Transaction; P: PumpRange;
      begin
        while {system running} do
          begin
            Nozzle.AwaitCustomer;
            StationOperator.NoteArrival (P);
            Pump.Start;
            Nozzle.AwaitCompletion;
            Pump.Stop;
            Display.GetTransaction (T);
            StationOperator.NoteTransaction (T, P)
          end
      end {PumpController};

   begin *** end {PumpStand};
```

The *pump controller* module in the design has been represented by a process and each of the other modules represented by monitors. The interactions identified in the design are expressed as procedure calls among the various program blocks.

The implementation of the monitors shown here is fairly straightforward and involves mostly devices operations of the type described in Chapter 9.

4.6 Hide-and-seek program

The *seeker* and *child* modules have a clearly motive role and so can be represented as processes. The other modules can be represented as monitors, leading to a program of the form:

```
program HideAndSeek;
   const NumberOfChildren = . . . ;
         NumberOfPlaces = . . . ;
   type  ChildRange = 1 . . NumberOfChildren;
         ChildCount = 0 . . NumberOfChildren;

   monitor module State in Library;

   monitor HidingPlace in Library;
   instance HidingPlaces: array [1 . . NumberOfPlaces] of HidingPlace;

   process module Seeker in Library;

   process Child in Library;
   instance Children: array [ChildRange] of Child;

   begin *** end {HideAndSeek}.
```

The individual modules might then be expressed as follows:

```
process Seeker;
   var ChildFound: Boolean;
       Try: 1 . . NumberOfPlaces;
   begin
     AllWaiting.Wait;
     repeat
       Try := RandomInteger (1, NumberOfPlaces);
       Places [Try].Inspect (ChildFound);
       if ChildFound then State.NoteChildFound
```

```
            until State.AllFound
         end {Seeker};

      process Child;
         var ChildFound, HiddenSuccessfully: Boolean;
             Try: 1..NumberOfPlaces;
         begin
            repeat
               Try := RandomInteger (1, NumberOfPlaces);
               Places [Try].TryToHide (HiddenSuccessfully)
            until HiddenSuccessfully;
            {now the child becomes a seeker}
            repeat
               Try := RandomInteger (1, NumberOfPlaces);
               Places [Try].Inspect (ChildFound);
               if ChildFound then State.NoteChildFound
            until State.AllFound
         end {Child};

      monitor HidingPlace;
         instance Hiding: Condition;

         procedure *TryToHide (var OK: Boolean);
            begin
               OK := Hiding.Empty;
               if OK then Hiding.Wait
            end {TryToHide};

         procedure * Inspect (var Found: Boolean);
            begin
               Found := not Hiding.Empty;
               if Found then Hiding.Signal
            end {Inspect};

         begin *** end {HidingPlace};

      monitor module State;
         var ChildrenFound: 0..NumberOfChildren;

         function *AllFound: Boolean;
            begin AllFound := ChildrenFound = NumberOfChildren end;

         procedure *NoteChildFound;
            begin ChildrenFound := ChildrenFound + 1 end;

         begin {State}
            ChildrenFound := 0;
            ***
         end {State};
```

Note that this is not a very useful simulation model as it produces no output! A
discussion of simulation modeling is given in Chapter 8, which covers the presentation of model behavior.

4.7 Parallel word search

There are three main modules in this program:

- A module *searcher*, to perform the search of individual lines – multiple instances
  of this module can be defined to run in parallel.

- A module *linefile*, to allocate lines to competing searchers.
- A module *wordcount*, to maintain the total count of the number of words found.

In Pascal Plus such a program might be expressed as follows:

```
program ParallelSearch (Output);
  const NumberOfSearchers = ...;

  monitor module WordCount;
    var Count: 0..Maxint;

    procedure *Increment;
      begin Count := Count + 1 end;

    begin {WordCount}
      Count := 0;
      ***;
      Writeln ('Total Number of Words Found = ', Count)
    end {WordCount};

  monitor module LineFile;
    type *Line = record
                   *Length: 0..80;
                   *Chars: array [1..80] of Char
                 end;
    var F: file of Line;

    procedure *TryToGetLine (var L: Line; var OK: Boolean);
      begin
        OK := not Eof (F);
        if OK then Read (F, L)
      end {TryToGetLine};

    begin
      Reset (F, 'InputFile');
      ***
    end {LineFile};

  process Searcher;
    var OK: Boolean;
        L: LineFile.Line;

    procedure SearchLine (L: LineFile.Line);
        ...
      begin
        {search line L and for each copy of the word found}
        {call LineCount.Increment.                        }
        ...
      end {SearchLine};

    begin {Searcher};
      repeat
        LineFile.TryToGetLine (L, OK);
        if OK then SearchLine (L)
      until not OK
    end {Searcher};
  instance Searchers: array [1..NumberOfSearchers] of Searcher;

  begin *** end {ParallelSearch}.
```

5. The testing of concurrent programs

5.1 Parallel record sort

The main change needed to the parallel sort program (described in Chapter 5) to enable it to handle records, is to modify the '<' comparison operations to pick out the appropriate key fields on which the sort is performed. These occur in both the Insert procedure of the Sublist envelope and in the TryToRemoveSmallestItem procedure of the TheSetOfSublists envelope. For maximum flexibility the '<' comparison is best handled by a function which is specified when the Sort and Merge processes are retrieved from the library. Thus, for a program that sorts records by student name the retrievals might take the form:

```
function NameLess (R1, R2: ItemType): Boolean;
   begin NameLess := R1. Name < R2.Name end;

process Sort in Library
   (Where function Lessthan = NameLess;);

process module Merge in Library
   (Where function Lessthan = NameLess;);
```

and for a version that sorts on the grade value:

```
function GradeLess (R1, R2: ItemType): Boolean;
   begin GradeLess := R1.Grade < R2.Grade end;

process Sort in Library
   (Where function Lessthan = GradeLess;);

process module Merge in Library
   (Where function Lessthan = GradeLess;);
```

5.2 Merge module as a monitor

If it is decided that the Merge module should be implemented as a monitor then the Sort process instances can pass sorted sublists directly to it. That is, the Merge and Exchange modules of the original solution can be combined to give a Merge monitor of the following form:

```
monitor module Merge;
   var Sublists: SetOfSublists;
        Next: 0 . . NumberOfSublists;

   procedure DoMerge;
      var Found: Boolean;
           Item: ItemType;

      procedure TryToRemoveSmallestItem
         (var I: ItemType; var Found: Boolean); . . . ;

      begin {DoMerge}
        repeat
           TryToRemovesSmallestItem (Item, Found);
           if Found then SortedList.DepositAnItem (Item)
        until not Found
      end {DoMerge};

   procedure *DepositASublist (S: ASublist);
      begin
        Next := Next + 1;
        Sublists [Next] := S;
```

```
        if Next = NumberOfSublists then DoMerge
      end {DepositASublist};

    begin Next := 0; *** end {Merge};
```

The testing of the program is now simplified because each module can be exercised using a sequential test harness since no explicit process suspension is involved.

5.3 General state module for the sort program

The State module is already in a reasonably flexible form and requires only the following simple changes:

```
    monitor module GeneralState;
      const IndentWidth = 4;
            ColumnWidth = 11;
      type *ProcessReferenceNumber= 1..Maxint;
            StepRange = 0..Maxint;
            LineRange = 0..Maxint;
      var Total: array [SorterRange] of 0..Maxint;
          NumberOfProcesses: 0..Maxint;
          TableWidth: LineRange;
          MergePosition: 0..Maxint;
      ...

    procedure Initialize;
        ...
      begin
        NumberOfProcesses := NumberOfSorters + 1;
        TableWidth := NumberOfProcesses * (ColumnWidth + 1);
        MergePosition := NumberOfSorters + 1;
        ...
      end {Initialize};
        ...
    begin ... end {GeneralState};
```

Most of this clumsiness could be avoided if standard Pascal permitted constant definitions to be given in terms of constant expressions, thus:

```
    const IndentWidth = 4;
          ColumnWidth = 11;
          NumberOfProcesses = NumberOfSorters + 1;
          TableWidth = NumberOfProcesses * (ColumnWidth + 1);
          MergePosition = NumberOfSorters + 1;
      ...
```

Note that this solution assumes that the output width is sufficient to deal with the number of processes involved.

5.4 Trace facility for temperature/humidity control program

One possible way to implement the trace facility is through a *state* module to which sensor processes report each value they measure. The *state* module, having access to the real-time clock and printer, might display values at some regular interval, say every minute. In addition, summary information might be given after longer intervals — possibly showing the temperature and humidity readings in a graphical form. Particular attention would also be drawn to any abnormal readings.

Another approach is to gather and present the information using an *observer* process. This is possible if the display modules make available the current values of temperature and humidity:

```
monitor module TemperatureDisplay;
    var *CurrentTemperature: Integer;
    procedure *Show (Temperature: Integer); ...;
    begin ··· end {TemperatureDisplay};
```

The *observer* process would then inspect these values periodically and present the results as described above.

6. Resource management

6.1 NamedOneFromN, MFromN and DatabaseAccess monitor tests

The description that follows assumes that each monitor is tested by using the techniques described in Chapter 5.

NamedOneFromN
(a) Objective:
       Check the basic allocation mechanism, namely that processes are allocated resources according to their priority status while those with the same status are allocated resources according to their arrival order.
    Possible method:
       (i)   With a single resource in the pool call Acquire four times and then Release four times – the allocation should follow the arrival order.
       (ii)   Repeat (i) with calls to PriorityAcquire using, say, priority values of 4, 3, 2, 1, respectively – for the three waiting processes the allocation order should be according to priority status, which here is the reverse of the arrival order.
       (iii) With a single resource in the pool call TryToAcquire twice – the first attempt should succeed and the second fail.
(b) Objective:
       Check that resource identities are acquired and released properly.
    Possible method:
       With three resources in the pool acquire all three and then release and reacquire them one at a time – this tests the acquisition of identities at the beginning middle and end of the range.

MFromN
(a) Objective:
       Check basic allocation mechanism.
    Possible method:
       Do as in (a) for the NamedOneFromN module, acquiring and releasing resources individually; repeat, acquiring and releasing resources in groups.
(b) Objective:
       Check that a process may take resources from the pool when a lower priority process is waiting.
    Possible method:

       (i) With two resources in the pool call PriorityAcquire requesting three re-sources and then twice requesting one resource, using priorities 2, 1 and 2 respectively – only the second call should succeed.

      (ii) Repeat (i) with the last two calls to PriorityTryToAcquire – the outcome should be the same.

(c) Objective:

Check the case where several calls to Release are needed before a waiting process is activated.

Possible method:

Clear the pool, call Acquire requesting three resources and then release three resources individually – the acquisition should only occur when the third Release call is made.

(d) Objective:

Check the case where one call to Release enables several waiting processes to be reactivated.

Possible method:

Clear the pool, make three calls to Acquire requesting one resource and then call Release to free two resources – the release should allow exactly two of the three waiting processes to proceed.

DatabaseAccess

(a) Objective:

Check basic allocation mechanism.

Possible method:

Do as in (a) for the NamedOneFromN module, acquiring and releasing *read* and *write* access alternately – the allocation order should be the same as for a single resource monitor.

(b) Objective:

Check that multiple readers are allowed.

Possible method:

Make three successive calls to obtained read access – all three calls should succeed.

(c) Objective:

Check that a writer does not proceed when there are current readers.

Possible method:

After (b) try to obtain access to write three times – all three attempts should not proceed.

(d) Objective:

Check that a reader does not proceed if there are current readers and a waiting writer.

Possible method:

After (c) try to obtain access to read twice – neither attempt should be successful.

(e) Objective:

Check that the last completing reader activates only one writer.

Possible method:

After (d) release access for three current readers – exactly one writer should proceed on the last release of read access.

(f) Objective:

Check that a reader does proceed if there is a current writer.

Possible method:

After (e) try to obtain access to read – access should be denied.
(g) Objective:
Check that a completing writer only activates one waiting writer.
Possible method:
After (f) release access for current writer – only the first of the two waiting writers should proceed.
(h) Objective:
Check that a completing writer can activate several readers.
Possible method:
After (g) release write access twice – on the second release three waiting readers should proceed.

6.2 BiasedMFromN module

This can be derived from the MFromN module by:

(a) introducing an ArrivalNumber variable, initialized to zero:

```
var ArrivalNumber: 0..Maxint;
```

(b) replacing the TryAllowed function by the procedure:

```
procedure CheckTryAllowed (var P: Priority;
                                Needed: ResourceSize;
                                var Allowed: Boolean);
  begin
    ArrivalNumber := ArrivalNumber + 1;
    P := P + Needed *WeightingFactor + ArrivalNumber;
    ConditionList.Empty
    if ConditionList.Empty
    then Allowed := True
    else Allowed := ConditionList.Priority > P
  end {CheckTryAllowed};
```

and replacing the calls to TryAllowed accordingly. The WeightingFactor should be supplied when the module is retrieved from the library.

To help avoid overflow the arrival number can be reset when there are no waiting processes (detected in Release). An explicit check for overflow should also be included in the CheckTryAllowed procedure.

6.3 NamedMFromN module

The interface operations for this module are the same as those for the MFromN module with the addition of a parameter to each routine identifying the set of resources involved. For example, Acquire, now has the form:

```
procedure *Acquire (Needed: ResourceSize; var SetGiven: ResourceSet);
  begin
    PriorityAcquire (PriorityLimit div 2, Needed, SetGiven)
  end {Acquire};
```

Internally, a ResourcePool module is required to control the allocation of the resources. It requires two operations, SelectAnyN and ReturnN in addition to those discussed in Chapter 6:

```
monitor module ExtendedResourcePool;
{assume const ResourceLimit = count of resources available}
{        type  Resource = 1..ResourceLimit              }
{        type  ResourceSize = 0..ResourceLimit           }
{        type  ResourceSet = set of Resource             }
    var *Pool: ResourceSet

    function *PoolSize: ResourceSize; ...;

    procedure *SelectAnyOne (var R: Resource); ...;

    procedure *SelectNamedOne (R: Resource); ...;

    procedure *ReturnOne (R: Resource); ...;

    procedure *SelectAnyN (Needed: ResourceSize; var R: ResourceSet);
        var Index: Resource;
            S: ResourceSize;
        begin
            Index := 1;
            R := [];
            for S := 1 to Needed do
                begin
                    while not (Index in Pool) do Index := Index + 1;
                    R := R + [Index]
                end;

            Pool := Pool − R
        end {SelectAnyN};

    procedure *ReturnN (R: ResourceSet);
        begin Pool := Pool + R end;

    begin Pool := [1..ResourceLimit]; *** end {ExtendedResourcePool};
```

The relevant changes to the MFromN monitor are then as follows:

```
monitor NamedMFromN;
{assume const PriorityLimit  = maximum priority value                          }
{        const ResourceLimit = count of resources available                    }
{        const ProcessLimit  = maximum number of processes using this monitor }
    type *PriorityRange = 0..Priority Limit;
         *ResourceSize = 0..ResourceLimit;
         *Resource = 1..ResourceLimit;
         *ResourceSet = set of Resource;

    monitor module ResourcePool = ExtendedResourcePool in Library
        {using ResourceLimit, ResourceSize, Resource and ResourceSet}

    monitor module ConditionList in Library
        (Where const QueueLimit = ProcessLimit;
                type  Requirements = ResourceSize;);

    function TryAllowed (P: PriorityRange): Boolean;
        begin
            ConditionList.Reset;
            if ConditionList.Empty
            then TryAllowed := True
            else TryAllowed := ConditionList.Priority > P
        end {TryAllowed};

    procedure *PriorityTryToAcquire (P: PriorityRange; var OK: Boolean;
                                     Needed: ResourceSize;
                                     var SetGiven: ResourceSet);
        begin
            OK := TryAllowed (P) and (Needed <= ResourcePool.PoolSize);
```

```
            if OK then ResourcePool. SelectAnyN (Needed, SetGiven)
         end {PriorityTryToAcquire};

      procedure *TryToAcquire (var OK: Boolean;
                                  Needed: ResourceSize; var SetGiven: ResourceSet);
         begin
            PriorityTryToAcquire (PriorityLimit div 2, OK, Needed, SetGiven)
         end {TryToAcquire};

      procedure *PriorityAcquire (P: PriorityRange;
                                  Needed: ResourceSize; var SetGiven: ResourceSet);
         begin
            if not TryAllowed (P) or (ResourcePool.PoolSize < Needed)
            then ConditionList.PWait (P, Needed);
            ResourcePool.SelectAnyN (Needed, SetGiven)
         end {PriorityAcquire};

      procedure *Acquire (Needed: ResourceSize;
                          var SetGiven: ResourceSet);
         begin
            PriorityAcquire (PriorityLimit div 2, Needed, SetGiven)
         end {Acquire};

      procedure *Release (SetGiven: ResourceSet);
         var StillAllocating: Boolean;
             Needed: ResourceSize;
         begin
            ResourcePool.ReturnN (SetGiven);
               . . .
         end {Release};

   begin *** end {NamedMFromN};
```

6.4 NamedMFromSubset module

The interface operations for this module are the same as those for the NamedMFromN
module with the addition of a parameter to each routine identifying the set of
acceptable resources. For example, Acquire, now has the form:

```
      procedure *Acquire (Needed: ResourceSize; Acceptable: ResourceSet;
                          var SetGiven: ResourceSet);
        begin
           PriorityAcquire (PriorityLimit div 2, Needed, Acceptable, SetGiven)
        end {Acquire};
```

The full implementation of the module can be expressed as follows:

```
   monitor NamedMFromSubset;
   { assume const PriorityLimit  = maximum priority value                          }
   {        const ResourceLimit = count of resources available                     }
   {        const ProcessLimit  = maximum number of processes using this monitor }
    type *PriorityRange = 0..Priority Limit;
         *ResourceSize = 0..ResourceLimit;
         *Resource = 1..ResourceLimit;
         *ResourceSet = set of Resource;
          ResourceDetails = record
                                  Needed: ResourceSize;
                                  Acceptable: ResourceSet
                            end;
   var SetJustFreed: ResourceSet;

   monitor module ResourcePool = Extended ResourcePool in Library
     {using ResourceLimit, ResourceSize, Resource and ResourceSet}
```

```
monitor module ConditionList in Library
  (Where const QueueLimit = ProcessLimit;
         type  Requirements = ResourceDetails;);

function TryAllowed (P: PriorityRange): Boolean;
  begin
    ConditionList.Reset;
    if ConditionList.Empty then TryAllowed := True
    else TryAllowed := ConditionList.Priority > P
  end {TryAllowed};

procedure LookForResources (Needed: ResourceSize; Acceptable: ResourceSet;
                            var SetGiven: ResourceSet;
                            var NumberGiven: ResourceSize);
  label 99;
  var R: Resource;
      OK: Boolean;
  begin
    NumberGiven := 0;
    SetGiven := [];
    for R := 1 to ResourceLimit do
      if R in (Acceptable * ResourcePool.Pool) then
        begin
          ResourcePool.SelectNamedOne (R);
          SetGiven := SetGiven + [R];
          NumberGiven := NumberGiven + 1;
          if NumberGiven = Needed then goto 99
        end;
  99:
  end {LookForResources};

procedure * PriorityTryToAcquire (P: PriorityRange; var OK: Boolean;
                                  Needed: ResourceSize; Acceptable: ResourceSet;
                                  var SetGiven: ResourceSet);
  var NumberGiven: ResourceSize;
  begin
    LookForResources (Needed, Acceptable, SetGiven, NumberGiven);
    OK := TryAllowed (P) and (NumberGiven = Needed);
    if not OK then ResourcePool.ReturnN (SetGiven)
  end {PriorityTryToAcquire};

procedure *TryToAcquire (OK: Boolean;
                         Needed: ResourceSize; Acceptable: ResourceSet;
                         var SetGiven: ResourceSet);
  begin
    PriorityTryToAcquire (PriorityLimit div 2, OK, Needed, Acceptable, SetGiven)
  end {TryToAcquire};

procedure *PriorityAcquire (P: PriorityRange;
                            Needed: ResourceSize; Acceptable; ResourceSet;
                            var SetGiven: ResourceSet);
  var OK: Boolean;
      Entry: ResourceDetails;
  begin
    PriorityTryToAcquire (P, OK, Needed, Acceptable, SetGiven);
    if not OK then
      begin
        Entry.Needed := Needed;
        Entry.Acceptable := Acceptable;
        ConditionList.PWait (P, Entry);
        SetGiven := SetJustFreed
      end
  end {PriorityAcquire};
```

```
    procedure * Acquire (Needed: ResourceSize; Acceptable: ResourceSet;
                            var SetGiven: ResourceSet);
      begin
        PriorityAcquire (PriorityLimit div 2, Needed, Acceptable, SetGiven)
      end {Acquire};

    procedure *Release (SetGiven: ResourceSet);
      var Entry: ResourceDetails;
          SetSaved: ResourceSet;
      begin
        ResourcePool.ReturnN (SetGiven);
        ConditionList.Reset;
        SetSaved := [];
        while ConditionList.InList and (ResourcePool.NumberFree <> 0) do
          begin
            ConditionList.Content (Entry);
            LookForResources (Entry.Needed, Entry.Acceptable, SetGiven, NumberGiven);
            if NumberGiven = Entry.Needed
            then
              begin
                SetJustFreed := SetGiven;
                ConditionList.Signal
              end
            else
            {Resources are not returned to the pool immediately}
            {as only resources not needed by higher priority     }
            {processes can be offered to those with a lower       }
            {priority to avoid starvation.                        }
              begin
                ConditionList.Next;
                SetSaved := SetSaved + SetGiven
              end
          end;
        ResourcePool.ReturnN (SetSaved)
      end {Release};

    begin *** end {NamedMFromSubset};
```

6.5 Banker's algorithm

```
  monitor module Banker;
  {assumes const PriorityLimit  = maximum priority value          }
  {         const ProcessLimit  = maximum number of processes}
  {                                using this monitor             }
  {         const ResourceLimit = count of resources available    }
  type
      ProcessRange = 1..ProcessLimit;
     *Key = ProcessRange;
    *PriorityRange = 0..PriorityLimit;
     Resource = 1..ResourceLimit;
     ResourceSize = 0..ResourceLimit;
     ResourceSet = set of Resource;
     ProcessDetails = record
                          TotalClaim, InUse: ResourceSet
                      end;
  var
     ResourcePool: ResourceSet;
     AllocationDetails: array [ProcessRange] of ProcessDetails;
     NextReference: 0..ProcessLimit;
```

```
monitor ConditionList in Library
  (Where const QueueLimit = ProcessLimit;
         type  Requirements = ProcessRange;);

instance
  Queues: array [Resource] of ConditionList;

procedure *NoteMaximumRequirement (Claim: ResourceSet; var Reference: Key);
  begin
    NextReference := NextReference + 1;
    Reference := NextReference;
    with AllocationDetails [Reference] do
      begin
        TotalClaim := Claim;
        InUse := []
      end
  end {NoteMaximumRequirement};

procedure *TryToAcquire (var OK: Boolean;
                              Reference: Key; R: Resource);
  var NotionalPool: ResourceSet;
      Completed: array [ProcessRange] of Boolean;
      ResourcesReturned: Boolean;
      P: ProcessRange;
  begin
    OK := R in ResourcePool;
    if OK then
      begin
      {make notional allocation}
        NotionalPool := ResourcePool − [R];
        with AllocationDetails [Reference] do
          InUse := InUse + [R];
      {check for possibility of deadlock}
        for P := 1 to ProcessLimit do Completed [P] := False;
        repeat
          ResourcesReturned := False;
          for P := 1 to ProcessLimit do
            if not Completed [P] then
              with AllocationDetails [P] do
                if (TotalClaim − InUse) − NotionalPool = [] then
                {the needs of this process can be satisfied}
                {− so complete its transactions and return  }
                {its resources                              }
                begin
                  NotionalPool := NotionalPool + InUse;
                  ResourcesReturned := True;
                  Completed [P] := True
                end
        until not ResourcesReturned;
        OK := NotionalPool = [1 . . ResourceLimit];
        if OK
        then {deadlock will not occur − make the allocation}
            ResourcePool := ResourcePool − [R]
        else {no allocation made − restore InUse details}
            with AllocationDetails [Reference] do InUse := InUse − [R]
      end
  end {TryToAcquire};

procedure *PriorityAcquire (P: PriorityRange;
                               Reference: Key; R: Resource);
  var OK: Boolean;
  begin
```

```
            TryToAcquire (OK, Reference, R);
            if not OK then Queues [R]. PWait (P, Reference)
         end {PriorityAcquire};

      procedure *Acquire (Reference: Key; R: Resource);
         begin
            PriorityAcquire (PriorityLimit div 2, Reference, R)
         end {Acquire};

      procedure *Release (Reference: Key; R: Resource);
         var WaitingProcess: ProcessRange;
            Index: Resource;
            OK: Boolean;
         begin
            ResourcePool := ResourcePool + [R];
            with AllocationDetails [Reference] do
               InUse := InUse − [R];
            for Index := 1 to ResourceLimit do
            if not Queues [Index].Empty and (Index in ResourcePool) then
               begin
                  Queues [Index].Content (Reference);
                  TryToAcquire (OK, Reference, Index);
                  if OK then Queues [Index].Signal
               end
         end {Release};

   procedure Initialize;
      var P: ProcessRange;
      begin
         NextReference := 0;
         ResourcePool := [1 . . ResourceLimit];
         for P := 1 to ProcessLimit do
            with AllocationDetails [P] do
               begin
                  TotalClaim := [];
                  InUse := []
               end
      end {Initialize};

   begin {Banker}
      Initialize;
      ***
   end {Banker};
```

6.6 Controlling access to multiple data items

```
   monitor module MultipleData;
   {assumes const ProcessLimit = maximum number of processes using}
   {                            this monitor                      }
   {        const ResourceLimit = count of resources available     }
    type *Resource = 1 . . ResourceLimit;
         *ResourceList = ↑ ResourceItem;
         *ResourceItem = record
                           *R: Resource;
                           *Next: ResourceList
                        end;
         ConditionRange = 1 . . ProcessLimit;
         WaitingEntry = ↑ WaitingRecord;
         WaitingRecord = record
                           ResourceNeeded: 0 . . Maxint;
```

```
                              WaitingQueue: ConditionRange
                        end;
            LinkEntry = ↑ LinkRecord;
            LinkRecord = record
                              Next: LinkEntry;
                              ProcessWaiting: WaitingEntry
                        end;
            ResourceEntry = ↑ ResourceRecord;
            ResourceRecord = record
                                R: Resource;
                                Next, Previous: ResourceEntry;
                                WaitingQueue: record
                                                   First, Last: LinkEntry
                                              end
                        end;
var Resources: ResourceEntry;
instance Conditions: array [ConditionRange] of Condition;

monitor module QueuePool = ResourcePool in Library
  (Where const ResourceLimit = ProcessLimit;
         type  Resource = ConditionRange;);

procedure TryToLocateResource (R: Resource; var Entry: ResourceEntry);

  function StillLooking (R: Resource; Entry: ResourceEntry): Boolean;
    begin
      if Entry = nil then StillLooking := False
      else StillLooking := Entry ↑ .R <> R
    end {StillLooking};

  begin
    Entry := Resources;
    while StillLooking (R, Entry) do Entry := Entry ↑ .Next
  end {TryToLocateResource};

procedure *Acquire (Needed: ResourceList);
{for each item needed do                                          }
{   if the item is not in the resource pool                       }
{   then                                                          }
{     add the item to the pool                                    }
{   else                                                          }
{     begin                                                       }
{       if this process is not awaiting other items then          }
{         create a process waiting record                         }
{       increment the count in the waiting record by one          }
{       add a process link to the list of links attached to       }
{           that item                                             }
{     end                                                         }
  var Index: ResourceList;
      TheResourceEntry: ResourceEntry;
      TheWaitingEntry: WaitingEntry;
      ItemsMissing: 0 . . Maxint;

  procedure SetUpResourceEntry (var Entry: ResourceEntry; R: Resource);
    begin
      New (Entry);
      Entry ↑ .Next := Resources;
      Entry ↑ .Previous := nil;
      if Resources <> nil then Resources ↑ .Previous := Entry;
      Resources := Entry;
      Entry ↑ .R := R;
      Entry ↑ .WaitingQueue.First := nil
    end {SetUpResourceEntry};
```

```
  procedure SetUpWaitingEntry (var Entry: WaitingEntry);
    begin
      New (Entry);
      QueuePool.SelectAnyOne (Entry ↑ .WaitingQueue)
    end {SetUpWaitingEntry};

  procedure SetUpLinkEntry (TheWaitingEntry: WaitingEntry;
                                  TheResourceEntry: ResourceEntry);
    var ALinkEntry: LinkEntry;
    begin
      New (ALinkEntry);
      ALinkEntry ↑ .ProcessWaiting := TheWaitingEntry;
      ALinkEntry ↑ .Next := nil;
      with TheResourceEntry ↑ .WaitingQueue do
        begin
          if First = nil
          then First := ALinkEntry
          else Last ↑ .Next := ALinkEntry;
          Last := ALinkEntry
        end
    end {SetUpLinkEntry};

begin {Acquire}
  Index := Needed;
  ItemsMissing := 0;
  while Index <> nil do
    begin
      TryToLocateResource (Index ↑ .R, TheResourceEntry);
      if TheResourceEntry = nil
      then SetUpResourceEntry (TheResourceEntry, Index ↑ .R)
      else {resource in use – prepare to wait}
        begin
          if ItemsMissing = 0 then
            SetUpWaitingEntry (TheWaitingEntry);
          ItemsMissing := ItemsMissing + 1;
          SetUpLinkEntry (TheWaitingEntry, The ResourceEntry)
        end;
      Index := Index ↑ .Next
    end;
  if ItemsMissing <> 0 then
    begin
      TheWaitingEntry ↑ .ResourcesNeeded := ItemsMissing;
      Conditions [TheWaitingEntry ↑ .WaitingQueue].Wait
    end
end {Acquire};

procedure *Release (Given: ResourceList);
{for each item released do                                      }
{   if its process waiting list is empty                        }
{   then                                                        }
{     delete the item from the pool                             }
{   else                                                        }
{     begin                                                     }
{       remove the link to the process at the head of the       }
{           waiting list                                        }
{       decrement the count in the corresponding process        }
{           record by one                                       }
{       if the count is zero then reactivate that process       }
{           and delete its waiting record                       }
{     end;                                                      }
```

```pascal
    var Index: ResourceList;
        TheResourceEntry: ResourceEntry;
        TheWaitingEntry: WaitingEntry;

    procedure DeleteResourceEntry (var Entry: ResourceEntry);
      begin
        if Entry = Resources
        then Resources := Entry ↑ .Next
        else Entry ↑ .Previous ↑ .Next := Entry ↑ .Next;
        if Entry ↑ .Next <> nil then
          Entry ↑ .Next ↑ .Previous := Entry ↑ .Previous;
        Dispose (Entry)
      end {DeleteResourceEntry};

    procedure DeleteWaitingLink (var Queue: LinkEntry;
                                 var TheWaitingEntry: WaitingEntry);
      var Entry: LinkEntry;
      begin
        Entry := Queue;
        Queue := Entry ↑ .Next;
        TheWaitingEntry := Entry ↑ .ProcessWaiting;
        Dispose (Entry)
      end {DeleteWaitingLink};

    procedure ActivateWaitingProcess (var Entry: WaitingEntry);
      begin
        Conditions [Entry ↑ .WaitingQueue].Signal;
        QueuePool.ReturnOne (Entry ↑ .WaitingQueue);
        Dispose (Entry)
      end {ActivateWaitingProcess};

    begin {Release}
      Index := Given;
      while Index <> nil do
        begin
          TryToLocateResource (Index ↑ .R, TheResourceEntry);
          if TheResourceEntry ↑ .WaitingQueue.First = nil
          then
            DeleteResourceEntry (TheResourceEntry)
          else {transfer access to first waiting process}
            begin
              DeleteWaitingLink (TheResourceEntry ↑ .WaitingQueue.First, TheWaitingEntry);
              with TheWaitingEntry do
                begin
                  ResourcesNeeded := ResourcesNeeded − 1;
                  if ResourcesNeeded = 0 then
                    ActivateWaitingProcess (TheWaitingEntry)
                end
            end;
          Index := Index ↑ .Next
        end
    end {Release};

begin
  Resources := nil;
  ***
end {MultipleData};
```

7. Communication management

7.1 SynchronizedChannel, SingleItemBuffer and MultipleItemBuffer monitor tests

The description that follows assumes that each monitor is tested using the techniques described in Chapter 5.

SynchronizedChannel
(a) Objective:
    Check that a process calling Send is delayed until another process calls either Receive or TryToReceive, and that the data item is passed correctly between the two processes.
    Possible method:
    (i) Call Send with an integer value (say) and then call Receive, displaying the value obtained.
    (ii) Repeat (i) where the second call is to TryToReceive.
(b) Objective:
    Check that a process calling Receive is delayed until another process calls either Send or TryToSend, and that the data item is passed correctly between the two processes.
    Possible method:
    (i) Call Receive and then call Send passing an integer value – again the value obtained can be displayed.
    (ii) Repeat (i) where the second call is to TryToSend.
(c) Objective:
    Check that calls to TryToSend and TryToReceive both return with False replies if no process is waiting.

SingleItemBuffer
(a) Objective:
    Check the basic send and receive synchronization mechanism.
    Possible method:
    (i) Call Receive and then call Send passing an integer value – the value obtained can be displayed.
    (ii) Repeat (i) where the second call is to TryToSend.
(b) Objective:
    Check that a call to TryToReceive returns with a False reply if no data item is present in the buffer.
(c) Objective:
    Check that a sending process has its data item accepted on calling either Send or TryToSend even if no receiver is waiting.
(d) Objective:
    Check that a call to TryToReceive obtains a value from the buffer if one is present.
    Possible method:
    After (c), call TryToReceive and display the value obtained.
(e) Objective:
    Check that only one data item can be held in the buffer.
    Possible method:
    Call Send to place an item in the buffer and then make successive calls to Send and TryToSend, neither of which should succeed in depositing a data item.

MultipleItemBuffer
Tests are the same as for the single item buffer except for (e), which differs only in that more than one item can be held.

7.2 Temperature/humidity control program variation

If the temperature of humidity display module is represented as a process then interaction with the corresponding sensor module can be performed through a synchronized or buffered channel. Using a single item buffer, for example, the temperature modules would take the form:

```
monitor module TemperatureSensorToDisplay = SingleItemBuffer in Library
   (Where type ItemType = Integer;);

process module TemperatureSensor;
      . . .
   begin
      . . .
      TemperatureSensorToDisplay.Send (T);
      . . .
   end {TemperatureSensor};

process module TemperatureDisplay;
   var Temperature: Integer;
   begin
      while True do
         begin
            TemperaturesSensorToDisplay.Receive (Temperature);
            {display temperature}
         end
   end {TemperatureDisplay};
```

The bell module may interact with both the **TemperatureSensor** and **HumiditySensor** processes. If the bell module is represented by a process and a separate communication channel is used for its communication with the sensor modules then it is obliged to poll the channels looking for possible interactions. The alternative is to use a single channel through which is passed the appropriate **Start** or **Stop** request, thus:

```
type BellAction = (Start, Stop);

monitor module BellCommunication = SingleItemBuffer in Library
   (Where type ItemType = BellAction;);

process module Bell;
   const NumberOfUsers = 2;
   var    BellRequests: 0..NumberOfUsers;
          Directive: BellAction;
   begin
      BellRequests := 0;
      while True do
         begin
            BellCommunication.Receive (Directive);
            case Directive of
            Start: begin
                     BellRequests := BellRequests + 1;
                     if BellRequests = 1 then {start bell}
                   end;
            Stop: begin
                     BellRequests := BellRequests − 1;
                     if BellRequests = 0 then {stop bell}
```

```
                  end
             end
          end
     end {Bell};

  process module TemperatureSensor;
     const LowBound = ...; HighBound = ...;
     var T: Integer;
     begin
        while True do
          begin
            {measure temperature T};
            TemperatureSensorToDisplay.Send (T);
            if (T < LowBound) or (T > HighBound) then
               begin
                 BellCommunication.Send (Start);
                 repeat
                    {measure temperature T};
                    TemperatureSensorToDisplay.Send (T);
                 until (T >= LowBound) and (T <= HighBound);
                 BellCommunication.Send (Stop)
               end
          end
     end {TemperatureSensor};
```

7.3 Message passing monitor

The interface to the message passing buffer might be defined as follows:

```
monitor MessageBuffer;
{assumes const MaxItems = number of messages in buffer     }
{         const MessageLimit = maximum length of message   }
{         const ProcessLimit = maximum number of processes }
{               using this monitor                         }
  type *ProcessIdentification = 1..ProcessLimit;
       *Message =
         record
            *Sender, *Receiver: ProcessIdentification;
            *Text: packed array [1..MessageLimit] of Char
         end;
procedure *TryToSend (M: Message; var OK: Boolean);
   {Send message if receiver waiting or buffer is nonfull;}
   {otherwise return                                      }
procedure *Send (M: Message);
   {Send message if receiver waiting or buffer is nonfull; }
   {otherwise wait until receiver arrives or space becomes }
   {available in buffer.                                   }
procedure *TryToReceive (var M: Message;
                               var OK: Boolean);
   {Receive message if one is present in buffer or held}
   {by waiting sender; otherwise return                }
   {Note: Reference of receiver is in M.Receiver       }
procedure *Receive (var M: Message);
   {Receive message - waiting if necessary        }
   {Note: Reference of receiver is in M.Receiver}
begin    {initially, buffer is empty} end {MessageBuffer};
```

Internally the implementation of the message buffer might use a MessageList module to
hold the buffered items:

```
monitor module MessageList;
{assumes type Message as defined in the message buffer      }
{          const MaxItems = maximum number of items held}
    function *Full: Boolean;
       {is there space in the list?}
    procedure *Insert (M: Message);
       {put a message into the list}
    procedure *TryToLocate (var M: Message; var Found: Boolean);
       {try to get a message for the given receiver (M.Receiver)}
    begin
       {initially, the message list is empty}
    end {MessageList};
```

The full implementation of the message buffer might be as follows:

```
monitor MessageBuffer;
{assumes const MaxItems = number of messages in buffer    }
{          const MessageLimit = maximum length of message }
{          const ProcessLimit = maximum number of process}
{                    using this monitor                         }

  type *ProcessIdentification = 1..ProcessLimit;
       *Message =
          record
             *Sender, *Receiver: ProcessIdentification;
             *Text: packed array [1..MessageLimit] of Char
          end;

  monitor module MessageList in Library
     {uses the definition of type Message and const MaxItems}

  instance Receivers: array [ProcessIdentification] of Condition;

  monitor module Senders = ConditionList in Library
     (Where const QueueLimit = ProcessLimit;
              type  Requirements = ProcessIdentification;
                    PriorityRange = 0..Maxint;);

  var MessageReceived: Message;
      MessagesWaiting: array [ProcessIdentification] of 0..Maxint;

  procedure *TryToSend (M: Message; var OK: Boolean);
    begin
      if not Receivers [M.Receiver].Empty
        then {receiver waiting}
          begin
            MessageReceived := M;
            Receivers [M.Receiver].Signal;
            OK := True
          end
        else {no receiver waiting}
          if MessageList.Full then OK := False
          else
            begin
              MessageWaiting [M.Receiver] := MessagesWaiting [M.Receiver] + 1;
              MessageList.Insert (M);
              OK := True
            end
    end {TryToSend};
  procedure *Send (M: Message);
    var OK: Boolean;
    begin
```

```
        TryToSend (M, OK);
      if not OK then
        begin
          MessagesWaiting [M.Receiver] := MessagesWaiting [M.Receiver] + 1;
          Senders.Wait (M.Receiver);
          if MessageList.Full
          then {receiver ready}
            MessageReceived := M
          else {buffer space now available}
            MessageList.Insert (M)
        end
    end {Send};

procedure *TryToReceive (var M: Message; var OK: Boolean);
  var Found: Boolean;

  procedure FindAndActivateSender (Receiver: ProcessIdentification);
    var Entry: ProcessIdentification;
    begin
      Senders.Reset;
      repeat
        Senders.Content (Entry);
        if Entry <> Receiver then Senders.Next
      until Entry = Receiver;
      Senders.Signal
    end {FindAndActivateSender};

  begin {TryToReceive}
    OK := MessageWaiting [M.Receiver] <> 0;
    if OK then
      begin
        MessagesWaiting [M.Receiver] := MessagesWaiting [M.Receiver] − 1;
        MessageList.TryToLocate (M, Found);
        if Found {in buffer}
        then
        {allow waiting sender to put item into buffer}
          begin
            Senders.Reset;
            Senders.Signal
          end
        else {reactivate sender in queue}
          begin
            FindAndActivateSender (M.Receiver);
            M := MessageReceived
          end
      end
  end {TryToReceive};

procedure *Receive (var M: Message);
  var OK: Boolean;
  begin
    TryToReceive (M, OK);
    if not OK then
      begin
        Receivers [M.Receiver].Wait;
        M := MessageReceived
      end
  end {Receive};

procedure Initialize;
  var P: ProcessIdentification;
  begin
```

```
        for P := 1 TO ProcessLimit DO
          MessagesWaiting [P] := 0
      end {Initialize};

  begin
    Initialize;
    ***
  end {MessageBuffer};
```

8. Discrete event simulation

8.1 Presentation of philosopher behavior

The behavior of the philosophers can be summarized in a *behavior table* as described for the laundry simulation in Chapter 8. This is produced by a *state* module to which the Philosopher processes pass activity information as they execute. The philosopher *state* module can be based on the equivalent module used in the laundry simulation program. The changes needed are relatively small:

- define the actions of the philosophers:

```
    Action = (Arrival, SeekFirstFork, SeekSecondFork, StartEating, StopEating);
```

- reduce the space available for each activity description (TextLimit) to ten characters (say) and set up the descriptions accordingly;
- set up the entity names;
- add code to accumulate and present statistics on each philosopher, such as his total eating time and his average and maximum time spent waiting for forks.

8.2 Pass-the-parcel with two parcels

The basic simulation model has already been given in Chapter 7. What remains is to decide how the simulation can be presented. This is a situation where a cartoon is ideal and where the effort required to produce it is not great. Given a terminal handling module which provides basic cursor addressing a pictorial representation of the children can be constructed using characters from the ASCII character set as suggested by Figure 8.8. The parcels can then be superimposed on this representation as numbers indicating the layers that remain. The numbers are then moved around the diagram to mirror the movement of the parcels. The current value of simulated time might also be shown in one corner of the screen together with some indication of whether or not music is playing.

8.3 Car wash simulation

The car wash simulation program takes the same form as the simulation programs discussed in Chapter 8. In addition to the usual *state*, *times*, and *clock* modules there are modules to model the cars and car wash.

A car might be represented as follows:

```
process Car;
  var Reference: CarRange;
  begin
    with State do
    begin
      Clock.Hold (Times.ArrivalTime);
```

```
              EntityReferences.GetReference (Reference);
              NoteAction (Arrival, Reference);
              CarWash.Acquire;
              NoteAction (StartWash, Reference);
              Clock.Hold (Times.WashTime);
              NoteAction (EndWash, Reference)
              CarWash.Release
          end
      end {Car};
```

Over a twelve-hour period about 120 cars are expected to arrive at the car wash so a larger number of processes (say 150) must be declared to ensure that every car is represented.

The car wash can be represented by an instance of the SingleResource monitor.

The maximum length of queue that forms can be determined from the information passed to the State monitor.

8.4 Supermarket queuing strategy simulation

Two versions of the program can be used to cover the two queuing schemes. The first version is as follows:

```
program QueueSimulation (Output);
{Time unit is MINUTES}
{Version 1: Separate queues for each checkout}
    const NumberOfCheckouts = 4;
          NumberOfCustomers = 100;
          NumberOfEntities = 104;
    type CustomerRange = 1..NumberOfCustomers;
         CheckoutRange = 1..NumberOfCheckouts;

    monitor module Times in Library;

    monitor module Clock in Library
      (Where const TimeLimit = Times.ObservedPeriod;
             const EntityLimit = NumberOfEntities;
             type  TimeType = Real;);

    monitor module CustomerIds in Library;

    monitor module State in Library
      (Where const Identification = 'Version 1: one queue per checkout';);

    monitor Queue in Library;
    instance Queues: array [CheckoutRange] of Queue;

    process CheckOut = Checkout1 in Library;
    instance Checkouts: array [CheckoutRange] of Checkout [(1), (2), (3), (4)];

    process Customer = Customer1 in Library;
    instance Customers: array [CustomerRange] of Customer;

    begin *** end {QueuesSimulation}.
```

The modules specific to this problem are those modeling the behavior of customers and checkouts, and one that deals with their synchronization. Only the *customer* and *checkout* modules differ in the two versions of the program.

The synchronization of the Customer and Checkout processes can be handled by the following monitor:

```
monitor Queue;
    instance CustomerQueue, Service, CheckoutWaiting: Condition;
```

```
function *Length: Integer;
{Return total length of waiting queue}
    begin Length := CustomerQueue.Length + Service.Length end {Length};

procedure *GetCustomer;
{Checkout either gets a customer from the queue or}
{waits for one to arrive                          }
    begin
      if CustomerQueue.Empty
      then CheckoutWaiting.Wait
      else CustomerQueue.Signal
    end {GetCustomer};

procedure *AwaitServiceComplete;
{Suspend customer until service complete}
    begin Service.Wait end;

procedure *SignalServiceComplete;
{Service complete – reactivate customer}
    begin Service.Signal end;

procedure *GetService;
{Wait for the checkout to become free or proceed if}
{the checkout is free.                             }
    begin
      if CheckoutWaiting.Empty
      then CustomerQueue.Wait else CheckoutWaiting.Signal
    end {GetService};

begin *** end {Queue};
```

In the first program, where there is a separate queue for each checkout, instances of the Queue monitor are associated with corresponding instances of each Checkout process. In the second program there is only one instance of the Queue monitor needed to model the single customer queue.

While there are no customers at a checkout the Checkout process concerned is suspended on the CheckoutWaiting condition.

When a Customer process arrives it is suspended. If the checkout is busy it is suspended awaiting service and if the checkout is not busy it is suspended for the time taken to be serviced at the checkout.

Note that the length of the waiting queue is taken to be the combined lengths of the CustomerQueue and Service condition queues.

With this definition of a queue the behavior of a customer can be modeled as follows:

```
process Customer1;
{Version 1: Separate queues at each checkout}
    var Shortest: record
                    Length: 0..Maxint;
                    Position: CheckoutRange
                  end;
        Index: CheckoutRange;
        Reference: CustomerRange;
    begin
    {Await arrival}
        Clock.Hold (Times.NextArrivalTime);
        CustomerIds.GetReference (Reference);
        State.NoteAction (Arrival, Reference);
        {Find the shortest queue}
        Shortest.Length := Queues[1]. Length;
        Shortest.Position := 1;
```

```
      for Index := 2 to NumberOfCheckouts do
        if Queues[Index].Length < Shortest.Length then
          begin
            Shortest.Length := Queues[Index]. Length;
            Shortest.Position:= Index
          end;
  {Now join it}
      Queues [Shortest.Position].GetService;
  {Service has started}
      State.NoteAction (StartedService, Reference);
      Queues [Shortest.Position].AwaitServiceComplete;
  {Service is complete}
      State.NoteAction (EndedService, Reference)
  end {Customer1};
```

The corresponding code for the Checkout process is:

```
process Checkout1 (C: CheckoutRange);
{Version 1: Separate queues at each checkout}
    begin
      repeat
        Queues [C].GetCustomer;
        Clock.Hold (Times.ServicesTime);
        Queues [C].SignalServiceComplete
      until False
    end {Checkout1};
```

In the second version of the program these modules have the following, simpler, structure:

```
process Customer2;
{Version 2: A single waiting queue for checkouts}
    var Index: CheckoutRange;
        Reference: CustomerRange;
    begin
      Clock.Hold (Times.NextArrivalTime);
      CustomerIds.GetReference (Reference);
      State.NoteAction (Arrival, Reference);
      Queue.GetService;
      State.NoteAction (StartedService, Reference);
      Queue.AwaitServiceComplete;
      State.NoteAction (EndedService, Reference)
    end {Customer2};


process Checkout2;
{Version 2: A single waiting queue for checkouts}
    begin
      repeat
        Queue.GetCustomer;
        Clock.Hold (Times.ServiceTime);
        Queue.SignalServiceComplete
      until False
    end {Checkout2};
```

The State module can, for each program, calculate and present the maximum and average customer queuing times. As a check, the distribution means for customer arrival interval and service time are calculated and displayed:

```
monitor module State;
{Assumes const Identification = string}
```

```
type *Action = ( *Arrival, *StartedService, *EndedService);
     TimeEntry = record
                       case IsSet: Boolean of
                              True: (Time: Real);
                              False: ()
                 end;
     CustomerDetails = record
                            Times: array [Action] of TimeEntry
                       end;
var Details: array [CustomerRange] of CustomerDetails;

procedure *NoteAction (A: Action; Customer: CustomerRange);
  begin
    with Details [Customer].Times [A] do
      begin
        IsSet := True; Time := Clock. PseudoTime
      end
  end {NoteAction};

procedure *NoteMeanServiceTime (Mean: Real);
  begin
    Writeln;
    Writeln ('Mean checkout service time = ', Mean:5:1, 'Minutes')
  end {NoteMeanServiceTime};

procedure *NoteMeanArrivalTime (Mean: Real);
  begin
    Writeln;
    Writeln ('Mean arrival interval = ', Mean:5:1, 'Minutes')
  end {NoteMeanArrivalTime};

procedure Finalize;
{Determine and display average and maximum queuing times}
  var Index: CustomerRange;
      CustomersProcessed: 0 . . NumberOfCustomers;
      LongestWait, Wait, TotalTime: Clock.TimeScale;
  begin
    TotalTime := 0; LongestWait := 0;
    CustomersProcessed := 0;
    for Index : = 1 to NumberOfCustomers do
      with Details [Index] do
      if Times [Arrival].IsSet and Times [StartedService].IsSet then
        begin
          Wait := Times [StartedService]. Time − Times [Arrival]. Time;
          if Wait > LongestWait then LongestWait := Wait;
          TotalTime := TotalTime + Wait;
          CustomersProcessed := CustomersProcessed + 1
        end;
    Writeln; Writeln;
    Writeln ('Average queuing time = ', TotalTime/CustomersProcessed:5:1, 'Minutes');
    Writeln;
    Writeln ('Maximum waiting time = ', LongestWait:5:1, ' Minutes');
    Writeln;
    Writeln ('Customers considered = ', CustomersProcessed:5);
    Writeln; Writeln;
    Writeln ('—— End of Simulation Output ——')
  end {Finalize};

procedure Initialize;
  var Index: CustomerRange;
      A: Action;
  begin
```

```
        Writeln ('Simulation of queuing strategy: ', Identification);
        for Index := 1 to NumberOfCustomers do
          for A := Arrival to EndedService do
            Details [Index].Times [A].IsSet := False
      end {Initialize};

    begin Initialize; ***; Finalize end {State};
```

Note that in working out the maximum and average queuing times only customers that have reached the checkout are considered.

8.5 Bar simulation

To provide the information required two versions of the program are used: one covering the case where each customer gets a fresh glass and the other where customers' glasses are refilled.

The overall program structure is as follows:

```
program Pub (Output);
{Basic time unit is SECONDS}
 const
    NumberOfCustomers = 50;
    NumberOfEntities = 52 {customers + barmaid + manager };
    DrinkLimit = 6;
    NumberOfGlasses = 30;
 type
    CustomerRange = 1..NumberOfCustomers;
    DrinkRange = 1..DrinkLimit;
    GlassRange = 1..NumberOfGlasses;
    GlassCount = 0..NumberOfGlasses;

 monitor module Times in Library;

 monitor module Clock in Library
    (Where const TimeLimit = Times.ClosingTime;
           const EntityLimit = NumberOfEntities;
           type  TimeType = Real;);

 monitor module Random = BasicDistributions in Library;

 monitor module State in Library;

 monitor module Sink in Library;

 monitor module Tables in Library;

 monitor module Stock in Library;

 monitor module Bar in Library;

 monitor module CustomerReferences in Library;

 process Customer in Library;

 instance Customers: array [CustomerRange] of Customer;

 process module Barmaid = Barmaid1 in Library;

 process module Manager in Library;

 begin *** end {Pub}.
```

The entities in the model are the *sink*, the *tables*, the *stock* of glasses, the *bar*, the *barmaid*, the *bar manager* and the *customers*. The first three entities can all be modeled by operations on shared variables, held in separate modules:

```
monitor module Sink;
  procedure *AddGlasses (Number: GlassCount);
  procedure *TryToWashAGlass (var OneWashed: Boolean);
  begin
    {initially, the sink is empty}
  end {Sink};

monitor module Tables;
  procedure *LeaveGlass;
  procedure *CollectGlassesPresent (var Number: GlassCount);
  begin
    {initially, the tables are clear}
  end {Tables};

monitor module Stock;
  procedure *TryToGetGlass (var Given: Boolean);
  procedure *AddGlass;
  begin
    {initially, the full stock is present}
  end {Stock};
```

The Times monitor might have the following form:

```
monitor module Times;
  const *ClosingTime = 7200;
        *TimeToPour = 60;
        *IdleTimeUnit = 5;
        *GlassWashTime = 30;
        *GlassCollectionTime = 300;
        *BarManagerInterval = 900;
  function *DrinkTime: Real; ...;
  function *NextArrivalTime: Real; ...;
  begin ... end {Times};
```

The behavior of the bar manager can then be described as follows:

```
process module Manager;
  var GlassesFound: GlassCount;
      CollectionTime, Interval: Real;
  begin {Manager}
    CollectionTime := Times.GlassCollection;
    Interval := Times.BarManagerInterval;
    Clock.Hold (Interval);
    repeat
      Tables.CollectGlassesPresent (GlassesFound);
      Clock.Hold (CollectionTime);
      Sink.AddGlasses (GlassesFound);
      Clock.Hold (Interval − CollectionTime)
    until False
  end {Manager};
```

The synchronization between customers and the barmaid is performed within the
Bar monitor:

```
monitor module Bar;
  instance ServiceComplete: Condition;

  monitor module BarQueue = ConditionList in Library
    (Where const QueueLimit = NumberOfCustomers;
           type Requirements = Boolean;
           type PriorityRange = 0..Maxint;);
```

```
    procedure *TryToGetCustomer (var Found, GlassReturned: Boolean);
      begin
        BarQueue.Reset;
        Found := not BarQueue.Empty;
        if Found
        then
          begin
            BarQueue.Content (GlassReturned);
            BarQueue.Signal
          end
        else GlassReturned := False
      end {TryToGetCustomer};

    procedure *SignalServiceComplete;
      begin ServiceComplete.Signal end;

    procedure *GetService (GlassReturned: Boolean);
      begin BarQueue.Wait (GlassReturned) end {GetService};

    procedure *AwaitServiceComplete;
      begin ServiceComplete.Wait end;

    begin *** end {Bar};
```

The synchronization involved here is similar to that of the customers and
checkouts in the previous problem. Each Customer process calling procedure
GetService is suspended on the BarQueue condition list with an indication of whether
or not the customer being modeled has returned a glass. When free, the Barmaid
process calls TryToGetCustomer. If the bar queue is nonempty the first customer is
activated; otherwise no action is taken. An activated Customer process is expected to
return with a call to AwaitServiceComplete where it is suspended for the time taken by
the barmaid to pour a drink. Finally, the Barmaid process calls SignalServiceComplete
when a drink has been poured to reactivate the waiting Customer process.

The behavior of each customer and the barmaid can be described thus:

```
process Customer;
  var
    D, DrinksRequired: DrinkRange;
    Reference: CustomerRange;
  begin {Customer}
    Clock.Hold (Times.NextArrivalTime);
    CustomerReferences.GetReference (Reference);
    DrinksRequired := Random.UniformInteger (1, DrinkLimit);
    for D := 1 to DrinksRequired do
      with State do
        begin
          NoteCustomerAction (JoinedQueue, Reference);
          Bar.GetService (D > 1);
          NoteCustomerAction (StartedService, Reference);
          Bar.AwaitServiceComplete;
          NoteCustomerAction (EndedService, Reference);
          Clock.Hold (Times.DrinkTime)
        end;
      Tables.LeaveGlass
    end {Customer};

process module Barmaid;
  var CustomerFound, GlassReturned, GlassFound: Boolean;
```

```
    procedure Idle;
      begin
        with State do NoteBarmaidAction (IsIdle);
        Clock.Hold (Times.IdleTimeUnit)
      end {Idle};

    procedure PourADrink;
      begin
        with State do NoteBarmaidAction (PouringDrink);
        Clock.Hold (Times.TimeToPour);
        Bar.SignalServiceComplete
      end {PourADrink};

    begin {Barmaid}
      repeat
        Bar.TryToGetCustomer (CustomerFound,GlassReturned);
        if CustomerFound
        then
          begin
            if GlassReturned then Sink.AddGlasses (1);
            Stock.TryToGetGlass (GlassFound);
            if not GlassFound then
              begin
                Sink.TryToGetAGlass (GlassFound);
                if GlassFound then
                  begin
                    with State do NoteBarmaidAction (WashingGlass);
                    Clock.Hold (Times.GlassWashTime);
                  end
              end;
            if GlassFound then PourADrink else Idle
          end
        else {no customer to serve}
          begin
            Sink.TryToGetAGlass (GlassFound);
            if GlassFound
            then
              begin
                with State do NoteBarmaidAction (WashingGlass);
                Clock.Hold (Times.GlassWashTime);
                Stock.AddGlass
              end
            else Idle
          end
      until False
    end {Barmaid};
```

where it is assumed that the interface to the State monitor is as follows:

```
monitor module State;
  type *CustomerAction = ( *JoinedQueue, *StartedService, *EndedService);
       *BarmaidAction = ( *IsIdle, *WashingGlass, *PouringDrink);
  procedure *NoteCustomerArrival (Customer: CustomerRange);
  procedure *NoteCustomerAction (Action: CustomerAction; Customer: CustomerRange);
  procedure *NoteBarmaidAction (Action: BarmaidAction);
  begin ... end {State};
```

A trivial change is needed to the Barmaid process to model the case where glasses of
returning customers are refilled.

8.6 The drunken porter problem

This problem has been defined in such a way that the normal clock mechanism is unnecessary – all that is required is that a process representing the porter be suspended after each delivery of mail until the processes representing the staff have stopped executing, i.e. they have all sorted the cards that they have received and returned, to the mailbox, those that have been delivered incorrectly.

The structure of the main program is as follows:

```
program PorterSimulation (Output);
   const NumberOfStaff = 8;
         NumberOfDeliveries = 72;
   type StaffRange = 1 . . NumberOfStaff;

   monitor module State in Library;

   monitor module CardSet in Library;

   monitor Office = SingleItemBuffer in Library
      (Where type ItemType = CardSet.Cards;);
   instance Offices: array [StaffRange] of Office;

   monitor module MailBox in Library;

   process StaffMember in Library;
   instance Staff: array [StaffRange] of StaffMember
                [(1), (2), (3), (4), (5), (6), (7), (8)];

   process module Porter in Library;

   begin *** end {PorterSimulation}.
```

All operations on sets of cards are performed through the module CardSet. All other modules correspond to entities in the model. Note that the staff offices are simply represented by instances of the standard SingleItemBuffer monitor.

The abstract operations needed by the CardSet module are:

```
monitor module CardSet;
   type *Cards = . . . ;
   procedure *Initialize (var C: Cards);
      {Initializes C to the empty state                             }
   function *IsEmpty (C: Cards): Boolean;
      {Returns True if C is empty and False otherwise               }
   procedure *Transfer (var Source, Destination: Cards);
      {Copies Source to Destination and clears Source.              }
      {Direct assignment of variables of type Cards is              }
      {permitted as long the source variable is not used            }
      {thereafter.                                                  }
   procedure *Combine (var Part, Main: Cards);
      {Returns Main + Part and clears Part                          }
   procedure *PrepareCardsToSend (var C: Cards; (Member: StaffRange);
      {Returns cards to be sent by specified staff member in C      }
   procedure *AcceptCards (var C: Cards; Member: StaffRange);
      {Deletes cards addressed to specified staff member from C     }
      {and also returns the number deleted                          }
   procedure *SelectAHandful (var C, Handful: Cards);
      {Extracts a random selection of cards from C and returns      }
      {them in Handful                                              }
   begin {no local data} end {CardSet};
```

These operations hide the representation of a set of cards from the rest of the program. One possible representation is as a linked list of records of the form:

```
Cards = CardList;
CardList = record
              Source, Destination: StaffRange;
              Next: Cards
           end;
```

Given these operations the other modules of the program can be expressed in a relatively simple form:

```
monitor module MailBox;
  var Mail: CardSet.Cards;

  procedure *Post (var C: CardSet.Cards);
    begin CardSet.Combine (C, Mail) end {Post};

  procedure *Collect (var C: CardSet.Cards);
    begin CardSet.Transfer (Mail, C) end {Collect};

  begin CardSet.Initialize (Mail); *** end {MailBox};


process Porter;
  label 99;
  var Mail, Handful: CardSet.Card;
      Cycle: 1..NumberOfDeliveries;
      StaffOffice: StaffRange;
  begin {Porter}
    for Cycle := 1 to NumberOfDeliveries do
      begin
        AllWaiting.Wait;
        MailBox.Collect (Mail);
        if CardSet.IsEmpty (Mail)
        then
          begin
            State.NoteDeliveryComplete;
            goto 99
          end
        else
          begin
            for StaffOffice := 1 to NumberOfStaff − 1 do
              begin
                Cardset.SelectAHandful (Mail, Handful);
                InOutTray [StaffOffice].Send (Handful)
              end;
            InOutTray [NumberOfStaff].Send (Mail)
          end
      end;
    99:
  end {Porter};


process StaffMember (Reference: StaffRange);
  var CardBatch: CardSet.Cards;
  begin
    CardSet.PrepareCardsToSend (CardBatch, Reference);
    repeat
      MailBox.Post (CardBatch);
      InOutTray [Reference].Receive (CardBatch);
      CardSet.AcceptCards (CardBatch, Reference)
    until False
  end {StaffMember};
```

9. Real-time systems

9.1 VDU handler modifications

(a) Suspending output

Screen output can be controlled by suspending and reactivating the Writer process on successive depressions of Control/S. This may be handled by the Arbiter monitor, thus:

```
monitor module VDUHandler;

  monitor module Arbiter;
    var DelayRequired: Boolean;
        ScreenOutput: Environment.Operation;
    instance Delay: Condition;

    procedure *DoScreenOutput (Character: Char);
      begin
        if DelayRequired then Delay.Wait;
        ScreenOutput.Character := Character;
        Perform (ScreenOutput)
      end {DoScreenOutput};

    procedure *ControlSPressed;
      begin
        if DelayRequired then Delay.Signal;
        DelayRequired := not DelayRequired
      end {ControlSPressed};

    begin {Arbiter}
      DelayRequired := False;
      ScreenOutput.Facility := Environment.VDUScreen;
      ***
    end {Arbiter};

  monitor module ScreenHandler;
      . . .
    process module Writer;
      var Character: Char;
      begin
        SetPriority (2);
        repeat
          ScreenBuffer.Receive (Character);
          Arbiter.DoScreenOutput (Character)
        until False
      end {Writer};

    begin *** end {ScreenHandler};

  monitor module KeyboardHandler;
      . . .
    process module Reader;
      var KeyboardInput: Environment.Operation; OK: Boolean;
      begin
        SetPriority (2);
        KeyboardInput.Facility := Environment.VDUKeyboard;
        repeat
          Perform (KeyboardInput);
          with KeyboardInput do
            if Character = Chr (ControlS) then Arbiter.ControlSPressed
            else
              begin
```

```
                    KeyboardBuffer.TryToSend (Character, OK);
                    if not OK then Arbiter.DoScreenOutput (Chr (BellCharacter))
                end
            end
        until False
    end {Reader};

  begin *** end {KeyboardHardler};
        ...

begin ... end {VDUHandler};
```

(b) Interrupting output

On receiving Control/Y this character can be passed up to the application level to
indicate that the operation in progress should be abandoned. In addition, a flag can
be set to prevent further output of characters to the screen until an acknowledgement character is passed down from the application level – say Control/Y again:

```
monitor module VDUHandler;

  monitor module Arbiter;
    var Interrupt, DelayRequired: Boolean;
        ScreenOutput: Environment.Operation;
    instance Delay: Condition;

    procedure *DoScreenOutput (Character: Char);
      begin
        if DelayRequired then Delay.Wait;
        ScreenOutput.Character := Character;
        if not Interrupt
        then Perform (ScreenOutput)
        else
          if Character = Chr (ControlY) then Interrupt := False
      end {DoScreenOutput};

    procedure *ControlSPressed;
      begin
        if DelayRequired then Delay.Signal;
        DelayRequired := not DelayRequired
      end {ControlSPressed};

    procedure *ControlYPressed;
    begin Interrupt := True end {ControlYPressed};

    begin {Arbiter}
      DelayRequired := False;
      Interrupt := False;
      ScreenOutput.Facility := Environment.VDUScreen;
      ***
    end {Arbiter};

  monitor module KeyboardHandler;
            ...

  process module Reader;
    var KeyboardInput: Environment.Operation;
        OK: Boolean;
    begin
      SetPriority (2);
      KeyboardInput.Facility := Environment.VDUKeyboard;
      repeat
        Perform (KeyboardInput);
        with KeyboardInput do
          if Character = Chr (ControlS)
          then Arbiter.ControlSPressed
```

```
                    else
                  begin
                      KeyboardBuffer.TryToSend (Character, OK);
                      if not OK
                      then DoScreenOutput (Chr (BellCharacter))
                      else
                          if Character = Chr (ControlY) then Arbiter.ControlYPressed;
                  end
              until False
          end {Reader};

      begin *** end {KeyboardHandler};
              . . .
      begin . . . end {VDUHandler};
```

Note that the output should not be interrupted until the Control/Y character has
been accepted by the keyboard buffer.

9.2 Lineprinter handler

To complete the module outlined in Chapter 6 we need to define an environment
operation record entry for the printers and also introduce a buffer for each device.
   The operation record entry might be defined as follows:

```
LPOperations = (PageThrow, LineOutput);
PrinterEntry = record
                    Printer: PrinterRange;
                    case LPOperation: LPOperations of
                    PageThrow: ( );
                    LineOutput: (ALine: Line)
                end;
                . . .
Operation = record
                case Facility: ExternalConnections of
                    . . .
                Printers: (P: PrinterEntry);
                    . . .
            end;
```

where it is assumed that:

(a) the definition of Line is as shown in the module outline in Chapter 6 but is now
     moved to the Environment monitor;
(b) the definition of PrinterRange is identical to that of PrinterPool.Resource.

   A buffer can then be declared for each printer, with an item type of
PrinterOperation:

```
monitor module PrinterBuffer = MultipleItemBuffer in Library
   (Where const MaxItems = . . .;
           type ItemType = Environment.PrinterOperation;);
instance
   Buffers: array [Environment.PrinterRange] of PrinterBuffer;
```

and the printer operations represented as follows:

```
monitor module Lineprinters;
   type *PrinterType = (*Full, *Reduced);

   monitor module PrinterPool = NamedOneFromSubset in Library
```

```
            (Where const ResourceLimit = Environment.NumberOfPrinters;
                   ProcessLimit   = ...;
              const PriorityLimit  = Maxint;);

        envelope *PrinterInterface (Required: PrinterType);
          var P: PrinterPool.Resource;
              NewPage, Print: Environment.Operation;

          procedure *PrintLine (L: Environment.Line);
            begin Print.P.ALine := L; Perform (Print) end {PrintLine};

          procedure *TakeNewPage;
              begin Perform (NewPage) end {TakeNewPage};

            begin {PrinterInterface}
              if Required = Full
              then PrinterPool.Acquire (P, [3, 5])
              else PrinterPool.Acquire (P, [1..NumberOfPrinters]);
              NewPage.Facility := Printers;
              NewPage.Printer := P;
              NewPage.LPOperation := Environment.PageThrow;
              Print.Facility := Printers;
              Print.P.Printer := P;
              Print.LPOperation := Environment.LineOutput;
              ***;
              TakeNewPage;
              PrinterPool.Release (P)
            end {PrinterInterface};

         begin *** end {Lineprinters};
```

The efficiency of this solution can be improved by passing references to lines (using
pointers) rather than copying the lines themselves through the system.

9.3 Real-time clock control

The operation record entry for controlling the real-time clock might take the form:

```
ClockOperations = (SetTime, InspectTime, AwaitTime);
TimeRange = 0..Maxint; {say}
ClockEntry = record
                ClockOperation: ClockOperations;
                Time: TimeRange
             end;
              . . .
Operation = record
              case Facility: ExternalConnections of
                         . . .
              RealtimeClock: (C: ClockEntry);
                         . . .
           end;
```

A module to handle clock operations might then be defined as follows:

```
envelope module Clock;

  procedure *DoSetTime (Time: Environment.TimeRange);
    var Entry: Environment.Operation;
    begin
      Entry.Facility := Environment.RealtimeClock;
      Entry.C.ClockOperation := Environment.SetTime;
      Entry.C.Time := Time;
```

```
        Perform (Entry)
      end {DoSetTime};

    procedure *DoInspectTime (var Time: Environment.TimeRange);
      var Entry: Environment.Operation;
      begin
        Entry.Facility := Environment.RealtimeClock;
        Entry.C.ClockOperation := Environment.InspectTime;
        Perform (Entry);
        Time := Entry.C.Time
      end {DoInspectTime};

    procedure *DoAwaitTime (Time: Environment.TimeRange);
      var Entry: Environment.Operation;
      begin
        Entry.Facility := Environment.RealtimeClock;
        Entry.C.ClockOperation := Environment.AwaitTime;
        Entry.C.Time := Time;
        Perform (Entry)
      end {DoAwaitTime};

    begin *** end {Clock};
```

Note that this module has been defined as an *envelope* rather than a *monitor*
because the use of Perform has no effect on monitor exclusion i.e. if the module is a
monitor the first process to invoke DoAwaitTime would shut out all others up to the
time specified. Instead, it is assumed that the underlying support software ensures
that there is exclusive access to its representation of the clock.

9.4 Simulation of filling station control program

An operation record to handle external interaction might be defined as follows:

```
ExternalConnections  = (ExternalIdentification, VDUScreen, VDUKeyboard, PumpStand);
PumpStandOperations = (Nozzle, Pump, Display);
PumpRange = 1..4;
Operation  = record
                  case Facility: ExternalConnections of
                  VDUScreen, VDUKeyboard:
                    (Character: Char);
                  PumpStand:
                    record
                      Reference: PumpRange;
                      case PumpOperation: PumpStandOperations of
                      Nozzle: {await nozzle signal}
                        ( );
                      Pump: {switch pump state}
                        ( );
                      Display: {show volume and cost of fuel}
                        (Volume, Cost: Integer {say});
                    end
                end;
```

The basic structure of the program is given in the solution to Exercise 4.5. Its
operation may be simulated by using the same technique as that described for the car
park control program in Chapter 9.

Index

Ada, 44, 187, 188, 249–56
AllWaiting condition, 69, 85–86, 161–2,
     245–6, 268
animation, 163
asynchronous input/output, 5–6,
     15–18

background processing, 210
banker's algorithm, 119–21, 138
BasicDistributions monitor, 175–7, 180–1
BasicGenerator monitor, 179–180
behavior presentation, 90–93,
     163–64
Boolean control variables, 237–8
Brinch Hansen, P., 240, 242
buffered communication, 6, 77, 139,
     144–52, 255
busy waiting, 62, 238

case studies
   car park, 56–61, 73, 202–207
   dining philosophers, 134–6, 181–2,
      183
   filling station, 38–42, 43, 73, 208
   Habermann's neighbor sort, 9–10
   hide-and-seek game, 37–8, 73,
      154–8
   launderette, 159–61, 164–71
   parallel sort, 8, 74–93, 94, 152
   pass-the-parcel game, 142–4, 150–1,
      173–9, 183–4
   temperature/humidity warning
      system, 27–33, 45–56, 70–1,
      94, 153, 189–94
   tool-box, 113–14, 121–3
   traditional operating system, 210–29

VDU handler, 195–202, 208, 213
circular dependency, 118, 121–3
clock module, 155, 158–63
command language, 210
command processor, 212, 214–15,
     225–42, 253
Communicating Sequential Processes,
     249
communication management, 139–53
communication monitors
   MultipleItemBuffer, 146–50, 153
   OneWayChannel, 140
   SingleItemBuffer, 145–6, 153
Concurrent Euclid, 44, 243–5
Concurrent Pascal, 44, 242–5
condition concept, 62–9, 267–8
conditional critical regions, 240–2, 253
ConditionList monitor, 105–11
configuration diagram, 28
continuous system simulation, 156
critical region, 54, 234–7, 240–2

data communications network, 229
deadlock
   avoidance, 118–23, 134–6, 218, 219
   definition, 4, 96–7, 113–14
   detection. 123–5, 219
design, 24–43
   functional, 26
   modular, 26–38
device driver, 195
Dijkstra, E.W., 120, 135, 238
discrete event simulation, 154–85
disk handler, 219–25
disk space manager, 217–18
distributed operating systems, 229–31

dominant modules, 31, 47, 50
driver module, 31
dynamic entities, 156

embedded systems, *see* real-time systems
entity processes, 157
envelope concept, 48–50, 260–1
environment level interaction, 187,
    189–94
environment module, 191–2
event driven simulation, *see* discrete
    event simulation
event queue, 158, 161–3
exclusion
    monitor, 54–5, 61, 63–9, 88–9,
        244–5, 266–8
    mutual, 54, 61
execution profile, 51–3
exponential distribution, 171–3, 176

fairness, 4, 14, 62, 98
feasibility study, 25
file access manager, 218–19
file server, 230
filing system, 211–12, 215–17, 231
foreground processing, 210
fork-and-join, 52

grain of concurrency, *see* scale of
    concurrency

Hoare, C.A.R., 44, 240, 242, 249

indefinite postponement, indefinite
    waiting, *see* starvation
information hiding, 32
inner statement, 49, 266
interrupts, 18

job control language, 210

library retrieval, 55, 259–60
local area network, 229–30

memory contention, 19, 255
memory interlock, 235
memory management, 133–4, 227
Modula-2, 44, 187, 188, 189, 246–9
module interface, 32, 48–9
monitor concept, 53–6, 243–5, 261
multiprocessors
    hybrid, 20–1
    loosely coupled, 15, 19–21
    tightly coupled, 15, 18–19

negative exponential distribution, *see*
    exponential distribution
nondeterminism, 3
normal distribution, 171–3, 176

occam, 249
operating systems, 5–6, 209–32
operational model, 29, 39–42

path name, 215
Perform operation, 189–94, 203,
    223–4, 268
priority, 98–9, 117–18, 130, 195,
    254–5
probability distribution, 156
process concept, 50–3, 261–2
process-oriented modeling, 157
processors
    central, 13
    input/output, 13–18
pseudotime, 157
public switched data network, 229

random number generators, 179–81
readers/writers, 126–33, 216–17
read-only variables, 49, 68–9
real-time clock, 18, 229
real-time systems, 6, 27–33, 38–42,
    45–64, 186–208, 209, 231
rendezvous, 251
requirements analysis, 24–5
resource management, 95–138
resource monitors
    BiasedMFromN, 117, 137
    DatabaseAccess, 126–30, 137
    MFromN, 114–17, 137
    monolithic, 118–19
    NamedMFromN, 117, 137
    NamedMFromSubset, 117–18, 137
    NamedOneFromN, 102–103, 137
    NamedOneFromSubset, 107–109, 112,
        136
    OneFromN, 101–102
    SingleResource, 100, 136
round robin scheduling, 18

scale of concurrency
    large-scale, 8–9
    small-scale, 9–10, 21–22
SIMD machines, 9
simulation systems, 6, 37–8, 121–3,
    135–7, 154–85, 202–207
specification, 24–25, 38, 69–71, 250
starvation, 4, 96–8, 117

state module, 27, 37–8, 86, 90–3, 154, 164–9
state variables, 156
stochastic models, 156, 171–9
subordinate modules, 31, 47–50, 53–6
synchronization, 3, 56–64, 234–7
synchronized communication, 139–44, 250–3, 255
system languages, 187
system state, 156

transputer, 15
termination, 69, 253–4, 268
test-and-set, 237–8
testing, 74–94
    incremental, 82

isolated, 82–90
time-dependent behavior, 3, 54, 256
time-slicing, 13
times module, 176–7
transient errors, 3, 54
type transfer, 220, 269

uniform distribution, 172
UNIX, 5
user accounts management, 212–13
user level interaction, 187–8

virtual resources, 133–4, 227
visible attributes, *see* module interface

wide area network, 229–30